ALMOST FROM SCRATCH

600 RECIPES FOR THE
NEW CONVENIENCE CUISINE

Andrew Schloss, CCP

SIMON & SCHUSTER

NEW YORK   LONDON   TORONTO   SYDNEY   SINGAPORE

SIMON & SCHUSTER
Rockefeller Center
1230 Avenue of the Americas
New York, NY 10020

For information regarding special discounts for bulk purchases, please contact
Simon & Schuster Special Sales at 1-800-456-6798 or business@simonandschuster.com

Designed by Jaime Putorti

Manufactured in the United States of America

10   9   8   7   6   5   4   3   2   1

Library of Congress Cataloging-in-Publication Data
Schloss, Andrew, 1951–
    Almost from scratch : 600 recipes for the new convenience cuisine / Andrew
       Schloss.
    p.   cm.
    Includes index.
    1. Quick and easy cookery. I. Title.
TX833.5.S33 2003
641.5′55—dc21   2003045432

ISBN 0-7432-2598-8

ACKNOWLEDGMENTS

This book could never have happened without the help of:

Cindy Ayers, who many years ago showed me that streamlining scratch recipes with manufactured ingredients is the next big step in the evolution of home cooking.

Lisa Ekus, who understood the power of this project right away and has helped to keep it on track with her uncommonly good common sense.

Sydny Miner, who gave this book life.

Laura Holmes, whose in-house enthusiasm for the book is contagious, and whose hard work and attention to detail makes everyone else's job easier.

Gabriel Weiss and Rose Anne Ferrick, who straightened out my prose, and Jaime Putorti, who tamed a massive manuscript into a clear and concise design.

Aileen Boyle and Erin Saunders, who took this project to heart and spread the word.

Blake Swihart, Robin Kline, Toni Allegra, Martha Johnston, Carol Moore, Phil Schulman, Joan Horn, Burt Horn, Ina Schecter, Deborah Shain, Murray Silberman, Adam Spielberg, Amy Herbig, Dana Schloss, Isaac Schloss, Ben Schloss, and most of all, my wife, Karen Shain Schloss, who listened with open minds and tasted with critical palates. Their input was essential in refining the direction and fine tuning the recipes.

Ken Bookman, who helped to hone the text.

Rux Martin, who saw the proposal for this book early on and encouraged it.

All of the recipe testers, who read, and cooked, and tasted, and advised. Thank you Judy Stern, Blake Swihart, Maryann Ochmanski, and most of all, Bonny Barry, whose culinary intelligence runs pervasively through these pages.

Karen and Richard Jacobson; none of this would have happened without their lack of flour.

In a world of too little time and too much to do,

this book is dedicated to all who still find pleasure

in cooking and sharing a homemade meal.

CONTENTS

ALMOST FROM SCRATCH

THE NEW CONVENIENCE CUISINE

Home cooking has changed, and cookbooks hardly noticed. But supermarkets did. Look at lettuce; whole heads have been replaced with prewashed, pretorn, pretossed, and crouton-studded cellophane sacks. Salad dressings have blended into marinades, mustards have morphed toward mayonnaise, and meats are sold stuffed, filleted, roasted, and grilled.

And still most cookbook recipes call for chopping carrots, mincing garlic, and tearing heads of lettuce. They ignore the myriad of Thai sauces, Jerk seasonings, Asian dressings, Mexican condiments, and Mediterranean pestos that crowd the shelves of every supermarket in every town. Cookbooks give directions for marinades and grill sauces that are clones of bottled dressings; they call for sifting dry ingredients or for sautéing vegetables when a bottled dressing, baking mix, or jar of salsa would yield the same results in a fraction of the time and with far fewer ingredients.

There has been an explosion of convenience foods in the American marketplace, and like the condensed mushroom soup, dehydrated onions, and French dressing of generations past, these foods are not just convenient facsimiles of finished dishes. They are high-powered ingredients in their own right.

A jar of tapenade doesn't just give us something new to spread on bread. It flavors a grilled chicken breast and seasons a salad dressing. It can be plopped atop a baked potato, swirled into vegetable soup, or used to thicken a lamb stew. With time and use, tapenade changes in our mind from an esoteric condiment to a kitchen staple that has elevated the way we cook and eat to another level.

The notion of using convenience ingredients to create powerfully flavored recipes is not new. American home cooks have been modifying scratch cooking for years with manufacturers' box-top recipes, but too often these are little more than dumbed-downed versions of family favorites. They fail to take advantage of the hidden power of the new generation of convenience ingredients: the ability to cook like a chef at home.

When a chef turns out Pesto-Stuffed Grilled Chicken Breast with Sun-Dried Tomato Sauce, the pesto has already been prepared, the sun-dried tomatoes have been soaked and puréed, the garlic has been chopped, the stock has been reduced, and the spice rub has been blended. A few years ago if you wanted to duplicate this dish at home, you would be facing half an afternoon in the kitchen. Now your local supermarket provides all the prep work. Pesto is available jarred, refrigerated, or frozen. Sun-dried tomatoes come puréed into pesto, minced to a powder, or chopped in a vinaigrette. There are spice rubs ranging from ancho-garlic to lemon-basil, and chicken breasts are trimmed in every conceivable form. The preparation that once took hours now takes minutes. It is the vision of *Almost from Scratch* that this is not a phenomenon confined to individual ingredients but rather is a new way of cooking that streamlines the way home cooks can prepare everything from soup to dessert.

THE CONVENIENCE KITCHEN

Several years ago we attended a family reunion. We were staying with cousins in Atlanta, and the first morning I woke early to make pancakes for everyone. Rummaging through the kitchen I found most of what I needed. There were the expected necessities for a family with young children: two gallons of milk, a dozen eggs, a giant jar of peanut butter, and even a calcified tin of baking powder, but there was no flour. I was getting dressed to run to the store when my wife's cousin awoke. She knew there was flour. She had just bought some in the hope that I might bake something. And sure enough she pulled out a package that I can only describe as an envelope of flour containing just two cups, enough for one cake or a pan of muffins, about 8 ounces.

I hadn't seen it because to my eye it was invisible. As a chef and an only-from-scratch home cook, I bought my flour in large sacks and used it not only for baking but for thickening sauces, browning meat, dusting pans, and frying chicken. What did it mean about the current state of American home cooking that this well-equipped kitchen was stocked with a dozen bottles of salad dressing but only a token packet of flour? What had happened to the American pantry while I was busy cooking from scratch?

Obviously things had changed. Scratch baking had become esoteric, and salad dressing had become an all-purpose sauce. Mayonnaise, enlivened with vinegar and herbs, had become de facto salad dressing, and mustard, spiked with honey, horseradish, or watercress, had become a mini convenience industry. Relish, reinforced with sun-dried tomatoes, mangoes, and lime, had become chic. Pesto was being peddled alongside ketchup, Thai sauces came canned, and Jack Daniels was manufacturing barbecue sauce. And all of these items were instantly ready to produce the kind of flavor that I needed a laundry list of ingredients to create. The world of scratch cooking had been usurped by the very preparations it had popularized.

For decades the amount of time spent preparing dinner has decreased, while opportunities for obtaining dinner in other ways has increased. The proliferation of chain restaurants, ethnic eateries, take-out shops, and dinner delivery services has made cooking from scratch just one option for getting dinner on the table. And as our options have expanded, so has our taste for exciting flavors and foreign cuisines, leading to a revolution at the supermarket.

The array can be mind-boggling and somewhat daunting, especially if you are new to the products. The following lists are offered to help you find your way and take charge.

THE CONVENIENCE PANTRY

The first task is to set up a pantry. Although I have tried to mine the depth and breadth of available ingredients in this book, it is helpful to keep a core group of items on hand. With them in your pantry you will be able to prepare a good number of the recipes in *Almost from Scratch* by adding one or two fresh ingredients, such as a chicken breast or a fish fillet. To assist in setting up your pantry, I have divided the list in two: what is essential and what is nice to have on hand.

ESSENTIALS
Marinated artichoke hearts
Tomato bruschetta
Canned beans, white and/or black
Instant black bean powder and/or powdered hummus

Capers
Garlic and herb cream cheese
Grated imported Parmesan cheese
Shredded cheddar cheese
Chicken broth
Coconut milk
Chopped or minced garlic
Minced ginger
Bottled organic lemon and/or lime juice
Marinara sauce
Spicy brown mustard
Nonstick oil spray (regular and/or olive)
Extra-virgin olive oil
Olive salad or muffuletta
Selection of dried pasta
Basil pesto
Roasted red peppers
Vinaigrette salad dressing and/or Caesar dressing
Chunky salsa (any heat level)
Curry sauce
Soy sauce
Sun-dried tomato pesto or purée
Tapenade (black olive purée)
Teriyaki or stir-fry sauce
Canned diced tomato
Tomato paste in a tube
Balsamic vinegar
Cider vinegar
V8 vegetable juice
Red wine and/or white wine
Spices: chili powder or Southwest seasoning, Italian seasoning,
    lemon pepper, crushed rosemary, ground coriander, and ground
    cumin

NICE TO HAVE ON HAND
Applesauce
Ready-to-serve precooked bacon
Nonstick oil spray with flour, such as Baker's Joy
Barbecue sauce or steak sauce
Bean dip

Bouillon cubes: fish and/or vegetable
Cornbread baking mix
Couscous
Chinese chili purée
Mango chutney or other fruit chutney
Cilantro pesto
Curry paste: red and/or green
Frozen eggplant cutlets
Fruit preserves (such as lemon, ginger, fig, orange, and/or cherry)
Hoisin sauce
Honey
Horseradish
Hot pepper sauce
Pickled ginger for sushi
Mole sauce (such as La Costeña or Goya)
Dried wild mushrooms, such as porcini or shiitake
Asian toasted sesame oil
Instant potato flakes
Peanut butter
Creamy salad dressing
Alternative salsas: fruit, pepper, verde, and/or corn and black bean
Demi-glace sauce concentrate (such as Aromont or More Than
    Gourmet)
Frozen shelled and cleaned shrimp
Sesame tahini
Thai peanut sauce
Risotto mix
Wasabi in a tube

GOING SHOPPING

The following directory will answer most of the questions you may have
about unfamiliar ingredients. In general I have avoided the mention of specific brands. The recipes were tested with as many brands of a specific item as
I was able to purchase at the time of testing, and although I found some differences in flavor and consistency among brands, most of the time the dispar-
ity was not great. Usually all the results were acceptable, and brand prefer-
ences were more a matter of taste than quality. When a particular brand did
make a difference, I have suggested its use. When a brand name precedes the

description of the product, I am making a strong suggestion and can't guarantee the proper results if another brand is used. However, when the brand is introduced with the phrase "such as" or "preferably," do not feel restricted by my recommendation. Other brands are likely to perform quite adequately, and I am only mentioning the brand to offer some guidance.

Most of the new convenience products fall into one of two groups:

- familiar ingredients that have been processed to be easier to use (such as bags of washed and torn lettuce leaves, shredded or sliced carrots, and diced or sliced potatoes);
- exotic or complex preparations that have been made more readily available (such as curry sauce, basil pesto, and Thai peanut sauce).

In regard to the first group, you probably already purchase the ingredients in a less prepared state (whole unwashed heads of lettuce, bunches of carrots, and unpeeled whole potatoes), and you may notice that the processed products seem more expensive. For example, a 10-ounce bag of washed and torn romaine leaves sells for the same price as an unwashed head of romaine that weighs twice as much. However, after you wash the head of romaine and discard its core, larger ribs, and any damaged leaves, you are left with about 12 ounces of servable lettuce—making it not much of a price difference after all.

The second group of ingredients is a different story. Not only is purchasing a jar of basil pesto cheaper than buying the ingredients needed to make it, but you are unlikely to ever prepare pesto, tapenade, curry sauce, or Thai peanut sauce outside of a specific recipe, which eliminates these preparations from your day-to-day cooking. By stocking your pantry with fully prepared sauces and condiments you give yourself the same tools used by professional chefs to create elaborate-sounding, highly flavored dishes. Just having them on hand will revolutionize the way you cook.

A word about cost: Some of the prepared ingredients can seem quite pricey. For instance, a 7-ounce container of demi-glace concentrate usually sells for about $12, which is a lot for a little jar. But since that jar yields more than sixty servings, the cost per serving is less than 20 cents. Also, the concentrate will keep for six months in the refrigerator and can be used to boost the flavor of almost any pan sauce, meat glaze, or soup.

Before buying any packaged product you should take a look at its ingredients list and nutrition label. You might be pleasantly surprised. Even though many manufacturers are more conscientious concerning the nutritional and ecological impact of their products than they used to be, you may want to use or avoid certain preparations or brands depending on your particular health concerns. The object is to determine the healthfulness or harmfulness of any food for you, whether it is manufactured or harvested. This can only be done by knowing your needs and seeing how well the qualities of that product meet them.

AT THE MARKET

The ingredients given below are grouped as they would be in your supermarket: produce; sauces; condiments; ethnic foods; grains and beans; meats, poultry, and seafood; dairy; desserts; seasoning; coffee and tea; and miscellaneous. Then they are alphabetical within each grouping.

Produce

The traditional image of whole heads of lettuce, bunches of beets, and ropes of garlic has been transformed. In every area of the market, produce has been cut and trimmed to fit the way you cook. The following list describes most of what you will find in a well-stocked produce area, as well as some produce options in other parts of the market. I have included only those products that I personally would use. For instance, I buy asparagus fresh and whole, because to my palate frozen and canned asparagus compromise the quality of the vegetable too much. On the other hand, I have described types of canned tomatoes in depth, because for most of the year the quality of tomatoes in the can is superior to what it is available fresh. Canned tomatoes are just cooked tomatoes, and if you are using a recipe in which your tomatoes will be cooked, the canned products give you a head start.

Artichoke hearts and bottoms: Fully trimmed and cooked artichokes (minus their leaves) are available canned and frozen. Hearts, comprising the inner core of leaves and a small piece of the bottom, are cheaper than bottoms and are more commonly available. The bottoms are creamier and slightly sweeter. When making dips, sauces, or spreads, you can use either canned or frozen, but if you are serving them as a side dish, frozen will give you fresher-tasting results.

Broccoli: Florets of fresh broccoli, loose and in bags, are ready to cook without further washing, trimming, or peeling. The stem section is sold shredded as broccoli slaw. It is both crisper and less acrid than the budding tops. Broccoli is also sold in bunches and as separate stalks, which are cheaper per pound than buying florets but require some trimming. Broccoli is also available frozen, but with the convenience of fresh trimmed broccoli stalks, there is no advantage; by the time you get it thawed and cooked, you could have fresh broccoli on the table.

Canned fruit and vegetables: Usually I don't use canned produce. The processing is too severe and destroys the color, texture, and flavor of all but the hardiest fruits and vegetables. There are some exceptions, such as tomatoes, corn, and beans. Canned yams make great pie and pudding, canned pumpkin makes better pumpkin pie than anything freshly cooked, and canned fruit in sugar syrup is ready-made for puréeing for a fruit sauce or to freeze for an instant sorbet. (See the individual entries for information on specific products.)

Carrots: Fresh carrots are available shredded, sliced, diced, cut into sticks, and trimmed into 2-inch lengths, when they are called baby carrots. Any fresh carrot product is ready to use in salads or for cooking. They are especially good for quick soups, stews, and stir-fries. Carrots in various cuts are also sold frozen and canned, but both processes compromise the texture and flavor of the vegetable.

Cauliflower: Cauliflower is related to broccoli, and the florets of both are often sold packaged together. Cauliflower florets are available loose and bagged. They usually cost about three times as much as heads of cauliflower, but when waste is considered, the cost is almost identical.

Celery: Fresh celery is sold trimmed into sticks and diced. It is fully cleaned and needs no further trimming or washing.

Cilantro: The leaf of coriander is an essential element in many cuisines. It is sold fresh by the bunch with other fresh herbs in the produce aisle but it is also available jarred in the form of pesto and chutney. Cilantro pesto is very versatile and will keep for several months in the refrigerator. The brand I buy most often is Trader Joe's; Stonewall Kitchen also produces a delicious cilantro pesto, but it costs a bit more. Cilantro chutney is an Indian relish that can be found with other ethnic ingredients in your market; it is spicy and should be used with some caution. Dried cilantro leaves are not very fragrant. Frozen leaves are hard to find but deliver more intense flavor.

Corn: Corn kernels are available canned and frozen. Both are convenient and of good quality, and I use both interchangeably. Whole hominy (soaked and skinned corn kernels), also called *posole,* has a unique flavor due to its processing, and it is essential for some Mexican and southwestern recipes. It is sold canned and dried. Although canned posole is softer and starchier than soaked and simmered dried posole, it is much more convenient because it reduces cooking time from several hours to a few minutes.

Eggplant: One of the most versatile vegetables, processed eggplant is available in several forms. Puréed roasted eggplant dip is the best source for eggplant purée. It is sold as baba ghanouj, eggplant dip, or eggplant caviar. I use eggplant purée to thicken and flavor soups, stews, and sauces, and I make eggplant mousse from baba ghanouj. Breaded frozen eggplant slices are also a convenient and versatile item to have on hand for throwing together a meatless entrée, topping pizzas, or tossing with pasta. They are sometimes called eggplant cutlets. Another option is jarred caponata, a marinated antipasto of eggplant, peppers, olives, and tomatoes. It is a great addition to vegetarian lasagna, makes a pungent pasta sauce, and is an inspired stuffing for leg of lamb.

Fruit: Although nothing compares to perfectly ripe fresh fruit, frozen, canned, and preserved fruit all have their place in a well-stocked kitchen.

- Frozen fruit, such as berries and peaches, are flash frozen in individual pieces when ripe. Upon thawing they lose their texture but retain their flavor and color, which makes them perfect for pies, cobblers, crisps, and sauce. Always thaw frozen fruit and drain it well before adding it to a recipe so that it doesn't leach its liquid into a batter or filling. Unless you are making a dessert sauce or sorbet that will be sweetened, try to buy frozen products unsweetened. Look for bags of frozen fruit in which you can feel that all the pieces are separate and firm. If part of the bag is a solid mass, the product was refrozen.
- Canned fruit is cooked in the can and is similar to poached fruit. For any preparation that calls for cooking fresh fruit in sugar, canned fruit can save time and effort. Canned fruit is categorized by the amount of sugar used in processing. The sweetest is packed in heavy syrup and is the best choice when making sorbet, mousse, or ice cream. Fruit in light syrup or in fruit juice concentrate has about half the sugar of heavy syrup and is good for sauces or stews. Canned pineapple is sold unsweetened, packed in juice. The least processed canned fruit is packed in jars, costs a bit more, but yields more whole unblemished pieces.
- Fruit preserves are cooked in enough sugar to permeate the fruit. They are thick, highly flavored, and very sweet, with only an occasional lump of recognizable fruit. Use preserves to make glazes or fruit fillings for cookies or pastries.

Garlic: There was a time when I avoided jarred chopped garlic. The amount of citric acid used to preserve the garlic left an acrid aftertaste that I disliked. And although some jarred garlic still has that problem, I have found several brands that deliver good, fresh garlic flavor. I recommend Christopher Ranch, which is sold as whole peeled cloves, chopped and minced in water, and roasted whole cloves. They do not sell chopped roasted garlic, so what I usually do is buy whole roasted cloves and chop them with an electric mini-chopper. The chopped garlic will keep when tightly sealed for up to one month in the refrigerator or for six months in the freezer. Frozen minced garlic, which contains no preservatives, is widely used by food manufacturers and food service establishments. Occasionally it can be found in the supermarket, usually in bubble packs containing a dozen or so teaspoon-size portions. It is an excellent product and very convenient to use. There's no need to defrost it; it thaws in seconds in a hot skillet. One whole clove of garlic equals about ½ teaspoon of minced garlic.

Gingerroot: Fresh ginger is hard to handle. First you have to peel it (scraping it with the edge of a spoon works best), and then you have to shred it or chop it, a task complicated by tough hairy fibers that refuse to break down. Jarred minced ginger eliminates all of that and is widely available. It can be found in either the Asian foods section of your market or near the minced garlic in the produce section. Use it as you would freshly grated gingerroot, or you can substitute it for dried ginger at about three times the volume. If substituting jarred ginger in a baking recipe, it should be added with the wet ingredients.

Ginger is also sold pickled for sushi. This thinly sliced marinated ginger can be found alongside the sushi in the prepared foods section of your market, or it can be bought in any Asian market. It is slightly sweet and lightly tangy. I use it as a flavor enhancer and garnish in salads or with grilled fish. Pickled ginger should be kept in its liquid in the refrigerator tightly sealed; it will stay usable for several months.

Lemon and lime juices: Most bottled lemon and lime juices have a pronounced aftertaste that makes them unsuitable substitutes for freshly squeezed juice. The exceptions are organic 100 percent lemon and lime juices bottled by Santa Cruz Natural. They have a clean citrus flavor that is very close to fresh. Once opened, the juice should be kept refrigerated; it will retain its quality for about a month. If storing longer than that, I suggest freezing the juice in ice cube trays.

Mushrooms: White mushrooms and Portobello mushrooms are the most commonly available washed and sliced mushrooms. They are ready to cook right out of the pack and will stay fresh in the refrigerator for up to five days. A few cultivated wild mushrooms are available washed and trimmed in medley packs, which usually include sliced crimini, shiitake, oyster, and enoki mushrooms. Most markets also sell a wide selection of loose wild mushrooms by the pound; they need gentle washing and trimming before they are ready for cooking. Dried wild mushrooms are also available and will keep indefinitely in a cabinet; they need only to be hydrated in hot water before using them. Their soaking liquid is a great addition to soups and sauces.

Onions: Chopped onions can be purchased refrigerated or frozen. The refrigerated product is treated with citric acid to prevent spoilage. This can leave a slight citrusy aftertaste when the onions are tasted alone, but the aftertaste dissipates when combined with other ingredients. Frozen chopped onions have no preservatives, although they are softer and moister than fresh onions, which makes them a little harder to brown but very similar to fresh after cooking. Recently, jarred caramelized onions, which are more like a sweet onion relish than caramelized roasted onions, have started to appear. Although they are too sweet and tart to be a substitute for fresh roasted onions, they can be a delicious addition to roasted chicken or beef gravy and make a surprisingly good sauce base for pasta.

Peppers: Roasted red and yellow bell peppers are available jarred, canned, and frozen, and all are excellent products. Look for packages in which the peppers are mostly whole. Those with visible pieces of burnt skin tend to be a bit smokier. Unopened jarred roasted peppers will keep almost indefinitely, but they should be used within a week after opening and stored in the refrigerator. Sometimes pickled roasted peppers are sold; they can be delicious but have a very different flavor.

Potatoes: There has been a revolution in the realm of processed potatoes since the days when dehydrated mashed potato flakes were the only option. In the freezer case you will find a myriad of options: fried, mashed, twice-baked, souffléed, roasted, and grilled. Crispy French fries make surprisingly good croutons in a salad; roasted and grilled potato wedges can be added to a stir-fry or give you a head start on a creative side dish; and mashed potatoes can be the basis for a soup, soufflé, vegetable pie, or creamy sauce.

In the refrigerator case there are many new options: shredded hashed browns, diced and sliced white potatoes, and wedges of red-skinned potatoes. These washed and sliced parcooked products have never been frozen and provide a convenient alternative that falls between fully prepared frozen potatoes and peeling and cooking from scratch. Most of the refrigerated products need some cooking.

One word about instant mashed potatoes: Although I would never use them to prepare mashed potatoes, they are very useful for thickening a watery soup or a thin sauce. Used in small amounts, they thicken liquid instantly without adding an off flavor or forming lumps the way flour and starch can.

Pumpkin: Canned pumpkin purée gives better results with less work than cooking pumpkin from scratch. This is partially because the canning process helps to break down tough fibers and concentrates the flavors of pumpkin more completely than simmering does, but it is also because canned pumpkin is made from a special breed of pumpkin that is unavailable to the average consumer. In recipes that call for pumpkin purée, do not use pumpkin pie filling, which is seasoned and sweetened.

Salad bar: The salad bar in your local supermarket is an ever-evolving source of fresh produce and condiments. There is no rule that says its contents are solely for salad. If you need only a small amount of sliced carrots, snapped green beans, or marinated artichoke hearts, the salad bar can be the most economical way to buy your vegetables.

Spinach: Frozen chopped spinach used to be one of my convenience staples, but prewashed spinach in a microwavable bag has changed my ways (although I usually keep a box or two of frozen on hand for emergencies). Years ago I switched to cooking spinach (frozen or fresh) in the microwave. It takes a few minutes and requires no additional water or pots, no stabbing at a frozen brick, and no stirring a mound of leaves to get a cup of cooked spinach. Now that fresh spinach comes fully cleaned in a package that goes right into the microwave, starting from frozen seems like backtracking.

When serving spinach in whole leaves or as a side dish, I prefer baby spinach because the stems are less noticeable, but for fillings, casseroles, and recipes that call for chopping spinach, I use less expensive mature spinach because the stems won't show after chopping. Bags of fresh spinach will keep for about five days in the refrigerator. Avoid those with wilted leaves or damp spots.

Squash: Frozen winter squash, made from a purée of acorn and butternut squashes, is a high-quality product that is helpful for thickening and sweetening vegetable sauces and soups.

Tomatoes: Tomatoes for canning are picked ripe and are usually in the can within a day or two of picking. Compared to the hothouse-grown specimens available in many markets, canned tomatoes are not only a better buy but are often of better quality. All canned tomatoes are minimally cooked in the can to sterilize the contents, and at most they are boiled down to a paste. The more cooking, the less the canned tomato will resemble fresh, and the more concentrated its flavor will be. If a recipe calls for cooking tomatoes, canned products give you a head start. The available canned tomato products from least to most cooked are as follows:

- *Whole tomatoes* are cooked in their own juice just long enough to kill any bacteria.
- *Diced or recipe-ready tomatoes* are the same as whole tomatoes but are cut up. They are much more convenient than whole tomatoes (who has ever used a canned tomato whole in a recipe?) and are sold with no salt added or seasoned with Italian herbs, jalapeños, garlic, or onion. If a recipe calls for fresh tomatoes, diced canned ones are the next best thing, and depending on the quality of the fresh tomatoes available, they may be a better choice.
- *Stewed tomatoes* are cut in wedges and cooked long enough so that some of the tomato pulp breaks down into the juices. Stewed tomatoes are usually seasoned with onion, garlic, and peppers. Because they are cooked more and seasoned, they can streamline the preparation of some stews and soups.
- *Crushed tomatoes* are pulverized and cooked until sterile. Use them when you want a smooth but lightly cooked sauce or soup.
- *Crushed tomatoes in purée* are cooked until the fiber of the tomato starts to break down. Use them when a thicker consistency is desired.
- *Tomato purée* is fully cooked until all the fiber disappears. Purée is good when you want to make a long-simmered sauce without cooking it for hours.
- *Tomato paste* is concentrated purée. Its flavor is so intense and its consistency so thick that it should only be used as a flavor enhancer. The best-quality tomato paste is packaged in tubes. Usually imported, these pastes are very sweet and aromatic, and are the only type of tomato paste I recommend. Best of all, the tube keeps air away from any leftover paste, allowing it to stay fresh for months in the refrigerator. No more throwing out half-used cans of tomato paste.

Vegetable juice (V8)—Vegetable juice is not technically a type of produce, but when streamlining a sauce, soup, or stew, it provides a balance of vegetable flavors so effortlessly that to my mind it should be given vegetable status. Although blended vegetable juices such as V8 look like tomato juice, their principal flavor profile is closer to the celery, onion, carrot, and bell pepper blend used so frequently in European and American recipes. I use sodium-reduced V8 as a base for soups, braised liquids, and gravies.

Sauces

Asian sauces: See entries under Ethnic Foods for specific sauces such as Curry (page 22), Hoisin (page 23), Thai peanut (page 25), and Soy sauce (page 24).

Barbecue sauce: There are hundreds of barbecue sauces out there, each proclaiming itself the best, and it really doesn't matter which one you use. Chances are it is tomato-based, sweet, tangy, and spicy (it might be a bit smoky, too). You can use it on grilled meats and braised ribs, but barbecue sauce also makes a great base for salad dressing, a seasoning for pot roast, or a flavor boost in a stir-fry. Almost any recipe that calls for ketchup can be made with barbecue sauce.

Broth: Chicken, vegetable, and beef broths are essential for making soups, sauces, and stews, braised dishes, and are available in many forms:

- Canned and boxed broths are ready to use. They are packed in a variety of sizes and packages, and many manufacturers sell fat-free and low-salt versions. Low salt is my preference because of its versatility (you can add salt to taste) and because you can't use salty broths to make a glaze (as they thicken, their salinity concentrates into brine). The brand I rely on is Swanson. It has a good balance of vegetables and meat flavors that is close to homemade, and the salt level is moderate. Most broth companies also sell broths flavored with onion, roasted garlic, and/or herbs. Although these may be convenient for specific recipes, the additional flavors limit their usefulness. I'd rather buy straight broth and add my own flavoring.
- Concentrated broth bases are often richer than canned broths and have the added advantage of allowing the cook to season a recipe to taste. If you followed only the package directions, you would think that the only thing these products provided was a way of making broth, but instead of diluting them you can use them full strength, a teaspoon at a time, to enrich a soup or turn watery pan drippings into a sauce. Bases can be found on the shelf, frozen, or refrigerated. They can vary greatly in price, and low price isn't always the best value. Look at the ingredients: If salt is high in the ingredients list, the salt may be taking the place of more expensive flavorful components such as meat and vegetables. The presence of yeast extract and/or hydrolyzed protein can mean the same thing; ingredients such as starch add bulk and thickness but no flavor.
- Powdered broth and bouillon cubes are the cheapest source of

broth, but they are also the saltiest. I keep them on hand because they don't need refrigeration and have a long shelf life. I also use them for broths that aren't available canned such as fish, seafood, ham, and vegetable. The brand I use most often is Knorr.

Marinade: Marinades are all about flavor. They are saturated with herbs, spices, salt, sugar, and acid, and their intensity is both their best asset and their greatest limitation. It gives them the strength to infuse dense meats with flavor or to glaze a grilled chop right out of the bottle, but the results are caustic if you use them as a pan sauce. If you want to use a bottled marinade to make a sauce, you must temper it with some broth, juice, wine, cream, or even water. With that caveat in mind, go wild. Marinades come in every flavor and for any cuisine you can think of.

Pasta sauce: Although there are literally hundreds of pasta sauces, all you need to know is that what is on your grocer's shelf falls into two broad groups: red and non-red. The bigger group is red, and red sauces can be one of two styles: ragù and marinara. Ragù is the Italian name for a long-simmered sauce containing meat. Ragùs are thick and rich, and usually lack any fresh vegetable flavor. Marinara sauces are lighter, fresher, and thinner than ragùs. They do not contain meat and often have chunks of vegetables. You can also think of ragùs as being an older style of sauce as the popular style for red sauce has evolved from being thick and pulpy to being thin and chunky.

When cooking with red sauce, I usually find thinner is better. Added to a sauté, a thin sauce allows you to cook meat in the sauce without fear of its scorching or becoming pasty. When a recipe requires a thinner sauce, I specify marinara; otherwise the brand and style are left up to you. Most red sauces are jarred, and most jarred sauces are thick. To find a thinner sauce, tilt the jar to see how fluid the sauce is before buying or look at refrigerated sauces, which don't have to cook as long as jarred sauces and therefore tend to be fresher and lighter. You will usually find them next to the refrigerated fresh pasta in your market.

Non-red sauces are either white or green. The most commonly found white pasta sauce is Alfredo, which is a cream sauce flavored with cheese and often nutmeg. It is convenient for making lasagna or a white pizza, and it can be helpful as a creamy soup base. Pesto, a blend of ground fresh basil, garlic, cheese, oil, and nuts, is the most well known green pasta sauce. Most jarred pestos are just that, but some pesto pasta sauce is really a white creamy sauce flavored with pesto. It cannot be used in a recipe in place of pesto.

Salad dressing: Salad dressings are very similar to marinades. They are intensely flavored and often highly acidic, and for the most part they can be used interchangeably with marinades in grilling and broiling. However, you cannot simmer them in a pan. Most salad dressings are designed to be used cold and they separate as soon as they are heated. If you want the flavor of a salad dressing in a pan sauce or stew, you can add it at the end of cooking, being careful not to use too much and keeping the heat low once the dressing is incorporated. Following these rules, you might be pleasantly surprised at how effortlessly a little blue cheese dressing can enliven a potato soup, or how a garlic vinaigrette can boost the flavor of a pasta sauce.

Sauce concentrates: For years restaurant chefs have had beautifully crafted sauce bases from which they create glistening, rich, silken sauces. These products have gradually become available to all of us. They are a bit pricey, but the results are truly professional. There are many types to choose from, including bases for duck and game sauces, but I would start with a demi-glace, either poultry or veal. Demi-glace is a rich, concentrated, all-purpose brown sauce that can transform the simplest sautéed chicken breast or pork chop into a four-star entrée. All you have to do is place a spoonful of sauce concentrate in the pan, add some water, and *voilá*.

Soups: Condensed soups have been used for sauces for more than half a century. In fact, at Campbell's Soup Company, where condensed soups were invented, they talk about their standard cooking soups (cream of mushroom, cream of chicken, and cream of tomato) as mother sauces. Because the results are well known and the recipes are already entrenched in American cooking, I have not spent a lot of time in this cookbook exploring condensed soup as sauce. But they still are a very convenient and flavorful way to prepare a silky, family-pleasing sauce base. They also make a surprisingly good risotto, the easiest cacciatore, and a better-than-average meatless moussaka.

Noncondensed, ready-to-serve soups are also useful for sauce making. Lentil soup is instant dal (beans) in a curried stew, and cream of corn, pumpkin, or onion soup can be a great base for a simple skillet sauce.

Wine: It is always helpful to have a bottle of white and a bottle of red wine on hand for sauce making. It doesn't really matter what kind. As long as it is drinkable, it will be cookable, too.

Condiments

Marinated artichoke hearts: Jars of completely trimmed artichoke hearts in a garlic and herb vinaigrette marinade are an essential convenience ingredient. They glorify vegetable lasagna, enrich a dip, enliven rice, and exalt pizza. If I had to limit my pantry to ten ingredients, this would be one of them. Marinated artichoke hearts come whole, halved, quartered, and chopped. When chopped, they are sold as artichoke spread or artichoke antipasto.

Bruschetta: Traditionally known as toast topped with a savory paste, bruschetta has become the name of the topping itself, and in particular the tomato variety. Tomato bruschetta can be found jarred, pouched, refrigerated, and fresh. It is an instant fresh pasta sauce, a sophisticated salad dressing, a topping for pizza, a garnish for rice pilaf, a pan sauce for chicken breast, a relish for broiled fish, and a base for vegetarian chili. Except for desserts, it plays a role in every aspect of cooking. Refrigerated bruschetta is totally unprocessed. It is like a finely chopped tomato salad and must be used within a few days of purchase. You will find it in the prepared foods case of your supermarket, at the deli section, with the produce, or in the dairy case. Bruschetta in a jar or pouch has been pasteurized, which means it has been cooked just long enough to destroy any pathogenic bacteria. It is similar in texture to salsa but has a different flavor profile. It is usually shelved with pasta sauces.

Capers: Capers are the unopened buds of a weedlike plant of the same name. They are native to the Mediterranean basin and have been part of Mediterranean cooking since ancient times. The buds are picked before they get a chance to open, and then are sun-dried and pickled in vinegar or salt. Capers are classified according to size. The smallest, nonpareils, are considered the best, but larger buds have a similar flavor and can be used in recipes without ill effect. Capers are quite pungent, and some recipes tell you to rinse them, although this is only necessary for capers that are packed in salt. Like olives, capers add a spark to sauces, salads, and pasta dishes. They can be scattered over grilled or sautéed meats and are traditionally paired with seafood.

Caper berries are much larger than capers and not nearly as pungent. They are the pickled fruit of the same plant and usually are sold with their stems attached. They are best used as garnish. Capers in brine will keep indefinitely unopened and will last for several months in the refrigerator after opening. Make sure they are covered with brine so that they stay moist.

Chutney: Chutney is the spicy sweet-and-sour relish used in Indian cuisine to give a lift to plain foods such as rice or dal (beans). It is usually made fresh and is largely a mixture of herbs and spices, vinegar, sugar, and fruit or coconut. A chutney made with green (under-ripe) mangoes was popular with British colonials and has become the prototype for the most well known commercial chutney, Major Grey's, which has evolved into a decidedly sweet, tangy, jamlike relish. Now you can find jarred chutneys made from onion, garlic, tomato, citrus, pineapple, apple, and pear. Just a dollop in a pan sauce or spread over a roasting meat will lend a sweet, tart, spicy tang that instantly boosts flavors. Chutney can be stirred into a stuffing or spooned over grilled meat. It can be a dip for fried foods or raw vegetables, and it is delicious paired with cheese.

Cilantro chutney: See Cilantro (page 8).

Honey: Honey ranges in flavor from mild to pungent. In general, color is a good indication of intensity; lighter honey tends to be milder, and darker honey is more robust. Honey also comes in several forms. Liquid honey is the most common, but honey is also sold in its comb, dehydrated into granules, or creamed. Although health claims for honey are common, it really has very few nutritional benefits. It is basically sugar and is best used when you want a honey flavor or when you need a liquid sweetener.

Hot pepper sauce: There are hundreds of hot pepper sauces, but all you need are three: fiery, mild, and chipotle. The fiery one I use most often is a Thai hot sauce called Sriracha Chili Sauce. It is available in Asian groceries and many supermarkets. If you can't find it, anything with flames on the label will do. You should also have a mild hot sauce such as Frank's RedHot Sauce or Crystal Hot Sauce for making Buffalo wings. A sauce containing chipotle peppers (smoked jalapeños) is also essential. Chipotle sauces are on the hot side and wondrously smoky. These three sauces will get you through a variety of recipes. Add them to taste and don't cook the dish much after the hot sauce is added. Hot sauces are meant to be eaten right out of the bottle; cooking destroys their more subtle flavors, leaving nothing but heat.

Ketchup: Sometimes an ingredient becomes so familiar that we lose track of what it actually is; this is the case with ketchup. Ketchups were originally salty fermented sauces from Asia, more akin to soy sauce or fish sauce than the sweet and tangy tomato-based condiment of today. But even though American ketchup is sweeter and thicker than the Asian original, it can have similar culinary uses. Like chutney, it adds a pleasant sweet and tangy kick to pan sauces, dressings, and marinades. A little bit of ketchup can round out flat flavors in a gravy or stew, or thicken a salad dressing without adding extra fat.

Mustard: Mustard has become its own mini-industry. Not only does it come creamy, coarse, spicy, sweet, and tangy, it ranges in color from school bus yellow to mahogany brown, hitting several shades of green and red along the way. It is flavored with fruit, molasses, honey, maple syrup, wine, horseradish, chiles, sweet peppers, smoke, forest herbs, and watercress. It comes crunchy with mustard seeds, stone-ground, and silkily seedless. Mustards are French, Bavarian, Polish, Hungarian, and good old American, and its unmistakable spark enhances bottled sauces, mayonnaise, salad dressings, barbecue sauces, relishes, stuffings, nuts, pretzels, and sardines. Any mustard can enliven your cooking.

Nut butters: Nut butters can lend their creaminess and richness to sauces and dressings without adding any dairy. I keep a good selection on hand, but the ones I use most are peanut butter, tahini (sesame butter), and almond or walnut butter. Except for hydrogenated peanut butter, opened jars of nut butter should be kept in the refrigerator to prevent them from turning rancid. Although most nut butters are sold in the same aisle as fruit preserves and jams, tahini is usually stored with Middle Eastern ingredients in the ethnic foods area of your market.

Oils: Although some oils are for cooking and others are specifically for flavoring, there are a few that can be used for both. I use pure olive oil as my all-purpose oil. When I want to emphasize the olive flavor, I switch to extra-virgin olive oil, and on rare occasions when its olive flavor doesn't go with what I'm cooking or when I'm deep-frying, I use regular vegetable oil. You will also find oils seasoned with herbs and spices. These are for adding flavor to recipes and should be used at the end of cooking and in small amounts. Heating these oils can cause their flavors to dissipate. Unusual oils such as walnut, almond, avocado, and sesame also don't respond well to heat and should be used as a flavoring or in a salad dressing that will not be cooked.

Purchase oils in an amount that you will use within a month or so. An open bottle of oil will eventually turn rancid. You can lengthen its life by storing it in the refrigerator, although it might become semi-solid when cold. To return it to a liquid state, warm it in a microwave or under warm running water.

The easiest way to coat a pan with oil for cooking is to use nonstick spray. Pam was the original oil spray, but now there are many more. Most brands include olive oil, canola oil, and vegetable oil in their product line. As far as I know, there is only one brand of oil spray with flour: Baker's Joy. It is sold for coating baking pans in recipes that call for greasing and flouring pans, but I also use it to coat meats for sautéing.

Olive salad: Also called muffuletta after the famous New Orleans sandwich in which it plays a definitive flavor role, olive salad is a mixture of chopped olives, bell peppers, garlic, olive oil, and herbs. It is usually used as a sandwich spread, but I also find it a wonderful addition to Mediterranean-style pan sauce and stews.

Pesto: A pesto is a flavorful paste that can be used to season everything from soup to bread. The most famous pesto is the one from Genoa, made with fresh basil, garlic, olive oil, pine nuts, and Parmesan cheese. It is also the most commonly available. You will find it refrigerated, frozen, and in jars.

Although refrigerated pestos are the freshest, jarred is more convenient and lasts longer. I also use cilantro pesto, artichoke pesto, red pepper pesto, and sun-dried tomato pesto. You can find most pestos in your market shelved with such condiments as capers and olives, in the produce case, or next to pastas and pasta sauces.

Red pepper spread: Also called rouille and red pepper pesto, red pepper spread can be roasted or not. It has a beautiful color and gives you an unadulterated flavor of the vegetable. I use it frequently, whenever I want the sweet fragrance of red pepper without having to clean, core, and chop. Once opened, red pepper spread will last about a month in the refrigerator.

Salsa: If your image of salsa has chips dipped in it, you're missing much of its culinary potential. After all, what is salsa? Tomatoes, onions, bell peppers, and chiles chopped together. That means anytime you need those ingredients in a recipe, a jar of salsa can simplify your labors. It's an obvious head start for chili or a tortilla soup, but it can also be part of a Chinese stir-fry, Caribbean shrimp and rice or a Moroccan stew. There is nothing in salsa which dictates that it can only be southwestern or Mexican. Many salsas are marketed by their heat level, but in most recipes heat is not the main attraction, and salsa is much more versatile. Mild or medium heat levels are the most malleable in a recipe; you can always add hot sauce to taste. But if you like your food incendiary and all you ever buy is hotter-than-heck salsa, feel free to use it. Salsas are also made from other ingredients. Some of the most useful alternative salsas are roasted red pepper salsa, corn and black bean salsa, chipotle salsa, pineapple or peach salsa, and mango salsa.

Sun-dried tomatoes: For nearly three hundred years Italians dried tomatoes in the sun for use in winter when fresh tomatoes were not available. Now sun-dried tomatoes are less important in Italy than they are in America, where they have been integrated into everything from salad dressing to potato chips. Sun-dried tomatoes come in many forms. The least processed is dried halves, which are sold prepackaged or loose; they are usually found in the produce section of your market. In this state the tomatoes need to be reconstituted before use. You can soak them in warm water until they are pliable, drain them (reserve the liquid for sauces of soups), and use them in a recipe. After soaking they can be kept in the refrigerator for up to two weeks.

It is more convenient to buy sun-dried tomatoes already reconstituted, packed in oil. They come as halves, quartered, sliced, chopped, and puréed. They are also available processed as salsa, pesto, relish, spread, or paste. Most forms are interchangeable, so if a recipe calls for sun-dried tomato pesto and all you have is sun-dried tomato salsa, chances are it will work fine—a little chunky but most likely delicious. Once opened, any sun-dried tomato product will stay usable for three months if kept in the refrigerator.

Tapenade: Tapenade is a black olive paste from southern France that is seasoned with garlic, olive oil, anchovies, and capers. It is typically used as a spread on bread, a flavorful sauce for pasta, or as a seasoning for grilled fish or poultry. You will find it freshly made in the refrigerator case of your market along with other dips, or in jars shelved beside the olives, or in the pasta aisle. Use tapenade whenever and wherever you want the flavor of olives. Although not as common, green olive tapenade is also sold in some stores.

Vinegar: Next to salt, vinegar is the most important flavor enhancer in your kitchen. With its innate ability to awaken the taste buds, a touch of vinegar can enliven meat flavors in a broth, heighten fruit flavor in a sauce, or calm a cacophonous curry. Because a little vinegar goes a long way, don't worry too much about price; even an aged balsamic that is $15 a bottle costs only pennies a serving to use. If you have only one vinegar in your pantry, it should be either a good-quality red wine vinegar or an apple cider vinegar. Both of these have some sweetness balancing their tartness. A bottle of balsamic is nice for sauces, and a fruit vinegar such as raspberry or orange is helpful for desserts. After that you can branch out to rice wine vinegar, herb vinegars, chili vinegar, or vanilla, one of my favorites.

Ethnic Foods

Asian noodles: There are five types of Asian noodles:

- Rice noodles (also called rice vermicelli) are white. They can be flat or round, medium thick or angel-hair thin. They do not need to be boiled. Just cover them with very hot water and let them soak for ten to fifteen minutes, depending on their thickness, and then drain them. After soaking, they will be flexible but remain a bit leathery. When you add them to a broth, sauce, or stir-fry, they will instantly soften.
- Bean thread noodles (also called cellophane noodles) are transparent. Made from mung bean starch and water, they are very brittle when dry but become soft and slippery after soaking. Treat them the same way as rice noodles, but they need only five to ten minutes of soaking.
- Soba noodles are made from buckwheat flour and look like buff-colored spaghetti or fettuccine. They should be boiled and cooked very quickly, about five minutes.

- Somen noodles are like soba except they are made from wheat flour and are creamy white. They are cooked in the same way as soba, and the two are often interchangeable.
- Udon noodles are flat, wide white noodles. Like other Asian noodles they cook quickly, in about five to eight minutes.

Baba ghanouj: A blend of roasted eggplant, garlic, and tahini, baba ghanouj is ubiquitous in the Middle East and nearly as common in the refrigerator cases of American markets. Similar to hummus, it is used mostly as a dip with flatbread but is also an excellent thickener for Arab-style stews or as a topping for vegetable pizza. It also makes a very easy baked eggplant mousse. Baba ghanouj is mostly sold fresh and will keep for about a week after opening.

Chili oil (also called hot pepper oil): This very fiery seasoning should be used as you would hot sauce, as a seasoning, not a cooking oil. It is made by steeping chiles in oil until the oil is permeated with their flavor. Sometimes toasted sesame oil is used, in which case the product is called hot sesame oil.

Chinese chili paste (also called chili sauce): This hot pepper paste is a mainstay of Chinese cooking. There are several different styles; it can either be made solely from hot peppers or bulked with fermented bean paste. It is frequently seasoned with garlic. All chili paste will keep indefinitely in the refrigerator.

Coconut milk: Coconut milk is made by mixing finely chopped coconut in hot water until it releases its richness and flavor. When you buy canned coconut milk, all this work has been done for you. It will keep for several years on the shelf and about a week in the refrigerator after opening. If you need to store it longer, it can be frozen. Light coconut milk is made by allowing the milk to settle into its thicker and more watery parts. The thicker "cream" has most of the fat, and when it is skimmed off, the more watery "skimmed milk" that remains is sold as light. It is lower in fat, which can cause it to separate more easily when it is heated. Both types of canned coconut milk are stored with Asian ingredients in your market. Either type can be used for sauces, soups, stir-fries, and stews.

Curry sauce (also called curry cooking sauce, masala simmer sauce, or curry simmer sauce): These Indian convenience foods simplify complex curry recipes down to browning the main ingredient and adding the sauce. They are easy to use and are of remarkably good quality. They are found in the ethnic foods section of your market or in specialty stores.

Curry paste: Red and green curry pastes are for making Thai curries. They are a blend of chiles, lemongrass, garlic, lime juice, and herbs. The only difference between the two is that one is made with red chiles and the other is made with green. Both are concentrated seasonings and need to be thinned with coconut milk, broth, or another liquid.

Fish sauce (also called nam pla): Made by fermenting salted fish, fish sauce is an ancient and important flavoring in Southeast Asian dishes. Fish sauces vary widely in quality, and lower-quality ones can have an off-putting aroma. Those made in China and Thailand are the best. The brand I use most often, called Tiparos, is from Thailand. It comes in both glass and plastic bottles, and the sauce in glass bottles holds up a bit longer. A Taste of Thai, a commonly available brand, is very good. Fish sauce should be a light amber color (the color of tea). It will darken with age. When it turns brown, discard it.

Hoisin sauce (also called plum sauce): A thick fermented soybean sauce, hoisin is dark brown, slightly sweet, and subtly spicy. It is a common seasoning in Chinese dishes and is best known as the sauce served in Chinese restaurants with Peking duck. It can be used like chutney to perk up the flavors of grilled and roasted meats or sweet vegetables, such as carrots, sweet potatoes, or winter squash. It comes jarred and canned; the jar is more convenient.

Hummus: A Middle Eastern blend of chickpeas, garlic, sesame tahini, lemon juice, and oil, hummus has broken into the mainstream. Sold in every market, you will usually find it near the produce area, although there are now so many hummus products, it might have its own mini refrigerator case. It is not unusual to find red pepper hummus, lemon hummus, herbed hummus, hot pepper hummus, kalamata olive hummus, and sun-dried tomato hummus. Hummus is typically used as a dip for crackers or vegetables. It is also a good thickener for soups, a binder for fish cakes, or a base for a creamy salad dressing.

Mole: Mole (pronounced moh-LAY) is an elaborate style of stew in Mexico that is flavored with a litany of chiles, spices, fruit, and nuts. The mole that is sold in jars is a concentrate designed to be turned into stew by adding water or broth. There are two types: brown mole, which is made from red chiles and often contains chocolate, and green mole (also called pipián), made from green chiles, herbs, and pumpkin seeds. The brown mole is usually cooked with meats and poultry. Green is for seafood. Mole is found alongside other Mexican ingredients. It keeps indefinitely in the refrigerator.

Nori: These thin seaweed sheets are best known as the wrappers for sushi. I use them as a garnish for seafood. You will find nori sheets in the Asian section of your market. Buy them toasted if you can. They keep indefinitely.

Oyster sauce: Like fish sauce, oyster sauce was originally made by fermenting oysters, but now it is a thickened, subtly sweet-salty brown sauce flavored with oyster extracts. It is not as fishy or as aromatic as fish sauce, but it is slightly more pungent than hoisin sauce, which it closely resembles. It is a traditional addition to Chinese chicken dishes, but it is equally good as a marinade or glaze for grilled meats, poultry, and seafood.

Pickled ginger: See Gingerroot (page 10).

Pipián: See Mole (page 23).

Ponzu sauce: This Japanese dipping sauce, a mixture of soy sauce and citrus juice, is used most often with seafood. It is very light and fresh, and is a good substitute for soy sauce when you want something more subtle. I prefer it to lite soy sauce, which I find bland and watery.

Sesame oil: There are two types of sesame oil. The pale yellow type, found mostly in health food stores, is made from raw sesame seeds, is very mild, and is used mostly for sautéing. It is shelved in your market with other oils. The second type, toasted or dark sesame oil, is Asian. It is made from toasted sesame seeds and is quite aromatic. It is used as a flavoring agent, usually in small amounts, and is added at the end of cooking. It is shelved with other Asian ingredients. When I call for sesame oil in my recipes, I am referring to the dark type.

Soy sauce: There are two types of soy sauce: thin and thick. Most of the soy sauces you will find are thin. They are watery, dark brown, and salty. You will find thick soy (also called dark) only in Asian markets. It is a thick paste, more fermented tasting, and less salty. I have not used it in this book. Of the thin soys, buy only those that say they are naturally brewed. They may be marked as premium, superior, or light. Do not confuse *light soy* with *lite soy,* which has reduced sodium. I only use lite soy for dipping and not for cooking because I find that I have to add twice as much to get enough flavor out of it. Chinese, Japanese, and Thai soy sauces taste somewhat different from one another, but for most recipes they are interchangeable. Soy sauces are generally cheap enough to experiment with different ones until you find the type you like. Tamari is Japanese soy sauce.

Stir-fry sauce: Stir-fry sauces are all-purpose, Asian-flavored sauces that are similar to teriyaki. They are combinations of soy sauce, vinegar, ginger, garlic, and sugar, which are all the ingredients one would have to assemble to make a typical stir-fry.

Tahini: A Middle Eastern sesame paste, tahini is sold in tins and jars, usually in the ethnic foods area of your market. Tahini is very creamy and can be used to thicken or enrich sauces. Be careful—it is quite intense; a little goes a long way.

Teriyaki: A traditional Japanese marinade and dipping sauce, teriyaki is a combination of soy sauce, sugar, vinegar, ginger, and garlic. There are many brands, but the one I buy exclusively is Soy Vay Veri Veri Teriyaki. It is slightly thicker than other bottled teriyaki sauces, much more flavorful, and loaded with sesame seeds.

Thai peanut Sauce: This sauce is a blend of coconut milk, peanuts, fish sauce, and spices, and it usually includes tamarind, chiles, lemongrass, and coriander. It comes dried in packets or jarred. Both are designed to be mixed with canned coconut milk to become a sauce, but the jarred product can be used as a marinade right out of the bottle. Thai peanut sauce is a traditional dip for grilled meats and seafood, but it is also useful as a stir-fry sauce and as a base for an exotic soup.

Tobiko: Tobiko is flying fish roe. Found in the sushi case of your market, these tiny, crunchy red orange balls are used more for their texture than their flavor, which is slightly salty. I use tobiko in salads and as a garnish for fish.

Wasabi: The green horseradish paste served with sushi is wasabi. It comes in two forms: powdered and fully prepared in a tube. Powdered wasabi must be rehydrated in water, so the prepared wasabi is much easier to use. Although wasabi is most often served with fish, it is a delicious seasoning for all types of meat and a great addition to mashed potatoes. The wasabi that is generally available in the United States is not really wasabi. Real wasabi is a rhizome in the mustard family and is cultivated mostly in Japan. It has some of the properties of horseradish (in particular, sinus-clearing), which is why horseradish is used as a common replacement. The wasabi that is commonly sold is a mixture of horseradish, mustard, and food coloring.

Grains and Beans

Canned beans: Almost any bean you can buy dried is also available in a can. Canned beans are slightly softer than the same beans cooked from scratch, but this is a small concession considering the hours saved by not having to soak and simmer them. During canning, protein from the beans sloughs into the liquid in the can, making it slightly slimy. Although there is nothing wrong with the liquid, many people think it has an unpleasant consistency, and there is some evidence that draining and rinsing canned beans makes them less flatulent.

Instant beans: Dried instant beans are an all-natural product made by cooking beans with spices and then drying and crushing them into powder. Then all you have to do is add boiling water to bring them back to life. These powders are typically sold for making bean dip or refried beans, but stopping there ignores their hidden potential as a thickener for countless sauces and broths. They make beautiful soups and form a crunchy seasoned crust on a sautéed fish fillet. You will find pinto, black bean, and falafel (chickpea) powders most often.

Cereal: Plain cereals such as Grape-Nuts, Rice Krispies, Chex, and Kix have a slightly sweet toasted grain flavor that makes them the perfect breading for fried foods and a flavorful low-fat topping for a fruit crisp. Packaged granola adds instant sweetness, fruit, and nuts to a cookie or spice cake recipe.

Couscous: Couscous is finely ground pasta that is precooked and dried so that all you need to do is soak it in boiling water. Couscous comes flavored in countless ways, and although flavored products make very easy side dishes, their added seasoning can make them less versatile in the kitchen. For that reason I almost always use plain couscous, but if all you have is a seasoned variety, you can use it and just discard the seasoning pack.

Edamame: Edamame (pronounced "ed-ah-mommy") are fresh green soybeans. Popular in Japan for centuries, they are now grown in the United States, but because their season is short and the fresh beans are relatively perishable, most edamame are frozen. They are usually in their pods but occasionally are already shelled. Edamame cook quickly, in about five minutes in boiling water or a microwave. They can be eaten as a snack right out of the pod, or the shelled edamame can be used in salads, soups, stews, pasta dishes, and stir-fries. Edamame have all the healthful properties of other soy products, including a significant amount of calcium, iron, potassium, B vitamins, and phytoestrogens, which are being touted as cancer-fighting agents.

Pasta: There are three types of pasta. Dried pasta can be stored indefinitely, but it must hydrate as it cooks, which can take time. Refrigerated and frozen pastas are fresh so they do not take as long to cook. This is a benefit when you are in a rush, but they must be frozen for extended storage. If you know you won't be using the pasta right away, it is best to buy it frozen and cook it right from the freezer. Some baked pasta shapes, such as lasagna noodles, are sold as no-boil. This means they do not need to be precooked before baking. They work well, but so does any dried pasta. In fact, you can make everything from baked ziti to lasagna without precooking noodles. Just add a little water with the sauce, and the pasta will cook while the casserole bakes.

Polenta: Polenta is Italian cornmeal mush. You can make it from scratch with coarse-ground cornmeal, or you can use one of the many processed polenta products. They range from instant dry polenta, which still needs to be simmered in water, to fully prepared polentas that are ready to slice and heat. All forms come in a variety of flavors, including garlic, herb, mushroom, pesto, and sun-dried tomato.

Rice and risotto: I am not a fan of instant rice. I find it mushy and bland, and since regular long-grain rice takes less than twenty minutes to cook, I don't see any reason for it. Quick-cooking brown rice does reach tenderness about fifteen minutes faster than regular brown rice, but it lacks the hearty flavor and chewy texture that is the hallmark of the real thing, so I don't use that, either. Boxed risottos are not much faster than using regular arborio rice (about five minutes' difference), and even though they seem easier because they don't require constant stirring, it isn't really necessary to stir regular risotto as much as traditional recipes tell you to (every five minutes or so is fine). So there's not much advantage there, either.

Seitan: Seitan is a vegetarian protein made from wheat gluten. Of all the meatless proteins it is the one that most closely resembles meat in texture and appearance. Seitan comes fully processed in refrigerated packages ready to be grilled, sautéed, or added to a stew.

Tabbouleh: Tabbouleh is an Arab-style parsley salad made with bulgur wheat, but because it is the sole exposure that most Americans have to bulgur, the name of the salad has become synonymous with the grain itself. Tabbouleh is cracked whole wheat that is steamed and dried. To cook it, just soak the grain in boiling water for a few minutes, a process so quick and easy that it is a natural convenience ingredient for time-pressed cooks. It is also good as a stuffing or as a grain for soups.

Tofu: Fermented soybean curd formed into cakes is the most accessible of the popular vegetarian proteins. It is designated by firmness. Extra-firm or firm tofu is best used for stir-frying, soups, and baking. Soft tofu is better for desserts and sauces. You will also find marinated tofu, which is flavored, pressed, and baked into a very firm cake. It needs only to be heated.

Veggie burgers: There are two types of nonmeat burgers. Those made from TVP (textured vegetable protein) have been processed to resemble meat, either ground beef or chicken, depending on the burger's design. They typically come frozen and can be heated in a microwave or skillet. They are good for sandwiches or meatless stews. The other type doesn't attempt to imitate meat in texture, flavor, or appearance. The burgers are made from grain and vegetables, and are more fragile than patties made from TVP.

Meats, Poultry, and Seafood

Precooked bacon: These all-natural bacon slices have been precooked and are ready to be crisped in a microwave or rendered in a skillet to start a hunter's style stew or a hearty potato salad. The quality is good, and they cost the same to use as raw bacon. The price per pound is usually four to five times the price of raw bacon, but since bacon loses about 80 percent of its weight during cooking, the usage costs are almost identical. Precooked bacon will last in the refrigerator for about two weeks after opening.

Beef: In the meat case alongside the steaks, roasts, and hamburger patties you will find packages of fully prepared beef dinners, such as pot roast and beef stew. Although these are designed to serve as is, they show their real culinary potential as a head start for more elaborate beef preparations such as goulash or a hearty soup.

Chicken: Americans' consumption of chicken continues to grow, with the latest figures hovering at 50 pounds per person per year, and manufacturers are heeding the call. It is now possible to purchase chicken in almost every conceivable form. Fresh raw chicken comes whole and cut into parts, but it also comes butchered, processed, and seasoned in ways that make it faster and easier to cook. Fully-cooked whole chicken is available rotisserie-roasted (a combination of steaming and roasting), and chicken parts are sold roasted or grilled. One word of warning: It has become common practice to pump chicken meat with salinated water to bulk up its weight and lengthen its shelf life. However, this process also toughens the meat and gives it a salty flavor. If you want your chicken unpumped (whether raw or cooked), you need to read the fine print on the label.

The following list covers the butchered and processed chicken products currently available at your local supermarket.

BONELESS AND SKINLESS BREASTS
- *Whole* is comprised of both lobes of the breast, still attached and only partially trimmed of fat; it is usually the cheapest.
- *Halves* are separate lobes, usually with some fat attached; they are best for sautéing.
- *Cutlets* are halves that are cut in half horizontally; they are especially good for sandwiches.
- *Tenders or tenderloins* are the strips of meat that lie under the large lobe of the breast. As the name implies, they are very tender and cook quickly. You can use them for sautéing or stir-frying.
- *Strips* are breast meat cut into thin strips for stir-frying or fajitas.
- *Seasoned* chicken is marinated and is available in a variety of flavors, such as Italian, teriyaki, lemon pepper, rosemary garlic, and herb. It is designed for grilling or broiling.
- *Fully-cooked* chicken breast is either roasted or grilled and seasoned in a variety of ways. It is good for salads, cold sandwiches, or topping a pizza.

CHICKEN THIGHS

- *Boneless and skinless* chicken thigh meat is moister than breast meat, and when boned and skinned, it cooks almost as quickly. Use it for soup, chili, stews, or grilling.
- *Roasted chicken thighs and drumsticks* are available completely cooked. They can be reheated in an oven or a microwave, and make a very quick chicken potpie.

CHICKEN WINGS

- *Wingettes* are chicken wings trimmed into sections with the tips discarded. They are designed for making Buffalo wings.
- *Drumettes* are the "drumstick" section of chicken wings. They are used for hors d'oeuvres or for upscale Buffalo wings.

CHICKEN SAUSAGE

- Many markets make their own chicken sausage with unusual flavorful additions, such as wild mushrooms, olives, cilantro, and sun-dried tomatoes. They are usually lower in fat than traditional pork sausage.

Cured Meats: Imported meats such as prosciutto and chorizo are more commonly available than they once were. Prosciutto comes prepackaged, and chicken and turkey low-fat chorizos are increasingly available.

Pork: In the meat case you will find marinated pork loins, spareribs, and pork tenderloins that are ready to be grilled or roasted. The same meats also come fully cooked, so all you have to do is warm them in a microwave or oven. You will find tubs of fully-prepared pork braised in gravy and pulled pork in barbecue sauce; they are designed to serve as is but are better used to speed up a stir-fry, assemble an enchilada, or jump-start a curry.

Seafood: The economics of commercial fishing dictates that all fish caught during a week's expedition are frozen on board, which means that unless you are buying your fish off the docks from small fishing companies who come into shore daily, you are buying seafood that has been frozen. With that in mind, if your market carries high-quality frozen seafood (not breaded fish fillets or sticks), you are likely to get a fresher product by buying it, especially if you are not going to serve it that day. Shrimp, in particular, are of better quality when purchased still frozen.

Smoked meat and fish: Small amounts of smoked meat and fish are an easy way to get a smoky nuance into a sauce, soup, or stew. There are many options: pork, turkey breast, smoked sausage, and many types of smoked fish, including salmon, trout, tuna, bluefish, sturgeon, carp, and whitefish. Smoked foods are better preserved than the fresh forms. If you keep them tightly wrapped in the refrigerator, the meat should last several weeks, and seafood about a week. If you freeze smoked products, they will lose their texture but keep their flavor, which is fine if you are using them finely chopped as a flavoring agent.

Turkey breast: The popularity of fresh turkey continues to rise. To both fuel and meet that demand, turkey producers keep finding new ways to divvy up the bird. In addition to whole turkeys and turkey parts, here is what you're likely to find:

- Boneless and skinless turkey breasts are available in lobes, sliced into cutlets (also called scalloppine), and butterflied into London broil. Turkey tenders (also called tenderloins) are the long cylindrical pieces of meat that run on the underside of the breast. They are very tender and can be broiled or grilled whole, or sliced for stir-frying or sautéing.
- Ground turkey is considered by many to be a low-fat alternative to ground beef. It is very lean and because of that can be dry when cooked thoroughly. It is best combined with condiments and bread crumbs to help boost flavor and maintain moisture, as when making burgers, meatballs, or meatloaf, or in a chili where it is surrounded by liquid. I also use it as a substitute for ground pork in a Thai meat salad.
- Many companies sell turkey sausage flavored like traditional pork sausage, such as Italian, chorizo, and breakfast links.

Dairy

Chèvre or goat cheese: The subtle tang and dairy sweetness of fresh goat cheese can add instant sophistication to a plate of spaghetti, a plain pizza, or a savory cheesecake. There are many types to choose from. Start with a nonaged fresh goat cheese. You will see several in your local market, and they are easy to spot. Creamy white and semisoft, they are usually made in the shape of small logs or disks and often have a goat on the label. Fresh chèvre will keep for several weeks in the refrigerator.

Flavored cream cheeses: Flavored cream cheeses can be savory or sweet. Savory flavors include garlic and herb, pesto, cracked pepper, horseradish, roasted garlic, jalapeño, garden vegetable, onion, and chive. Melt them over pasta, swirl them into risotto, whisk them into a sauce, blend them into spinach, or stuff them into a chicken breast for instant flavor and a creamy richness. Sweet cheeses include a variety of fruit flavors, cheesecake, honey-nut, and cinnamon. Whip them into a quick mousse, ice cream, or cheesecake.

Grated and shredded cheese: Almost any cheese that is used in cooking is available grated or shredded. If you have a choice between the two, choose grated or finely shredded (also called *fancy*) for making sauces or for recipes where you need the cheese to disperse quickly and evenly, as when making whipped potatoes or risotto. Use regular shredded cheese when the dish will be cooked for any length of time. Cheese has a tendency to separate if it is heated too much, and the finer the cheese is shredded, the greater the chance that that will happen. When adding finely shredded cheese to a sauce, heat the sauce to simmering and remove it from the heat as soon as you add the cheese. Stir until the cheese is incorporated, allowing the residual heat in the sauce to melt it gently.

Ricotta cheese: Ricotta cheese makes instant mousse and delicious ice cream. All you have to do is purée it in a food processor with fruit, chocolate, maple syrup, or rum, and refrigerate or freeze the resulting cream until thick. On the savory side, there is ricotta cheese enriched with Parmesan, mozzarella, and Romano, which is designed to be used as an easy lasagna filling. It is equally good in stuffed shells and cannelloni, or tossed with pasta and vegetables.

Desserts

Baker's Joy No Stick Spray with Flour: See Oils (page 19).

Baking mixes: Baking mixes, whether for cookies, cakes, muffins, or breads, are nothing more than dry ingredients sifted together. Each one is designed to simplify the preparation of a specific baked good, but in actuality most mixes are fairly generic and more versatile than you might think. Brownie mix, given the right additions, makes a high-flying dessert soufflé, and bran muffin mix makes excellent biscotti. The crumble mix for apple crisp is both pastry and topping for a bar cookie, and cornbread mix is just waiting to be a crunchy, creamy whole grain coffee cake.

Pastry: Although preparing pastry dough is simple, it is not easy. Doing it well takes practice, and those who don't practice, purchase. Fortunately there are lots of options: frozen pie shells in pans, both baked and unbaked; refrigerated pie dough rolled into rounds; paper-thin layers of filo (phyllo); boxes of piecrust mix; and frozen puff pastry sheets that are of such high quality and so easy to use that only a culinary masochist would choose to make them from scratch. There are cookie, cracker, and cereal crumbs for making nonpastry crusts, and even bean powders and potato flakes for alternative savory crusts.

Pie filling: The quality of frozen fruit is so good that I see little reason to use products sold as pie filling. For my taste they are overly starchy and overly sweet.

Pudding mix: Like baking mixes, pudding mix is nothing more than the dry ingredients for a pudding sifted together. Use stove-top pudding mixes to streamline bread puddings, custard pies, or mousse. Do not use instant pudding mix in a recipe that calls for heating.

Seasoning

The biggest change in the spice aisle has been the growth of seasoning blends designed to provide you with the flavors of a cuisine or a specific preparation in a single jar. The selection of blends is varied, and you should choose those that best suit your palate and the kind of cooking you like to do. I recommend the following as a start:

- A Mexican-style blend such as fajita seasoning, Southwest seasoning, or chili powder;
- A Mediterranean herb blend such as Italian, pesto, Greek, or herbes de Provence;
- A curry blend such as curry powder, garam masala, red curry, or madras powder;
- An Asian blend, such as Thai or Szechwan;
- A pepper blend, such as lemon pepper or pepper medley.

Another evolution in seasonings has been the emergence of more convenient ways of purchasing gourmet seasonings. For instance, Saigon (or Vietnamese) cinnamon, which was once so esoteric you had to order it from Asia, is now available in your supermarket in a shaker bottle. Rosemary leaves only came whole and ground, but recipes usually asked for them crushed. Now McCormick sells crushed rosemary, and OXO sells rosemary in its own adjustable grinder.

Inevitably your inventory of seasonings will expand as you use more recipes. When your spice shelf grows, try to purchase spices in as small a package size as you can. In general, a little spice goes a long way, and if you have excess, it can go bad. You can tell if a seasoning is over the hill by smelling it. If it smells like sawdust, it probably tastes like sawdust and should be discarded. Whole-leaf dried herbs will last about six months; whole dried spices will last about a year. After grinding, the flavor of both herbs and spices diminishes rapidly.

Coffee and Tea

Instant espresso: Instant espresso crystals are the easiest way to get a pronounced coffee flavor in desserts and sauces without adding additional liquid. Buy a small jar because only a small amount is usually needed and the crystals can become stale after several months.

Tea bags: Teas provide a kaleidoscope of flavors for dessert sauces, poaching liquids, and glazes. I use tea for simmering shrimp and fish, for flavoring sorbets, and for poaching fruit. Try green tea for seafood, spice teas for hydrating dried figs, and hibiscus tea for simmering poultry.

Tea concentrates: Liquid iced tea concentrates come flavored with a variety of fruit and honey. They are intensely flavored and quite sweet, perfect for chilling into a sophisticated sorbet or mousse. With the addition of a drop of vinegar they can be a glaze for a roasting chicken or duck.

Miscellaneous

Smoker bags: A smoky nuance improves the flavor of almost any roasted or grilled meat. To get it in the past you either had to build a campfire or sprinkle on some Liquid Smoke. Now there is another alternative. Savu smoker bags are a Finnish product sold in many gourmet grocery stores (Whole Foods Markets and Trader Joe's, for example), cookware stores, and on the Internet at www.thestoreforcooks.com. They leave no bad odor in your house, there is no mess, and they work in the same time it would take to cook the ingredient by any other method. Just layer your ingredients in a standard baking dish, slip the whole thing in the smoker bag, close the top, and bake. While the food cooks, wood dust trapped in the interior of the walls of the bag starts to smoke. The smoke is channeled through tiny holes in the inner wall inside the bag where it permeates the ingredients. When cooking is done, you just slit open the bag, remove the dinner, and throw away the remnants.

Tube food: It started with anchovy paste. Now garlic, mushrooms, sweet peppers, hot peppers, tomatoes, sun-dried tomatoes, pesto, and wasabi are all packaged in tubes. Why? The products are high quality, and tubes keep them that way. By reducing the amount of air that touches the ingredient, the surface doesn't dry out, grow mold, or go bad. Tubed foods will stay fresh in the refrigerator for several months after opening.

CHAPTER 1

ELEGANT APPETIZERS AND SPUR-OF-THE-MOMENT SNACKS

Herbed Artichoke Dip or Spread
Warm White Bean and Brie Dip
Hot Pepper Hummus
Salsa Hummus
Sesame Ginger Hummus
Provençal Baba Ghanouj
Roasted Onion Dip
Smoked Eggplant Dip
Anchovy Eggplant Cream
Muddy Chèvre
Sage Cheese with Toasted Walnuts
Baked Chèvre and Prosciutto
Garlic Figs and Brie
GARLIC FIGS AND BRIE I
GARLIC FIGS AND BRIE II
Mango Brie Quesadillas
Potato Chip Blue Cheese Nachos
Shrimp and White Bean Nachos
Mozzarella with Bruschetta Vinaigrette

Charred Polenta Bruschetta

Sweet and Hot Almonds

Chilied Edamame

Garlic-Ginger Sesame Popcorn

Sweet Chipotle Popcorn Cakes

Parmesan Shortbread

Spinach and Cheese Cupcakes

Chèvre Figs and Prosciutto

Tomato Tarragon Tart

Spanikupicakes

Blue Cheese Quiche with Potato Crust

Roasted Peppers and Anchovies with Pesto Drizzle

Sautéed Seafood Tart

Knish for a New Millenium

FONTINA POLENTA KNISH

ANCHOVY POTATO KNISH

Grilled Pesto Shrimp

Curried Shrimp with Toasted Coconut Salt

Fried Sardines with Horseradish Vinaigrette

Shrimp with Peach Mustard Sauce

Lemon Olives

Garlic Chèvre and Roasted Pepper Baguette

Baked Artichoke Bruschetta

Thai Peanut Crudité

Hoisin Eggs with Sesame Salt

Roasted Grapes, Garlic, and Walnuts

Chicken Wings Many Ways

STICKY WINGS

SMOKY HOT 'N' HONEY WINGS

BOMBAY WINGS

SPICY THAI WINGS

SWEET SESAME WINGS

HOT HOT MUSTARD WINGS

Herbed Artichoke Dip or Spread

Marinated artichoke hearts should be a staple in every kitchen. With almost no effort they can become a pasta sauce, a pizza topping, a condiment for grilled meats, or the finishing touch for a salad. When mixed with a little herbed cream cheese, they make this dynamite dip.

Makes 6 servings (about 1¼ cups)

1 jar (6 ounces) marinated artichoke hearts
1 package (6 ounces) garlic and herb cream cheese
¼ teaspoon lemon pepper

Place the artichoke hearts, half their liquid, and the cream cheese in the bowl of a food processor and purée. Mix in the lemon pepper. Serve as a spread for bread or crackers, or as a dip for vegetables or chips.

Warm White Bean and Brie Dip

What a miraculous amalgam. Spicy, meaty, earth-bound bean dip is set aloft with a creamy addition of warm Brie. The effect is as unimaginable as it is addictive. If you have any left over (an unlikely possibility), it can be stored in the refrigerator for several days. During that time it will degenerate into an inedible lump, but give it a few seconds in the microwave, and it will regain its silken consistency.

Makes 6 servings (about 1¾ cups)

8 ounces Brie cheese
1 container (8 ounces) bean dip, preferably white bean or hummus

Remove the rind from the Brie and cut the cheese into chunks. Place the Brie and bean dip in a microwave-safe bowl. Microwave at full power for 1 minute, until the cheese melts. Stir with a fork until well combined. Serve warm with tortilla chips, bread, or crackers.

Hot Pepper Hummus

Garlicky, lemony, loamy hummus is given a whole new personality and an attractive rosy blush with the simple addition of Asian chili paste. Chili paste is a basic staple of the Chinese kitchen and is widely available in the Asian aisle of your local market. It will stay fresh for months if it is refrigerated after opening.

Makes 4 servings (about 1 cup)

1 container (8 ounces) hummus
1 tablespoon Chinese chili purée

Combine the hummus and chili purée. Serve with flatbread or vegetables for dipping.

Salsa Hummus

The chunkiness of salsa completely transforms the appearance and personality of hummus. Together they become something more like a condiment or a salad. You can vary the formula almost endlessly by changing the heat level or flavor of the salsa you use. Fruit salsas, for example, bring out the lemon and garlic in the hummus. Chipotle salsa gives the hummus a sexy, smoky redolence.

Makes 6 servings (about 1 cup)

1 container (8 ounces) hummus
¼ cup salsa, any heat level or flavor

Combine the hummus and salsa. Serve with tortilla chips, flatbread, or vegetables for dipping.

Sesame Ginger Hummus

An inspired drizzle of toasted sesame oil, a significant swirl of chopped ginger, and a hint of cardamom coax this hummus from its Middle Eastern roots and give it a Far Eastern disguise. The lemon and garlic in the hummus turn out to be a natural background for the Asian ingredients, and the richness of the sesame oil blends seamlessly with the creaminess of the hummus. Make sure you use dark, toasted Asian sesame oil. Untoasted sesame oil, which looks more like vegetable oil, does not have enough flavor.

Makes 6 servings (about 1 cup)

1 container (8 ounces) hummus
1 teaspoon Asian toasted sesame oil
2 teaspoons chopped ginger, jarred or fresh
⅛ teaspoon ground cardamom

Combine the hummus, sesame oil, ginger, and cardamom. Serve with flatbread, vegetables, apples, or pears for dipping.

Provençal Baba Ghanouj

Ingredients such as eggplant, olives, garlic, and lemon are ubiquitous in the Mediterranean basin, so it is only natural that the eggplant dip of one coast should move smoothly into an adjoining cuisine. In this dip, Middle Eastern baba ghanouj takes a voyage to southern France with an addition of tapenade, sun-dried tomatoes, and pesto.

Makes 6 servings (about 1 cup)

1 container (8 ounces) baba ghanouj
2 teaspoons tapenade (black olive spread)
2 teaspoons jarred sun-dried tomato pesto or sun-dried tomato paste
2 teaspoons basil pesto, jarred or fresh

Combine the baba ghanouj, olive spread, sun-dried tomato pesto, and basil pesto. Serve with flatbread.

Roasted Onion Dip

Roasted garlic products abound, so why not roasted onion? I long for a savvy manufacturer to start marketing high-quality refrigerated roasted onions, but until then we'll have to roast our own. Roasted onions will stay usable for up to a week in the refrigerator, and they freeze spectacularly.

Makes 6 servings (about 1¼ cups)

3 medium onions, diced (about 2½ cups)
Nonstick olive oil spray
Salt and black pepper to taste
2 tablespoons balsamic vinegar
⅓ cup extra-virgin olive oil
¼ to ⅓ cup chicken broth

Preheat the oven to 400°F. Scatter the onions in a baking dish, spray with oil, and season with salt and pepper. Roast for 30 minutes, until browned and tender. This step can be done several days in advance. Purée the roasted onions in a food processor. Add the vinegar and olive oil, and purée until smooth. Add enough broth to thin to the consistency of a dip.

Smoked Eggplant Dip

The delicious smokiness of this concoction comes from two places: the roasted onion and the chipotle hot sauce. Chipotle peppers are smoked jalapeños. If you can't find chipotle hot sauce, substitute the same amount of ground chipotle pepper or use a small amount of chipotle pepper en adobo.

Makes 6 servings (about 1¾ cups)

¾ cup chopped onion, frozen or fresh
Nonstick olive oil spray
Salt and black pepper to taste
1 container (8 ounces) baba ghanouj
¼ teaspoon chipotle hot sauce

Preheat the oven to 400°F. Scatter the onion in a baking pan, spray with oil, and season with salt and pepper. Roast for 15 to 20 minutes, until browned and tender. This step can be done several days in advance. Combine the baba ghanouj, onion, and hot sauce. Serve with chips, flatbread, or vegetables for dipping.

Anchovy Eggplant Cream

Puréed eggplant isn't pretty. Bland at best, it is the perfect background for other, more assertive ingredients. In this streamlined recipe, Middle Eastern eggplant dip is made creamier and fluffier by beating in a bit of fragrant olive oil, and the flavor is enlivened with a hefty squeeze of anchovy paste. Depending on the amount of garlic in the baba ghanouj that you start with, you might want to add a little minced garlic to taste.

Makes 6 servings (about 1 cup)

1 container (8 ounces) baba ghanouj
1 tablespoon anchovy paste
1 tablespoon extra-virgin olive oil

Combine the baba ghanouj, anchovy paste, and oil. Serve with pita chips, flatbread, or vegetables for dipping.

Muddy Chèvre

You know the old adage about inner beauty being more valuable than the flashy, superficial sort. I beg you to remember it now. This dip is ugly. It needs your love and support, and if you give it, you will be forever hooked. Its flavor is intense and intoxicating, an artful blend of tangy cheese, acid-sweet tomato, unctuous olives, pungent garlic, and perfumed virgin olive oil. Dig in; it won't let you down.

Makes 8 servings (about 1½ cups)

1 log (8 ounces) fresh chèvre cheese
3 tablespoons sun-dried tomato pesto or paste
3 tablespoons tapenade (black olive spread)
3 tablespoons extra-virgin olive oil

Mash the cheese with the back of a fork. Mix in the pesto, tapenade, and oil. Refrigerate up to 5 days.

Sage Cheese with Toasted Walnuts

This contemporary "cheese ball" has the dusty aroma of sage and enough garlic to keep demons at bay. It will keep for several days in the refrigerator. Serve it with black bread or any type of flatbread or cracker.

Makes 8 servings

8 ounces farmer's cheese
¼ teaspoon rubbed sage
1 teaspoon minced garlic, jarred or fresh
Salt and black pepper to taste
2 ounces toasted walnut pieces, finely
　　chopped (½ cup)

Mash the cheese with the back of a fork. Mix in the sage, garlic, salt, and pepper. Refrigerate for at least 1 hour. Form the cheese into a mound and cover with the chopped walnuts. Serve with crackers or bread.

Baked Chèvre and Prosciutto

Tiny pillows of marinated goat cheese are wrapped in a skin of prosciutto and baked, which is when the alchemy begins. The chèvre gets puffy; its belly goes pudgy. In contrast, the prosciutto thins, stiffens, and dries, becoming a lacquered shell that cracks tinnily between the teeth. Although it is perfectly fine to assemble the ingredients ahead, don't let the bundles linger after baking or the contrasts will diminish as they sit.

Makes 6 to 8 servings

1 log (8 ounces) fresh chèvre cheese
2 tablespoons extra-virgin olive oil
¼ teaspoon minced garlic, jarred or fresh
1 ounce prosciutto, cut into 8 paper-thin
　　slices

Preheat the oven to 425°F. Cut the cheese in 8 rounds. Combine the oil and garlic, and dip the cheese into the mixture, turning the rounds to coat them evenly. Wrap each round of cheese with a slice of prosciutto and place on a sheet pan. Bake for 5 minutes, until the prosciutto is slightly crisp and the cheese is warm.

Garlic Figs and Brie

The combination of figs, garlic, balsamic vinegar, and Brie is so spectacular that I had to do it twice. The first presentation is a little more complex in flavor—savory, sweet, tangy, and pungent all at once. It calls for Adriatic fig spread, which is an imported fig preserve. It is sold at fine food shops and many supermarkets, including Whole Foods, but if you can't find it, any fig preserve will do. The second variation uses fresh figs. It is equally delicious, somewhat less sweet, and requires more assembly.

GARLIC FIGS AND BRIE I

Makes 12 servings

1 large round of Brie cheese
1 jar (8 ounces) Adriatic fig spread or other fig preserve (see Note)
1 tablespoon minced garlic, jarred or fresh
1 tablespoon balsamic vinegar (fig balsamic if you can find it)
12 slices crusty bread

Preheat the oven to 350°F. Cut the Brie in half horizontally. Combine the fig spread, garlic, and balsamic vinegar. Spread over the surface of one of the Brie halves and place the other Brie half on top. Set the cheese on a sheet pan surrounded with the bread slices. Bake about 10 minutes, until the cheese is soft and the bread is toasty. Serve immediately.

NOTE: If you cannot find fig spread or fig preserves, substitute 6 dried Calimyrna figs, puréed with a little boiling water until mushy.

GARLIC FIGS AND BRIE II

Makes 4 to 6 servings

8 ounces fresh figs, halved vertically
2 tablespoons extra-virgin olive oil
1 teaspoon chopped garlic, jarred or fresh
1 small round of Brie cheese, at room temperature
12 slices crusty bread
2 teaspoons aged balsamic vinegar

Preheat the oven to 375°F.

Toss the figs with the oil and garlic in a baking dish just large enough to fit the figs in a single layer. Place the Brie on a sheet pan, surrounded by the bread slices. Bake the cheese, bread, and figs for 8 minutes, until the fig skin is lightly toasted, the Brie is barely soft, and the bread is toasty.

Remove from the oven and drizzle the balsamic vinegar over the figs. Serve warm. To eat, spread a slice of bread with some cheese and top with figs.

Mango Brie Quesadillas

It is not accidental that mango is the fruit of choice for salsa. Apples are more popular and bananas more common, but mangoes fit the requirements best. They have a meaty texture that maintains its integrity when chopped but still holds the liquid in the salsa in suspension; a sweet taste that is not cloying when paired with more savory peppers, onions, and garlic; and a color so vibrant that no one will miss the visual absence of the standard tomatoes or tomatillos. Fortunately for this recipe, they are also perfectly paired with the richness of a creamy surface-ripened cheese like Brie.

Makes 4 servings

6 tablespoons mango salsa
½ teaspoon hot pepper sauce
1 teaspoon cilantro pesto or chutney, or
    1 tablespoon chopped cilantro leaves
    (optional)
4 large flour tortillas
8 ounces Brie cheese, cut in 8 slices, rind
    removed
Nonstick olive oil spray

Combine the salsa, hot pepper sauce, and cilantro pesto, if desired. Spread ¾ tablespoon of the mixture on each of the 4 tortillas and place 2 slices of Brie to one side of each tortilla. Fold the tortilla so that one side covers the cheese. Press gently but firmly to help the quesadillas hold together.

Coat a large skillet with oil spray and place it over medium-low heat. Cook the quesadillas gently on both sides until the tortillas are lightly browned and the Brie is softened but not fully melted. Cut each quesadilla in 3 or 4 wedges. Serve immediately.

Potato Chip Blue Cheese Nachos

These are incredible—crunchy, salty, tangy, creamy. Make them with Yukon Gold potato chips or any thick-cut gourmet chip. There is nothing complicated about the preparation even though the results appear to be the most sophisticated of bar snacks.

Makes 4 servings

1 package (5 ounces) Yukon Gold potato
    chips or other thick-sliced gourmet
    potato chips
¼ teaspoon garlic powder
2 ounces blue cheese, crumbled (about ½
    cup)

Pile the chips on a microwave-safe dish and sprinkle with the garlic powder. Scatter the cheese over the top. Microwave at full power until the cheese is melted, about 1 to 2 minutes.

Shrimp and White Bean Nachos

This flavorful, colorful, imaginative combination of ingredients is not your everyday nacho. You can cook your own shrimp, though the preparation is almost effortless with precooked shrimp. And now, thanks to high-quality frozen shrimp that is available almost everywhere, there is no reason not to.

Makes 4 servings

8 ounces cooked shrimp, peeled and tails
    removed, cut in 3 or 4 pieces each
1 cup canned white beans, rinsed and
    drained
1 cup fruit salsa, such as peach, mango,
    or pineapple
2 teaspoons extra-virgin olive oil
2 scallions, roots trimmed, thinly sliced
4 ounces (4 cups) spicy blue corn chips,
    such as Red Hot Blues
2 ounces fresh chèvre or feta cheese,
    broken in pieces (about ½ cup)

Combine the shrimp, beans, salsa, oil, and scallions. Mound the chips on a large microwave-safe platter, pour the shrimp mixture on top, and dot with the cheese pieces. Microwave at full power for 2 minutes, until the mixture is heated through and the cheese has melted.

Mozzarella with Bruschetta Vinaigrette

The word "bruschetta," which originally meant a toast topped with a savory paste, has devolved into the name of the topping itself, and in particular the tomato variety, which has become the most ubiquitous of bruschettas. Tomato bruschetta can be found jarred, pouched, refrigerated, and fresh. Any of its forms will work well in this fragrant, chunky sauce that gilds slices of fresh water-packed mozzarella. Although you can substitute the firmer shreddable form of mozzarella (the kind that goes on pizza), the results will not be nearly as good.

Makes 4 servings

¾ cup (6 ounces) bruschetta, jarred,
    refrigerated, or fresh
2 teaspoons red wine vinegar
2 teaspoons extra-virgin olive oil
1 teaspoon basil pesto, jarred or fresh
Kosher salt and freshly ground black
    pepper to taste
1 ball (8 ounces) fresh water-packed
    mozzarella cheese, cut in ¼-inch-thick
    slices
1 tablespoon chopped Italian (flat-leaf)
    parsley

Combine the bruschetta, vinegar, oil, and pesto, and season with salt and pepper. Arrange the mozzarella slices on a plate and spoon the bruschetta sauce over the slices. Scatter the chopped parsley over the cheese. Serve at room temperature.

Charred Polenta Bruschetta

Polenta, the homiest of Italian starches, can turn the simplest sauce or relish into a meal. Here fully prepared polenta in a tube replaces bread in a bruschetta. All you do is slice, broil, and gild with one or more toppings. The amount of each topping listed in the recipe is enough to top all the polenta slices by itself. If you choose to use more than one, adjust the amounts accordingly.

Makes 8 servings

1 tube (16 ounces) refrigerated polenta
Nonstick olive oil spray

TOPPINGS:
1½ cups (12 ounces) bruschetta
6 tablespoons pesto, jarred or fresh
6 tablespoons tapenade (olive spread), jarred or fresh
1 jar (8 ounces) olive salad
1 cup pasta sauce, jarred or fresh
½ cup grated imported Parmesan cheese
4 ounces fresh goat cheese or Gorgonzola

Preheat the broiler. Cut the polenta into 16 slices, each about ⅜ inch thick. Place on a broiler pan and coat with olive oil spray. Set as close to the broiler as possible and toast the polenta on both sides until it is spotted. Top each slice with a portion of one or more of the toppings and serve immediately.

Sweet and Hot Almonds

Black and white. Hot and cold. Loud and quiet. Put them together and what do you get? Gray. Tepid. Subdued. But try the same thing with spicy, salty, and sweet, and watch out! Instead of uniting, they fight, and in their wake, culinary sparks start to fly. These nuts are prime examples of the phenomenon. They are utterly addictive and make a great gift.

Makes 4 servings

8 ounces (about 1½ cups) whole almonds in their skins
½ cup sugar
1 teaspoon ground cinnamon
1 teaspoon salt
¼ teaspoon cayenne pepper

Place a nonstick skillet over high heat for 1 minute. Add the almonds and lower the heat to medium. Stir until the almonds toast lightly. Add the sugar and keep stirring until the sugar melts and browns, about 30 seconds. Be careful; caramelized sugar can give a nasty burn.

Immediately scrape onto a sheet pan, spread into a single layer, and sprinkle with cinnamon, salt, and cayenne pepper. Wait for a few minutes, until the almonds are just cool enough to touch. Break them into individual almonds. Do not wait too long, or the sugar will harden and it will be difficult to separate them.

Chilied Edamame

The popularity of soy and soy products has transformed edamame (fresh soybeans) from an obscure Japanese snack food into the trendiest healthy snack. Edamame come frozen in two forms: in their pods or shelled. The pod form is more common, but shelled edamame are increasingly available. For this recipe use shelled beans. Just drop them, still frozen, into boiling water and cook until tender.

Makes 6 servings

1 tablespoon kosher salt
1 bag (16 ounces) frozen shelled
    edamame
2 tablespoons jarred chili purée
½ teaspoon minced garlic, jarred or fresh
½ teaspoon minced ginger, jarred or
    fresh
1 teaspoon Asian toasted sesame oil
1 teaspoon organic lemon juice, bottled
    or fresh

Heat water in a medium saucepan until boiling. Add the salt and edamame, and simmer until the edamame are tender, about 4 minutes. Meanwhile, combine the chili purée, garlic, ginger, sesame oil, and lemon juice. Drain the edamame and toss with the sauce.

Garlic-Ginger Sesame Popcorn

I'm a big fan of popcorn, and I pop corn the old-fashioned way—in oil, over high heat, using a big, heavy pan. That is how I have written this recipe, but if you would rather air-pop your corn or use the microwave, those methods will also work, although I don't think the results are nearly as good. If you do use another method of popping, omit the vegetable oil and add the flavorings while the popcorn is still hot. But under no circumstances should you use butter-flavored popcorn for this recipe.

Makes 11 cups

1 tablespoon vegetable oil
½ cup (4 ounces) popcorn
1 tablespoon dark Asian sesame oil
½ teaspoon minced garlic, jarred or fresh
1 teaspoon minced ginger, jarred or
    fresh
Pinch of cayenne pepper
½ teaspoon salt

Heat the vegetable oil in a large, heavy saucepan over high heat. Add 3 popcorn kernels. When the kernels pop, add the remaining popcorn. Cover the pan and shake occasionally. When the popping subsides, turn off the heat; when the popping stops, pour the popped corn into a large bowl. Add the sesame oil, garlic, ginger, cayenne, and salt. Toss to coat thoroughly.

Sweet Chipotle Popcorn Cakes

These are ingenious snacks—caramel sweet, lightly buttered, smoky hot. Because caramelizing sugar is difficult and slightly hazardous, I devised a method, utilizing marshmallows. The method is similar to making Rice Krispies treats except that you cook the marshmallows a little longer before you add the grain. And you form the batter into a log, rather than a sheet. After cooling and slicing, the finished product resembles a rice cake rather than a brick.

Makes 20 cakes

1½ tablespoons butter
2 tablespoons water
½ bag (about 5 ounces) marshmallows
1 teaspoon ground chipotle pepper
11 cups salted popcorn
1 cup (4 ounces) pecan pieces
Nonstick oil spray

Bring the butter and water to a boil in a heavy saucepan. Stir in the marshmallows and continue stirring until they melt and brown lightly. Remove the pan from the heat and stir in the chipotle pepper. Combine the popcorn and pecans in a large bowl. Scrape the marshmallows into the bowl and mix until the popcorn and pecans are completely coated with the melted marshmallow. Allow to rest for 1 minute.

Scrape the popcorn mixture onto a cutting board. Coat your hands with oil spray and use them to form the mixture into a tightly packed 20-inch-long log. Allow to set. Cut into 1-inch-wide rounds.

Parmesan Shortbread

"Melt in your mouth" doesn't come close to capturing the velvety richness of these savory cookies. Like all shortbreads, their construction is simple: fat, flour, and flavoring. The difference here is in the flavoring. Imported Parmesan cheese replaces any sweetener, transporting these delicate cookies from the dessert table to the cocktail party.

Makes 2 dozen cookies

½ pound (2 sticks) lightly salted butter
¾ cup grated imported Parmesan cheese
Pinch of cayenne pepper
½ teaspoon minced garlic, jarred or fresh
2 cups flour

Preheat the oven to 325°F. Place the butter in a microwave-safe bowl and soften it in a microwave oven at full power for 30 seconds. Mix in ½ cup of the Parmesan, the cayenne, and garlic. Mix in 1¾ cups of the flour and stir until a soft dough forms.

Spread the remaining flour on a clean work surface. Scrape the dough onto the floured surface, and with floured hands pat the dough into a rectangle about ¼ inch thick. Cut the dough into 24 rounds using a 1½-inch round biscuit cutter. Place the rounds on a baking sheet and sprinkle with the remaining cheese. Bake for 20 minutes, until firm and lightly browned.

Spinach and Cheese Cupcakes

These miniature spinach potato puddings have a skin of flaked potatoes and a cheesy custard enriched with potato purée. High-quality prepared mashed potatoes are widely available as either refrigerated or frozen products, which makes infinite sense. If you think about it, nothing in mashed potatoes is either damaged by storage or improved by immediate consumption.

Makes 12 servings

Nonstick olive oil spray
½ cup bread crumbs or instant potato flakes
½ cup chopped onion, frozen or fresh
1 cup refrigerated prepared mashed potatoes
10 ounces frozen chopped spinach, thawed and squeezed dry, or 1 bag (10 ounces) fresh spinach, cooked, squeezed dry, and chopped
1 teaspoon minced garlic, jarred or fresh
½ teaspoon salt
¼ teaspoon freshly ground black pepper
2 cups milk, 2% or whole
2 large or extra-large eggs
1 cup grated imported Parmesan cheese or shredded Swiss cheese

Preheat the oven to 375°F. Coat the cups of a mini-muffin tin with oil spray and dust with bread crumbs or instant potato flakes. Coat a nonstick skillet with oil spray and warm the skillet over medium heat. Add the onions and sauté until ten-der, about 4 minutes. Combine the sautéed onions, mashed potatoes, spinach, garlic, salt, and pepper. Mix in the milk and eggs until blended and stir in the cheese. Fill each muffin cup with ⅔ cup of the potato mixture and bake for 25 minutes, until browned and set.

Chèvre Figs and Prosciutto

Sometimes the right ingredients require no more from a cook than an introduction to one another. Here's a case in point. The fig is for sweetness, the chèvre lends richness, and the ham is for salt, the punctuation that sets off the parts so that we sense each of them with greater clarity.

Makes 6 to 8 servings

1 ounce fresh chèvre cheese
12 dried or fresh figs, halved lengthwise
2 ounces thinly sliced prosciutto, cut in ½ × 3-inch strips

Place about ½ teaspoon of chèvre in the seed cavity of each fig half. Wrap each stuffed fig half with a strip of prosciutto.

Tomato Tarragon Tart

Culinary convenience can materialize in the most unusual places. A recent arrival has been the chopped tomato salad sold as bruschetta in delis and gourmet shops. Taking its name from the toasted garlic bread that it typically garnishes, bruschetta makes an instant sauce for pasta, or a garnish for grilled chicken. Here it is balanced with creamy chèvre and sweet tarragon in a savory tomato pie.

Makes 6 servings

⅓ cup grated imported Parmesan cheese
One 9-inch baked pastry shell
6 ounces fresh chèvre, crumbled (about 1 cup)
8 sprigs fresh tarragon, leaves only, or ¼ teaspoon dried tarragon
3 cups tomato bruschetta topping, jarred or fresh, drained

Preheat the oven to 375°F. Sprinkle half of the Parmesan on the bottom of the pastry shell. Top with half of the crumbled chèvre and half of the tarragon leaves. Top with half of the bruschetta topping, followed by the remaining Parmesan and tarragon. Cover with the remaining bruschetta and scatter the remaining chèvre over the top. Bake for 35 minutes, until it is bubbling at the edges and the cheese is melted. Cool at least 10 minutes before serving. Slice in wedges.

Spanikupicakes

These tiny phyllo quiches look as if they took half the day to prepare, but they actually took only minutes. The custard is made from prepared mashed potatoes, precleaned spinach, and sautéed onion. It is nestled in petite phyllo shells that come frozen and preformed.

Makes 15 servings

2 teaspoons olive oil
⅓ cup chopped onion, frozen or fresh
½ teaspoon chopped garlic, jarred or fresh
1 bag (8 ounces) cleaned baby spinach
Salt and black pepper to taste
⅔ cup refrigerated prepared mashed potatoes
1 large or extra-large egg
⅔ cup milk, 2% or whole
Pinch of ground nutmeg
30 mini phyllo dough shells (two 2.1-ounce boxes)

Preheat the oven to 350°F. Heat the oil in a skillet. Add the onion and sauté until tender, about 1 minute. Add the garlic and spinach, and cook until the spinach is wilted and almost dry. Season with salt and pepper. Stir the spinach mixture into the potatoes and mix in the egg, milk, and nutmeg. Fill the phyllo shells with the potato mixture, place the shells on a sheet pan, and bake for 12 minutes. Serve immediately.

Blue Cheese Quiche with Potato Crust

Prepared refrigerated shredded potatoes form a crunchy, lacy crust for this flavor-packed pie layered with sautéed onions, crisp bacon, and blue cheese custard.

Makes 12 servings

5 large or extra-large eggs
2 cups (half of a 20-ounce package) refrigerated shredded hash brown potatoes
2 tablespoons flour
Salt and black pepper to taste
Nonstick oil spray
3 strips ready-to-serve prepared bacon, chopped
¼ medium onion, thinly sliced (about ⅓ cup)
¼ cup milk, 2% or whole
¼ cup crumbled blue cheese

Preheat the oven to 375°F. Combine one of the eggs with the potatoes, flour, salt, and pepper. Coat a 9-inch pie plate with oil spray, and press the potato mixture into the plate to form a crust. Bake for 15 minutes, until the crust is set and the surface is browned. Remove from the oven and press with the back of a spoon to firm any loose spots.

Heat a skillet over medium heat. Place the bacon strips in the skillet and sauté until the bottom of the pan is coated with a thin film. Add the onion and sauté until the bacon and onion are browned, about 3 minutes.

Beat the remaining eggs and the milk together, and season with salt and pepper. Stir in the onion mixture and the blue cheese. Pour into the crust and bake for 20 minutes, until the top is browned and the filling is set. Cut into 12 wedges.

Roasted Peppers and Anchovies with Pesto Drizzle

The flavors of Provence meet simply and elegantly in this colorful salad. Basil, garlic, olive oil, and orange juice are whisked into a pale green sauce that is dripped over a tangle of roasted red pepper strips and slivers of marinated anchovy.

Makes 6 to 8 servings

3 tablespoons basil pesto, jarred or fresh
1 teaspoon minced garlic, jarred or fresh
⅓ cup extra-virgin olive oil
2 tablespoons orange juice
1 jar (16 ounces) roasted red bell peppers, cut in strips
1 can (2 ounces) anchovy fillets in olive oil, drained and cut in slivers
Kosher salt and coarsely ground black pepper to taste

Combine the pesto, garlic, oil, and orange juice. Combine the pepper strips and anchovies, and mound them on a plate. Season with salt and pepper, and drizzle with the pesto mixture.

Sautéed Seafood Tart

Pepperidge Farm frozen puff pastry is one of the great convenience ingredients. It's a high-quality product that is ready to use. Only the most accomplished home cook would ever try to make puff pastry from scratch. In this elegant appetizer it becomes the flaky base for seafood that is sautéed with Portobellos and layered, pizza-style, with a prepared bruschetta, tapenade, and Parmesan.

Makes 4 servings

2 tablespoons extra-virgin olive oil
½ cup chopped onion, frozen or fresh
6 ounces Portobello mushrooms, sliced
Salt and black pepper to taste
1 package (about 16 ounces) frozen
    seafood, such as shrimp, bay scallops,
    squid rings, or a combination
1 sheet (about 9 × 9 inches) frozen puff
    pastry, such as Pepperidge Farm,
    thawed according to package direc-
    tions
½ cup grated imported Parmesan cheese
1 jar (12 ounces) tomato bruschetta,
    drained
1 teaspoon tapenade (black olive spread)

Preheat the oven to 400°F. Heat the oil in a large skillet, add the onion, and sauté until tender. Add the mushrooms and sauté until the onion and mushrooms are lightly browned. Season liberally with salt and pepper. Remove from the skillet and set aside.

Add the seafood to the skillet, return the skillet to the heat, and cook until the seafood is barely cooked. Remove the seafood from the skillet with a slotted spoon and set aside.

Place the sheet of defrosted puff pastry on a sheet pan and cut into a 9-inch circle. Sprinkle with half of the Parmesan. Combine the bruschetta and tapenade, and spread over the pastry, leaving a ½-inch rim exposed. Top the bruschetta mixture with the sautéed seafood, onions, and mushrooms, and top with the remaining Parmesan.

Bake for 20 minutes, until the pastry is browned and the topping is bubbling. Cut into 8 wedges.

Knish for a New Millennium

The knish, that preternaturally dense dumpling stacked in the corner of deli cases from Brooklyn to Berkeley, is little more than a peasant pastry made from flaky dough and wrapped around a filling. Its preparation, complicated by centuries of tradition, has been streamlined by the advent of prepared mashed potatoes, chopped liver, and polenta for filling, and of frozen puff pastry shells for dough.

FONTINA POLENTA KNISH

Makes 6 servings

1 tablespoon extra-virgin olive oil
½ cup chopped onion, frozen or fresh
8 ounces prepared garlic-flavored
   polenta
1 egg, any size
1 tablespoon water
1 package (about 1 pound) frozen puff
   pastry shells, thawed
3 ounces Italian Fontina cheese, cut in 6
   chunks

Preheat the oven to 400°F. Heat the oil in a small skillet, add the onion, and sauté until tender, about 2 minutes. Combine the onion and polenta with a fork. Combine the egg and water to make an egg wash.

Roll each pastry into a ½-inch circle. Brush each pastry with the egg wash. Divide the filling among the pastries and press a piece of Fontina in the center of each mound of filling. Wrap the dough around the filling, gathering the edges together to form puffy pillows with a small indentation in the center. Place the pastries with the indentations facing up on a sheet pan and brush the tops with additional egg wash. Bake for 20 to 25 minutes, until the pastries are golden brown and puffed.

ANCHOVY POTATO KNISH

Makes 6 servings

1 tablespoon extra-virgin olive oil
½ cup chopped onion, frozen or fresh
1 teaspoon minced garlic, jarred or fresh
1 cup (8 ounces) refrigerated prepared
   mashed potatoes
2 teaspoons anchovy paste
1 egg, any size
1 tablespoon water
1 package (about 1 pound) frozen puff
   pastry shells, thawed

Preheat the oven to 400°F. Heat the oil in a small skillet, add the onion, and sauté until tender, about 2 minutes. Using a fork, combine the onion, garlic, potatoes, and anchovy paste. Combine the egg and water.

Follow the method for forming and baking the knish from the previous recipe, eliminating the cheese.

Grilled Pesto Shrimp

These fragrant herbed shrimp are simple, straightforward, and delicious. They are marinated in a pesto vinaigrette, which doubles as the sauce. Make sure that your grill is very hot and that the shrimp are close to the flame; a little charring helps their flavor and appearance.

Makes 4 to 6 servings

¼ cup basil pesto, jarred or fresh
¼ cup red wine vinegar
¼ cup extra-virgin olive oil
1 teaspoon chopped garlic, jarred or fresh
1 pound peeled and cleaned jumbo shrimp (21 to 25 count), thawed if frozen
Nonstick oil spray

Combine the pesto, vinegar, oil, and garlic. Toss the shrimp in half of the marinade to coat and refrigerate for at least 20 minutes. Reserve the remaining marinade. While the shrimp are marinating, heat the grill and coat the rack of the grill with oil spray. Remove the shrimp from the marinade and grill until firm and opaque, about 2 to 3 minutes per side. Serve with the reserved marinade as a sauce.

Curried Shrimp with Toasted Coconut Salt

This exotic, aromatic shrimp cocktail needs only a tiny bit of cooking in a microwave. The sauce is a combination of curry sauce, of which there are a myriad of brands and flavors (any will do), and just enough vinegar to transform it from a curry gravy to a curry vinaigrette.

Makes 4 to 6 servings

½ cup (4 ounces) curry sauce
¼ cup cider vinegar
Salt and black pepper to taste
¼ cup sweetened shredded coconut
¼ teaspoon coarse sea salt or kosher salt
1 pound peeled and cleaned cooked jumbo shrimp (21 to 25 count), thawed if frozen
1 teaspoon lemon juice, organic bottled or fresh

Combine the curry sauce, vinegar, salt, and pepper. Scrape the mixture into a small bowl and set the bowl in the center of a platter. Spread the coconut on a microwave-safe plate and microwave at full power for 30 seconds. Toss with a fork and microwave 20 seconds more, until the coconut is spotted with brown. Toss with the salt. Arrange the shrimp around the bowl of dip on the platter. Drizzle the shrimp with the lemon juice and sprinkle with the toasted coconut salt. Serve with toothpicks or small forks.

Fried Sardines with Horseradish Vinaigrette

The best sardines are whole and packed in oil, usually olive oil. In this recipe sardines are floured lightly and sautéed just until the surfaces are crisp. Because the fish are already cooked in the can, there is no need to worry about cooking them through. The crisp, fatty fish are served drizzled with an easily prepared sweet and pungent vinaigrette. Scrumptious!

Makes 6 servings

1 tablespoon spicy brown mustard
2 tablespoons white horseradish
2 tablespoons apple cider vinegar
½ teaspoon honey
5 tablespoons extra-virgin olive oil
½ cup flour
Salt and black pepper to taste
4 to 5 tablespoons vegetable oil
3 cans (3.75 ounces each) whole sardines, packed in oil, preferably olive oil

Combine the mustard, horseradish, vinegar, and honey, and slowly whisk in the olive oil until the horseradish vinaigrette is smooth and creamy. Set aside.

Season the flour with salt and pepper, and place on a plate or a sheet of foil. Heat half of the vegetable oil in a large nonstick skillet. Dredge the sardines in the seasoned flour and sauté them in the hot oil until both sides are browned and crisp. Add more oil if needed. Transfer the fried sardines to several layers of paper towels. Blot them quickly and transfer to a serving plate. Drizzle with the horseradish vinaigrette.

Shrimp with Peach Mustard Sauce

Here is a dip made from an unlikely pair of ingredients: peach preserves and spicy brown mustard. One goes on scones and the other on franks; one is for breakfast, the other is for lunch; one is florally sweet, the other is tearfully tangy. They say that opposites attract. Occasionally they have to be right.

Makes 6 servings

⅔ cup peach preserves
3 tablespoons spicy brown mustard
2 teaspoons hot-pepper sauce, such as Tabasco
1 teaspoon salt
1 pound cooked large or jumbo shrimp, peeled and chilled, thawed if frozen

Combine the peach preserves, mustard, pepper sauce, and salt. Serve as a dip with the shrimp.

Lemon Olives

A whole chopped lemon, rind and all, is the flavorful and colorful pizzazz in this vibrant condiment. Make sure you use oil-cured olives. Their rich consistency and subtle bitterness is the proper foil for the bright acidity and sweet-and-sour flesh of the lemon.

Makes about 8 servings

1 small lemon
8 ounces (1½ cups) pitted oil-cured black olives
1 teaspoon minced garlic, jarred or fresh
Large pinch of crushed red pepper flakes
1 tablespoon extra-virgin olive oil

Cut the lemon in half on its equator and remove the seeds with the tip of a knife. Cut the lemon halves in slices and chop the slices into small pieces. Toss the lemon pieces with the olives. Combine the garlic, pepper flakes, and oil, and mix with the olives and lemons. This can be stored in the refrigerator for several weeks.

Garlic Chèvre and Roasted Pepper Baguette

The crackled crust and air-pocketed innards of a loaf of artisan French bread is the real star of this appetizer sandwich. The bread is halved and then flavored with your choice of prepared sauces and cheese. I have chosen to stuff the bread with fresh goat cheese, a Provençal-style vegetable spread, and a salve of roasted garlic. After the loaf is reassembled, it is baked to crisp the crust and soften the cheese, and is served in thick slices.

Makes 12 servings

1 log (about 12 ounces) fresh chèvre cheese
⅓ cup roasted red pepper spread or pesto
2 teaspoons minced roasted garlic, jarred or fresh
Salt and black pepper to taste
1 French bread baguette

Preheat the oven to 400°F. Using the back of a fork, combine the cheese with the red pepper spread or pesto, minced garlic, salt, and pepper. Cut the baguette in half lengthwise. Spread one piece of bread with the chèvre mixture and place the other piece on top. Place the sandwich on a sheet pan and bake for 15 minutes, until the bread is crisp and the cheese is warmed through. Cut in ½-inch thick slices, about 24 per loaf.

Baked Artichoke Bruschetta

Bruschetta isn't always tomato. The topping for these toasts is made simply by combining herbed cream cheese, an artichoke spread or relish, and some Parmesan cheese. Different brands of herbed cheese—garlicky, basil-laden, or peppery—will yield different results, but all will work well in this preparation.

Makes 12 servings

1 package (about 5 ounces) herbed
    cream cheese, such as Boursin
¾ cup finely chopped marinated arti-
    choke hearts
¼ cup grated imported Parmesan cheese
1 French bread baguette, cut in ½-inch-
    thick slices (about 24 slices)
1 tablespoon extra-virgin olive oil

Preheat the oven to 400°F. Combine the cream cheese, artichoke, and half of the Parmesan. Place the bread slices on a sheet pan and brush with a thin film of the oil. Mound 1 tablespoon of the artichoke mixture on each slice of bread. Divide the remaining Parmesan among the bread slices and bake for 10 minutes, until the tops are lightly browned.

Thai Peanut Crudité

Dozens of brands and styles of Thai peanut sauce are available in your supermarket. Use any of them for this recipe. Depending on the sauce you choose, this dip might be spicy, aromatic, or sweet— or all three. Taste of Thai is the brand I use most often and the one I find most widely available. A note about vegetables: The amount given is approximate. It will yield about ½ cup per person, but feel free to make more or less depending on your guests' appetites.

Makes 8 servings

1 cup jarred Thai peanut sauce
¾ cup coconut milk
3 tablespoons lime juice, organic bottled
    or fresh
Salt and black pepper to taste
1 quart uncooked fruit and vegetables
    (such as baby carrots, snow peas, bell
    pepper, scallions, peeled broccoli stem
    strips, apple wedges, barely ripe pear
    wedges, mango slices, etc.)

Combine the peanut sauce, coconut milk, lime juice, salt, and pepper. Use as a dip for the fruit and vegetables.

Hoisin Eggs with Sesame Salt

Pickling eggs takes practically no effort or time to set up. However, once the eggs are in the pickling brine, they should be refrigerated for at least two days before serving. They are served with a spicy and delicious seasoned salt made by toasting Szechwan seasoning and sesame seeds. The flavored salt is also delicious on everything from roasted vegetables to popcorn.

Makes 12 servings

12 eggs
1 bottle (15 ounces) stir-fry sauce
¾ cup rice wine vinegar
1 teaspoon Szechwan seasoning
1 teaspoon sesame seeds
½ teaspoon coarse sea salt or kosher salt

Place the eggs in a large saucepan, cover with water, and bring to a boil. Lower the heat, cover the pan, and simmer for 10 minutes. Remove from the heat and allow to rest until the water is warm to the touch, about 2 hours. Run the eggs under cold water and peel them. Place the eggs in a jar with a tight-fitting lid.

Combine the stir-fry sauce and vinegar in the same saucepan used for cooking the eggs. Bring to a boil and pour over the eggs. Seal the jar and shake gently to coat the eggs with liquid. Refrigerate for 2 to 3 days, turning and shaking the jar every day.

To make the salt, combine the Szechwan seasoning, sesame seeds, and salt, and toast in a dry skillet over medium heat until the seeds pop, about 2 minutes, or in a microwave at full power for 90 seconds. Serve the eggs whole, halved, or sliced and sprinkled with the salt.

Roasted Grapes, Garlic, and Walnuts

Seduce me with a roasted grape—plump to bursting and with a dribble of caramelized juice oozing through a crack in the petrified skin. The scent of virgin olive oil, a few fragrant shards of garlic, and a dusting of roasted nuts complete the charm. Served warm or chilled with aged chèvre and fresh bread.

Makes 6 to 8 servings

1 pound seedless grapes
16 cloves garlic, peeled, jarred or fresh
1 cup (about 3½ ounces) walnut halves
2 tablespoons extra-virgin olive oil
½ teaspoon kosher salt
¼ teaspoon dried thyme leaves
½ teaspoon balsamic vinegar

Preheat the oven to 400°F. Toss the grapes, garlic, walnuts, oil, salt, and thyme in a baking dish suitable for serving. Bake for 15 minutes. Remove from the oven, smash the garlic, and drizzle with balsamic vinegar. Toss lightly and serve warm or at room temperature.

Chicken Wings Many Ways

You can tell by the following recipe that I have a deep appreciation of winged appendages and the snacking possibilities they inspire. Most of them are baked. I prefer baking wings using convection because it crisps the skin better and cooks large batches of wings more evenly. The wings should be cut into sections, and the tip section should be discarded or saved for stock.

STICKY WINGS

These wings are a takeoff on an old convenience-ingredient recipe using apricot preserves, onion soup mix, and French dressing. In this reincarnation the dressing is replaced with barbecue sauce.

Makes 8 appetizer servings

Nonstick oil spray
3 pounds chicken wings, cut in sections
1 envelope onion soup mix
1 cup apricot preserves
1 cup spicy barbecue sauce

Preheat a convection oven to 400°F or a regular oven to 450°F. Cover a sheet pan with heavy-duty foil and coat the foil with oil spray. Lay out the wing pieces in a single layer with as much space between the pieces as possible. Bake for 20 minutes, or until lightly browned. While the wings are cooking, blend the soup mix, apricot preserves, and barbecue sauce. Brush the wings with the sauce and bake for 5 minutes. Turn and brush with more sauce. Bake for another 5 minutes. Turn, brush, and bake in 5-minute intervals two more times. The wings should brown deeply.

SMOKY HOT 'N' HONEY WINGS

The star of the sauce is chipotle salsa, which adds a jolt of hotness with a hefty dose of smoke.

Makes 8 appetizer servings

Nonstick oil spray
1 jar (16 ounces) chipotle salsa
⅓ cup honey
3 pounds chicken wings, cut in sections
¼ cup chopped cilantro

Preheat a convection oven to 375°F or a regular oven to 400°F. Cover a sheet pan with heavy-duty foil and coat the foil with oil spray. Combine the salsa and honey in a blender or food processor and toss the wing pieces in the mixture. Place the pieces on the sheet pan in a single layer with as much space between the pieces as possible. Bake for 30 minutes, turn, and bake for another 15 minutes, until both sides are browned and the wings are cooked through. Remove the wings from the baking pan and toss with the cilantro.

BOMBAY WINGS

These tangy wings are very fruity, a little sweet, a little spicy, and intriguingly tart.

Makes 8 appetizer servings

Nonstick oil spray
3 pounds chicken wings, cut in sections
1 cup pineapple salsa
1 jar (about 8 ounces) mango chutney
2 tablespoons honey

Preheat a convection oven to 400°F or a regular oven to 450°F. Cover a sheet pan with heavy-duty foil and coat the foil with oil spray. Place the wing pieces in a single layer with as much space between the pieces as possible. Bake for 20 minutes, or until lightly browned. Turn and bake another 20 to 25 minutes, until golden brown and crisp.

While the wings are cooking, blend the salsa, chutney, and honey in a blender or food processor. When the wings are done, toss the pieces in the sauce. Lift with tongs or a slotted spoon and serve.

SPICY THAI WINGS

Sriracha sauce is quite fiery. If you'd like to make a tamer version of these wings, feel free to substitute a less assertive hot sauce. At the same time I encourage you to give these a try. Sriracha is not just hot, it is full of tart, fruity undertones that give great nuance to the chicken.

Makes 8 appetizer servings

Nonstick oil spray
3 pounds chicken wings, cut in sections
¼ cup hoisin sauce
2 tablespoons Thai hot sauce, such as
  Sriracha
¼ cup apple cider vinegar

Preheat a convection oven to 400°F or a regular oven to 450°F. Cover a sheet pan with heavy-duty foil and coat the foil with oil spray. Place the wing pieces on the foil in a single layer with as much space between them as possible. Bake for 20 minutes, or until lightly browned. Turn and bake another 20 to 25 minutes, until golden brown and crisp. While the wings are baking, combine the hoisin sauce, hot sauce, and vinegar. When the wings are done, toss them in the sauce and then remove them with tongs or a slotted spoon and serve.

SWEET SESAME WINGS

I try not to specify brands for a product as generic as teriyaki sauce, but Soy Vay Veri Veri is so unusual that I have to share it with you. It's not too sweet, and has a full, rounded, fermented soy flavor, a little acid, a jolt of ginger, and lots of sesame seeds. It is an essential ingredient in these wings.

Makes 8 appetizer servings

Nonstick oil spray
3 pounds chicken wings, cut in sections
¼ cup Chinese plum sauce or duck sauce
¼ cup Soy Vay Veri Veri Teriyaki Sauce
2 teaspoons Asian toasted sesame oil

Preheat a convection oven to 400°F or a regular oven to 450°F. Cover a sheet pan with heavy-duty foil and coat the foil with oil spray. Place the wing pieces in a single layer on the foil with as much space between the pieces as possible. Bake for 20 minutes, or until lightly browned. While the wings are cooking, combine the plum sauce, teriyaki sauce, and sesame oil.

Brush the wings with the sauce and bake for 5 minutes. Turn the wings and brush with more sauce. Bake for another 5 minutes. Turn, brush, and bake in 5-minute intervals two more times. The wings should brown deeply.

HOT HOT MUSTARD WINGS

Mustard is a whole new direction for wings, but don't let the novelty deter you. These are tangy and fiery. The fire comes from the Chinese chili purée, so feel free to adjust the amount to suit your taste.

Makes 8 appetizer servings

Nonstick oil spray
3 tablespoons spicy brown mustard
2 tablespoons Chinese chili purée
3 tablespoons apple cider vinegar
3 pounds chicken wings, cut in sections

Preheat a convection oven to 375°F or a regular oven to 400°F. Cover a sheet pan with heavy-duty foil and coat the foil with oil spray. Combine the mustard, chili purée, and vinegar, and toss the wing pieces with the sauce. Place the wings on the prepared sheet pan in a single layer with as much space between the pieces as possible. Bake for 30 minutes. Turn and bake another 15 minutes, until both sides are browned and the wings are cooked through.

CHAPTER 2

SOUPS UNCANNED

Ten-Minute Chicken Noodle Soup
Thai Big Noodle Bowl
Chinese Chicken Noodle Soup
Tomato Tortellini Soup
Tuscan Clam and White Bean Soup
Roasted Chowder
Corn and Black Bean Clam Chowder
Three-Corn Chowder
Smoked Turkey and Chickpea Chili
Five-Minute Five-Ingredient Bean Soup
Red Bean Soup with Barbecued Pork
Potato Spinach Bisque
Cheddar Bacon Potato Soup
Broccoli-Spinach-Potato Soup with Cheddar
Smoked Salmon Vichyssoise
Smoked Salmon Congee
Purée of White Bean Soup with Cilantro
Hearty Sweet-and-Sour Beef Borscht
Salad Bar Minestrone
Creamy Roasted Pepper Tomato Soup
Tomato Tarragon Consommé

Sun-Dried Tomato Tortilla Soup
Moroccan Porridge
Turkey Posole Soup
Shrimp and Black Bean Mole
Hot and Sour Chicken Soup
Mulligatawny in Minutes
Curried Shrimp and Sweet Potato Tagine
Coconut Curry Tomato Soup
Red Curried Pork Soup
Garden Pea Soup
Easy African Peanut Soup
Cream of Pumpkin Soup with Asiago Cheese
Pumapple Bisque
Italian Clam Soup
Chestnut Brandy Bisque
Easy Beet Borscht
Chilled Cucumber Soup
Garden-Free Gazpacho
Cardamom Apricot Soup
Honeydew Mint Soup
Mango Raspberry Soup

Ten-Minute Chicken Noodle Soup

There is nothing like a slow-cooked chicken soup radiating a head of healing steam, but this one comes pretty close, and in just about ten minutes. There are three tricks, all essential. First, start with a good prepared chicken broth. I like Swanson Natural Goodness because of its balanced flavor and moderate salt level. Second, add a little unflavored gelatin to keep the broth from being thin and watery. Third, use fresh pasta instead of dried noodles. The quality is a little better, and they cook in less than a minute.

Makes 6 servings

1 large can (49 ounces) chicken broth
¼ teaspoon unflavored gelatin
½ cup chopped onion, frozen or fresh
½ cup shredded carrot
1 boneless, skinless chicken breast half, cut in ½-inch pieces
1 package (9 ounces) refrigerated fresh angel-hair pasta, strands cut in half
1 tablespoon chopped fresh Italian (flat-leaf) parsley, or 1 teaspoon dried parsley flakes

Combine the broth and gelatin in a large saucepan. Heat to simmering, stirring occasionally. Add the onion, carrot, and chicken, and simmer about 5 minutes, until the vegetables are just tender. Add the pasta and parsley, and simmer about 1 minute, until the pasta is tender.

Thai Big Noodle Bowl

Add tons of noodles to your soup and you transform it from just another nourishing meal into the gastronomic equivalent of a slip-and-slide. This is what happens to good old American chicken noodle soup when it is internationalized with an extra dose of bean thread noodles, ginger, a jolt of hot sauce, and some lime juice.

Makes 4 servings

2 ounces cellophane (bean thread) noodles
1 jar (32 ounces) or 2 cans (19 ounces each) ready-to-serve chicken noodle soup
1 teaspoon minced garlic, jarred or fresh
1 teaspoon minced ginger, jarred or fresh
1 lime
1 to 2 teaspoons hot pepper sauce, to taste

Place the noodles in a bowl, cover them with very hot tap water, and set aside. Combine the soup, garlic, and ginger in a saucepan and bring to a simmer. Grate the lime skin on the finest teeth of a grater and add it to the soup. Cut the lime in half, and when the soup is hot, squeeze the juice into the soup. Stir in the hot pepper sauce. Drain the noodles and divide among 4 soup bowls. Ladle the soup on top of the noodles.

Chinese Chicken Noodle Soup

The layers of flavor and the bulk of the ingredients in this simple yet complex soup come from a relatively new but ubiquitous convenience item: Asian noodle salad. You will find it prepackaged in the refrigerator case or freshly made in your market's salad bar. I call this soup Chinese Chicken Noodle, but if you buy Thai or Vietnamese noodles, the ethnicity of the soup will change according to the flavor of the salad.

Makes 4 servings

1 can (about 14 ounces) chicken broth
1 boneless, skinless chicken breast half (about 6 ounces), cut in ½-inch pieces
1 container (8 to 10 ounces) Asian noodle salad
1 tablespoon teriyaki sauce
¼ teaspoon hot pepper sauce

Bring the broth to a simmer in a medium saucepan. Add the chicken and simmer for 5 minutes. Add the noodle salad and teriyaki sauce, and return the mixture to a simmer. Stir in the hot sauce and serve.

Tomato Tortellini Soup

This herb-laced tomato soup can be assembled in seconds, and it cooks in minutes. Because it relies on a long-simmered prepared marinara sauce as its base and gets instant flavor from jarred pesto and chopped garlic, the soup requires very little time to release its flavor. Refrigerated tortellini is used in this recipe, but if you wish, substitute frozen or dried, or another small stuffed pasta such as ravioli or cappelletti.

Makes 4 to 6 servings

¼ cup extra-virgin olive oil
2 teaspoons chopped garlic, jarred or fresh
2 cups (16 ounces) marinara sauce
1 large container (32 ounces) chicken broth
2 teaspoons basil pesto, jarred or fresh
1 package (9 ounces) refrigerated spinach tortellini
1 bag (8 to 10 ounces) baby spinach

Bring a large pot of salted water to a boil. Heat the oil in a saucepan, add the garlic, and sauté for 10 seconds. Add the marinara sauce and simmer until thick. Add the broth and simmer for 5 minutes. Stir in the pesto. Meanwhile, cook the tortellini in the boiling water until tender, about 7 minutes. Add the spinach and simmer until wilted, about 20 seconds. Drain. Stir the tortellini and spinach into the soup.

Tuscan Clam and White Bean Soup

Sometimes just a few ingredients can transform something familiar into something exotic. Such is the case with this recipe, which transports New England clam chowder to the Tuscan countryside with the simple addition of cannellini beans, garlic, hot pepper, and parsley. Be sure to use Italian (flat-leaf) parsley, which has real parsley flavor; use the curly kind for garnishing.

Makes 4 servings

1 jar (32 ounces) or 2 cans (19 ounces each) ready-to-serve New England clam chowder, or 2 cans (10 ounces each) condensed New England Clam Chowder, reconstituted with milk
1 can (15 ounces) cannellini beans, rinsed and drained
1 teaspoon minced garlic, jarred or fresh
Pinch of crushed red pepper flakes
¼ cup chopped Italian (flat-leaf) parsley

Bring the soup to a simmer in a large pot. Add the beans, garlic, pepper flakes, and parsley, and heat through.

Roasted Chowder

Forgive me, foodies, but this soup is delicious. Toss six packaged products in a pot and turn on the stove. The flavors are amazing, consisting of charred roasted pepper, caramelized roasted chicken, and sweet corn simmered in a rich chicken broth. It is thickened with a true miracle product, but it's a miracle only if you never use it as it was intended. I'm talking about instant mashed potatoes. The mashed potatoes that come from those flakes have nothing to do with the real thing, but whisk a little into a watery soup, and—*voilà!*—you have perfect consistency instantly. Every kitchen needs a box of instant mashed potatoes in the cupboard.

Makes 6 servings

1 jar (16 ounces) roasted pepper salsa
8 ounces roasted red peppers, diced (about 1 cup)
8 ounces prepared roasted chicken breast, cut in ½-inch pieces (about 1¾ cups)
1 cup canned or frozen corn kernels
1 large container (32 ounces) chicken broth
⅓ cup instant mashed potato flakes

Combine the salsa, peppers, chicken breast, corn, and broth in a large saucepan. Heat until simmering. Add the potato flakes and stir to incorporate. Simmer for 5 minutes.

Corn and Black Bean Clam Chowder

This effortless, spicy, tomato-based clam chowder is chock-full of clams and garden vegetables: onions, peppers, corn, beans, and tomatoes. The vegetables and beans come from a jar of corn and black bean salsa, and the minced clams are in a can. The only work (if you can call it that) is making rice, but once that's done, all you have to do is pour, heat, and enjoy.

Makes 4 servings

1 cup water
¼ cup long-grain or basmati rice
½ teaspoon Italian seasoning
2 bottles (8 ounces each) clam juice
¾ cup (about 6 ounces) corn and black bean salsa, refrigerated or jarred
1 can (6½ ounces) minced clams
12 ounces (about 1½ cups) crushed tomatoes
Salt and pepper to taste

Combine the water and rice in a saucepan and bring to a boil. Lower the heat, cover, and simmer until the rice is tender, about 12 minutes. Uncover and add the seasoning, clam juice, salsa, clams and their broth, tomatoes, salt, and pepper. Heat until boiling.

Three-Corn Chowder

This chunky, creamy soup gets its corn flavor from three ingredients: corn and black bean salsa, corn kernels, and crushed corn chips. The effect is a combination of a bisque, a chowder, and a tortilla soup—a truly sophisticated soup that requires just minutes to assemble.

Makes 4 servings

1 jar (11 ounces) corn and black bean salsa
1½ cups canned or frozen corn kernels
1 can (about 14 ounces) chicken broth
24 corn tortilla chips, ground or finely crushed
Salt and pepper to taste
⅓ cup light cream

Combine the salsa, corn, and broth in a medium saucepan and heat until simmering. Add the corn chips and stir to incorporate. Simmer for 5 minutes. Season with salt and pepper, and stir in the cream. Heat through.

Smoked Turkey and Chickpea Chili

A curry cooking sauce is the secret behind this exotic, colorful chili. It has the floral fragrance of coriander and ginger, the sweet acid and spicy bite of salsa, and a smoky redolence from smoked turkey breast and ground chipotle pepper. If you can't find ground chipotle, substitute a bit of chipotle hot sauce or use a chipotle salsa for part of the salsa in the recipe. The soup is thickened with powdered spiced chickpeas, sold for making falafel.

Makes 4 servings

1 jar (15 ounces) curry sauce
1 jar (16 ounces) chunky salsa, medium or hot
¼ to ½ teaspoon ground chipotle pepper, to taste
2 teaspoons ground cumin
4 ounces smoked turkey breast, finely chopped (about ¾ cup)
1 can (about 14 ounces) chicken broth
¼ cup instant falafel powder (page 25)

Combine the curry sauce, salsa, chipotle pepper, cumin, turkey breast, and broth in a large saucepan. Heat to boiling, stirring often. Whisk in the falafel powder and simmer for 1 minute. Remove from the heat and let sit for 2 minutes.

Five-Minute Five-Ingredient Bean Soup

As a radicchio-toting, classically trained chef, I am appalled, intrigued, insulted, and humbled that you can make a soup this hearty and healthful without wielding a knife or lifting a whisk. All you need are three cans, one box, and one bottle. How embarrassing. How delicious.

Makes 4 servings

1 can (about 14 ounces) chicken or beef broth
1 can (15 ounces) crushed tomatoes
1 can (15 ounces) black beans, rinsed and drained
1 box (7 ounces) instant black beans (page 25)
1 to 2 teaspoons hot pepper sauce, to taste
Salt to taste

Combine the broth, tomatoes, black beans, and 1 can of water in a large saucepan. Bring to a boil. Stir in the black beans and cook about 2 minutes, until lightly thickened. Stir in the hot pepper sauce and salt.

Red Bean Soup with Barbecued Pork

Fully prepared roasted meats have moved from meal-replacement restaurants to supermarket food courts to refrigerated meat cases. And for the most part their quality is good. This soup starts with a package of barbecued pork and then is transformed with chicken broth and V8 juice into a down-home barbecue bean soup that is hearty enough to serve as a main course.

Makes 8 appetizer servings or 4 entrée servings

*1 package (about 1 pound) refrigerated
    pulled pork with barbecue sauce
2 cups V8 vegetable juice
1 large container (32 ounces) chicken
    broth
½ teaspoon ground chipotle pepper
2 cans (15 ounces each) red kidney
    beans, rinsed and drained
⅓ cup instant refried bean powder
    (page 25)
Salt and pepper to taste*

Combine the pork, V8 juice, broth, and chipotle pepper in a large saucepan. Bring to a simmer, stirring often. Stir in the kidney beans, bean powder, salt, and pepper. Bring to a boil, stirring often. Let sit for 5 minutes so that the instant beans will thicken the broth.

Potato Spinach Bisque

A few recipes ago I decried the use of instant mashed potato flakes for making mashed potatoes. But there is an easy-to-use and natural alternative: fully prepared refrigerated or frozen mashed potatoes. These products are made from real cooked potatoes and are mashed with butter and milk into something that looks and tastes like real mashed potatoes. I use them frequently for concocting delicious potato soups. This one contains spinach, which adds color and a vegetable, and onion dip for richness.

Makes 4 servings

*1 bag (7 ounces) baby spinach, coarsely
    chopped
1 container (8 ounces) refrigerated
    French onion dip, any brand
1 can (about 14 ounces) chicken broth
1 package (16 ounces) prepared mashed
    potatoes, refrigerated, or frozen and
    thawed
Dash of grated nutmeg
Pepper to taste (you probably won't
    need additional salt)*

Combine the spinach, onion dip, and broth in a large saucepan. Add the potatoes, nutmeg, and pepper, and bring to a simmer, stirring often.

Cheddar Bacon Potato Soup

Cheesy potato soups have become standard fare in casual-dining restaurants. This recipe allows you to duplicate the rich, bacon-laden, cheddar-infused crocks that we have come to love at our neighborhood T.G.I. Applebennihouligans. The bacon in this recipe is precooked and ready to eat.

Makes 4 servings

2 strips ready-to-serve bacon, finely chopped
1 cup chopped onions, frozen or fresh
1 large container (32 ounces) chicken broth
1 package (16 ounces) prepared mashed potatoes, refrigerated, or frozen and thawed
1 cup light or heavy cream
Salt and pepper to taste
4 ounces (1 cup) shredded sharp cheddar cheese
1 tablespoon dried chives

Cook the bacon and onions in a large saucepan until the onions are tender. Do not allow the onions to brown. Stir in the broth and potatoes, and simmer for 5 to 10 minutes, until the onions are soft. Add the cream, salt, and pepper, and return to a simmer. Remove from the heat and stir in the cheese and chives until the cheese melts.

Broccoli-Spinach-Potato Soup with Cheddar

When frozen vegetables are cooked in a soup, they are almost indistinguishable from fresh vegetables. When puréed in a soup, they are superior. I'm not sure why. It may be because the freezing slightly breaks down the fiber in the vegetable so that it doesn't need as much cooking to get to a consistency where it can be puréed. The result is a brighter color and fresher flavor.

Makes 6 servings

1 tablespoon butter
1 cup chopped onions, frozen or fresh
½ teaspoon chopped garlic, jarred or fresh
1 large container (32 ounces) chicken broth
1 box (10 ounces) frozen broccoli
1 box (10 ounces) frozen chopped spinach
¾ cup instant mashed potato flakes
3 ounces (¾ cup) shredded sharp cheddar cheese

Melt the butter in a large, heavy saucepan. Add the onions and sauté until tender. Stir in the garlic and broth, and bring to a simmer.

Add the broccoli and simmer until almost tender, about 4 minutes. Add the spinach and simmer for another 3 minutes. Purée in a food processor until smooth, return to the saucepan, and bring to a simmer.

Stir in the potato flakes and simmer for 2 to 3 minutes, until the soup thickens slightly. Remove from the heat to very low, add the cheese, and stir until melted. Do not allow the soup to boil.

Smoked Salmon Vichyssoise

I have never understood the la-di-dah reputation of vichyssoise. Isn't it just cold potato soup? I know it is enriched with heavy cream and has the consistency of wet velvet, but it's still mashed potatoes. This version couldn't be simpler. All you do is mix everything together and chill. (The smoked salmon makes it very la-di-dah.)

Makes 4 servings

1 package (16 ounces) prepared mashed potatoes, refrigerated, or frozen and thawed
½ teaspoon minced garlic, jarred or fresh
½ teaspoon dried dill weed
1 can (about 14 ounces) chicken broth
8 ounces (1 cup) plain yogurt or sour cream
4 ounces smoked salmon, finely chopped

Whisk together all the ingredients until well blended and refrigerate until cold. Serve chilled.

Smoked Salmon Congee

Congee is Chinese rice soup. It is made by cooking rice in liquid until it breaks down into a slightly thickened, slightly sweet porridgelike broth with tiny pearls of very soft rice. In this recipe saffron risotto creates a radiant golden congee.

Makes 4 servings

7 cups water
2 (9 grams each) fish bouillon cubes
1 box (about 6 ounces) saffron risotto (Milanese)
1 tablespoon minced gingerroot, jarred or fresh
½ teaspoon minced garlic, jarred or fresh
¼ teaspoon dried basil
1 tablespoon lemon juice, organic bottled or fresh
Pepper to taste (you probably won't need more salt)
4 ounces smoked salmon, chopped in medium pieces

Bring the water to a boil and stir in the bouillon until dissolved. Stir in the risotto with its flavor packet. Simmer for 15 minutes, until the rice is tender, stirring once or twice. Stir in the ginger, garlic, basil, lemon juice, and pepper, and simmer for 5 minutes, until the rice is very soft and the soup is the consistency of thin porridge. Divide the chopped salmon among 4 soup bowls and ladle the hot soup over it. Stir to disperse the salmon evenly.

Purée of White Bean Soup with Cilantro

This very simple soup is all about the heavenly pairing of white beans and cilantro. If you have any reservations about either ingredient, move on to another recipe. But if you are like me, you will find this the lightest and cleanest of all bean soups. Don't allow the soup to sit long once the cilantro is added. It will oxidize and turn dark, which doesn't affect the flavor but will make the soup look muddy. If you prepare the soup ahead add the cilantro just before serving.

Makes 6 servings

1 large container (32 ounces) chicken broth
2 cans (about 19 ounces each) white beans (any type), rinsed and drained
½ cup chopped onion, frozen or fresh
2 teaspoons chopped garlic, jarred or fresh
Salt and pepper to taste
Pinch of ground allspice
2 tablespoons cilantro pesto or chutney, or ¼ cup chopped cilantro

Combine the broth, beans, onion, garlic, salt, pepper, and allspice in a large saucepan. Simmer until the onion is tender, about 10 minutes. Remove from the heat and purée in a food processor. Stir in the cilantro and serve immediately.

Hearty Sweet-and-Sour Beef Borscht

Beef borscht, the robust beef and cabbage soup of Eastern Europe, traditionally cooks for hours until the meat collapses into a rich tangy pulp. In this recipe the cooking time is compressed without sacrificing any of the long-simmered flavor. By relying on prepared beef and potatoes, sauerkraut (for the cabbage and the tang), V8 juice (for vegetable flavors), and a little brown sugar, all the elements of a traditional beef borscht are in the pot before the cooking even begins. It is all right to make this soup a day ahead. It gets better with age.

Makes 4 servings

1 package (1 pound) refrigerated beef and gravy entrée, such as pot roast, sirloin tips, or roast beef
1 pound refrigerated sauerkraut, drained
About 10 ounces refrigerated diced potatoes (2 cups)
¼ cup brown sugar
3 cups V8 vegetable juice
1 can (about 14 ounces) beef broth
Black pepper to taste (you probably won't need more salt)

Combine all the ingredients in a large saucepan and simmer over medium heat, stirring often, for about 20 minutes, until the flavors are blended.

Salad Bar Minestrone

The greatest source of prepared ingredients in your market isn't in the freezer
or packed into cans—it's the salad bar.
Chopped vegetables, marinades, condiments, and meats are all waiting to be
built into a salad or transformed into a
glorious freshly made soup. This minestrone comes together in minutes, cour-
tesy of that salad bar. If your salad bar
doesn't have the exact ingredients
listed in the recipe, make substitutions
freely and use more vegetables if you
wish.

Makes 4 servings

¼ cup Italian salad dressing
1 cup chopped onion, or 1 small onion
16 baby carrots, or ¾ cup sliced carrot
1 cup sliced celery
2 cups sliced mushrooms
1 cup diced red pepper, or ½ medium
    pepper
2 teaspoons minced garlic, jarred or
    fresh
1½ tablespoons Italian seasoning
1 can (about 15 ounces) diced tomato,
    fresh or canned
1 quart water
2 (11 grams each) vegetable bouillon
    cubes
1 tablespoon tomato paste in a tube
Salt and pepper to taste
1 cup canned or cooked beans, such as
    chickpeas, white kidney beans, or
    pinto beans
1 jar (6 ounces) marinated artichoke
    hearts, broken in pieces

Combine the dressing, onion, carrots, and
celery in a soup pot. Cook until the onion
becomes translucent and the carrots start
to soften, about 5 minutes. Add the
mushrooms and red pepper, and cook
until they lose their raw look, about 3
minutes. Stir in the garlic and seasoning,
add the tomato and water, and heat until
simmering. Stir in the bouillon cubes,
tomato paste, salt, and pepper, and simmer for 5 minutes. Stir in the beans and
artichoke hearts, and heat through.

Creamy Roasted
Pepper Tomato Soup

I'm not a big fan of creamy tomato soup,
but add a roasted pepper, and I lick the
bowl. Maybe it's the flavor of char bal-
ancing the dairy in the soup, or maybe it's
the natural sweetness in the pepper
rounding out the soup's slight sugary
edge. At any rate, this soup is great, and
it's easy enough for a spur-of-the-
moment meal.

Makes 4 servings

1 container (32 ounces) Campbell's
    Ready-to-Serve Cream of Tomato Soup
1 jar (6 ounces) roasted red pepper pesto
    or purée
½ cup chicken or vegetable broth
⅛ teaspoon Italian seasoning

Combine all the ingredients and heat
until simmering.

Tomato Tarragon Consommé

As I mentioned in the recipe for Ten-Minute Chicken Noodle Soup (page 65), one way to make a canned broth taste homemade is to add a touch of unflavored gelatin. When making consommé, which is clarified concentrated broth, the gelatin is even more important. The slight stickiness you want in a homemade broth should become dominant in a consommé, hence the full packet of gelatin in this recipe. The results are very close to a classically prepared consommé—spare, clean, and elegant. It is flavored with tomato and garnished with a few fresh tarragon leaves. If you don't have tarragon, almost any fresh herb can be substituted.

Makes 4 servings

1 packet (7 grams) unflavored gelatin
1 large can (49 ounces) chicken broth
¼ cup tomato paste in a tube
4 fresh tarragon leaves, finely chopped

Soften the gelatin in ½ cup of the broth. Heat the remaining broth in a large saucepan until boiling. Skim off any foam that rises to the surface and simmer until the broth is reduced by about one-third, to about 1 quart. Whisk in the gelatin and tomato paste. Simmer another minute, add the tarragon, and serve.

Sun-Dried Tomato Tortilla Soup

It took almost twenty years for sun-dried tomatoes to travel from relative obscurity to mass acceptance. Now their pungent supersaturated flavor is part of our culinary vernacular, headlining in salad dressings, marinades, soups, and sauces. Their ubiquity has certainly made it easy to get high-powered flavor with very little effort. This tortilla soup is a delicious example. Sun-dried tomatoes are used in two ways: Sun-dried tomato pesto adds herbs and garlic as well as an overriding tomato sensation, and sun-dried tomato pieces give a visual and a textural dimension.

Makes 6 servings

1 jar (6 ounces) chunky salsa, any heat
    level
½ cup sun-dried tomato purée or pesto
¼ cup sun-dried tomato pieces in oil
1½ cups canned or frozen corn kernels
1 container (32 ounces) chicken broth
24 corn tortilla chips, crumbled coarsely
1 teaspoon cilantro pesto or chutney, or
    1 tablespoon chopped fresh cilantro

Combine the salsa, sun-dried tomato purée, sun-dried tomato pieces, corn, and broth in a saucepan and heat until simmering. Add the chips and stir to incorporate. Simmer for 5 minutes. Season with cilantro and heat through.

Moroccan Porridge

This soup has all the sensual charm of a traditional Moroccan couscous but arrives at the table in a fraction of the time it takes to prepare couscous from scratch. The complex seasoning is built from a combination of spice blends, salsa, and hummus, which along with a handful of couscous helps thicken the broth.

Makes 6 servings

1 large container (32 ounces) chicken broth
½ cup chopped onion, frozen or fresh
½ cup chunky salsa, medium or hot
2 teaspoons chopped garlic, jarred or fresh
1 cup shredded carrots or sliced baby carrots
8 ounces prepared roasted chicken breast, cut in ½-inch pieces
1 teaspoon ground coriander
¼ teaspoon pumpkin pie spice
¼ teaspoon poultry seasoning
1 container (8 ounces) hummus
⅔ cup chopped Italian (flat-leaf) parsley,
½ cup couscous

Combine the broth and onion in a large saucepan and simmer for 5 minutes. Add the salsa, garlic, carrots, chicken breast, coriander, pumpkin pie spice, and poultry seasoning. Simmer for 5 minutes. Stir in the hummus and parsley, and return to a simmer. Stir in the couscous and let rest for 3 minutes.

Turkey Posole Soup

Posole is Mexican hominy. It is sold dried and canned. Both are easy to cook, but dried hominy needs over an hour on the stove, so I use canned exclusively. Posole has a unique flavor that is enhanced by hot pepper, cumin, and cilantro, all of which figure significantly in this soup. It is finished with crushed corn tortilla chips, which thicken the broth and lend a toasty sweetness.

Makes 6 servings

1 jar (16 ounces) salsa, medium or hot
1 can (15 ounces) posole (whole hominy), drained
1 large container (32 ounces) chicken broth
½ teaspoon ground cumin
1 teaspoon chopped garlic, jarred or fresh
4 ounces roasted turkey breast, cut in ½-inch pieces
24 corn tortilla chips (about 2 ounces), ground or finely crushed
1 teaspoon cilantro pesto or chutney, or 1 tablespoon chopped cilantro

Combine the salsa, posole, broth, cumin, garlic, and turkey breast in a large saucepan. Heat until simmering. Add the corn chips, stir to incorporate, and simmer for 5 minutes. Season with the cilantro and heat through.

Shrimp and Black Bean Mole

Shrimp and black beans might just be the new surf and turf. The earthiness of the beans creates the perfect foil for the sweet meatiness of the shrimp, and the color contrast is striking. The combination is seasoned with mole paste, an amalgam of nuts, fruit, chiles, and spices. Mole recipes typically have many steps and lengthy preparation time, but we bypass much of the work by using the prepared product.

Makes 6 servings

1 cup chopped onions, frozen or fresh
1 large container (32 ounces) chicken broth
1 teaspoon chopped garlic, jarred or fresh
1 cup shredded carrots or sliced baby carrots
1 can (19 ounces) black beans, rinsed and drained
¼ cup jarred mole
1 pound small shrimp, peeled and cleaned
Salt and pepper to taste

Combine the onions and broth in a large saucepan. Simmer for 5 minutes. Add the garlic, carrots, black beans, and mole, and simmer for another 3 minutes. Stir in the shrimp and simmer for 1 minute. Season with salt and pepper.

Hot and Sour Chicken Soup

Hot and sour soup is eaten so often in restaurants that home cooks just assume it is outside their milieu. Not true. It takes no longer to cook than boiling broth, and it's no more difficult. Miso is fermented soybean paste used to flavor stir-fries, stews, sauces, and cooked grains. It can be kept in the refrigerator for up to a year if tightly wrapped.

Makes 4 servings

1 large container (32 ounces) chicken broth
1 tablespoon miso paste
1 tablespoon cornstarch
1 cup shredded carrots or sliced baby carrots
1 can (15 ounces) straw mushrooms, drained
8 ounces prepared roasted chicken breast, cut in ½-inch pieces
¼ cup rice vinegar
½ to 1 teaspoon hot pepper or chili oil, to taste
2 scallions, roots trimmed and thinly sliced
Salt to taste

Place 1 cup of the broth in a large saucepan. Add the miso and mash with a fork. Whisk in the cornstarch until thoroughly combined. Add the remaining broth, carrots, mushrooms, and chicken. Simmer about 3 minutes, until the vegetables are tender and the soup is slightly thickened. Add the vinegar, hot pepper oil, and scallions. Season with salt.

Mulligatawny in Minutes

This curried soup is an Anglo-Indian con-coction, made from a mixture of spices, vegetables, and meat (most often chicken) cooked in broth that has been enriched with cream (Anglo) or coconut milk (Indian). There are as many recipes for this soup as there are people who love it. This one could not be easier.

Makes 6 servings

1 tablespoon vegetable oil
1 carrot, peeled and sliced
1 celery rib, peeled and sliced
1 skinless, boneless chicken breast (6 ounces), cut in ½-inch cubes
2 cans (19 ounces each) ready-to-serve chicken and rice soup
1 jar (15 ounces) curry sauce
2 teaspoons coriander pesto or chutney, or 1 tablespoon chopped cilantro
½ teaspoon freshly ground black pepper
1 cup regular coconut milk or light cream

Heat the oil in a large saucepan. Add the carrot and celery, and sauté until barely tender, about 3 minutes. Add the chicken and sauté until the chicken loses its raw look, about 1 minute. Add the soup, curry sauce, coriander pesto, pepper, and coconut milk. Simmer for 5 to 8 minutes, until the vegetables are tender and the flavors are blended.

Curried Shrimp and Sweet Potato Tagine

Tagine is a stew named for the conical earthenware pot in which it is tradition-ally prepared. I use the name to denote a hearty soup or stew that has North African roots. Although this recipe arrives at its Arabic character using an array of international ingredients, all the essential elements are there: lots of caramelized onions, rice, tomatoes, hot peppers, a swirl of yogurt, and a healthy handful of parsley.

Makes 4 servings

2 cans (10¾ ounces each) Campbell's con-densed French onion soup
1 can water
¼ cup long-grain or basmati rice
1 can (15 ounces) yams or sweet pota-toes, drained and mashed
1 cup curry sauce, any type
½ cup canned diced tomato
2 tablespoons chopped Italian (flat-leaf) parsley
8 ounces shrimp, shelled, cleaned, cooked, and cut in bite-size pieces
1 cup (about 8 ounces) plain yogurt or whole milk

Heat the onion soup and water in a large saucepan until boiling. Add the rice and simmer until almost tender, about 10 minutes. Add the yams, curry sauce, tomatoes, and parsley. Simmer for 5 min-utes. Turn the heat to low and stir in the shrimp and yogurt.

Coconut Curry Tomato Soup

This chunky, exotic tomato soup has Caribbean notes. Sweet coconut, spicy salsa, tangy mustard, and a fragrant curry all exert their influence on a jar of humble tomato soup. The effect is at once friendly and foreign. You can use it as a base for almost any meat or seafood, whether fresh or precooked.

Makes 6 servings

½ cup shredded coconut
2 teaspoons curry powder
1 jar (16 ounces) chunky salsa, medium or hot
1 container (32 ounces) Campbell's Ready-to-Serve tomato soup
1 can (15 ounces) regular coconut milk
1 teaspoon spicy brown mustard
8 ounces meat or seafood, such as small cleaned and shelled shrimp, cooked diced chicken breast, or smoked ham

Place a large saucepan over medium-high heat for 30 seconds. Add the coconut and stir until it toasts lightly. Stir in the curry powder. Immediately add the salsa, tomato soup, coconut milk, and mustard. Stir until incorporated and bring to a simmer. Stir in the meat or seafood and heat another 2 minutes.

Red Curried Pork Soup

When I see a package of pulled pork barbecue, I ask myself, "What's in there?" Hmmm, there's pork, vinegar, hot pepper, sugar, and some tomato. "What could I make from that?" I wonder. Let's see, I could put it on a bun, but anyone can do *that*. I ask myself, "What else has those ingredients?" Lots of curries do. Well, you get the picture.

Makes 6 servings

1 package (about 1 pound) pulled pork with barbecue sauce
1 large container (32 ounces) chicken broth
1 jar (15 ounces) curry sauce
2 teaspoons spicy brown mustard
2 teaspoons red curry powder or Thai red curry paste
1 can (19 ounces) chickpeas, rinsed and drained

Combine all the ingredients in a large saucepan and simmer for 5 minutes, stirring often.

Garden Pea Soup

The first time I ate mint with peas was a revelation. Until then I took my peas like vitamin tablets, one at a time, swallowed and not chewed. But the mint transformed them. All at once they found an inner sweetness, almost like candy that was good for you, and I became a pea aficionado. A few years later I ordered a green pea soup at a restaurant. There was the mint again, but this time there was something else that turned the soup into what I can only describe as a liquid garden: The secret ingredient was lettuce. Here is my recreation of that soup, updated with the greatest innovation of the last decade: prewashed lettuce.

Makes 6 servings

1 tablespoon butter
1 cup chopped onions, frozen or fresh
1 tablespoon dried mint, or 3 tablespoons chopped fresh mint leaves
2 boxes (10 ounces each) frozen peas, thawed
1 bag (7 ounces) butter lettuce salad blend
1 large container (32 ounces) chicken broth
1 tablespoon sugar
Salt and pepper to taste
1 cup light cream

Melt the butter in a large saucepan. Add the onions and sauté until tender, about 2 minutes. Add the mint, peas, lettuce, broth, sugar, salt, and pepper, and simmer until the peas are tender and the flavors have blended, about 7 minutes.

Purée the soup in a blender or food processor, return it to the saucepan, add the cream, adjust the seasoning, and heat through.

Easy African Peanut Soup

Peanuts are an important protein source in the cooking of West Africa. In this recipe, peanut butter, spicy salsa, and ginger enhance chicken and rice soup to make a pungent and very convincing West African–style peanut soup.

Makes 4 servings

Nonstick oil spray
1 cup shredded carrots
1 teaspoon minced ginger, jarred or fresh
1 cup chunky salsa, medium or hot
1 can (about 14 ounces) chicken broth
1 can (19 ounces) ready-to-serve chicken and rice soup
Salt and pepper to taste
½ cup peanut butter

Coat the bottom of a large saucepan with oil spray, add the carrots, and sauté until soft, about 2 minutes. Add the ginger, salsa, broth, and chicken and rice soup. Heat to a simmer, season with salt and pepper, and simmer until the vegetables are tender, about 5 minutes. Whisk in the peanut butter.

Cream of Pumpkin Soup with Asiago Cheese

In America, pumpkin is only sweet. It goes in cakes and pies and muffins, and even when we put it in a soup, we tend to add cinnamon and sweeten it as much as possible. Get ready to change your mind. This savory, creamy, pungently cheesy pumpkin soup is not only a gorgeous pale orange but is fragrant with garlic and Asiago cheese.

Makes 4 servings

2 tablespoons butter
½ cup finely chopped onion, frozen or fresh
1 teaspoon chopped garlic, jarred or fresh
1 can (15 ounces) pure pumpkin
1 large container (32 ounces) chicken broth
Pinch of grated nutmeg
Salt and white pepper to taste
1 cup light or heavy cream
¼ cup grated Asiago cheese
1 tablespoon chopped Italian (flat-leaf) parsley

Melt the butter in a large saucepan, add the onion, and sauté until tender. Do not brown. Add the garlic and sauté a few seconds more. Stir in the pumpkin, broth, nutmeg, salt, and pepper. Simmer for 5 minutes, until the flavors combine. Stir in the cream and heat through. Stir in the cheese and parsley.

Pumapple Bisque

I love when two ingredients blend so perfectly that regardless of how hard the palate may try, it can't coax them apart. That's what happens to the applesauce and pumpkin purée in this sweet and savory soup. The pumpkin gives the apple substance, and the apple makes the pumpkin sweet and tangy. Eaten together, they become a totally new ingredient. Pumapple, anyone?

Makes 4 servings

2 tablespoons butter
½ cup finely chopped onion, frozen or fresh
1 tablespoon chopped ginger, jarred or fresh
Pinch of cinnamon
Pinch of crushed red pepper flakes
1 jar (16 ounces) unsweetened applesauce
1 can (15 ounces) pure pumpkin
1 container (32 ounces) chicken broth
2 tablespoons honey
Salt to taste
1 cup whole milk, half-and-half, or light cream

Melt the butter in a large saucepan. Add the onion, and sauté until soft. Add the ginger, cinnamon, and pepper flakes, and sauté a few seconds more. Stir in the applesauce, pumpkin, broth, honey, and salt. Simmer for 5 to 7 minutes, until the flavors combine. Stir in the milk and heat through.

Italian Clam Soup

Sometimes Old World recipes are so easy and straightforward that streamlining them for convenience is pointless. This traditional Italian shellfish soup is a perfect example. Clams are simmered in a simple marinara sauce until they release their juices, flavoring the sauce, and thinning it to a perfect soup consistency.

Makes 4 servings

⅓ cup extra-virgin olive oil
2 teaspoons minced garlic, jarred or fresh
½ cup white wine
1 jar (26 to 28 ounces) marinara sauce
2 tablespoons chopped Italian (flat-leaf) parsley
Tiny pinch of crushed red pepper flakes
3 dozen littleneck clams, cleaned (see Note)

Heat the oil in a large saucepan with a cover. Add the garlic and sauté about 10 seconds. Add the wine and boil for 1 minute. Add the marinara sauce and heat until warm. Add the parsley, pepper flakes, and the clams. Cover the pan, and boil until the clams open, about 5 minutes. Serve with crusty bread.

NOTE: Clams can be sandy and hard to clean, but better seafood stores sell prewashed clams. If you buy clams unwashed, place them in cold water and scrub with a nylon pad, changing the water as it gets cloudy. Repeat until the water is clear.

Chestnut Brandy Bisque

This rich, creamy bisque should be reserved for the chilliest nights and the most elegant occasions. It has a subtle nutty flavor and an aroma of sweet vegetables. Chestnut purée is generally sold along with baking supplies or in the gourmet food aisle, between the caviar and the cornichons.

Makes 6 servings

1 container (32 ounces) vegetable broth
1 can (15 ounces) chestnut purée
1 can (about 14 ounces) chicken broth
Pinch of ground cloves
Salt and white pepper to taste
1 cup heavy cream
2 tablespoons brandy

Whisk the vegetable broth and chestnut purée together in a large, heavy saucepan until smooth. Mix in the chicken broth, cloves, salt, and pepper. Heat until simmering, stirring often. Stir in the cream and brandy, and keep warm.

Easy Beet Borscht

There's no cooking here. None, not even a spoon for stirring. And if you don't mind serving out of the blender jar, there's hardly any cleanup, either. It's the perfect soup for a summer lunch or for starters at a picnic. Plus, its color is outrageous.

Makes 4 servings

1 jar (16 ounces) pickled beets
2 cups buttermilk
2 tablespoons chopped fresh dill, or 1
*   teaspoon dried dill*
1 tablespoon prepared horseradish
1 cup ice water
Salt and pepper to taste

Chop the beets and their liquid finely in a blender. Add the buttermilk, dill, horseradish, ice water, salt, and pepper, and blend. Chill if needed. Serve chilled.

Chilled Cucumber Soup

Here's another soup that is perfect when it's just too hot to cook but you can't get out of the kitchen. Tzatziki is a Greek cucumber dip that is sold in many delis. If you can't find it, substitute a creamy cucumber salad. You might want to add a spoonful or two of sour cream, depending on how creamy the salad is.

Makes 4 servings

1 large container (12 ounces) tzatziki or
*   creamy cucumber salad*
1 can (about 14 ounces) chicken broth
½ teaspoon dried dill weed
2 tablespoons lemon juice
Salt and pepper to taste

Whisk all the ingredients together and chill thoroughly.

Garden-Free Gazpacho

V8 juice is almost gazpacho all by itself, so the notion of turning it into the classic Andalusian soup can hardly be considered creative. Still, it is one of the most refreshing of chilled soups, and with this recipe it can be made even when fresh produce is unavailable.

Makes 4 servings

1 slice stale bread, cubed (about 1 cup)
1 cucumber, peeled and cubed
1 teaspoon crushed garlic
¼ cup diced onion, frozen or fresh
2 cups V8 vegetable juice
1 to 2 teaspoons hot pepper sauce,
  preferably green Tabasco, to taste
1 tablespoon extra-virgin olive oil
2 tablespoons red wine vinegar
Salt and pepper to taste
6 ice cubes

Combine the bread, cucumber, garlic, onion, and V8 juice in a blender or food processor and process until finely chopped. Pour into a serving bowl and stir in the hot pepper sauce, oil, vinegar, salt, pepper, and ice. Stir occasionally, until the ice cubes have melted and the soup is chilled. Serve immediately or refrigerate until you're ready to serve.

Cardamom Apricot Soup

There are two styles of fruit soup. Summer fruit soups tend to be uncooked or barely cooked purées. Cold-weather varieties are cooked and often contain dried fruit. This is an example of the latter. It is slightly tart and very rich, and is made from a combination of apricots, golden raisins, candied ginger, and a bit of ground cardamom. If cardamom is unfamiliar to you, I encourage you to try it. Similar to ginger but a bit more floral, it is an exotic spice that's very easy to love.

Makes 4 servings

1 bottle (24 ounces) apricot nectar
3 cups water
2 (11 grams each) vegetable bouillon
  cubes
8 dried apricots, cut in ¼-inch pieces
⅓ cup golden raisins
3 slices crystallized ginger, minced (about
  2 tablespoons)
3 tablespoons honey
¼ teaspoon ground cardamom
¼ cup sour cream (optional)

Combine the apricot nectar and water in a medium saucepan and bring to a boil. Add the bouillon, apricots, raisins, ginger, honey, and cardamom. Simmer for 5 minutes. Serve hot or chilled, topping each serving with 1 tablespoon of sour cream if desired.

Honeydew Mint Soup

Think of this soup as drinkable melon. The only challenge is finding a ripe honeydew. Look for specimens with a golden blush that are slightly soft and that radiate a strong perfume when sniffed at one end. If the melons you find don't meet these criteria, don't buy them. They will be bland and hard.

Makes 4 servings

1 large or 2 small ripe honeydew melons, halved, seeds removed
3 tablespoons lime or lemon juice, organic bottled or fresh
Pinch of salt
1 teaspoon crushed, dried mint leaves, or 1 tablespoon chopped fresh mint leaves

Scoop the flesh from the rind of the honeydew and purée it in a food processor or blender until smooth. Mix with the juice, salt, and mint. Chill before serving.

Mango Raspberry Soup

This is a brilliant first course for a meal of grilled seafood or poultry—or a spectacular dessert served with cookies or cake. The choice is yours, and you can't go wrong. Frozen mango purée is increasingly available, but if your market doesn't have it, substitute frozen mango pieces or fresh mango puréed in a food processor. If you use fresh mango, chill the soup before serving.

Makes 4 servings

½ cup white wine
1 tablespoon honey
1 package (10 ounces) frozen mango purée, cut into pieces
1 cup orange juice
Pinch of salt
½ pint raspberries

Heat the wine in a saucepan, or microwave it until boiling. Add the honey and stir until it dissolves. Remove from the heat. Add the mango purée and stir until it melts but is still cold. Stir in the juice and salt, and taste for sweetness and temperature. Add more honey if needed. Chill if needed. Stir in the raspberries just before serving.

CHAPTER 3

SAUCES:
LOTS OF FLAVOR, LITTLE WORK

Herbed Cheese Sauce
Creole Cream Sauce
Triple Tomato Mascarpone
Carrot Potato Puddle
Wasabi Potato "Cream"
Hummus "Hollandaise"
Baba-Latté
Pineapple Mustard Salsa
Grapefruit Ponzu Sauce
Artichoke and Feta Relish
Salsa Butter
Salsa Aioli
Curried Avocado Ketchup
Tahini Lime Sauce
Guacamaise
Thai Peanut Vinaigrette
Ancho Duck Sauce
Balsamic Black Bean Sauce
Tomato Raita

Easy-Does-It Marinara

Tomato Gravy

Roasted Pepper Tomato Sauce

Mediterranean Tonno Sauce

Mole Demi-Glace

Wild Mushroom Sauce

Sun-Dried Beurre Rouge

Sun-Dried Tomato Balsamic Glaze

Brown Butter Caper Vinaigrette

Ginger Steak Sauce

Olive Beurre Noire

Olive Olive Aioli

Tapenade "Butter"

Hot and Sour Sauce

Tomato Hoisin Sauce

Sweet-and-Sour Ginger Sauce

Spicy Orange Sesame Sauce

Szechwan Barbecue Sauce

Cardamom Apricot Glaze

Sweet-and-Sour Molasses

Roasted Pepper Mayonnaise

Major Grey's Cranberry Sauce

Herbed Cheese Sauce

Light and creamy, and brightened by the fruity acidity of white wine and a jolt of garlic, this simple sauce owes much of its nuance to a single ingredient that you have probably used a hundred times, although probably not in sauce making: garlic and herb cream cheese. It doesn't matter which of the many brands you use for this sauce, but taste the cheese before you start; you might want to add a bit of garlic at the end.

Makes about 2 cups (4 servings)

1 cup white wine
1 cup chicken or seafood broth
2 packages (6 ounces each) garlic and
    herb cream cheese, such as Boursin
Salt and pepper to taste

Combine the wine and broth, and boil over high heat until reduced to about ½ cup. Turn the heat to low and whisk in the cheese until smooth and melted. Add salt and pepper if necessary. Use as a sauce with grilled chicken or turkey, or grilled or poached fish.

Creole Cream Sauce

This versatile recipe juxtaposes seemingly disparate ingredients to make a sophisticated multidimensional sauce. The bruschetta contributes herbs, fragrant olive oil, and chunks of tomato while the cream brings sweetness and richness. It is all balanced by a glow of pepper and a bright spark of vinegar from the Tabasco. The broth determines the sauce's destiny: seafood or poultry.

Makes about 2 cups (4 servings)

1 cup tomato bruschetta, jarred or
    refrigerated
1 cup clam juice or chicken broth
1 cup heavy cream
1 to 2 teaspoons Tabasco sauce, to taste
1 to 2 teaspoons Pernod or other anise-
    flavored liqueur, to taste (optional)

Boil the bruschetta and clam juice or chicken broth in a skillet over high heat until reduced by half. Add the cream and boil until the sauce thickens slightly, about 3 minutes. Stir in the Tabasco and the Pernod if desired. Serve with seafood (if made with clam juice) or with chicken or veal (if made with chicken broth).

Triple Tomato Mascarpone

Mascarpone is a fresh cheese made from cream. Its fat content gives it a consistency more like very thick sour cream than cheese. This recipe builds on the richness of the mascarpone with three types of tomato products: fresh-tasting bruschetta, long-simmered and highly concentrated tomato paste, and turbo-flavored sun-dried tomatoes.

Makes about 2 cups (4 servings)

1½ cups (12 ounces) tomato bruschetta,
    jarred, refrigerated, or fresh
1 tablespoon tomato paste in a tube
1 tablespoon sun-dried tomato pesto or
    paste
8 ounces (about 1 cup) mascarpone
Salt and black pepper to taste

TO PREPARE A COLD SAUCE:

Drain the bruschetta. Stir in the tomato paste, pesto, and mascarpone until thoroughly blended. Add salt and pepper. Serve with grilled fish or chicken, or toss with pasta.

TO PREPARE A HOT SAUCE:

Heat the bruschetta in a skillet until the liquid is almost gone. Stir in the tomato paste and pesto. Over low heat, stir in the mascarpone and heat until a creamy sauce develops, about 1 minute. Adjust the seasoning with salt and pepper. Serve with sautéed seafood, chicken or turkey breast, veal, or stuffed pasta.

Carrot Potato Puddle

Vegetable purées are the basis for some of the most refined restaurant sauces. In a home kitchen, though, purées are hard to come by. Enter mashed potatoes, a culinary chameleon if there ever was one. In this pale, carrot-tinted sauce, refrigerated prepared mashed potatoes are seasoned with garlic and onion and thinned with carrot juice and milk. The result is a silken sauce with the consistency of heavy cream but only a fraction of its fat.

Makes 6 servings (about 3 cups)

1 pound refrigerated prepared mashed
    potatoes
2 teaspoons minced roasted garlic, jarred
    or fresh
⅛ teaspoon onion powder
¾ cup carrot juice, bottled or fresh
⅓ cup milk, 2% or whole
2 tablespoons chopped Italian (flat-leaf)
    parsley
1 tablespoon butter

Combine the potatoes, garlic, onion powder, carrot juice, and milk in a large saucepan. Heat until simmering, stirring often. Stir in the parsley and butter. (The sauce should have the consistency of barely beaten cream.) If necessary, thin it with a bit more milk or thicken it by simmering a bit longer. Serve with grilled or poached seafood, sautéed chicken, or roasted vegetables.

Wasabi Potato "Cream"

Here's another creamy potato sauce, but this one is somewhat bolder and is bolstered with a jolt of wasabi horseradish, some ginger, and a whiff of garlic. The potatoes acquire a sauce consistency with the use of chicken broth and milk. The resulting sauce is the palest of greens and radiates the peppery scent of wasabi.

Makes 6 servings (about 3 cups)

1 pound refrigerated prepared mashed
   potatoes
2 teaspoons wasabi powder
½ teaspoon minced garlic, jarred or fresh
½ teaspoon minced ginger, jarred or
   fresh
¾ cup chicken broth
⅓ cup milk, 2% or whole

Combine all the ingredients in a large saucepan. Heat until simmering, stirring often. (The sauce should have the consistency of barely beaten cream.) If necessary, thin it with a bit more milk or thicken by simmering a bit longer. Serve with grilled or poached seafood, sautéed chicken, or roasted vegetables.

Hummus "Hollandaise"

While not really hollandaise (there's no egg yolk, heating, whisking, breaking, or fear of saturated fat), this easy sauce gets its creamy consistency from hummus and added richness from olive oil.

Makes ¾ cup (4 servings)

4 ounces hummus with herbs or spices
2 tablespoons lemon juice
2 tablespoons extra-virgin olive oil

Combine all the ingredients. Serve with grilled, roasted, or sautéed fish, chicken, lamb, or shellfish.

Baba-Latté

This light, creamy sauce is perfect for broiled or poached fish, plainly roasted meats, or a grilled chicken breast. The recipe calls for *za'atar*, a Middle Eastern spice blend made from thyme leaves, sumac berries, and sesame seeds. It is available in Middle Eastern markets, on the Internet, or in spice catalogs (see Ingredient Sources, page 399). If you cannot find *za'atar*, substitute a bit of lemon juice and some thyme.

Makes about ¾ cup (4 servings)

4 ounces baba ghanouj
¼ cup ranch salad dressing
2 teaspoons lime juice, organic bottled or fresh
1 teaspoon za'atar, or ½ teaspoon dried thyme leaves
Salt and black pepper to taste

Combine all the ingredients. Serve with grilled or roasted meats, poultry, seafood, or vegetables.

Pineapple Mustard Salsa

Although the tangy, sweet spiciness of this salsa is reminiscent of chutney, this mixture is not cooked, so it boasts a freshness that is missing in processed chutneys. The recipe yields a lot. It will keep in the refrigerator for about a week and can be frozen.

Makes about 2¾ cups (8 servings)

1 can (15 ounces) crushed pineapple, drained
1 tablespoon spicy brown mustard
1 jar (12 ounces) fruit salsa (any type, such as peach, pineapple, mango, etc.)
1 teaspoon honey

Combine all the ingredients. Serve with roasted or grilled meats, poultry, or fish. It is especially good with turkey, pork, and salmon.

Grapefruit Ponzu Sauce

Ponzu, a sauce made from citrus and soy, is the sparest and cleanest of Japanese condiments. It is drizzled over sashimi or used as a dressing for vinegared dishes *(sunomono)*. This untraditional ponzu is made from grapefruit juice that is flavored with ginger, garlic, and soy sauce. It will store well for several weeks in the refrigerator.

Makes about ¾ cup (4 servings)

¾ cup unsweetened grapefruit juice
2 teaspoons minced ginger, jarred or fresh
1 teaspoon chopped garlic, jarred or fresh
2 teaspoons soy sauce

Combine all the ingredients. Serve with grilled or poached seafood, or with grilled or broiled chicken breast.

Artichoke and Feta Relish

Not all sauces flow. Some are syrupy glazes, some are cloudlike foams, and others, such as this one, are so full of flavorful chunks that they are more like diminutive side dishes than sauces. It has just three ingredients, but its flavors are intense and multifaceted: sweet artichoke, fragrant olive oil, pungent garlic (all from the marinated artichoke hearts), plus the spike of hot pepper and the creamy tang from the fresh feta cheese.

Makes about ¾ cup (4 servings)

1 jar (6 ounces) marinated artichoke hearts
½ cup crumbled feta cheese
½ teaspoon minced garlic, jarred or fresh

Finely chop the artichoke and mix it with the cheese and garlic. Serve with grilled or poached seafood; grilled, sautéed, or broiled chicken breast; or sautéed veal.

Salsa Butter

Salsa has become so common that our appreciation for its natural complexities has dulled. It is a cacophony, bringing together the sweet acidity of fresh tomatoes, the eye-tearing pungency of onion, the burning glow of jalapeño, the fragrance of lime, and the distinctive scent of cilantro. This composed sauce adds yet another sensory level, taming the assertive ingredients with a balm of sweet butter.

Makes about ¾ cup (4 servings)

1½ cups salsa, any heat level
3 tablespoons unsalted butter, cut in
   pieces

Bring the salsa to a boil in a small saucepan or skillet and cook until most of the liquid has evaporated. Remove from the heat and whisk in the butter until the sauce is smooth. Serve with grilled or poached seafood; grilled, sautéed, or broiled chicken breast; or baked pork chops.

Salsa Aioli

Think of Russian dressing radiating with jalapeño, or of Thousand Island dressing with salsa replacing the relish. Either way, this aromatic mayonnaise may take the place of your favorite dressing for cold meats, seafood, and poultry.

Makes about ¾ cup (4 servings)

1 tablespoon mayonnaise
½ cup salsa, any heat level, drained
1 teaspoon chopped garlic, jarred or
   fresh
2 tablespoons extra-virgin olive oil

Combine the ingredients. Serve with grilled or poached seafood; grilled, sautéed, or broiled chicken breast or turkey breast; or any cold meat.

Curried Avocado Ketchup

Wherever Indian cuisine alights, convenient curry sauces are quick to follow. It took a long time for Indian food to filter into the mainstream of the American kitchen, but it has definitely arrived. If you have any doubts, count how many ways there are to make a curry with the ingredients found on the shelves of your supermarket. This recipe uses one of the most available and versatile of the easy curry crowd: curry sauce. You will find several flavors and styles of curry cooking sauces. Use any of them for this exotically spiced ketchup that is seasoned with curry and thickened with guacamole.

Makes about ¾ cup (4 servings)

½ cup refrigerated guacamole
¼ cup (2 ounces) curry sauce

Combine both ingredients until smooth. Refrigerate. Serve chilled with grilled or roasted meats, poultry, seafood, or vegetables; baked or fried potatoes; or meatloaf or burgers.

Tahini Lime Sauce

Tahini (sesame butter) is used extensively in eastern Mediterranean sauces. It is best known in the United States as part of the sauce for falafel and as that "other thing" in hummus besides the chickpeas. In this simple pan sauce, the tahini provides richness and the central flavor. Its nutty, creamy velour is brightened by lime juice and garlic. It goes beautifully with grilled or sautéed sea scallops. Warning: The sauce is intense; a little goes a long way.

Makes about ½ cup (4 servings)

2 tablespoons butter
¼ cup chopped onion
½ teaspoon minced garlic, jarred or fresh
3 tablespoons lime juice, bottled organic
  or fresh
3 tablespoons water
2 tablespoons tahini
Salt and black pepper to taste

Melt the butter in a small skillet over medium heat. Add the onion and sauté until lightly browned. Stir in the garlic, lime juice, and water, and bring to a simmer. Turn the heat to low and whisk in the tahini until smooth. Season with salt and pepper. Serve with grilled or roasted seafood or with vegetables.

Guacamaise

A warning about refrigerated prepared guacamole: There's a wide range of quality out there. Some products are so saturated with ascorbic acid that they taste more like a vitamin C tablet than an avocado. I have found one brand (Avo Classic) that is widely available in my region and is consistently high in quality. There may well be other good brands around, so I wish you the same good fortune.

Makes 4 servings (about ¾ cup)

1 cup refrigerated guacamole
1½ tablespoons lemon juice, organic bottled or fresh
¼ cup extra-virgin olive oil

Combine the guacamole and lemon juice, and slowly whisk in the oil. Serve with grilled or poached seafood; grilled, roasted, or sautéed chicken or turkey breast; roasted or sautéed vegetables; baked or fried potatoes; or as a sauce for tuna, chicken, or shrimp salad.

Thai Peanut Vinaigrette

Thai peanut products have arrived. You can buy them ready to eat as a sauce in a jar or as a flavor in a packet. In any form, the blend of aromatic spices, citrus tang, sweet coconut, and down-to-earth peanut has captivated the American palate. This mix-and-serve sauce utilizes jarred Thai peanut sauce, but if you have a dry packet, substitute it for the jarred. The only adjustment you'll have to make is adding more coconut milk to make up for the lost liquid. It's delicious poured over grilled or roasted anything.

Makes about 1 cup (4 servings)

½ cup jarred Thai peanut sauce
½ cup coconut milk
4 teaspoons lime juice, organic bottled or fresh
Salt and black pepper to taste

Combine all the ingredients. Serve heated or chilled with grilled meats, seafood, or poultry.

Ancho Duck Sauce

This sweet, jamlike Chinese sauce has many names and just as many variations. Most of us know it as the ever-present super-orange, super-sweet, super-tangy condiment that accompanies Chinese-American restaurant food. Whether it's called plum sauce or duck sauce, it is made from fruit, preserved ginger, spices, vinegar, and sugar. Although it is most often seen as a dip, it is a recipe ingredient in Chinese cooking and is used to glaze spareribs or to act as a base for sweet-and-sour preparations. The addition of ancho chiles and cumin gives this version greater depth and a subtle personality shift.

Makes about 1 cup (4 servings)

1 cup (8 ounces) Chinese duck sauce or
   plum sauce
1 teaspoon ground ancho chili pepper
½ to 1 teaspoon hot pepper sauce
1 tablespoon apple cider vinegar
1 teaspoon soy sauce
¼ teaspoon ground cumin

Combine all the ingredients in a small saucepan and heat until simmering. Serve with grilled or roasted meat, seafood, or poultry.

Balsamic Black Bean Sauce

This pungent purple purée, redolent with cumin and garlic, the scent of cilantro, and a molasseslike tang of aged balsamic vinegar, is the logical evolution of black bean dip. One of the most versatile of the new generation of convenience ingredients, we've already seen how black bean dip can become a soup or a coating for fried food. Here is its incarnation as a sauce.

Makes about 1¾ cups (4 servings)

½ cup chicken or vegetable broth
1 jar (10 ounces) black bean dip
1 tablespoon balsamic vinegar or apple
   cider vinegar
1 teaspoon cilantro pesto or chutney, or
   1 tablespoon chopped cilantro
2 tablespoons shredded cheddar cheese,
   sharp or mild

Heat the broth until boiling in a medium saucepan. Mix in the bean dip and vinegar, and heat until simmering, stirring often. Mix in the cilantro and cheese until the cheese is melted. Serve with seafood, poultry, or pork.

Tomato Raita

A raita is a North Indian yogurt salad. As in most Indian recipes, a raita has an extensive ingredients list that is loaded with spices and vegetables. This one has been streamlined by starting with salsa, which contains all the necessary vegetables and several of the spices. Raita is typically served with dal (a bean sauce usually made from lentils) as an accompaniment to a meal. If you wish, serve this one teamed with the recipe for Balsamic Black Bean Sauce (page 97).

Makes 1 cup (4 servings)

1 cup chunky salsa, medium or hot
½ teaspoon ground coriander
¼ cup plain yogurt

Combine all the ingredients. Serve with grilled meats, poultry, or seafood. Refrigerate for up to two days.

Easy-Does-It Marinara

Italian tomato sauce comes in two basic types: ragù, which is thick and meaty and requires the better part of an afternoon to simmer to perfection, and marinara. A marinara is made from vegetables only, is thinner and lighter than a ragù, and takes less than an hour to cook. By starting with crushed tomatoes (which have already simmered for a while), this recipe gives you a marinara in a little more than 10 minutes—about the time needed to grill or sauté a chicken breast or a veal chop, or to cook pasta.

Makes about 3 cups (4 servings)

3 tablespoons olive oil
½ cup chopped onion
2 cloves garlic, minced, jarred or fresh
1 can (28 ounces) crushed tomatoes
1 tablespoon tomato paste in a tube
Salt and black pepper to taste
1 tablespoon basil pesto, jarred or fresh

Heat the oil in a large saucepan over medium heat. Add the onion and sauté until tender, about 3 minutes. Do not brown. Add the garlic and sauté a few seconds. Add the tomatoes, tomato paste, salt, and pepper, and simmer for 10 minutes. Stir in the pesto and simmer 1 minute more. Serve with pasta or grilled meats, poultry, or fish.

Tomato Gravy

In a genuine Italian ragù, tomatoes and meat simmer together for hours. The meat is then removed and served as its own course while the remaining meaty sauce is served with pasta, gnocchi, or polenta. This recipe for tomato gravy replicates the flavor of a ragù after it has been delivered of its meat. It uses a fairly new product, of which I have become wholeheartedly enamored: demi-glace concentrate. Demi-glace is the highly refined super-meaty elixir essential for making any brown sauce in a classic French kitchen. The concentrate is quite pricey, but a little goes a long way and the flavor is absolutely authentic.

Makes 4 cups (8 servings)

2 tablespoons demi-glace concentrate
  (page 16)
1 cup water
1 jar (26 ounces) marinara sauce

Whisk together the demi-glace concentrate and water, and bring to a boil. Stir in the marinara sauce and simmer for 5 minutes. Serve with grilled, sautéed, or roasted beef, pork, or veal, or with cooked pasta.

Roasted Pepper Tomato Sauce

When roasted red pepper is used in a fresh tomato sauce, barely simmered with a hint of basil and a tickle of garlic, it embodies the essence of a summer garden. In this recipe the magic emerges from the marriage of two ingredients. It couldn't be simpler.

Makes about 3 cups (6 servings)

½ cup roasted red pepper purée or pesto
1 jar (26 ounces) marinara sauce

Combine both ingredients and simmer for 5 minutes. Serve with grilled, sautéed, or poached seafood, chicken, or veal, or with pasta.

Mediterranean Tonno Sauce

In Italy, canned tuna is employed without apology whenever fresh tuna is hard to come by. Hence, home-style tuna sauces abound. Some are made from tomatoes, and others are mayonnaise-based. This one is a creamy version that combines many of the elements of the northern shore of the Mediterranean: olives, fish, tomatoes, and basil.

Makes about 3 cups (6 servings)

1 jar (16 ounces) Alfredo sauce
1 can (6 ounces) solid-packed white tuna, packed in water, drained and crumbled
1 can (about 15 ounces) Italian-style stewed tomatoes
¼ cup tapenade, olive salad, or olive purée
Black pepper to taste

Combine the Alfredo sauce, tuna, tomatoes, and tapenade in a medium saucepan. Heat through, stirring often. Add, the pepper. (You probably won't need salt.) Serve with sautéed chicken or turkey breast, fish, or veal, or serve over pasta.

Mole Demi-Glace

This intercontinental concoction merges the preeminent sauces of France and Mexico. Imagine a silken, suave demi-glace energized by Latin fire, and you will begin to sense the gastronomic tremors set off by this sauce.

Makes about 1½ cups (4 servings)

2 tablespoons jarred mole sauce (page 23)
2 cups water
3 tablespoons demi-glace concentrate (page 16)
½ teaspoon ground ancho chili pepper
Salt and black pepper to taste

Dissolve the mole in half the water in a small saucepan. Add the remaining water and heat until boiling. Add the demi-glace and chili pepper, and simmer until slightly thickened, about 2 minutes. Season with salt and pepper. Serve with roasted, grilled, or broiled meats or poultry, especially beef, lamb, turkey, or duck.

Wild Mushroom Sauce

Wild mushrooms used to be rarities, but now they are easily obtained in so many forms and from so many sources that I'm surprised the gourmet community has not shunned them for their commonality. Every supermarket carries half a dozen exotic mushrooms, a dozen or more dried varieties, and an array of wild mushroom soups, sauces, and condiments. This recipe uses dried wild mushrooms for their concentrated flavor, and fresh or frozen mushrooms for meatiness and bulk. Notice that this sauce contains very little liquid. It is really a sort of mushroom ragout that could be a side dish as well as a sauce.

Makes about 2 cups (4 servings)

½ ounce dried wild mushrooms (any type)
1 cup very hot water
1 tablespoon unsalted butter
½ cup chopped onion, frozen or fresh
1 package (1 pound) frozen or fresh mushroom medley
½ teaspoon dried crushed rosemary
1 tablespoon demi-glace concentrate or poultry stock (page 16)
1 cup (about 6 ounces) canned Italian-style diced tomatoes, drained
1 tablespoon chopped Italian (flat-leaf) parsley
Salt and black pepper to taste

Soak the dried mushrooms in the hot water until tender, about 10 minutes. Drain and reserve the soaking liquid. Chop the mushrooms coarsely and set aside.

Melt the butter in a skillet and sauté the onions until soft. It's okay if they brown a little. Add the soaked mushrooms and mushroom medley, and sauté until the liquid is almost gone. Add the rosemary and stir.

Slowly add the mushroom soaking liquid. Try to keep any debris in the bottom of the cup from getting into the sauce (pouring through a coffee filter will help). Heat until boiling. Stir in the demi-glace concentrate and tomatoes. Heat until simmering. Stir in the parsley, salt, and pepper, and simmer until the liquid is thick enough to cling to the mushrooms.

Serve with any roasted or grilled meat, roasted poultry, or even a meaty fish such as salmon or swordfish. It is especially good with roasted beef rib.

Sun-Dried Beurre Rouge

Beurre rouge (red wine butter sauce) is a traditional sauce of French cooking that has been overshadowed by its more famous sibling, beurre blanc (white wine butter sauce). Both are made the same way, from a reduction of wine swirled with butter. Reduce the wine ahead of time, if you wish, but the butter should be added just before serving.

Makes 1½ cups (4 servings)

¼ pound (1 stick) unsalted butter, cut in 8
   pieces
1 cup chopped onions, frozen or fresh
2 cups red wine
2 tablespoons sun-dried tomato pesto
Salt and black pepper to taste

Melt 1 tablespoon of the butter in a small skillet over medium heat. Add the onions and sauté until tender. Do not brown. Add the wine and boil over high heat. Reduce to about ½ cup. Stir in the pesto. The sauce can be made ahead to this point.

Over low heat, whisk in the remaining butter a piece at a time. Season with salt and pepper. Serve with steak, a meaty fish such as tuna or salmon, sautéed wild mushrooms, or roasted beets.

Sun-Dried Tomato Balsamic Glaze

Very intense and very simple, this glaze gilds anything it touches with the acidic sweet syrup of aged balsamic vinegar mixed with sun-dried tomato pesto.

Makes ⅔ cup (about 5 servings)

¼ cup sun-dried tomato pesto
5 tablespoons aged balsamic vinegar
2 tablespoons water

Combine all the ingredients. Serve with grilled seafood, chicken, veal, or pork, or drizzle over sautéed or roasted vegetables.

Brown Butter Caper Vinaigrette

This sauce, like beurre rouge, is an emulsification of a concentrated acidic base and butter, but unlike traditional butter sauces, it takes its flavor direction from a vinaigrette. Pungent and semisweet, it marries the raucous combination of garlic, capers, and balsamic vinegar with the velvety nut-brown cloak of butter, yielding a sauce that hovers between the piquancy of a salad dressing and the richness of a butter sauce.

Makes about 1¼ cups (4 servings)

1 cup balsamic vinegar
1 cup chopped onions, frozen or fresh
1½ teaspoons minced garlic, jarred or fresh
1 tablespoon nonpareil capers
¼ pound (1 stick) unsalted butter, cut in small pieces
Salt and black pepper to taste

Heat the vinegar, onions, garlic, and capers in a medium skillet until the vinegar is reduced by about half. Remove from the heat and mix in the butter until melted. Season with salt and pepper, but you probably won't need much salt. Serve with fish, shellfish, chicken, pork, or veal.

Ginger Steak Sauce

Steak sauces can be flavored in any number of ways, but at heart they are built from three ingredients: butter, Worcestershire sauce, and mustard. This one asserts its individuality with a generous infusion of ginger, which makes it suitable for poultry and seafood as well as beef.

Makes 8 servings (about 2 cups)

¼ pound (1 stick) butter
¼ cup Worcestershire sauce
2 tablespoons spicy brown mustard
1 tablespoon minced ginger, jarred or fresh
½ teaspoon chopped garlic, jarred or fresh
2 tablespoons ketchup

Melt the butter in a small saucepan over medium heat or in a microwave-safe bowl at full power in a microwave oven. Whisk in the Worcestershire sauce, mustard, ginger, garlic, and ketchup. Heat until well blended. Serve warm with grilled or sautéed meats, poultry, or hearty seafood, such as tuna or salmon.

Olive Beurre Noire

The flavor of olives is older than history, and all those millennia are concentrated in this pungent purple-black composed butter. To use it, toss a portion with hot food or place on top of a steak or chop and allow the "sauce" to melt across the surface.

Makes 6 servings (about 6 tablespoons)

4 tablespoons (½ stick) butter
¼ cup tapenade (black olive spread), jarred or fresh
1 teaspoon chopped garlic, jarred or fresh

Soften the butter by heating it for 10 seconds in a microwave oven at full power, and mash with a fork until soft and creamy. Stir in the tapenade and garlic. Use within 1 hour or refrigerate. After refrigeration, allow to sit at room temperature for at least 30 minutes before serving. Serve with grilled shrimp, seared scallops, grilled or sautéed fish, or grilled or roasted poultry, veal, or pork.

Olive Olive Aioli

This garlicky olive-laced condiment uses olives from two sources. It gets its appearance, consistency, and color from olive salad or olive spread, and it gets its fragrance from olive oil. If you choose to use olive salad, your sauce will be chunky and colorful. Tapenade will yield a smooth, velvety, pale purple sauce with a more pronounced olive flavor. The choice is yours, and you can't go wrong.

Makes 1 cup (4 to 6 servings)

¼ cup mayonnaise, regular or reduced-fat
¼ cup olive salad, or 2 tablespoons tapenade (olive spread)
2 teaspoons chopped garlic, jarred or fresh
¼ cup extra-virgin olive oil
Salt and black pepper to taste

Combine the mayonnaise, olive salad, and garlic. Whisk in the oil a tablespoon at a time and season with salt and pepper. Serve with grilled meats or any seafood, as a sandwich spread, as a sauce for tuna or chicken salad, or as a dip for vegetables or pita chips.

Tapenade "Butter"

The only thing buttery about this blue-black sauce is the unctuous olive purée, called tapenade, from which it springs. Once a regional specialty of the Mediterranean coast of France, tapenade is now everywhere and readily available in American markets. This sauce starts with the olive, garlic, and herbal flavors of tapenade and extends them with more garlic and enough olive oil to turn the tapenade into a sauce. If you prefer your "butter" spreadable rather than fluid, refrigerate it overnight. The oil will solidify, giving the sauce a creamy, buttery consistency.

Makes 5 or 6 servings (about ⅔ cup)

½ cup tapenade (black olive spread), jarred or fresh
1 tablespoon chopped garlic, jarred or fresh
¼ cup extra-virgin olive oil
Salt and black pepper to taste

Combine the tapenade, garlic, and oil. Season with salt and pepper. Serve with poached or grilled seafood, poultry, or veal.

Hot and Sour Sauce

Drizzle this pale, clear, water-thin sauce over seafood or grilled chicken. You'll get the pungent glow of hot and sour soup with none of the work. The heat comes from hot pepper oil, also known as chili oil or hot oil. These oils are made by infusing vegetable oil with hot peppers, and they can vary greatly in heat level and flavor.

Makes ⅔ cup (6 servings)

½ cup rice wine vinegar
1 tablespoon chopped ginger, jarred or fresh
2 teaspoons chopped garlic, jarred or fresh
4 teaspoons hot pepper oil

Combine the vinegar, ginger, and garlic. Whisk in the oil. (You can use all chili oil, or a combination of chili oil and vegetable oil, depending on how hot you want the sauce to be and how hot your chili oil is.) Drizzle over grilled meats, fish, shellfish, or poultry.

Tomato Hoisin Sauce

Hoisin sauce has been essential to Chinese food for millennia. Here it joins forces with an equally complex sauce from Mexico to create a pungent, chunky, fiery tomato gravy that ignites the flavors of grilled or roasted seafood, chicken, meat, or vegetables.

Makes about 1¾ cups (6 servings)

¼ cup salsa, any heat level
½ cup hoisin sauce
1 cup chicken or vegetable broth

Combine all the ingredients. Place in a small saucepan and bring to a simmer over medium heat, or place in a covered microwave-safe bowl and microwave at full power for 3 minutes. Serve with poached or grilled seafood, poultry, or veal, or with grilled or roasted vegetables.

Sweet-and-Sour Ginger Sauce

You will find ginger preserves in the jams and jellies aisle of your market. They are sweet enough to spread on bread, but they also pack enough ginger to add pungency to a meat glaze or become the basis for a sweet-and-sour sauce. Because the ginger preserves provide both sweetness and spice, this needs only a splash of vinegar and some seasoning to evolve into a sauce.

Makes about ⅔ cup (5 servings)

½ cup ginger preserves
⅓ cup apple cider vinegar
1½ teaspoons chopped garlic, jarred or fresh
1 teaspoon chopped Italian (flat-leaf) parsley, or a pinch of dried parsley flakes
Salt and black pepper to taste

Combine the ginger preserves, vinegar, and garlic in a small saucepan and heat until simmering, stirring often. Stir in the parsley, salt, and pepper. Serve with any shellfish or fish, chicken breast, turkey breast, or pork.

Spicy Orange Sesame Sauce

This sweet and spicy Chinese-style sauce can replace plum sauce or duck sauce in any recipe. For variations try it with other marmalades, such as lemon or lime.

Makes ⅔ cup (5 servings)

¼ cup orange marmalade
1 teaspoon chopped ginger, jarred or fresh
½ teaspoon minced garlic, jarred or fresh
½ teaspoon teriyaki sauce, preferably Soy Vay Veri Veri Teriyaki Sauce
2 tablespoons apple cider vinegar
4 teaspoons hot pepper sesame oil (see Note)

Combine the marmalade, ginger, garlic, teriyaki sauce, and vinegar. Whisk in the oil. Drizzle over or use as a glaze for grilled fish, shellfish, or poultry. It's great tossed with roasted beets.

NOTE: You can also use a combination of hot pepper sesame oil and toasted sesame oil, depending on how hot you want the sauce to be and how hot your oil is.

Szechwan Barbecue Sauce

There are as many recipes for barbecue sauce as there are grill jockeys armed with a basting brush. Obviously, the finished flavor of this sauce will depend on the barbecue sauce you start with, but I have yet to find one that is not enhanced by the floral fragrance and hidden fire in Szechwan pepper, a little ginger, a touch of garlic, and the sweet-and-sour magic of rice wine vinegar.

Makes 1½ cups (6 servings)

1 jar (about 18 ounces) barbecue sauce, any type
⅓ cup rice wine vinegar
¼ cup lime juice, organic bottled or fresh
2¼ teaspoons Szechwan seasoning
3 tablespoons chopped ginger, jarred or fresh
2 tablespoons chopped garlic, jarred or fresh
1 tablespoon soy sauce
Salt and black pepper to taste

Combine the barbecue sauce, vinegar, lime juice, seasoning, ginger, garlic, and soy sauce in a medium saucepan. Bring to a simmer, stirring often. Season with salt and pepper if needed. Serve with anything grilled.

Cardamom Apricot Glaze

By the time you finish cooking your way through this book, you will see that I am somewhat partial to cardamom, and I hope that you join me in my affection. It is a wonderful spice—lightly gingered, slightly peppery, decidedly sweet—that pleases even when you don't know quite what it is doing. I especially like to use it with apricot in desserts, which led me to this sweet and meaty aromatic glaze.

Makes about 2 cups (6 servings)

1 jar (12 ounces) apricot preserves
2 cups chicken broth
1 teaspoon chopped garlic, jarred or
    fresh
½ teaspoon ground cardamom
1 teaspoon Worcestershire sauce

Combine all the ingredients in a medium saucepan and bring to a simmer. Use as a glaze for roasted poultry or pork.

Sweet-and-Sour Molasses

This is the simplest sweet-and-sour sauce I know. It relies on the mildly burnt flavor of molasses for its nuance and is especially good as a glaze for roasted, grilled, or sautéed salmon.

Makes 1⅓ cups (6 servings)

1 cup molasses (not blackstrap)
½ cup apple cider vinegar
¼ teaspoon ground cinnamon
2 teaspoons chopped garlic, jarred or
    fresh
Salt and black pepper to taste

Combine all the ingredients in a small saucepan and warm over medium heat until simmering, or place in a microwave-safe mixing bowl and microwave at full power about 3 minutes, until simmering. Serve with grilled or roasted beef, pork, chicken, or full-flavored fish, such as salmon.

Roasted Pepper Mayonnaise

Roasting your own peppers is easy enough, but the availability of high-quality roasted pepper products makes doing the work yourself seem somewhat masochistic. The smokiness of the red pepper in this mayonnaise is enhanced by another smoked pepper, chipotle, which is simply a smoked jalapeño. Chipotles can be quite fiery, but that is not why they're used here. You want just enough chipotle to enhance the smoky flavor, but not so much as to cause pain.

Makes 1 cup (4 to 6 servings)

¾ cup mayonnaise, regular or reduced-fat
3 ounces jarred or fresh roasted red pepper, finely chopped (⅓ cup), or ⅓ cup roasted pepper pesto
1 teaspoon minced roasted garlic, jarred or fresh
¼ teaspoon ground chipotle chiles, or ½ teaspoon chipotle hot sauce
Salt and black pepper to taste

Combine the mayonnaise, red pepper, garlic, and chipotle chiles. Season with salt and pepper if needed. Serve with grilled meats, seafood, poultry, or vegetables, or use as a sauce for making tuna or chicken salad.

Major Grey's Cranberry Sauce

Raw cranberries pucker the palate and hurt the tongue, but heat them with sugar and they burst into a tantalizing sweet-tart companion to roasted chicken or char-grilled meat.

Makes 1½ cups (6 servings)

1 bag (12 ounces) fresh cranberries
1 jar (15 ounces) Major Grey's Mango Chutney
1 tablespoon minced ginger, jarred or fresh

Combine everything in a food processor and chop coarsely. Transfer to a saucepan and cook, stirring often, until the berries soften and the sauce turns bright red. Serve warm or cold with roasted meat or poultry.

CHAPTER 4

MEAT MEALS IN MINUTES

Steak with Wasabi Steak Sauce
Steak au Poivre from Hell
Red Hot Rib Steaks
Sirloin Steak with Peppers and Olives
Beef with Espresso Jus
Deep Dark Pot Roast
Sweet-and-Sour Cranberry Brisket
Beef Stewed with Thirty Cloves of Garlic
Deviled Short Ribs
Broiled Chipotle Short Ribs
Smoked Sausage and Greens
Salsa Meatloaf
Mango Spareribs
Moroccan Ribs
Pork Chops Braised with Mustard Fruit
Pork Saltimbocca with Pesto Vinaigrette
Pork Chops with Pepper Cream
Pork Chops with Chipotle Peanut Sauce
Pork Chops in Spicy Corn Bread Crust
Lemon Pork Chops on Artichoke Bruschetta
Pork Chops Stuffed with Apples and Gingersnaps

Pork Chops with Balsamic Beurre Noire
Broiled Barbecued Pork Chops Stuffed with Chutney
Sweet Corn Pork
Pork Chops Smoked with Sauerkraut, Apples, and White Beans
Lemon Pesto Veal Chops
Pork or Veal Chops with Merlot Fig Demi-Glace
Spicy Tomato Veal Chops with Feta Cheese
Salsa Veal Chops on Black Bean Purée
Potato-Crusted Veal with Horseradish Marinara
Veal Stew with Artichokes
Streamlined Osso Buco
Calf's Liver Glazed with Cherries and Balsamic Vinegar
Honey Mustard Lamb Chops
Rack of Lamb with Horseradish Crust
Provençal Stuffed Lamb
Roasted Leg of Lamb with Fig Jam

Steak with Wasabi Steak Sauce

Wasabi, the pale green, sinus-scouring Japanese rhizome that is similar to horse-radish, is most often paired with fish; this recipe shows that it also naturally complements beef.

Makes 4 servings

1 teaspoon Szechwan seasoning
2 tablespoons olive oil
1 to 1½ pounds boneless tenderloin, sir-loin, or loin steak
2 tablespoons butter, softened (see Note)
2 tablespoons Asian toasted sesame oil
1½ tablespoons Worcestershire sauce
1 tablespoon prepared wasabi in a tube
2 teaspoons ketchup

Combine the Szechwan seasoning and olive oil, rub into the surface of the steak, and set aside for 10 to 20 minutes. Preheat a grill or broiler. Meanwhile, make the sauce by whisking together the butter and sesame oil until smooth. Mix in the Worcestershire sauce, wasabi, and ketchup. Grill or broil the steak to the desired doneness, about 5 to 7 minutes per side for medium, depending on thickness. Serve the steak with the sauce.

NOTE: The fastest way to soften refrigerated butter is to microwave it on the defrost setting for 30 seconds.

Steak au Poivre from Hell

Just as a good steak needs fire to char its skin and seal in its juices, it needs fiery spices to cut through its fat and enliven its meatiness. In this recipe the spice flares on two levels: with a pepper-laced seasoning blend that's rubbed into the surface of the meat, and a hot salsa in a chilied butter sauce.

Makes 4 servings

4 sirloin strip steaks, 7 to 8 ounces each
Nonstick olive oil spray
1¼ teaspoons spicy steak seasoning, such as McCormick Spicy Montreal Steak Seasoning
1 cup chunky salsa, hot
6 tablespoons butter, cut in pieces

Preheat a grill or broiler. Coat the steaks with oil spray and season each one with ¼ teaspoon of the steak seasoning. Bring the salsa to a boil in a small skillet and add the remaining seasoning. Remove from the heat and mix in the butter until completely incorporated. Set aside. Grill or broil the steaks about 2 inches from the flame to desired doneness. Serve the steaks topped with the sauce.

Red Hot Rib Steaks

There are two styles of enchilada sauce. The authentic one is made from puréed chiles, while the Americanized version has a tomato base. These lightly braised rib steaks are delicious with either. No steak tastes better than a rib eye, and if you cook it in sauce for a few minutes, its natural toughness melts away.

Makes 4 servings

4 boneless rib eye steaks, each about 8
  ounces and ¾ inch thick
Salt and black pepper to taste
1 tablespoon chili powder
3 cups medium enchilada sauce
1 tablespoon ground chipotle chiles, or 1
  tablespoon chipotle hot sauce
½ cup sour cream for garnish

Season the steaks on both sides with salt, pepper, and chili powder. Place a large skillet (preferably iron) over high heat for 2 minutes. Add the steaks and cook until seared on both sides, about 3 minutes per side.

Lower the heat to medium, add the enchilada sauce and chipotles, and lift the steaks to allow the sauce to cover the bottom of the pan. Cover and simmer for 2 minutes. Flip the steaks and cook 2 minutes more, or until cooked to desired doneness.

Transfer the steaks to a platter. Pour the sauce over the steaks and top each one with 2 tablespoons of sour cream.

Sirloin Steak with Peppers and Olives

Iron skillets take a long time to get hot, but once they do they stay that way. In this recipe, garlic-crusted steaks are seared in a super-heated iron skillet and topped with blackened peppers. Be careful when the steaks hit the hot pan; it is apt to flare.

Makes 4 servings

4 sirloin strip steaks, 7 or 8 ounces each
1 teaspoon garlic spice blend
Nonstick olive oil spray
1 jar (8 ounces) roasted red peppers,
  drained and cut in strips
2 tablespoons jarred pesto
2 teaspoons tapenade (black olive spread)

Place an iron skillet over high heat until the skillet is extremely hot. Meanwhile, season each steak with the spice blend and coat liberally with oil spray. Sear the steaks for about 3 minutes per side and finish cooking to desired doneness, about 1 more minute per side for rare to 3 more minutes per side for medium-well. Remove to a warm platter. Add the roasted peppers to the skillet and stir until they blacken, about 30 seconds. Remove from the heat and stir in the pesto and tapenade. Top the steaks with the peppers.

Beef with Espresso Jus

The beef is roasted at the highest temperature setting of the oven. That maximizes browning and ensures a rare interior, even as the surface chars. Deglazing the pan drippings with espresso enhances the dark, roasted flavor. So instead of tasting coffee, you taste roasted meat.

Makes 6 servings

1 standing beef rib roast, 3½ to 4 pounds (2 ribs)
1 teaspoon kosher salt
½ teaspoon black pepper
1½ cups brewed espresso
¼ teaspoon dried thyme
1 teaspoon minced garlic, jarred or fresh
1 tablespoon chopped parsley
¼ cup orange juice

Preheat the oven to 500°F. Season the beef with salt and pepper, stand the roast on its rib side in a metal roasting pan, and roast for 30 minutes. Lower the oven temperature to 350°F and roast 15 minutes more for rare, 25 minutes for medium-rare, and 35 minutes for medium. Remove the roast to a cutting board and let sit for 5 minutes.

Spoon the fat from the pan drippings and discard. Place the roasting pan over medium heat on the stovetop and heat until boiling. Add the espresso, thyme, garlic, and parsley, and boil for 2 minutes, stirring and scraping to incorporate any browned bits into the jus. Stir in the orange juice and adjust the seasoning with salt and pepper. Slice the roast and serve with the espresso jus.

Deep Dark Pot Roast

If you think of pot roast as homey but bland, think again. This one sings with robust mole, piercing hot pepper, fruity salsa, and sultry chocolate.

Makes 6 servings

3 pounds brisket or chuck roast
1 teaspoon Southwest seasoning
¼ cup jarred mole sauce (page 23)
2 cups hot water
1 jar (16 ounces) mango salsa
1 jar (8 ounces) olive salad
1 ounce semisweet chocolate

Sprinkle the beef with the seasoning. Heat a Dutch oven until smoking. Add the beef, fat side down, and brown on both sides. Dissolve the mole in the water and add it to the browned beef along with the salsa and olives. Heat to simmering, cover, and simmer for 2 hours, or until the meat is tender. Add more water if the sauce gets too thick.

When the beef is tender, remove it from the sauce and spoon off the fat. Stir in the chocolate until melted. Slice the beef against the grain and cloak it in sauce.

Sweet-and-Sour Cranberry Brisket

Nothing could be easier than this family favorite. It is nearly effortless and is delicious and extremely versatile. The directions below are for oven and stovetop, but if you want to use your slow cooker, just reduce the liquid by half and let it sit. Or speed it up in a pressure cooker using half the liquid and full pressure for forty-five minutes, and letting it rest for fifteen minutes before releasing the steam.

Makes 6 servings

Nonstick oil spray
1 beef brisket, about 3 pounds
2 teaspoons lemon pepper
12 small yellow onions, halved and
   peeled
1 cup red wine, any type
1 can (about 15 ounces) beef broth
1 can (about 15 ounces) whole-berry
   cranberry sauce
Prepared horseradish

Preheat a broiler and coat the broiler pan with oil spray. Season the brisket on both sides with the lemon pepper and place, fat side up, on the pan. Scatter the onions, rounded side up, around the brisket and coat the onions with oil spray.

Broil 3 inches from the flame about 10 minutes. Turn the onions, which should now be browned, and broil the brisket and onions for another 10 minutes, until the brisket is deeply browned and the onions are cooked through. Remove the onions and set aside. Turn the brisket and brown it well on the other side, about 15 minutes.

Place the brisket in a large, heavy pot and surround it with the onions. Pour the wine and broth into the broiler pan, scraping up any brown bits clinging to the rack or the pan. Add the cranberry sauce and mix it with the pan juices. Pour the sauce over the brisket and heat until simmering. Cover and simmer for 2 hours, until the brisket is fork-tender.

Place the meat on a cutting board and boil the liquid in the pan until it is lightly thickened. Slice the brisket against the grain and return the slices to the pan. (Do not boil once the meat has been returned to the pan.) Serve the sliced brisket slathered with juices and onions. Serve horseradish on the side.

Beef Stewed with Thirty Cloves of Garlic

This stew is loaded with garlic, but don't let the number of cloves scare you. Garlic has a split personality. When finely chopped and cooked in oil, it is pungent and odoriferous, but left whole and simmered in liquid, its sugars emerge, and an assertive aroma never develops.

Makes 6 servings

2 pounds beef cubes, chuck or round
Salt and black pepper to taste
1 tablespoon olive oil
1 tablespoon chopped garlic, jarred or fresh
30 peeled cloves garlic (about half of a 4-ounce jar or 2 heads fresh)
1 cup white wine
1 can (15 ounces) Italian-style diced tomatoes, with their juice
1 can (about 15 ounces) beef broth
½ cup prepared baba ghanouj

Season the beef cubes with salt and pepper. Heat the oil in a wide pot or Dutch oven over high heat. Brown the beef on all sides in two batches.

Add the chopped garlic and sauté for 30 seconds. Add the garlic cloves and wine, and heat to boiling. Add the diced tomatoes and broth, cover the pan, and simmer until the beef is tender, about 1 hour. Stir in the baba ghanouj and adjust the seasoning with salt and pepper.

Deviled Short Ribs

Baker's Joy, the nonstick spray with flour that is sold to coat cake and bread pans, is not just for baking. I have been using it to flour meat for browning. Not only does it form a thin, even skin on the surface, but it provides a film of oil as well, making it unnecessary to grease the pan.

Makes 4 to 6 servings

6 short ribs, about 3 pounds
Salt and black pepper to taste
Baker's Joy No Stick Spray with Flour
1 jar (about 15 ounces) curry sauce
1 tablespoon spicy brown mustard

Remove the meat from the bones by sliding a thin-bladed knife along the bone under the meat. Discard the bones. Season the meat with salt and pepper and coat it on all sides with the flour spray.

Place a large skillet over high heat for 1 minute. Add the meat and brown well on all sides. Add the curry sauce and mustard, and stir to combine. Bring to a simmer, cover, and simmer about 20 minutes, until the sauce is thick and the meat is tender. Turn the meat several times as it cooks. Serve the meat covered in sauce.

Broiled Chipotle Short Ribs

The first thing to understand about short ribs is that they are part of a rib roast. They have the flavor and quality of prime ribs for a fraction of the cost.

Makes 6 servings

Nonstick oil spray
6 short ribs, about 3 pounds
1 teaspoon garlic spice blend
1 cup boiling water
1 cup chipotle salsa
2 tablespoons demi-glace concentrate
  (page 16)

Coat a broiler pan with oil spray. Sprinkle the ribs with the spice blend (there's no need to season the bone side). Place in the pan and brown under the broiler about 8 minutes on each of the three seasoned sides. When browned, place the ribs on a cutting board to cool.

Pour the water in the pan and stir, scraping any browned bits clinging to the pan. Place over medium heat and stir in the salsa and demi-glace; simmer for 5 minutes.

While the sauce is simmering, remove the meat from the bones by sliding a thin-bladed knife under the meat along the bone. Discard the bones. Cut each piece of meat in half lengthwise. Place in the sauce and simmer for a few minutes. Do not overcook.

Smoked Sausage and Greens

This hearty one-pot meal is colorful and redolent with smoky, meaty flavor, but much of its flavor depends on which sausage you use. I recommend kielbasa or andouille. Both are traditionally made from pork (which will work fine in this dish), but I have found lots of kielbasa- and andouille-style sausages made from beef, turkey, or even chicken. Use any one you want.

Makes 4 servings

1 tablespoon vegetable oil
1 cup chopped onions, frozen or fresh
1 pound smoked sausage, cut in 8 pieces
1 cup long-grain rice
3 cups chicken broth
1 can (about 15 ounces) black-eyed peas,
  rinsed and drained
1 package (16 ounces) frozen chopped
  collard greens
Salt and black pepper to taste

Heat the oil in a large skillet. Add the onions and sauté until tender, about 2 minutes. Add the sausage pieces and sauté until they are browned at the edges and heated through. Add the rice, stir it to coat, and stir in the broth. Bring to a boil, stir in the peas and greens, cover, and simmer about 20 minutes, until the rice is tender and the broth has been absorbed. Add the salt and pepper.

Salsa Meatloaf

The simple truth is that the sensory charm of any meatloaf is in the filler, not the meat. Once the meat is ground, any moisture or textural quality it had is gone. Baking it can only dry up what's left into the equivalent of edible gravel. With filler you add flavor, moisture, and consistency; without it all you have is desiccated hamburger.

Makes 4 servings

1¼ pounds meatloaf mix (ground beef, veal, and pork)
1 large or extra-large egg
1 cup salsa, any heat level
½ cup black bean dip
½ cup crushed tortilla chips

Preheat the oven to 350°F. Thoroughly combine all the ingredients, form into a loaf on a sheet pan, pack down well, and square off the ends. Bake for 45 minutes, until the loaf is browned and firm, and a meat thermometer inserted in the center reads 160°F. Remove the meat from the oven, let sit for 5 minutes, and slice. It is also great cold.

Mango Spareribs

Spareribs pose a problem. We think of them on the grill, quick and effortless, but ribs are tough, bony, and gristly. So, yes, finish them on the grill, but start them in a microwave. Your microwave is like a steamer. Giving a rack of ribs fifteen or twenty minutes in a microwave will soften their tough fibers, moisten their meat, and ensure that they cook through without scorching. *Then* they're ready to finish up on the grill, slathered with your favorite sauce or condiment.

Makes 4 servings

3 pounds pork spareribs
Salt and black pepper
Nonstick oil spray
1 jar (10 ounces) mango chutney
¼ cup prepared white horseradish

Season the spareribs with salt and pepper, cut them into 2- or 3-rib sections, place them in a microwave-safe baking dish, and cover with plastic wrap. Microwave at full power for 20 minutes. While the ribs are in the microwave, preheat a broiler and coat a broiler pan with oil spray. Combine the chutney and horseradish, transfer the ribs to the broiler pan, and spread the mixture over the ribs. Broil the ribs until browned on both sides, about 5 minutes per side.

Moroccan Ribs

Every cuisine has a seasoning palate. In China it's soy sauce, ginger, and garlic; in Greece, olive oil, lemon, and oregano. Morocco's is much more complex: a blend of cumin, coriander, cinnamon, ginger, tomato, onion, and lemon. It's a combination that takes a shelf full of ingredients—unless you combine pumpkin pie spice, coriander, lemon, and salsa. *Voilà!* Moroccan ribs.

Makes 4 servings

Nonstick oil spray
1 tablespoon pumpkin pie spice
2 teaspoons ground coriander
1½ tablespoons lemon pepper
3 pounds pork spareribs or lamb riblets
1 jar (16 ounces) chunky salsa, any heat level
¼ cup lemon juice, organic bottled or fresh

Preheat a grill or broiler and coat the rack with oil spray. Combine the pumpkin pie spice, coriander, and lemon pepper. Season the spareribs with 2 tablespoons of the mixture. Grill or broil the ribs about 10 minutes per side, until they are browned on both sides.

While the ribs are browning, combine the salsa, lemon juice, and the remaining seasoning mix. Place the ribs in a microwave-safe baking dish, pour the sauce over the top, cover with plastic wrap, and microwave at full power for 15 to 20 minutes, until the meat is fork-tender.

Pork Chops Braised with Mustard Fruit

Mustard with fruit is an Old World combo that never fails to surprise the uninitiated and intrigue the palate. Although you can buy jarred mustard fruit imported from Italy at exorbitant prices, the sauce in this recipe expertly imitates the flavor of the original at a fraction of the cost by combining chutney and spicy brown mustard.

Makes 4 servings

1 teaspoon red or yellow curry powder
2 tablespoons brown sugar
Salt and black pepper to taste
4 boneless center-cut pork chops, ¾ inch thick
Nonstick oil spray
1 cup chicken broth
1 jar (8 ounces) mango chutney
2 tablespoons spicy brown mustard

Combine the curry, sugar, salt, and pepper, and rub the mix into all surfaces of the meat. Heat a large nonstick skillet over medium-high heat, coat with oil spray, and brown the pork on both sides. Add the broth and simmer about 5 minutes, until the pork is not quite firm in the center. Place the pork on a serving platter and keep warm. Bring the broth in the pan to a full boil and stir in the chutney and mustard. Pour the sauce over the chops.

Pork Saltimbocca with Pesto Vinaigrette

In the fat-fearing 1990s, pork was rebuilt. All the little piggies were put on a diet, and they became leaner and a wee bit meaner. The fat that had lent them their flavor and succulence was gone. Our traditional pork recipes, which had really been designed to kill trichinae rather than cook meat, gave utterly inedible results. The new pork needs new recipes, and I have a dilly. When pork is marinated with sun-dried tomato and Caesar vinaigrette, sauced with more of the same, and spiked with pesto, you'll never miss the fat. But your waistline might.

Makes 4 servings

8 thinly cut boneless pork chops
1½ cups flour, seasoned liberally with salt
    and black pepper
¼ cup sun-dried tomato pesto or spread
½ cup Caesar dressing
¼ cup olive oil
2 tablespoons jarred basil pesto
½ lemon, cut in 4 wedges

Place the pork chops between sheets of plastic wrap and pound until very thin, about ⅛ inch thick. Place the seasoned flour in a pie plate or on a large sheet of plastic wrap or foil. Combine the sun-dried tomato and half of the Caesar dressing. Brush the meat with the mixture and dredge in the flour until the pieces are coated thoroughly and uniformly.

Heat a large nonstick skillet over medium-high heat. Add the oil and cook the pork until it browns on both sides, about 4 minutes. It should be not quite firm in the center. Combine the remaining dressing and pesto, and dollop each portion with 2 tablespoons of this sauce. Garnish each portion with a wedge of lemon for squeezing over the meat.

Pork Chops with Pepper Cream

Boneless pork chops cook faster and more evenly than bone-in chops. Their one disadvantage is that they tend to become dry as they approach doneness. This recipe guarantees moist results by stopping the cooking when the pork is still lightly pink, and then napping the chops in rich, flavorful cream.

Makes 4 servings

4 boneless center-cut pork chops, ¾ inch
thick
Salt and black pepper to taste
2 teaspoons chopped garlic, jarred or
fresh
Nonstick olive oil spray
1½ cups light cream
¼ cup red pepper pesto or spread
1 tablespoon chopped Italian (flat-leaf)
parsley

Season the pork with salt and pepper on both sides and rub each piece with ½ teaspoon of chopped garlic.

Heat a large skillet over medium-high heat. Coat with oil spray and brown the pork on both sides. Turn the heat to medium-low, cover, and cook about 10 minutes, until the chops are brown but not quite firm in the center and a thermometer inserted through the side of the chop into its center registers 145°F (see headnote). Remove the pork from the pan and arrange on serving plates. Add the cream to the pan and simmer until slightly thickened. Remove from the heat, whisk in the red pepper pesto, season with salt and pepper, and stir in the parsley. Pour the sauce over the pork.

Pork Chops with Chipotle Peanut Sauce

Chipotle salsa and Thai peanut sauce are cooking ingredients in their own right, but when paired, they form a truly remarkable union—smoky, spicy, chunky, and sweet.

Makes 4 servings

4 boneless center-cut pork chops, ¾ inch
thick
1 teaspoon garlic spice blend
1 tablespoon olive oil
1 cup chipotle salsa
½ cup water
¼ cup jarred Thai peanut sauce
1 tablespoon chopped Italian (flat-leaf)
parsley

Season the pork on both sides with the spice blend. Heat a large skillet over medium-high heat. Add the oil and brown the pork on both sides. Add the salsa and water, stir, cover, and simmer about 5 minutes, until the chops are not quite firm in the center. Transfer the pork to a serving plate. Stir the peanut sauce and parsley into the sauce, bring to a boil, and pour over the pork.

Pork Chops in Spicy Corn Bread Crust

Stuffing mix is more than just an easy way to amend chicken. It is a breading par excellence. In this recipe crushed corn bread stuffing spiced with chili and cumin coats baked pork chops. The results are slightly sweet, buttery, and golden brown, with a hint of hot pepper lingering after each bite.

Makes 4 servings

Nonstick oil spray
1 cup crumbled corn bread stuffing
1 tablespoon chili powder
1 tablespoon ground cumin
⅓ cup ranch dressing or plain yogurt
4 pork chops, each about ¾ inch thick
2 tablespoons mild hot sauce

Preheat the oven to 400°F. Coat a roasting rack with oil spray and set on a sheet pan.

Combine the stuffing, chili powder, and cumin on a sheet of foil. Brush the chops with half of the dressing and dredge in the stuffing mixture to coat them completely. Place on the prepared rack and bake for 30 minutes, until the crumbs are browned and crisp. The chops should be not quite firm in the center, and a thermometer inserted through the side of the chop into its center should register 145°F. While the chops are baking, combine the hot sauce and the remaining dressing. Serve the chops topped with a portion of sauce.

Lemon Pork Chops on Artichoke Bruschetta

Thin pork chops are fast. Especially now that pork is bred so lean, by the time the chops are seared the interior will be pearly pink. Here they are served atop a relish of artichoke and tomato.

Makes 4 servings

1 large jar (12 ounces) marinated artichoke heart quarters
1 cup tomato bruschetta, jarred or refrigerated
2 tablespoons lemon juice, bottled organic or fresh
8 thinly cut pork chops
1 teaspoon lemon pepper
Nonstick olive oil spray

Coarsely chop half of the artichoke heart quarters and mix with the bruschetta and the remaining artichoke quarters. Stir in 2 teaspoons of the lemon juice. Set aside. Season the pork chops with lemon pepper.

Heat a large skillet over medium-high heat. Coat with oil spray, add the pork chops, and brown on both sides, about 5 minutes, until the chops are not quite firm in the center. Transfer the chops to a serving plate. Add the artichoke mixture to pan and heat through.

To serve, place about ½ cup of the artichoke sauce on a plate and top with a pork chop. Sprinkle with the remaining lemon juice.

Pork Chops Stuffed with Apples and Gingersnaps

Most butchers will cut pockets into thick pork chops if you ask, but if you must cut the pockets yourself, here's how: Insert a thin-bladed knife, such as a paring knife or boning knife, into the middle of the rounded edge of a chop. Move the point of the knife inside the center of the meaty part, cutting an opening that runs parallel to the surface.

Makes 6 servings

1 tablespoon butter
1 cup chopped onions, frozen or fresh
1 box (12 ounces) frozen escalloped
  apples, cooked
¼ teaspoon crushed dried rosemary
Salt and black pepper to taste
4 gingersnap cookies, coarsely crushed
6 extra-thick (about 1 inch) pork chops,
  with a pocket cut into each chop (see
  headnote)
½ teaspoon poultry seasoning
1 tablespoon vegetable oil

Preheat the oven to 350°F. Melt the butter in a large skillet with a metal handle. Add the onions and sauté until tender. Add the apples, rosemary, salt, pepper, and gingersnaps. Stir to combine.

Stuff each pork chop with a quarter of the apple mixture. Season with salt and pepper and poultry seasoning. Wipe out the skillet, add the oil, and heat over a high flame. Brown the pork chops on both sides. Place the skillet in the oven and bake for 20 minutes.

Pork Chops with Balsamic Beurre Noire

This classic is easy and fast but the juxtaposition of salty capers, nutty brown butter, and sweet, tangy balsamic vinegar wouldn't be better if it had simmered for hours.

Makes 4 servings

8 thinly cut pork chops
Kosher salt and coarsely ground pepper
  to taste
3 tablespoons unsalted butter
2 tablespoons nonpareil capers
⅓ cup aged balsamic vinegar

Season the pork chops with the salt and pepper. Heat a large nonstick skillet over medium-high heat. Add 2 teaspoons of the butter and brown the chops on both sides, about 5 minutes, until they are not quite firm in the center. Transfer to a serving plate. Place the capers and the remaining butter in the hot pan. Add the vinegar and boil until slightly thickened, less than 1 minute. Pour the sauce over the chops.

Broiled Barbecued Pork Chops Stuffed with Chutney

This simple broiled meat develops intense flavor inside and out. Tangy, hot, sweet chutney is placed inside each chop while dark, rich Chinese black bean sauce glazes the outside. About all you have to do is turn on the broiler and wait for the magic.

Makes 4 servings

Nonstick oil spray
¼ cup chutney, any type
4 center-cut pork chops, each about ¾ inch thick and cut with a pocket for stuffing (see headnote on page 124)
½ cup Chinese black bean sauce or bottled barbecue sauce

Coat the rack of a broiler pan with oil spray and preheat the broiler. Spoon 1 tablespoon of chutney in the pocket of each pork chop.

Place the chops on the rack and spread 1 tablespoon of black bean sauce on each one. Broil 2 inches from the flame until the chops are deeply browned on one side, about 5 to 7 minutes. Turn the chops, spread 1 tablespoon of black bean sauce on each, and broil until browned on the second side. They should be not quite firm in the center. Do not overcook.

Sweet Corn Pork

Corn is a culinary chameleon. On the cob it is a fresh vegetable. Dried and ground, it is a muffin. Soaked and skinned, it is posole or hominy. In this recipe it is a sauce, and corn soup is the perfect launch pad. All you do is brown your meat and add the soup. As the meat simmers, the soup thickens into a sauce.

Makes 4 servings

Nonstick oil spray
4 boneless center-cut pork chops, ¾ inch thick
1 teaspoon garlic spice blend
1 container (32 ounces) creamy corn soup
3 tablespoons mild hot pepper sauce
1 tablespoon chopped Italian (flat-leaf) parsley

Heat a large skillet over medium-high heat and coat with oil spray. Season the pork with the spice blend and brown on both sides. Add the soup, lower the heat, cover, and simmer about 8 minutes, until the chops are not quite firm in the center. Transfer the chops to a serving plate.

The sauce will thicken while the chops cook. If it is still thin, boil until it thickens slightly. Remove from the heat and stir in the pepper sauce and parsley. Pour any juices that have collected around the chops back into the sauce and stir. Pour over the chops.

Pork Chops Smoked with Sauerkraut, Apples, and White Beans

Smoking is messy, difficult, and time-consuming. And, quite literally, it stinks. When you are done, everything and everybody—you, your walls, your kids, your pets—smell as if they just survived a three-alarm fire. You need to try smoker bags, ingenious disposable smokers from Scandinavia that work in your oven, infusing any ingredient you want with sweet aromatic smoke. Just layer everything in a standard baking dish, slip the whole thing in the smoker bag, close the top, and bake. (For more information on smoker bags, see page 33.)

Makes 4 servings

4 boneless center-cut pork chops, ¾ inch thick
2 teaspoons seasoning salt
1 bag (16 ounces) refrigerated sauerkraut, drained
1 can (15 ounces) small white beans
½ cup dried apple slices

You'll need one Savu Original Food Smoker Bag, medium smoke (page 33). Preheat the oven to 475°F. Sprinkle the pork chops on both sides with seasoning salt. Combine the sauerkraut, beans, and apples in an 11 × 7-inch baking dish. Arrange the chops in a single layer on top of the sauerkraut mixture. Place the smoker bag on a sheet pan. Slip the baking dish into the bag and seal the open end. Bake for 45 minutes. Remove from the oven and let sit for 10 minutes. Remove the baking dish from the bag and serve. Discard the bag.

Lemon Pesto Veal Chops

This simple combination of sweet and mild veal, lemon juice, and basil pesto is straightforward, down to earth, and easy to love.

Makes 4 servings

4 rib veal chops, ½ inch thick
1½ teaspoons lemon pepper
Nonstick oil spray
½ cup basil pesto, jarred or fresh
¼ cup lemon juice, organic jarred or fresh

Season the veal chops with lemon pepper. Place a large skillet over medium-high heat and coat with oil spray. Sauté the chops on both sides until browned. Lower the heat and continue cooking about 8 minutes, until the chops are not quite firm in the center and a thermometer inserted through the side of the chop into its center registers 140°F. Transfer the chops to a platter. Combine the pesto and lemon juice, and top each chop with a portion of the mixture.

Pork or Veal Chops with Merlot Fig Demi-Glace

This elegant sauce is also exceptionally easy. The secret is demi-glace concentrate, which is discussed extensively in the Introduction (page 16) and in Chapter 3 (page 99). Here it is flavored with a peppery fruity merlot and fig preserves.

Makes 4 servings

4 rib or loin pork chops or veal chops,
    each ¾ inch thick
Salt and black pepper to taste
1 tablespoon olive oil
½ cup merlot or other bold red wine
2 cups water
3 tablespoons demi-glace
    concentrate
2 tablespoons fig preserves

Season the chops with salt and pepper. Heat the oil in a large skillet and brown the chops on both sides. Add the wine, bring it to a boil, and lower the heat so that the liquid simmers. Simmer for a few minutes, until the wine is reduced to a glaze. Add the water and heat until boiling. Stir in the demi-glace until smooth.

Cover and simmer until the chops are not quite firm in the center and a thermometer inserted through the side of the chop into its center registers 145°F for pork or 140°F for veal, about 5 minutes. Transfer the chops to a serving plate.

Stir the fig preserves into the sauce in the pan and boil until the desired consistency is reached; the sauce should be shiny and just thick enough to coat a spoon. Season to taste with salt and pepper, and spoon over the chops.

Spicy Tomato Veal Chops with Feta Cheese

The seemingly complex construction of this recipe has been simplified by an herbed stuffing of feta cheese, which melts into a sauce as the chops cook, and a pungent glaze of salad dressing, hot sauce, and chopped basil. If your butcher will not cut pockets in the chops for stuffing (most are glad to), follow the directions in the headnote on page 124.

Makes 4 servings

4 rib veal chops, ¾ inch thick, cut with a pocket for stuffing
¼ cup herbed feta cheese spread
Salt and black pepper to taste
2 tablespoons olive oil
¾ cup sun-dried tomato vinaigrette
1 tablespoon Green Pepper Tabasco sauce
12 fresh basil leaves, chopped, or ½ teaspoon dried basil

Stuff the pocket in each chop with 1 tablespoon of cheese and press the opening closed. Season the outsides of the chops with salt and pepper. Place a large skillet over medium-high heat. Add the oil and sauté the chops on both sides until browned. Lower the heat and cook about 10 minutes, until the chops are not quite firm in the center. Transfer the chops to a platter. Add the vinaigrette, Tabasco, and basil to the skillet, and bring to a boil. Pour the sauce over the chops.

Salsa Veal Chops on Black Bean Purée

This recipe vibrates with carnival colors and raucous flavors. You may prepare the black bean purée ahead and reheat it while the chops cook.

Makes 4 servings

4 rib veal chops, ½ inch thick
Salt and black pepper to taste
Nonstick oil spray
1 jar (16 ounces) chunky salsa, any heat level
1 teaspoon ground cumin
1 cup corn kernels, frozen or canned
1 box (7 ounces) instant black beans (page 25)
2 cups boiling water
½ bunch cilantro, chopped

Season the chops with salt and pepper. Place a large skillet over medium-high heat and coat with oil spray. Sauté the chops on both sides until browned. Add the salsa, cumin, and corn. Lower the heat, cover, and simmer about 8 minutes, until the chops are not quite firm in the center. Transfer the chops to a platter. Meanwhile, combine the black beans, boiling water, and half of the cilantro. Cover and let sit for 5 minutes.

Serve each chop on a mound of black bean purée topped with sauce, and some cilantro.

Potato-Crusted Veal with Horseradish Marinara

I don't know what is more surprising, the crispy richness of the potato crust made from instant mashed potato flakes or the addition of horseradish to marinara sauce.

Makes 4 servings

1 cup flour
1½ cups instant mashed potato flakes
1 egg
8 pieces veal scallopine, 2 to 3 ounces
    each
¼ teaspoon lemon pepper
2 tablespoons extra-virgin olive oil
½ cup jarred marinara sauce
4 teaspoons prepared white horseradish

Spread the flour on one sheet of foil and spread the potato flakes on another sheet. Beat the egg in a bowl. Sprinkle each piece of veal with lemon pepper, dredge in the flour, shaking off any excess. Dip the veal in the egg, coating both sides. Dredge in the potato flakes until completely coated.

Heat a large nonstick skillet over high heat. Add the oil. Brown the veal on both sides until the meat is firm to the touch. Transfer to a platter. Remove the skillet from the heat, add the marinara sauce, and stir until heated through. Stir in the horseradish and spoon over the veal.

Veal Stew with Artichokes

Even the toughest cuts of veal are relatively tender, which is why veal stew is so quick to prepare. This stew gets instant flavor from seasoned broth and a jar of marinated artichoke hearts.

Makes 4 or 5 servings

1½ pounds veal stew meat
Salt and black pepper to taste
2 tablespoons olive oil
2 cups chopped onions, frozen or fresh
4 ounces sliced mushrooms
2 tablespoons flour
½ cup white wine
2 cans (14 ounces each) Italian herb
    chicken broth
1 large jar (12 ounces) marinated arti-
    choke hearts
1 can (15 ounces) chickpeas, drained
1 tablespoon chopped Italian (flat-leaf)
    parsley

Season the veal with salt and pepper. Place a large skillet over high heat. Add the oil and brown the veal on all sides. Add the onions and mushrooms, and lower the heat to medium. Sauté until brown. Stir in the flour, add the wine and the broth, and stir to combine. Lower the heat and simmer until the veal is tender, about 40 minutes.

Add the artichoke hearts and their liquid, and chickpeas. Cover and simmer 5 minutes more. Stir in the parsley.

Streamlined Osso Buco

Osso buco, the regal braised veal shank from Milan, takes very little work, but it does take time. It's worth every minute. As the shanks simmer, the meat becomes velvety and falls from the bones at the touch of a fork. At the same time, nubbins of marrow dissolve into the sauce, giving it the creamy, meaty consistency that is the hallmark of this dish. It is all snapped back to life at the last minute with a jolt of garlic and a swirl of herb. This is a great dish to prepare in a slow-cooker if you have one. It takes longer, but who cares? You're out of the kitchen.

Makes 4 servings

4 pieces veal shank, cut for osso buco, about 2 inches thick
Salt and black pepper to taste
Baker's Joy No Stick Spray with Flour
1 cup white wine
1 jar (12 ounces) garlic salsa
1 can (about 15 ounces) chicken broth
1 teaspoon dried Italian seasoning
1 teaspoon dried lemon peel
¾ cup shredded carrot
1 tablespoon pesto, jarred or fresh
½ teaspoon chopped garlic, jarred or fresh

Season the veal shanks with salt and pepper, and coat liberally with the flour spray. Heat a large, deep skillet over high heat for 1 minute. Brown the shanks on both sides in the hot skillet. Add the wine to the pan and heat to boiling. Add the salsa, broth, Italian seasoning, lemon peel, and carrot. Heat to a simmer, cover the pan, and simmer gently until the veal is very tender, about 2 hours.

The osso buco can also be made in a slow-cooker: Brown the veal as described above and transfer to the slow-cooker. Deglaze the pan with the wine and pour the liquid over the veal, scraping into the cooker any brown bits clinging to the bottom of the pan. Add the salsa, half of the broth, the Italian seasoning, lemon peel, and carrot to the cooker and cook on low for 8 hours. Because there is less evaporation in this method, you will not need the rest of the broth.

Whichever method you use for cooking the meat, combine the pesto and garlic before the meat is finished. Transfer the shanks to a warm platter. For skillet cooking, boil the liquid in the pan until slightly thickened. In a slow-cooker, raise the setting to high and boil until thickened, as desired. Stir in the pesto mixture and pour the liquid over the veal.

Calf's Liver Glazed with Cherries and Balsamic Vinegar

Liver is destroyed by overcooking. Its natural sweetness becomes bitter, its creamy flesh turns to gravel, its color goes from mahogany red to khaki gray, and its mild aroma becomes an acrid stench. Years of abuse have so marred its reputation that liver has become the poster child for the inedible, but in the age of the ten-minute dinner, liver is a winner. If you remove it from the heat as soon as it is firm, it will be sweet-tasting and creamy.

Makes 4 servings

1 pound calf's liver, thinly sliced
Salt and black pepper to taste
3 tablespoons unsalted butter
1 teaspoon minced garlic, jarred or fresh
6 tablespoons whole cherry preserves
¼ cup balsamic vinegar
1 tablespoon chopped Italian (flat-leaf)
   parsley

Season the liver with salt and pepper. Melt the butter over medium-high heat in a large skillet. Add the liver and sauté until the surface is browned and the interior is springy, about 3 minutes. Do not overcook; remove to a platter. Add the garlic, preserves, vinegar, and parsley to the skillet. Swirl to mix and pour over the liver.

Honey Mustard Lamb Chops

I have long thought that crushed pretzels with their salty tang would make a natural breading ingredient, but not until the emergence of honey mustard pretzels did I make the connection with lamb. They give it a savory, crusty casing reminiscent of mustard crumbs.

Makes 4 servings

1½ cups broken honey mustard pretzels
1 tablespoon crushed dried rosemary
3 tablespoons mayonnaise
1 tablespoon Dijon mustard
8 rib or loin lamb chops, each about 1
   inch thick
Nonstick oil spray

Preheat the oven to 500°F. Coat a rack with oil spray and set on a sheet pan. In a food processor, grind the pretzel pieces and rosemary to a fine powder. Spread evenly over a sheet of foil. Combine the mayonnaise and mustard.

Brush the sides and edges of the lamb chops with the mayonnaise mixture and coat each chop on all sides with the pretzel crumbs. Place the chops on the oiled rack and roast for 15 minutes, until the crumbs are browned. The chops should be medium-rare, about 140°F.

Rack of Lamb with Horseradish Crust

Lamb loves pungent associations such as pepper, anchovies, or, as in this recipe, horseradish and mustard. The challenge is to crisp the crust before the meat is overcooked. I suggest Grape-Nuts cereal to ensure crispness and to give a sweet counterpoint to the combination of mustard and horseradish.

Makes 4 or 5 servings

2 trimmed racks of lamb, each about 2
    pounds with 8 chops
1 tablespoon olive oil
3 tablespoons (2 ounces) prepared white
    horseradish
1 tablespoon Dijon mustard
2 teaspoons dried thyme leaves
¾ cup Grape-Nuts cereal

Remove the lamb from the refrigerator one hour before roasting and trim any excess fat. Preheat the oven to 475°F. Place a rack on a sheet pan. Combine the oil, horseradish, mustard, and thyme. Place the cereal on a sheet of foil. Brush the meaty parts of the lamb with the horseradish mixture and dip the coated sections in the cereal until the meat is thoroughly coated.

Place the lamb on the rack and roast for 25 minutes, until a thermometer inserted in the center of the meat registers 140°F for medium-rare to 150°F for medium. Remove the meat from the oven and let it sit for 5 minutes before carving into chops.

Provençal Stuffed Lamb

Artichoke, eggplant, and lamb—the combination is traditional, and now it's easy, too, with artichoke and eggplant spreads so commonplace.

Makes 10 to 12 servings

5 pounds boneless leg of lamb
1 teaspoon kosher salt
½ teaspoon black pepper
1 teaspoon minced garlic, jarred or fresh
1 cup artichoke spread
1 jar (about 8 ounces) eggplant spread
2 teaspoons herbes de Provence

Preheat the oven to 500°F. Open the lamb out as flat as it will go. Make slits in the thicker parts so that the lamb opens into an even layer about 1 inch thick. Season with salt, pepper, and garlic. Combine the artichoke and eggplant spreads and spread the mixture over the lamb. Reroll the lamb and secure with string. Place, seam side down, in an oiled roasting pan. Rub with the herbes de Provence.

Roast for 1 hour, until the meat is deeply browned and a meat thermometer inserted in the thickest part has an internal temperature of 140°F for rare or 150°F for medium. Let the meat rest for 10 minutes before carving.

Roasted Leg of Lamb with Fig Jam

This is a glorious roast that should be reserved for a grand occasion. A leg of lamb is roasted in a hot oven for a crisp, crackled skin and a moist, rare interior. While the lamb is roasting, prepare a glaze of garlic fig and balsamic vinegar for a dish that is tangy, sweet, savory, pungent, and incredible.

Makes 8 servings

1 trimmed whole leg of lamb (about 7 pounds) or boned, rolled, and tied (about 5 pounds)
50 cloves roasted garlic, jarred or fresh
2 tablespoons olive oil
2 tablespoons crushed dried rosemary
Salt and black pepper to taste
1 jar (8 ounces) fig preserves
1 tablespoon balsamic vinegar
1 tablespoon Worcestershire sauce

With a small, sharp knife, make slits in the meaty sections of the lamb every 2 inches, about 25 in total, and insert a clove of the roasted garlic in each slit. Rub the surface of the lamb with the oil and sprinkle with 4 teaspoons of the rosemary, salt, and pepper. Place the lamb, fat side up, on a rack in a roasting pan and let sit at room temperature for 1 hour. In the meantime, preheat the oven to 500°F.

Roast the lamb for 45 minutes, or until a meat thermometer inserted in the thickest section (without touching any bone) registers 140°F for rare or 150°F for medium. While the lamb roasts, mash the remaining 25 cloves of roasted garlic with the back of a fork. Make the jam by combining the garlic with the fig preserves, vinegar, the remaining rosemary, and Worcestershire sauce. When the lamb has finished roasting, remove it from the oven and brush it with the fig jam. Let the lamb sit for 10 to 15 minutes, then carve it and serve.

CHAPTER 5

ESCAPING THE CHICKEN RUT

Garlic Chicken

Peking Chicken

Lemon Chicken with Dried Plums

Orange-Spiced Game Hens

Wok-Fried Chicken

Spicy Vanilla Chicken

Chicken Cacciatore

Deviled Chicken Breast with Bacon and Cheese

Chicken Wellington

Chicken in Honey Mustard Cream Sauce

Blackened Chicken with Tomato Jam

Black Bean Chicken with Salsa Syrup

Lemon Poppy Seed Chicken Paillard

Olive-Crusted Chicken on Fattoush

Curried Chicken with Lentil Dal

Chicken Chili with Guacamole Cream

Chicken Chickpea Chili

Curried Chicken Chili

Sautéed Lemon Chicken Tenders

Instant Chicken Fajitas

Chicken Fingers with Cumin Yogurt

Chicken Braised in Enchilada Sauce
Braised Anise Chicken
Chicken Thighs Braised with Posole
Chicken Braised with Roasted Peppers
Chicken Braised in Sun-Dried Tomato Vinaigrette over Greens
Mahogany Drumsticks
Balsamic-Glazed Drumsticks
Chicken Primavera Pizza
Molasses and Fire Baked Chicken Wings
Waco Wings
Southwest Chicken Baked with Rice and Beans
Smoked Chicken with Chorizo Rice
Molasses Mustard Roast Turkey Breast
Turkey with Fruit
Chèvre Turkey Burgers with Olive Relish
Roasted Turkey Fajitas
Easy Turkey Mole

Garlic Chicken

The secret to this simple broiled chicken is garlic oil. Its scent permeates the flesh while the oil crisps its skin and keeps the white meat moist.

Makes 4 servings

1 chicken (about 4 pounds), cleaned
2 teaspoons seasoning salt
3 tablespoons garlic oil
15 whole cloves garlic, jarred or fresh
1 cup white wine

Preheat the oven to 450°F. Sprinkle the interior cavity of the chicken with the seasoning, and rub the exterior with the garlic oil. Place, breast side down, in a metal roasting pan. Roast for 30 minutes, until the back of the chicken is crisp and brown. Turn the chicken breast side up. Scatter the garlic cloves around the chicken and roast for another 20 minutes, until a thermometer inserted in the thickest part of the thigh reads 165°F.

Remove the chicken to a cutting board. Add the wine to the roasting pan and set on a burner. Bring to a boil, scraping any brown bits into the juices. Carve the chicken into serving pieces and place the pieces on a platter. Moisten with the pan drippings and garlic.

Peking Chicken

Peking duck is one of the glories of the Chinese kitchen. Although this chicken doesn't quite match the crackling skin of the original, it is a pretty good imitation. The skin is glazed and is appropriately tawny, and the flavor captures the characteristic flavor of caramelized sugar and salty hoisin.

Makes 4 servings

1 chicken (4 pounds), cleaned
Salt and black pepper to taste
1 tablespoon Asian toasted sesame oil
¼ cup honey
¼ cup hoisin sauce
1 teaspoon Chinese chili purée

Preheat the oven to 450°F. Sprinkle the interior cavity of the chicken with salt and pepper, and rub the exterior with the oil. Place, breast side down, on a rack in a roasting pan and roast for 25 minutes. Meanwhile, combine the honey, hoisin sauce, and chili purée. Brush this mixture over the top of the chicken and roast for another 5 minutes.

Loosen the chicken from the rack with a spatula. Turn it breast side up and roast 20 minutes more. Brush with the glaze and roast 5 minutes more, until a thermometer inserted in the thickest part of the thigh reads 165°F. Remove from the oven, brush with glaze, and rest for 5 minutes before carving.

Lemon Chicken with Dried Plums

Dried plums (which used to be called prunes) are stuffed inside a bird with garlic, capers, and lemon sauce. Your market carries many lemon cooking sauces—some marinades, others (like piccata sauce) designed specifically for chicken. If you don't have a lemon sauce, substitute some lemon juice mixed with a little olive oil.

Makes 4 servings

1 chicken (3 to 4 pounds), cleaned
½ teaspoon herb seasoning blend
12 pitted dried plums (prunes)
12 whole cloves roasted garlic, jarred or
   freshly made
2 tablespoons nonpareil capers
1 jar (about 11 ounces) lemon cooking
   sauce, such as Consorzio
1 tablespoon olive oil

Preheat the oven to 450°F. Sprinkle the interior cavity of the chicken with the seasoning. Toss the dried plums, garlic cloves, half of the capers, and ¼ cup of sauce together, and spoon into the cavity of the chicken. Rub the outside of the chicken with the oil and place, breast side down, in a metal roasting pan. Roast for 30 minutes, turn breast side up, pour another ¼ cup of the sauce over the chicken, and roast another 20 minutes, until the internal temperature of the thigh meat is 165°F.

Transfer the chicken to a carving board. Remove the fat from the roasting pan and set the pan over medium-low heat. Add the remaining sauce and the capers to the pan, and using a spatula, scrape any browned bits in the pan into the simmering sauce. Cut the chicken into serving pieces and serve with the dried plums and sauce.

Orange-Spiced Game Hens

Game hens are diminutive chickens. Look for small ones (about 1 pound) so that you can serve a whole hen per person. If the only ones you find are closer to 2 pounds cut them in half lengthwise before roasting and serve one half per person.

Makes 4 servings

4 game hens (1 pound each), cleaned
1 teaspoon lemon pepper
½ cup spicy barbecue sauce
½ cup orange marmalade
¼ cup apple cider vinegar

Preheat the oven to 450°F. Sprinkle the interior cavities of the hens with lemon pepper. Place, breast side down, on an oiled rack in a roasting pan and roast for 15 minutes.

Meanwhile, combine the barbecue sauce, marmalade, and vinegar. Brush on the hens. Roast for another 5 minutes. Remove from the oven, turn the hens breast side up, and roast 20 minutes more, basting with sauce halfway through. The hens are done when the internal temperature of the thigh meat is 165°F.

Wok-Fried Chicken

It's time to relax about frying. Done right, frying draws moisture from the food into the oil; it doesn't draw oil into the food. The only additional fat in fried food clings to the surface, and most of that is easily removed by blotting with paper towels.

Makes 4 servings

1 cup plain yogurt, any kind
1¼ teaspoons dried crushed rosemary
2½ teaspoons poultry seasoning
2½ teaspoons dried granulated garlic
Salt and black pepper to taste
1½ pounds chicken tenders
1 cup flour
1 cup vegetable oil, for frying
1 lime, cut in 8 wedges

Combine the yogurt, ¼ teaspoon of the rosemary, ½ teaspoon of the poultry seasoning, ½ teaspoon of the garlic, and the salt and pepper. Toss the chicken pieces in the mixture to coat completely, cover, and set aside for at least 15 minutes (or refrigerate up to 12 hours).

Combine the flour, salt and pepper, and the remaining rosemary, poultry seasoning, and garlic on a sheet of foil. Remove the chicken from the marinade and coat each piece with the flour mixture.

Heat the oil in a large wok to 375°F, or until a chopstick or wooden spoon inserted in the oil begins to bubble immediately. Fry the chicken in the hot oil in 2 or 3 batches until the coating is golden brown and the chicken is cooked through, about 2 minutes per batch.

Remove the chicken with tongs or a slotted spoon and blot on a double-thick layer of paper towels. Season with more salt and pepper if desired. Serve with lime wedges.

Spicy Vanilla Chicken

Like most commonplace things, we have come to take vanilla for granted. Slang for insipid, ordinary, and bland, "plain vanilla" means dull. But that's only because we use it in dull ways. Taste vanilla out of context, and its true character blossoms. Vanilla is the fruit of a jungle orchid, and that's the exotic flower you taste in this spicy, fruity glaze for chicken.

Makes 4 servings

4 boneless, skinless chicken breast halves
*   (about 6 ounces each)*
Nonstick oil spray
½ teaspoon lemon pepper
1 cup mango salsa
1 tablespoon vanilla extract
1 teaspoon hot pepper sauce

Preheat a grill or broiler. Coat the chicken breasts with oil spray and season with lemon pepper. Coat the rack of a grill or broiler with oil spray and grill or broil the chicken 2 to 3 inches from a high flame, about 4 minutes per side. While the chicken cooks, combine the salsa, vanilla, and hot pepper sauce. Place half of the salsa mixture on top of the chicken and grill 2 minutes more. Serve with the remaining salsa mixture.

Chicken Cacciatore

Cacciatore usually has mushrooms, herbs, tomatoes, and wine. They're all here, bound together with the queen mother of convenience ingredients: Campbell's Cream of Mushroom Soup.

Makes 4 servings

*4 chicken breast halves, bone in (about
  12 ounces each)*
1 teaspoon Italian seasoning
2 tablespoons olive oil
*1 can (10¾ ounces) Campbell's
  Condensed Cream of Mushroom Soup*
*2 cans (14½ ounces) Italian-style stewed
  tomatoes*
¼ teaspoon black pepper
1 cup white wine
1 teaspoon anchovy paste
*1 tablespoon chopped Italian (flat-leaf)
  parsley*

Sprinkle the chicken with the Italian seasoning. Heat the oil in a large skillet over medium-high heat and brown the chicken on both sides. While the chicken is browning, combine the soup, tomatoes, and pepper. When the chicken is well browned, add the wine to the pan and stir to scrape up any brown bits clinging to the skillet. Add the soup mixture and move the chicken to allow the liquid to settle in the pan. Lower the heat so that the liquid simmers.

Cover and cook until the chicken is cooked through, about 30 minutes. Remove the lid and simmer until the liquid thickens slightly, about 5 minutes. Transfer the chicken to a platter. Stir the anchovy paste and parsley into the sauce and pour over the chicken.

Deviled Chicken Breast with Bacon and Cheese

Deviling can be a glaze of mustard, a crust of hot pepper, a relish of horseradish, or, as in this recipe, all of the above. A slightly smoky and spicy crust is broiled on top of a chicken breast, crowned with cheddar, and gratinéed just until the cheese melts. The dominance of any of the spicy ingredients can be modified to suit your taste and/or what you have on hand; just keep the total quantity the same so that you can coat all the chicken.

Makes 4 servings

2 tablespoons spicy brown mustard
1 tablespoon prepared white horseradish
2 teaspoons Chinese chili paste with garlic
1 strip precooked ready-to-serve bacon
½ teaspoon minced garlic, jarred or fresh
*4 boneless, skinless chicken breast halves
  (about 6 ounces each)*
Nonstick oil spray
*⅓ cup shredded Monterey Jack or Pepper
  Jack cheese*

Preheat the broiler. Combine the mustard, horseradish, chili paste, bacon, and garlic. Brush the chicken pieces with this mixture and coat with oil spray. Broil the chicken 2 inches from the flame for 5 minutes per side. Top each breast half with a portion of the cheese and broil 1 minute more, until the cheese melts.

Chicken Wellington

Beef Wellington has fallen out of vogue—too heavy, too rich, too stodgy, and too often poorly done. Yet there is something celebratory about dinner wrapped in pastry; it is like receiving an elegant gift. In that spirit I'll try to renovate the warhorse of banquets past: in place of beef, a boneless chicken breast; instead of duxelle, sautéed Portobellos; and for the foie gras, well, foie gras, because nothing else is quite so plush. The trick is to avoid sogginess. Cool the chicken before wrapping to keep the juices in place and the pastry crisp. You can prepare much of this recipe in advance and bake the Wellingtons right out of the refrigerator.

Makes 4 servings

4 boneless, skinless chicken breast halves
    (about 6 ounces each)
Salt and black pepper to taste
Nonstick olive oil spray
4 ounces sliced Portobello mushrooms
1 box (1 pound or 2 sheets) Pepperidge
    Farm Puff Pastry Sheets, thawed
4 ounces liver pâté or pâté de foie gras,
    preferably refrigerated, but if not,
    canned

Season the chicken with salt and pepper. Place a large nonstick skillet over high heat, coat the skillet with olive oil spray, and brown the chicken on both sides. Transfer the chicken to a serving plate and refrigerate for at least 10 minutes. Coat the skillet with more oil spray, add the mushroom slices, and brown the mushrooms on both sides. Refrigerate.

Roll the sheets of puff pastry slightly to make them roughly 8 × 11 inches. Cut each sheet in half so that you have 4 sheets, each about 8 × 5½ inches. Divide the pâté to 8 portions, each about ½ ounce.

TO MAKE THE WELLINGTONS:

Place a sheet of pastry with a short side toward you and brush the edges with water. Spread a portion of pâté just below the center line, top with a piece of chicken, and spread another portion of pâté on top of the chicken. Top with 3 mushroom slices, fold the empty pastry half over the chicken, and pinch the edges together. Trim away any excess. Repeat with the remaining ingredients. Place the four wrapped pastries on a sheet pan. The Wellingtons can be prepared to this point up to 24 hours ahead, as long as they are well wrapped and kept in the refrigerator.

Preheat the oven to 375°F. Bake the Wellingtons for 40 minutes, until the pastry is golden brown. Serve as is or with Wild Mushroom Sauce (page 101).

Chicken in Honey Mustard Cream Sauce

This preparation is the essence of elegant, easy cooking. Pounding the chicken breasts is important, for it ensures that the chicken will cook through quickly and evenly. By spraying the chicken with oil before pounding, you ensure it will flatten without tearing.

Makes 4 servings

4 boneless, skinless chicken breast halves
   (about 6 ounces each)
Salt and black pepper to taste
Nonstick oil spray
2 teaspoons minced garlic, jarred or
   fresh
1 tablespoon nonpareil capers
1 cup sour cream or heavy cream
3 tablespoons honey mustard

Season the chicken with salt and pepper, coat with oil spray, and pound between sheets of plastic wrap to an even thickness of about ¼ inch. Place a large skillet over high heat, coat with oil spray, and sauté the chicken breasts until they are browned on both sides and cooked through, about 3 minutes per side. Do not crowd the pan. Cook in 2 skillets or in batches, if needed. Transfer to a serving plate and keep warm.

Lower the heat to medium-low, add the garlic and capers to the pan, and stir briefly. Add the sour cream and mustard, and stir until a sauce forms. Pour over the chicken.

Blackened Chicken with Tomato Jam

Tomato is a fruit, and like all fruit, it makes beautiful jam. Forget your prejudice. A tomato is just as sweet as an apple or a strawberry; the only difference is its overt acidity, the very quality that makes it maintain its flavor when simmered into a preserve. It is the perfect counterpoint to the charred surface of a blackened chicken breast.

Makes 4 servings

⅓ cup jalapeño jelly
⅓ cup tomato purée
1 tablespoon tomato paste in a tube
2 teaspoons red or white wine vinegar
½ teaspoon salt
4 boneless, skinless chicken breast halves
   (about 6 ounces each)
Nonstick olive oil spray
1 teaspoon Szechwan seasoning

Heat the jelly until it melts and stir in the tomato purée, tomato paste, vinegar, and salt.

Coat the chicken breasts with oil spray and season with the Szechwan seasoning. Flatten the chicken breasts between sheets of plastic wrap to an even thickness of about ½ inch.

Heat a large iron skillet and coat the pan with oil spray. Cook the chicken on both sides in the hot skillet until the surfaces are blackened and the meat feels firm to the touch. Brush the chicken on both sides with the tomato jam and serve.

Black Bean Chicken with Salsa Syrup

And now for something completely different. Boneless chicken breasts are embedded in a crust of cooked, seasoned, dehydrated black beans and glazed with a buttery smooth piquant salsa.

Makes 4 servings

4 boneless, skinless chicken breast halves (about 6 ounces each)
Salt and black pepper to taste
Nonstick oil spray
1 box (7 ounces) instant black beans
½ cup yogurt
2 tablespoons olive oil
¾ cup salsa, any heat level
2 tablespoons butter

Season the chicken with salt and pepper, coat with oil spray, and pound between sheets of plastic wrap to an even thickness of about ½ inch. Place the beans on a sheet of foil. Brush the chicken with the yogurt and dredge in the beans until thoroughly coated.

Heat the oil in a large skillet, add the chicken pieces in a single layer, and cover the pan. Cook until the chicken is well browned, about 5 minutes. Turn the chicken, cover the pan, and cook 5 minutes more, until the chicken is firm.

While the chicken is cooking, purée the salsa in a food processor. When the chicken is done, transfer it to a warm platter with a spatula. Discard any excess oil from the skillet and add the salsa. Boil for 2 minutes and swirl in the butter. Serve each piece of chicken with 2 to 3 tablespoons of the salsa syrup.

Lemon Poppy Seed Chicken Paillard

A paillard (pronounced pie-*yard*) is an extremely thin fillet that is delicate and tender. It welcomes almost any sauce or seasoning, and cooks in seconds. The only hitch is the pounding. Pounding equalizes thickness, ensuring quick and even cooking.

Makes 4 servings

4 boneless, skinless chicken breast halves (about 6 ounces each)
¼ cup bottled oil and vinegar dressing
2 teaspoons poppy seeds
Nonstick oil spray
¼ cup lemon juice, bottled organic or fresh

Coat the chicken pieces with 1 tablespoon of the dressing. Place them between sheets of plastic wrap and pound to an even thickness of about ⅛ inch. Sprinkle with the poppy seeds. Heat 2 large skillets until very hot. Coat with oil spray, add the chicken, and sauté until golden brown and firm, about 1 minute per side. Transfer the chicken to a serving platter. Add the remaining dressing and the lemon juice to one of the pans, bring to a boil, and pour the sauce over the chicken.

Olive-Crusted Chicken on Fattoush

The exotic juxtaposition of flavors and textures in this recipe is Arab-inspired. Fattoush, or bread salad, is common fare in the Middle East, and when it is served with grilled meat and olives, it is nothing less than Arabian soul food. There are countless recipes for fattoush, so treat this one as a point of departure rather than destination. The one essential rule is to add the toasted pita just before serving. That way, its crunch offsets the juiciness of the vegetables in the salad.

Makes 4 servings

4 pita breads, each cut in 8 wedges
Nonstick olive oil spray
4 chicken breast halves, bone in (about 12 ounces each)
Salt and black pepper to taste
¼ cup tapenade (black olive spread)
1 jar (12 ounces) tomato bruschetta
1 tablespoon extra-virgin olive oil
1 teaspoon chopped garlic, jarred or fresh
1 tablespoon chopped Italian (flat-leaf) parsley
2 tablespoons lemon juice, organic bottled or fresh

Preheat the oven to 375°F. Place the pita wedges on a sheet pan, coat with oil spray, and bake for 5 minutes, until crisp and lightly toasted. Remove the bread and turn the oven to the broiler setting to preheat the broiler. Set a rack about 4 inches from the flame and coat the broiler pan with oil spray. Season the bone side of the chicken with salt and pepper. Lift the skin from the breast halves and rub 1 tablespoon of tapenade into the meat of each breast half. Replace the skin and coat the chicken on both sides with oil spray. Set the chicken, skin side down, on the broiler pan and broil for 12 to 15 minutes, until deeply browned.

Meanwhile, make the fattoush. Toss the toasted pita wedges with the bruschetta, oil, garlic, parsley, half of the lemon juice, salt, and pepper. Turn the chicken breasts and broil 5 to 7 minutes more, until the skin is crisp and golden brown, and the chicken is cooked through, registering an internal temperature of 160°F. Serve the chicken breasts on a bed of fattoush, drizzled with the remaining lemon juice.

Curried Chicken with Lentil Dal

Curries are stews. Like all stews, they do not call for complex cooking, yet they often require numerous spices and so many bouts of precooking (boiling beans for dal, roasting vegetables or whole spices, and so forth) that they feel cumbersome and complex. In this surprisingly easy curry, spices are replaced with a curry sauce (see curry sauces on page 22).

Makes 4 servings

4 boneless, skinless chicken breast halves
   (about 6 ounces each)
Salt and black pepper to taste
1 tablespoon olive oil
1 can (14.5 ounces) lentil soup
1 cup curry sauce
1 can (15 ounces) lentils, rinsed and
   drained
1 teaspoon minced garlic, jarred or fresh
1 teaspoon minced ginger, jarred or
   fresh
2 teaspoons cilantro pesto or chutney, or
   2 tablespoons chopped fresh cilantro

Season the chicken pieces with salt and pepper. Heat a large skillet, add the oil, and brown the chicken on both sides. Add the lentil soup, curry sauce, lentils, garlic, and ginger. Simmer until the chicken is cooked through, about 5 minutes. Adjust the salt and pepper, stir in the cilantro, and serve.

Chicken Chili with Guacamole Cream

Chipotle peppers, white beans, cilantro pesto, a square of chocolate, and a swirl of creamy avocado come together to disarm the notion that this is just another humdrum chili. Its construction, though, is quite ordinary: The chicken is browned, simmered for five minutes, mixed with beans, and served. But if you don't tell, I won't, either.

Makes 4 servings

Nonstick oil spray
1 pound boneless, skinless chicken breast
   halves, cut in bite-size chunks
1 jar (about 16 ounces) chipotle salsa
½ cup chicken broth
2 teaspoons ground cumin
1 ounce bittersweet chocolate
1 can (about 15 ounces) white beans,
   rinsed and drained
1 tablespoon cilantro pesto or chutney,
   or 3 tablespoons chopped cilantro
1 cup refrigerated guacamole
½ cup sour cream

Place a large skillet over high heat, coat the interior with oil spray, and sauté the chicken until lightly browned. Add the salsa, broth, and cumin. Bring to a boil and simmer until the chicken is done. Stir in the chocolate until it melts. Stir in the beans and cilantro, and heat through. Combine the guacamole and sour cream. Serve bowls of chili topped with the guacamole cream.

Chicken Chickpea Chili

This chicken chili has been lightened by using salsa in place of a long-simmered tomato product and by thickening the sauce with Israeli couscous, the pearl-shaped pasta from the Middle East, and a small amount of instant falafel powder.

Makes 4 servings

1½ pounds boneless, skinless chicken
   breast halves, cut in 1-inch cubes
Salt and black pepper to taste
1 tablespoon olive oil
1 package Israeli couscous
1 teaspoon ground cumin
1 teaspoon chili powder
1 can (about 15 ounces) chicken broth
1 large jar (32 ounces) salsa, any heat
   level
1 can (about 12 ounces) chickpeas, rinsed
   and drained
1 tablespoon instant falafel powder
   (page 25)

Season the chicken with salt and pepper. Heat the oil in a large, heavy saucepan, add the chicken, and sauté until browned. Add the couscous and sauté until lightly toasted, about 2 minutes more. Add the cumin and chili powder. Add the broth and stir until simmering, scraping up any brown bits clinging to the pan. Add the salsa and return to a simmer.

Mash about one-third of the chickpeas with the back of a fork. Stir both the whole and the mashed chickpeas and the falafel into the chili and simmer until the couscous is tender, the chicken is cooked through, and the broth is slightly thickened, about 10 minutes more. Adjust the seasoning and serve.

Curried Chicken Chili

I've always thought of chili as American curry. It has the same layering of flavors, love of heat, and willingness to sacrifice appearance in pursuit of complex, provocative flavor. The basic difference is that curry sauce takes the place of tomatoes, chickpeas stand in for kidney beans, and, in this case, the meat is chicken rather than beef. The only other adjustment is changing your mind.

Makes 4 servings

1 tablespoon vegetable oil
1½ pounds boneless, skinless chicken
   breast halves, cut in chunks
1 jar (16 ounces) curry sauce
1 teaspoon chili powder
1 teaspoon ground cumin
1 can (about 15 ounces) chickpeas,
   drained
2 teaspoons cilantro pesto or chutney, or
   2 tablespoons chopped fresh cilantro

Heat the oil in a large skillet. Add the chicken and sauté until the pieces are browned on all sides. Add the curry sauce, chili powder, cumin, and chickpeas, and simmer for 5 minutes. Stir in the cilantro and serve.

Sautéed Lemon Chicken Tenders

There must a word to capture the extreme "lemonosity" of this simple sauté. "Lemony" won't do, "lemon-scented" is so-o-o subdued, and "citro-mania" is just too yellow. But no matter how you describe it, the results are equally intense. Lemon enters the dish in three ways: sweetly in marmalade, aromatically as lemon peel, and tartly as lemon juice.

Makes 4 servings

1½ pounds chicken tenders or boneless, skinless chicken breasts, cut into fingers
Salt and black pepper to taste
1 tablespoon vegetable oil
1 medium onion, peeled and thinly sliced
1 cup chicken broth
¼ cup lemon marmalade
½ teaspoon dried lemon peel
3 tablespoons lemon juice, organic bottled or fresh
1 tablespoon dried chives, or 2 tablespoons freshly chopped chives

Season the chicken with salt and pepper. Place a large skillet over high heat until the skillet is very hot. Add the oil, chicken, and onion, and brown. Add the broth and scrape up any brown bits clinging to the pan. Simmer until the chicken is cooked through, about 1 minute. Add the marmalade and lemon peel, and boil until slightly thickened. Stir in the lemon juice and chives, and serve.

Instant Chicken Fajitas

Most of the work in making fajitas is chopping, so for the knife-impaired I make the following offering: chop-free fajitas. The chicken comes ready to cook in tenders, the vegetables are all in the salsa, the lime juice is bottled, and the guacamole is premade. All you have to do is put down the knife and get cooking.

Makes 4 servings

1½ pounds chicken tenders or boneless, skinless chicken breasts, cut into fingers
Salt and black pepper to taste
1 tablespoon vegetable oil
1 teaspoon fajita seasoning
½ cup chunky salsa, any heat level
1 tablespoon lime juice, organic bottled or fresh
8 flour tortillas, warmed in an oven or microwave
1 cup refrigerated guacamole
½ cup sour cream, regular or reduced-fat

Season the chicken with salt and pepper. Place a skillet over medium-high heat until the skillet is hot. Add the oil and sauté the chicken until it is browned and almost cooked through. Add the fajita seasoning and salsa, bring to a boil, and stir in the lime juice. Serve with warm tortillas and guacamole and/or sour cream.

Chicken Fingers with Cumin Yogurt

The secret to the highly seasoned, super-crispy batter in this recipe is instant falafel powder. Sold as part of a kit for making deep-fried falafel patties, it is also an instant breading ingredient.

Makes 4 servings

2 cups plain yogurt
2 tablespoons ground cumin
2 teaspoons Southwest seasoning
1½ pounds chicken tenders
Vegetable oil for frying
1 box (10 ounces) falafel mix

Combine the yogurt, cumin, and seasoning. Marinate the chicken in half of this mixture for 30 minutes. Heat 2 inches of the oil in a deep skillet to 375°F, or until a wooden spoon inserted in the oil bubbles immediately. Place a cooling rack on a sheet pan and set near the fryer.

Place the falafel mix on a sheet of foil. Remove the chicken pieces from the yogurt and coat them thoroughly with falafel mix. Cook several pieces of chicken at a time in the hot oil until the chicken is browned and cooked through, about 3 minutes per batch. Transfer with a slotted spoon to the rack. Cook the remaining chicken in the same way. Serve with the remaining cumin yogurt as a dip.

Chicken Braised in Enchilada Sauce

This simple stew has a robust flavor that comes from two complementary ingredients: stone-ground cornmeal and Mexican-style enchilada sauce. There are two types of enchilada sauce. The Mexican style is made principally from ground chiles and vinegar, while the American style has a tomato base. Either one will work in most recipes, but in this recipe stick to the Mexican style. The combination of acrid sauce and sweet cornmeal makes the flavors distinctive.

Makes 4 servings

3 pounds chicken pieces, drumsticks and
    thighs separated, and breasts halved
⅓ cup stone-ground yellow cornmeal
2 tablespoons olive oil
1 jar (12 ounces) red or green Mexican-
    style enchilada sauce
½ cup chicken broth
Salt and black pepper to taste

Place the chicken and cornmeal in a plastic bag. Seal the bag and shake it until the chicken is coated with the cornmeal. Heat a large skillet over medium-high heat. Add the oil and brown the chicken pieces on all sides. Add the cornmeal remaining in the bag, the enchilada sauce, and broth. Heat until the sauce is simmering and season with salt and pepper. Cover and cook until the chicken pieces are cooked through, about 20 minutes.

Braised Anise Chicken

Star anise, the dried fruit of the anise bush, is a standard flavoring in Chinese braised dishes, and its licorice perfume is the principal aromatic in Chinese five-spice powder. The pods are quite beautiful, forming a five-pointed star when whole. Although the anise pods are inedible, it is traditional to leave them in the sauce as a natural garnish.

Makes 4 servings

⅓ cup hoisin sauce
½ teaspoon minced garlic, jarred or
     fresh
½ teaspoon minced ginger, jarred or
     fresh
2 whole pieces star anise (the equivalent
     in broken pieces is fine, but the dish
     won't be as pretty)
2½ to 3 pounds chicken pieces, drum-
     sticks and thighs separated, and
     breasts halved
Flour seasoned with salt and pepper
Nonstick oil spray
½ cup chopped onion, frozen or fresh
1 cup chicken broth
8 dried shiitake mushrooms or other
     dried exotic mushroom

Combine the hoisin sauce, garlic, ginger, and star anise. Sprinkle the chicken with the seasoned flour. Heat a large skillet and coat with oil spray. Sear the chicken pieces in the skillet on all sides. Add the onion and stir-fry until lightly browned. Add the broth and mushrooms, and bring to a boil. Stir in the hoisin mixture. Lower the heat to medium-low, cover, and cook until the chicken pieces are cooked through, about 20 minutes.

Remove the lid and cook over high heat until the sauce has thickened and the chicken is thoroughly coated. Turn the chicken frequently to make sure the sauce doesn't burn.

Chicken Thighs Braised with Posole

Posole and whole hominy are different names for the same grain. The one you find depends on where you live. Posole has a unique flavor stemming from the alkaline used to process it, which is complemented by hot peppers, cilantro, and lime juice. It is this medley of flavors that gives posole stews their character.

Makes 4 servings

*2 pounds (8 to 10 pieces) boneless, skin-
   less chicken thighs*
Salt and black pepper to taste
2 tablespoons olive oil
1 jar (16 ounces) salsa, any heat level
1 can (15 ounces) posole, drained
*1 teaspoon cilantro pesto or chutney, or
   1 tablespoon chopped fresh cilantro*
*1 teaspoon lime juice, organic bottled or
   fresh*

Season the chicken with salt and pepper. Place a large skillet over medium-high heat until hot. Add the oil and brown the chicken thighs on all sides. Add the salsa and posole, and simmer until the chicken is cooked through, about 20 minutes or until the thighs register an internal temperature of 170°F. Stir in the cilantro and lime juice.

Chicken Braised with Roasted Peppers

The bold Mediterranean flavor for this chicken stew is instant, emerging from a jar of roasted peppers, a jar of basil pesto, a jar of tapenade, and a bottle of wine.

Makes 4 servings

*2½ to 3 pounds chicken pieces, drum-
   sticks and thighs separated, and
   breasts halved*
Salt and black pepper to taste
1 tablespoon olive oil
1 cup chopped onions, frozen or fresh
*¾ cup roasted peppers, jarred or fresh,
   cut in strips*
1½ cups white wine
1 tablespoon pesto, jarred or fresh
*1 tablespoon tapenade (black olive
   spread)*

Season the chicken pieces liberally with salt and pepper. Heat a large skillet, add the oil, and brown the chicken on all sides. Do not crowd the pan. When the chicken is almost done, add the onions and continue sautéing until the onions are lightly browned. Add the roasted peppers and wine. Cover and simmer until the chicken pieces are cooked through, about 20 minutes. Transfer the chicken to a serving plate. Stir the pesto and tapenade into the skillet, adjust the seasoning, and pour the sauce over the chicken.

Chicken Braised in Sun-Dried Tomato Vinaigrette over Greens

The wonderful gift of braising is that you end up with two foods in one: meat brimming with falling-from-the-bone flavor plus an equally flavorful broth. In some classic braised dishes the two are served separately—the broth as a soup or a pasta sauce, the meat as the main course. Here, chicken thighs are braised in a winey, vinegary broth that acts as a sauce for the chicken and a dressing for a salad of hearty lettuce.

Makes 4 servings

1 pound (4 or 5 pieces) boneless, skinless
    chicken thighs
Salt and black pepper to taste
1 tablespoon olive oil
½ cup white wine
1½ cups chicken broth
1 tablespoon red wine vinegar
1 tablespoon sun-dried tomato paste or
    pesto
1 tablespoon chopped Italian (flat-leaf)
    parsley
1 bag (8 to 10 ounces) hearty lettuce mix

Season the chicken with salt and pepper. Heat a large skillet. Add the oil and brown the chicken thighs on both sides. Deglaze the pan with the wine and boil until the wine is reduced by half. Add the broth and simmer until the chicken is cooked through, about 20 minutes.

Transfer the chicken to a cutting board. Stir the vinegar, tomato paste, and parsley into the pan.

To serve, cut each chicken thigh into 3 or 4 slices. Toss the greens with half of the liquid in the pan and mound on dinner plates. Top each mound with chicken slices and spoon the remaining pan liquid over the top.

Mahogany Drumsticks

In Chinese cooking, braising in soy sauce or other dark liquid is called red-cooking, because it tints the food as it simmers. In this version, chicken drumsticks are braised in teriyaki sauce until they turn a deep, dark red-brown color.

Makes 4 servings

1 teaspoon chopped garlic, jarred or fresh
1 tablespoon minced ginger, jarred or fresh
Pinch of crushed red pepper flakes
⅓ cup teriyaki sauce, preferably Soy Vay Veri Veri Teriyaki Sauce
⅓ cup water
1 tablespoon apple cider or rice wine vinegar
2 pounds (8 to 10 pieces) chicken drumsticks
2 teaspoons Asian toasted sesame oil

Combine the garlic, ginger, pepper flakes, teriyaki sauce, water, and vinegar in a large skillet with a lid. Arrange the drumsticks in a single layer in the sauce. Cover and simmer for 10 minutes. Turn the chicken and simmer, uncovered, until the drumsticks are cooked through, and the pan liquid has reduced to a glaze. Turn the chicken as needed to glaze evenly. Drizzle with sesame oil and serve.

Balsamic-Glazed Drumsticks

Balsamic vinegar is fascinating. For braising, any balsamic will do. The best balsamics are aged in wooden casks for decades until they develop a deep color and become more like syrup than vinegar—very fruity, sticky sweet, and mildly acidic. Save these vinegars for drizzling on fruit, a beautiful roasted meat, or a wonderfully aged cheese. In this preparation, any balsamic will do.

Makes 4 servings

2 pounds chicken drumsticks (8 to 10 pieces)
Salt and black pepper to taste
2 tablespoons olive oil
1 teaspoon chopped garlic, jarred or fresh
1½ cups chicken broth
¾ cup balsamic vinegar
1 tablespoon sugar

Season the chicken with salt and pepper. Heat a large skillet, add the oil, and brown the chicken on all sides. Add the garlic and broth, and bring to a boil. Add the vinegar and sugar, and simmer, uncovered, until the drumsticks are cooked through and the pan liquid has reduced to a glaze. Turn the drumsticks as needed to ensure that they cook uniformly and are glazed evenly.

Chicken Primavera Pizza

Precooked pizza rounds, which are really a type of focaccia, have revolutionized the notion of home-baked pizzas. This one is a colorful one-dish meal that combines starch, vegetable, meat, and sauce. Fresh plum tomatoes are used because they are the meatiest of the commonly available tomatoes. Other tomatoes may be too juicy, causing puddles to form when they bake.

Makes 4 servings

4 individual prebaked pizza rounds, or 2
   large pizza rounds, such as Boboli
1 cup jarred Alfredo sauce
8 ounces sliced roasted chicken breast
8 ounces roasted red pepper, jarred or
   fresh, sliced
½ small onion, thinly sliced
2 plum tomatoes, each cut in 6 slices
1 cup (about 5 ounces) frozen chopped
   spinach, thawed and squeezed dry
1 jar (6 ounces) quartered marinated
   artichoke hearts, drained

Preheat the oven to 400°F. Place the pizza rounds on a foil-covered sheet pan and spread the sauce over the top to ½ inch from the edge. Arrange the chicken, pepper, onion, tomatoes, spinach, and artichoke hearts on top, and bake for 15 minutes, until the sauce bubbles and the bottom of the crust is crisp.

Molasses and Fire Baked Chicken Wings

Refining sugar results in three grades of molasses: light (for pancake syrup), dark (for cooking and baking), and blackstrap (eaten mostly for health benefits). In this recipe the rich, bittersweet caramel of dark molasses blends with hoisin sauce, chili paste, and garlic into a fiery, lip-sticking barbecue sauce for wings.

Makes 4 servings

Nonstick oil spray
3 pounds chicken wings, cut in sections,
   tips discarded
¼ cup dark molasses
2 tablespoons hoisin sauce
2 tablespoons Chinese chili purée
2 teaspoons minced garlic, jarred or
   fresh

Preheat the oven to 450°F. Cover a sheet pan with heavy-duty foil and coat with oil spray. Lay out the wing pieces in a single layer, leaving space between the pieces. Bake for 20 minutes, or until lightly browned. While the wings are cooking, combine the molasses, hoisin sauce, chili purée, and garlic.

Brush the wings with the sauce and bake for 5 minutes. Turn, brush with more sauce, and bake for another 5 minutes. Turn, brush, and bake twice more, each time for 5 minutes. The wings should brown deeply and even blacken in spots.

Waco Wings

This rendition of Buffalo chicken wings, given to me by a friend from Waco, Texas, is baked, not fried. The salsa adds a chunky vegetable dimension without taking away the magical butter-hot sauce combination of the Yankee original.

Makes 4 servings

*3 pounds chicken wings, cut in sections,
    tips discarded
5 tablespoons butter, melted
1 cup spicy salsa
2 tablespoons mild hot pepper sauce*

Preheat the oven to 450°F. Toss the wing pieces with 1 tablespoon of the butter, place them in a 9 × 13-inch baking pan, and bake until crisp, about 45 minutes. Toss the remaining melted butter with the salsa and hot sauce. When the wings are cooked, toss them with the sauce and serve.

Southwest Chicken Baked with Rice and Beans

This is the perfect stop-at-the-market-after-work dinner. It has everything: protein, starch, and vegetable. It is assembled in five minutes, and while it's in the oven, you can throw together a salad and still have time to relax.

Makes 4 servings

*Nonstick oil spray
1 can (10¾ ounces) Campbell's
    Condensed Cream of Chicken Soup
1 cup chunky salsa, medium or hot
1½ cups very hot water
1 can (11 ounces) Mexican-style corn,
    drained
½ cup canned black beans, rinsed and
    drained
1¼ cups converted rice
4 boneless, skinless chicken breast halves
    (about 6 ounces each)
1 cup shredded cheddar cheese*

Preheat the oven to 375°F. Coat a 9 × 13-inch baking dish with oil spray. Combine the soup, salsa, water, and corn in a large mixing bowl. Fold in the beans and rice, and pour into the prepared baking dish. Smooth the top. Place the chicken on top of the rice and bake for 25 minutes. Sprinkle the cheese over each chicken breast and bake for another 10 minutes, until the cheese is melted and the chicken is firm or registers an internal temperature of 160° F.

Smoked Chicken with Chorizo Rice

Here's another recipe using smoker bags (page 33). Because the bag provides a closed cooking space, juices collect in the bottom of the baking dish, providing a smoky broth for steaming rice along with the chicken. The resulting one-pot meal needs only a side salad.

Makes 4 servings

1 cup long-grain rice
1 can (about 15 ounces) chicken broth
1 cup frozen corn kernels
8 ounces chorizo sausage, chopped
1 chicken (3 to 4 pounds), excess fat removed and cavity cleaned
1 tablespoon Southwest seasoning
2 scallions, finely sliced

You will need one Savu Original Food smoker bag, medium smoke (page 33). Preheat the oven to 475°F. Combine the rice, broth, corn, and sausage in a 7 × 11-inch baking dish. Rub the chicken inside and out with the seasoning and place it on the rice. Place the baking dish in the smoker bag. Seal the opening of the bag with a double fold, and place on a sheet pan.

Bake for 1¼ hours. Remove from the oven and let rest for 10 minutes. Remove the baking dish from the bag and discard the bag. Lift the chicken from the rice, carve it into serving pieces, fluff the rice, and serve.

Molasses Mustard Roast Turkey Breast

The roasted, slightly bitter tones of molasses are brightened by the spice and tang of brown mustard. Together they enhance the sweetness of roast turkey breast. Be sure to glaze the turkey after the oven temperature has been lowered. Otherwise, the molasses will burn.

Makes 4 servings

Nonstick olive oil spray
1 boneless turkey breast half (about 4 pounds)
Coarse salt and pepper to taste
1 pound new potatoes, scrubbed
4 ounces baby carrots
8 peeled cloves garlic, jarred or fresh
¼ cup molasses
3 tablespoons spicy brown mustard

Preheat the oven to 425°F. Coat a baking dish with oil spray. Season the turkey with salt and pepper. Scatter the potatoes, carrots, and garlic in the baking dish, top with the turkey breast, and coat with more oil spray. Roast for 30 minutes.

While the turkey is roasting, combine the molasses and mustard. Lower the oven temperature to 375°F. Brush the turkey with half of the molasses-mustard mixture. Bake for 10 minutes, brush with the remaining molasses-mustard mixture, and bake for another 10 minutes, until the internal temperature of the turkey registers 160°F. Slice the turkey and serve.

Turkey with Fruit

The complex flavors and aromas of this sweet and savory turkey pot roast belie its simplicity. The secret is the combination of browned turkey, dried fruit, and marsala wine. Because the turkey is braised, it cooks in record time, and because the meat is continually steeped in liquid, it never dries out.

Makes 6 servings

1 boneless, skinless turkey breast half
   (about 4 pounds)
Salt and black pepper to taste
1 tablespoon vegetable oil
¼ cup dried cranberries
⅓ cup dried apricots, quartered
5 pitted prunes, quartered
4 dried figs, stems removed, quartered
   lengthwise
½ teaspoon minced garlic, jarred or fresh
2 cups marsala or other sweet wine

Season the turkey breast liberally with salt and pepper. Heat the oil in a large, deep skillet or Dutch oven over medium-high heat and brown the turkey breast on both sides. Add the cranberries, apricots, prunes, figs, and garlic, and stir briefly. Add the marsala, cover, and simmer until the turkey is cooked through, about 25 minutes, or until the internal temperature registers 165°F. Transfer the turkey breast to a cutting board. Boil the wine until it has thickened slightly. Slice the turkey and serve with the sauce.

Chèvre Turkey Burgers with Olive Relish

Turkey burgers are light and sweet, and because the meat is relatively lean, they'll be dry unless you take measures to increase their moisture. You do that here by stuffing the patties with goat cheese, which softens into a creamy sauce as the burgers cook.

Makes 4 servings

1½ pounds ground turkey
1 teaspoon salt
½ teaspoon black pepper
1½ teaspoons minced garlic, jarred or
   fresh
4 ounces fresh chèvre, cut into 4 pieces
½ cup jarred tomato bruschetta
1 tablespoon tapenade (black olive
   spread)
Toasted buns (optional)

Preheat a broiler. Combine the turkey, salt, pepper, and garlic. Divide into 8 golf-ball-size pieces and flatten 4 of them. Place a piece of chèvre in the center of each flattened piece, top with one of the remaining meatballs, and mold into 4 burgers. Broil 4 inches from a hot flame to desired doneness, about 8 minutes per side. While the meat broils, combine the bruschetta and tapenade. When the burgers are done, top each one with 1 tablespoon of the sauce. Serve on toasted buns, if desired.

Roasted Turkey Fajitas

Fajitas are typically grilled. These are roasted, which allows you to stick them in the oven and walk away.

Makes 4 servings

1½ pounds turkey cutlets
1 large onion, cut in thin wedges
Salt and black pepper to taste
¼ cup extra-virgin olive oil
1 jar (12.5 ounces) salsa verde
½ teaspoon minced garlic, jarred or fresh
2 tablespoons lime juice, organic bottled
    or fresh
8 flour tortillas, warmed in an oven or
    microwave
1 cup shredded Monterey Jack cheese

Preheat the oven to 500°F. Toss the turkey and onion with salt and pepper and 3 tablespoons of the oil on a large sheet pan. Spread everything out and roast for 25 minutes, until all is browned and the turkey is cooked through. Meanwhile, mix the salsa, garlic, lime juice, and remaining oil together. Toss with the roasted fajita ingredients and serve with warm tortillas and cheese.

Easy Turkey Mole

Mole poblano made with turkey is the most traditional of Mexican moles, but this one is anything but traditional. A butterflied, skinless, boneless turkey breast, sold as turkey London broil, is broiled to doneness and then sliced and simmered in a sauce made from the turkey drippings, chipotle salsa, and jarred mole sauce. The results are lighter and more contemporary than the classic mole.

Makes 6 servings

1 turkey London broil, about 3½ pounds
1 tablespoon Southwest, Cajun, or fajita
    seasoning
Nonstick oil spray
1 cup boiling water
1 cup chipotle salsa, any heat level
¼ cup jarred mole sauce (page 23)
Cooked rice, warm bread, or tortillas

Preheat the broiler. Rub the turkey with the seasoning and coat with oil spray on all sides. Place on a broiler pan. Broil about 4 inches from the flame until browned and a thermometer inserted in a side registers 160°F, about 8 minutes per side. Transfer the turkey to a cutting board and cover with foil to keep warm.

Pour the water in the pan and stir, scraping any browned bits clinging to the pan. Stir in the salsa and mole. Place over medium-high heat and simmer for 5 minutes. While the sauce is simmering, cut the turkey in thin slices. Slip the slices into the sauce, heat through, and serve with rice, warm bread, or tortillas.

CHAPTER 6

SEAFOOD ELABORATED

Seafood Risotto with Black Beans and Basil
Paella con Polenta
Seafood Bolito Misto
Twelve-Minute Bouillabaisse
Shrimp Cakes Florentine
Shrimp Fried in Creamy Polenta Batter
Express Checkout Scampi
Nacho-Crusted Fried Shrimp and Guacamole
Shrimp and Black Bean Chili
Shrimp in Clam Sauce
Seared Scallops with Spicy Tomato Butter
Hot and Sour Clams
Seared Sesame and Soy Scallops
Tex-Mex Mussels
Tea-Smoked Clams and Mussels
Salmon Smoked with Rice and Corn
Poached Salmon with Sake Beurre Blanc
Grilled Salmon with Olive Vinaigrette
Salmon Stuffed with Smoked Salmon Mashed Potatoes
Southwest Blackened Salmon with Escabeche
Caribbean Salmon Couscous

Mexican Monkfish

Escabeche of Sole

Flounder in Orange-Tomato Marinara

Parmesan Flounder with Caesar Sauce

Wok-Seared Tuna on Thai Noodles

Tuna Seared in a Wasabi Crust

Maki Tuna Burgers

Bluefish Baked with Lemon and Mustard

Caramelized Catfish

Catfish Corn Burgoo

Fish Steaks with Sesame Rouille

Pesto Fish Stew

Fish in Green Curry

Fried Fish in Chickpea Batter with Citrus Dressing

Fish Stick Fajitas

Tuna Enchiladas Verde

Seafood Risotto with Black Beans and Basil

The ephemeral nature of risotto has convinced many home cooks that it's difficult to prepare—and most recipes don't help. True, risotto can degenerate from silken cream to concrete while sitting on your plate, but when a recipe tells you that it must be stirred constantly and takes far longer to cook than regular rice, that's nonsense. Risotto can be cooked in 20 minutes from start to finish, and though it takes some attention, a stir every 5 minutes or so is more than sufficient. This risotto can be one course in an elaborate meal or an entrée in a casual dinner.

Makes 6 servings

1 tablespoon olive oil
1 cup chopped onions, frozen or fresh
2 cups arborio rice (risotto)
1 cup white wine
2 bottles (8 ounces each) clam juice
3 cups water
1 jar (16 ounces) mild chunky salsa
1 pound ready-to-cook seafood, thawed
   if frozen (shrimp, scallops, squid, etc.)
1 cup canned black beans, rinsed and
   drained
3 tablespoons basil pesto, jarred or fresh
Salt and black pepper to taste
¼ cup toasted pumpkin seeds (optional)

Heat the oil over medium heat in a large, deep skillet. Add the onions and sauté until tender. Add the rice and stir to coat with the oil. Add the wine and stir until absorbed. Combine the clam juice and water, and add the mixture to the rice in 3 increments, about 1½ cups at a time, stirring occasionally, until all the liquid is absorbed.

Add the salsa, seafood, and black beans. Stir occasionally and simmer about 5 minutes, until the liquid has reduced to a sauce and the seafood is cooked through. Stir in the pesto and season with salt and pepper. Top with pumpkin seeds if desired.

Paella con Polenta

One key substitution can turn a beloved classic into a whole new dish. Paella, the golden saffron rice extravaganza from Spain, is loaded with seafood, poultry, sausage, and vegetables. But finely minced prepared polenta gives you the correct golden hue, creaminess without hours of cooking, and a corn flavor that combines naturally with the chorizo, tomatoes, and peppers.

Makes 4 servings

1 package (about 16 ounces) precooked ready-to-serve polenta
1 tablespoon olive oil
2 boneless, skinless chicken breast halves, cut in chunks
8 ounces chorizo sausage, sliced
1 teaspoon chopped garlic, jarred or fresh
1 jar (16 ounces) chunky salsa, any heat level
1 teaspoon Italian seasoning
1 teaspoon ground coriander
1 tablespoon lemon juice, organic bottled or fresh
1 cup olive salad
1 can (about 14 ounces) chicken broth
8 ounces ready-to-cook seafood, thawed if frozen (shrimp, scallops, squid, etc.)
⅔ cup frozen baby peas

Cut the polenta into chunks and finely chop it with a knife or a food processor. Heat the oil in a large skillet. Add the chicken and sausage, and sauté until browned. Add the garlic, salsa, Italian seasoning, coriander, lemon juice, olive salad, and broth. Simmer for 5 minutes. Stir in the seafood and simmer 3 minutes more, until the seafood is barely cooked. Stir in the peas and polenta, and heat through.

Seafood Bolito Misto

Bolito misto contains meats and poultry simmered in a flavorful broth and served with a selection of vinaigrettes and pestos—after a course of the broth with a small pasta. In the tradition of improving on tradition, I've designed this elegant one-course dinner soup with seafood poached in a tomato and herb-infused vegetable broth, ladled over couscous, and swirled with basil pesto.

Makes 4 servings

1 container (32 ounces) vegetable broth
1 jar (12 ounces) tomato bruschetta
1 pound ready-to-cook seafood, thawed if frozen (shrimp, scallops, squid, etc.)
¾ cup (5 ounces) couscous
8 teaspoons basil pesto, jarred or fresh

Heat the broth and bruschetta in a large saucepan. When it is simmering, add the seafood and bring to a boil. Place 3 tablespoons of couscous in each of 4 wide, shallow soup bowls, and ladle 2 cups of the boiling stew into each bowl. Stir to moisten the couscous and let rest for 3 minutes. Stir 2 teaspoons of the pesto into each bowl and serve.

Twelve-Minute Bouillabaisse

The down-to-earth roots of bouillabaisse have been subverted by a gourmet mystique. There is no official recipe for this colloquial fish stew, but for the best results use a combination of seafood and lean and fatty fish.

Makes 4 servings

1 tablespoon olive oil
1 cup diced onions, frozen or fresh
1 teaspoon herbes de Provence
1 tablespoon dried orange peel
2 teaspoons chopped garlic, jarred or fresh
1 cup white wine
1 cup boiling water
1 large (9 grams) seafood bouillon cube
⅔ cup orange juice
1 can (14½ ounces) diced tomatoes with juice
Salt and black pepper to taste
1 pound ready-to-cook seafood, thawed if frozen (shrimp, scallops, squid, fish fillets)

Heat the oil over medium-high heat in a large saucepan. Add the onions and sauté until tender, about 2 minutes. Add the herbes de Provence, orange peel, and garlic, and stir to combine. Add the wine and bring to a boil. Add the boiling water and bouillon cube, and stir until the cube dissolves. Add the orange juice, tomatoes, salt, and pepper, and simmer for 1 minute. Add the seafood and simmer until cooked through, about 3 minutes.

Shrimp Cakes Florentine

These shrimp cakes are so ostentatiously opulent, so chock-full of shrimp, so precisely seasoned and striated with spinach that no one would ever guess they were concocted with just a few ingredients.

Makes 4 servings

1 pound peeled, cleaned, and cooked shrimp, thawed if frozen
1 package (10 ounces) frozen chopped spinach, thawed and squeezed dry
1 package (about 5 ounces) herbed cream cheese, such as Boursin
⅔ cup seasoned bread crumbs
2 tablespoons olive oil
1 lemon, cut in 4 wedges

Chop the shrimp into small pieces (if you use a food processor, be careful not to pulverize the shrimp). Combine with the spinach, herbed cheese, and half of the bread crumbs. Place the remaining bread crumbs on a sheet of foil. Divide the shrimp mixture into 8 balls. Place the shrimp balls, one at a time, in the bread crumbs, flattening and turning several times to coat each cake thoroughly. Heat the oil in a large skillet over medium heat and brown the cakes on both sides until they are golden brown and heated through, about 4 minutes per side. Serve with lemon wedges.

Shrimp Fried in Creamy Polenta Batter

Crispy and fried aren't always synonymous. This silken batter of polenta and Parmesan browns subtly at the edges while remaining fluffy and creamy underneath, like a savory corn pudding scattered with cheese.

Makes 4 entrée servings or 6 appetizer servings

8 ounces prepared polenta
¾ cup milk
1 large or extra-large egg, or ¼ cup liquid egg substitute
¼ cup grated imported Parmesan cheese, plus additional for garnish
Flour or cornstarch for dredging
24 peeled and cleaned jumbo shrimp, thawed if frozen and backs sliced so shrimp open like a book
Vegetable oil or a combination of olive and vegetable oils for frying
2 cups Roasted Pepper Tomato Sauce (page 99) or other marinara sauce

Chop the polenta in a food processor until crumbly. Add the milk, egg, and Parmesan, and process in pulses into a smooth batter. Transfer to a bowl.

Place the flour and shrimp in a plastic bag, close the bag tightly, and shake until the shrimp are coated. Place the coated shrimp in a strainer set over a large bowl and shake the strainer vigorously to remove all excess flour. Place the shrimp in the batter and toss gently. Place the strainer back over the bowl.

Pour 1 inch of oil in a saucepan and heat to 350°F. (At that temperature the end of a wooden spoon dipped into the hot oil will bubble within 5 seconds.) Fry about 6 shrimp at a time in the hot oil until firm and lightly browned. Remove with tongs or a slotted spoon and place in the strainer to drain. Serve 6 shrimp per person in a pool of Roasted Pepper Tomato Sauce and scatter additional Parmesan on top.

Express Checkout Scampi

"Scampi" is Italian for a lobsterlike critter native to the western Atlantic and the Mediterranean. In America the term has come to mean big shrimp prepared with a lot of garlic. There is no such thing as a classic recipe for scampi, so I've created my own with just enough ingredients to get you through the express checkout line in record time.

Makes 4 servings

4 tablespoons (½ stick) butter
1 pound peeled and cleaned shrimp, thawed if frozen
1 tablespoon chopped garlic, jarred or fresh
1 cup white wine
2 tablespoons chopped Italian (flat-leaf) parsley
Cooked rice or pasta

Melt the butter in a large skillet over medium heat. Sauté the shrimp until firm and opaque, about 2 minutes, and transfer to a plate with a slotted spoon. Add the garlic to the pan and sauté for 10 seconds. Add the wine and boil until the sauce thickens slightly. Return the shrimp to the pan along with any liquid on the plate. Add the parsley and heat through. Serve with rice or pasta.

Nacho-Crusted Shrimp and Guacamole

Exactly when nacho started to be a flavor and not just a dish is unclear, but by now it is so deeply entrenched in contemporary food history that a notion as bizarre as nacho pizza seems almost reasonable. Without going to that extreme, I decided to bread some shrimp in ground nacho chips, and believe it or not, they're fabulous.

Makes 4 servings

4 ounces nacho-flavored corn chips
1 pound peeled and cleaned jumbo shrimp, thawed if frozen
¼ cup mayonnaise
1 cup refrigerated guacamole
⅓ cup chunky salsa, any heat level
Oil for frying

Crush the nacho chips to a fine powder in a food processor or with a rolling pin. Place on a sheet of foil. Coat the shrimp with mayonnaise and then with the nacho crumbs. Set on a sheet of foil. Combine the guacamole and salsa, and set aside.

Heat 2 inches of oil in a large deep skillet to 350°F. (At that temperature the end of a wooden spoon dipped into the hot oil will bubble within 5 seconds.) Fry the shrimp until firm and the coating is brown and crispy. Remove from the oil with a slotted spoon and drain for a few seconds. Serve with the guacamole mixture for dipping.

Shrimp and Black Bean Chili

The secret to cooking shrimp is knowing when to stop. Unlike meat chiles that get better with time, seafood chiles are ruined by overcooking. In this quick and easy stew, a flavorful broth is assembled, shrimp are added along with some bean powder for thickening, and within minutes the chili is ready.

Makes 4 servings

1 jar (16 ounces) roasted pepper salsa, medium or hot
1½ teaspoons ground cumin
1½ teaspoons ground coriander
1 bottle (8 ounces) clam juice
1 can (15 ounces) black beans, rinsed and drained
1 pound peeled and cleaned medium or large shrimp, thawed if frozen
¼ cup instant black beans
1 tablespoon lemon or lime juice, organic bottled or fresh
1 tablespoon cilantro pesto or chutney, or 3 tablespoons chopped cilantro
Salt and black pepper to taste

Combine the roasted pepper salsa, cumin, coriander, clam juice, and black beans in a large saucepan and bring to a boil. Add the shrimp and instant black beans, and simmer until the sauce thickens lightly and the shrimp turn opaque, 1 to 2 minutes. Remove from the heat and stir in the juice and cilantro pesto. Adjust the seasoning with salt and pepper, and serve.

Shrimp in Clam Sauce

Clam sauce is so simple and yet so easy to mess up. Combine clams, oil, garlic, and wine in the proper proportions and you get a silken sauce as clean as sea air. But if the recipe is off-balance, it can fail in a dozen ways. Some tricks: (1) Reserve about half of the oil for the end. Cooked oil has a different flavor and consistency. (2) Boil the wine to concentrate the flavor and reduce the volume of liquid. Too much will make the sauce watery. (3) Fresh clams are best, but don't worry about shells. Fresh chopped clams are available at the seafood department of your supermarket.

Makes 4 servings

2 tablespoons extra-virgin olive oil
1 pound peeled and cleaned medium or large shrimp, thawed if frozen
1 cup white wine
1 can (15 ounces) clam sauce
1 container (16 ounces) fresh chopped clams, drained
¼ cup chopped Italian (flat-leaf) parsley
Cooked rice or pasta

Heat half of the oil in a skillet over medium-high heat. Add the shrimp, sauté until firm and opaque, about 2 minutes, and transfer to a plate with a slotted spoon. Add the wine to the skillet and reduce by half. Add the sauce and bring to a boil. Stir in the remaining oil, the clams, and cooked shrimp along with any liquid on the plate. Return to a boil and serve over rice or pasta.

Seared Scallops with Spicy Tomato Butter

Fresh scallops smell and taste sweet and range in color from pearly pink to creamy white. Stark white scallops have been soaked in preservatives; avoid them. Soaked scallops release a lot of water and shrink substantially when they cook.

Makes 4 servings

3 tablespoons butter, softened
1½ tablespoons tomato paste
⅛ teaspoon Chinese chili purée
¼ teaspoon garlic salt
1½ pounds sea scallops .
2 teaspoons extra-virgin olive oil
1 tablespoon lime juice, fresh or organic bottled
1 tablespoon chopped cilantro leaves

Combine the butter, tomato paste, chili purée, and half of the garlic salt. Trim any tough strips attached to the sides of the scallops. Flatten the scallops gently but firmly between your palms to about ½ inch thickness. Rub the scallops with the oil and season with the remaining garlic salt.

Meanwhile, place a large iron skillet over high heat for 5 minutes. Sear the scallops for 1½ minutes per side, until crusty and lightly browned but still soft in the center. Remove to a platter, drizzle with lime juice, and top with the tomato butter. Scatter the cilantro over the top.

Hot and Sour Clams

Hot and sour is nothing more than vinegar and chili peppers. It is very simple—and very potent. Here, hot and sour works its magic on clams. Look for small, clean clams that are tightly closed, and use them within forty-eight hours.

Makes 4 servings

4 dozen cleaned littleneck clams in their shells
½ cup rice wine vinegar
2 tablespoons hot pepper sesame oil
2 teaspoons Chinese chili purée
¾ cup chicken broth
4 scallions, roots trimmed, sliced

Place the clams in a large bowl and fill with very cold water. Swirl the clams around for 1 minute. The water will become cloudy; drain it. Repeat until the water remains clear.

Meanwhile, combine the vinegar, oil, and chili purée. Bring the broth to a boil in a large saucepan. Add the clams, cover, and cook over medium-high heat, shaking the pan periodically, until the clams open, about 4 minutes. If most of the clams are wide open but some are open only slightly, pry them open with a knife. Discard any clams that are still tightly closed. Pour the hot and sour sauce over the clams, sprinkle with scallions, and shake the pan to distribute.

Seared Sesame and Soy Scallops

When you sear scallops, stop cooking them while they are still soft in the center. Residual warmth from the surface will firm the center as they sit. If you leave them on the heat until they are cooked through, they will toughen and dry out.

Makes 4 servings

1 teaspoon Asian toasted sesame oil
1 teaspoon minced ginger, jarred or fresh
1 teaspoon minced garlic, jarred or fresh
Salt and black pepper to taste
1½ pounds sea scallops
1 tablespoon vegetable oil
¼ cup toasted sesame seeds
¼ cup teriyaki sauce
2 tablespoons sesame tahini
1 tablespoon lime juice, organic bottled or fresh

Trim any tough strips attached to the sides of the scallops. Combine the sesame oil, ginger, garlic, salt, and pepper. Toss the scallops in this mixture and set aside for 10 minutes. Heat the vegetable oil in a large skillet until smoking. Lift the scallops from their marinade and cook on both sides in the hot oil until the edges are browned but they are still soft in the center, about 2 minutes per side. Transfer to a serving plate.

Pour off any excess oil, stir in the sesame seeds, any remaining marinade, the teriyaki sauce, and tahini. Stir until the tahini melts. Do not overcook, or the tahini will split. Remove from the heat, stir in the lime juice, and pour over the scallops.

Tex-Mex Mussels

Mussels are highly perishable, so buy them no more than a day ahead. Look for mussels that are shiny and tightly closed. If they are open tap them. If they don't close immediately, they should be discarded. In this recipe mussels steam in a combination of spicy salsa, cumin, and lemon. As the mussels open, their juices create a delicious broth.

Makes 4 servings

4 dozen (about 5 pounds) cleaned mussels in their shells
1 jar (16 ounces) chunky salsa, hot
1 teaspoon ground cumin
1 teaspoon chili powder
1 tablespoon lemon juice, organic bottled or fresh
1 tablespoon chopped cilantro

Place the mussels in a large bowl. Run cold water in the bowl and swirl the mussels around until the water in the bowl is clear. Drain. Discard any opened mussels.

Heat the salsa, cumin, and chili powder to a boil in a large saucepan. Add the mussels and cover. Cook until all the mussels open, about 2 minutes. Stir in the lemon juice and cilantro.

Tea-Smoked Clams and Mussels

The acrid smoke from tea leaves seems culinarily destined for shellfish, and the cleanest, fastest, most trouble-free place to unite them is under a grill cover. Just throw the cleaned shellfish over the hottest fire you can make. Within a few minutes the juices inside the shell start to steam, the shells pop open, and the tender meat absorbs whiffs of smoke and charcoal-grilled flavor.

Makes 4 servings

2 dozen cleaned littleneck clams, in their shells
2 dozen (about 2½ pounds) cleaned mussels, in their shells
¼ pound (1 stick) butter
1 tablespoon lemon or lime juice, organic bottled or fresh
½ cup loose orange-spice tea leaves

Place the clams and mussels in a large bowl and fill with very cold water. Swirl the shellfish around for 1 minute. The water will become cloudy; drain. Repeat with more water and more swirling until the water remains clear. Discard any clams and mussels that aren't tightly closed. Place them in separate bowls. Heat a covered grill and set a rack about 3 inches from the fire.

While the coals are heating, melt the butter over medium heat and simmer until it browns slightly. Add the lemon juice and keep the mixture warm.

Steep the tea leaves in about 1 cup of boiling water for 10 minutes. Drain the leaves and place them on a sheet of heavy-duty foil. Place in the center of the rack on the grill. Cover the grill until the tea leaves start to smoke, about 5 minutes. Open the grill cover and scatter the clams directly on the grill grate around the smoking tea. Cover again and cook for 1 minute. Add the mussels and cook 3 minutes more, until all are open. Remove the shellfish with tongs and serve with the brown butter for dipping.

Salmon Smoked with Rice and Corn

One advantage of cooking fish in a smoker bag is that the closed environment prevents the fish from drying out. This recipe has the added benefit of infusing rice with the juices of the salmon, as the fish absorbs smoky fumes and a spicy sweet glaze of mustard and brown sugar. If you can't find Chinese chicken broth, substitute any chicken broth enhanced with 1 teaspoon of minced gingerroot and ¼ teaspoon of minced garlic, both either freshly chopped or from a jar.

Makes 4 servings

1 cup long-grain rice
2 cups Chinese chicken broth, such as Annie Chun's Ginger Chicken Broth (see headnote)
1 cup corn kernels, frozen or canned
1 tablespoon spicy mustard
½ teaspoon minced garlic, jarred or fresh
2 tablespoons dark brown sugar
1½ pounds salmon fillet, skinned
2 scallions, finely sliced

You will need one Savu Orginal Food smoker bag, medium smoke (page 33). Preheat the oven to 475°F. Combine the rice, broth, and corn in a 7 × 11-inch baking dish. Combine the mustard, garlic, and sugar. Place the salmon fillet on the rice and brush the salmon with the mustard mixture.

Place the smoker bag on a sheet pan. Slip the casserole into the bag and seal the open end. Bake for 40 minutes. Remove from the oven and let rest for 10 minutes. Remove the casserole from the bag, lift the fish from the rice with a spatula, stir the sliced scallions into the rice, and serve.

Poached Salmon with Sake Beurre Blanc

Besides the requisite flaky fish fillet, poaching salmon produces a far more important culinary perk: fish broth, the base for a myriad of sauces. In this recipe it is turned into a simple and surprising butter sauce—simple because the technique is quick and uses a single pan, and surprising because the fish is poached in sake and the sauce is derived from it.

Makes 4 servings

1½ pounds salmon fillet
Salt and black pepper to taste
1 tablespoon chopped garlic, jarred or
    fresh
1 tablespoon chopped ginger, jarred or
    fresh
1 cup sake or white wine
2 tablespoons lime juice, organic bottled
    or fresh
1 tablespoon dry chives
4 tablespoons (½ stick) unsalted butter

Season the salmon with salt and pepper, and set aside. Combine the garlic, ginger, and sake in a medium nonstick skillet and bring to a simmer. Add the salmon, skin side down, cover, and simmer about 10 minutes, until the fish flakes to gentle pressure.

Use a slotted spatula to transfer the salmon to a warm platter. Add the lime juice to the liquid in the skillet and boil over high heat until it is bubbling vigorously and it measures ½ cup. Add the chives and turn the heat to low. Whisk in the butter, a tablespoon at a time, until slightly thickened. Pour over the salmon and serve.

Grilled Salmon with Olive Vinaigrette

Olive salad is the basis for this chunky Mediterranean sauce. It is spooned, unheated, over grilled salmon, but it is also delicious on grilled chicken breasts, sautéed shrimp, and broiled pork chops.

Makes 4 servings

Nonstick oil spray
2 teaspoons tomato paste
⅓ cup olive salad
¼ cup extra-virgin olive oil
2 tablespoons red wine vinegar
1½ pounds salmon fillet
Salt and black pepper to taste

Preheat the grill and coat the grate with oil spray. Set the grate 3 to 4 inches from the flame. Combine the tomato paste, olive salad, olive oil, and vinegar. Season the salmon with salt and pepper, and grill until browned and the flesh flakes to gentle pressure, about 6 minutes per side. Divide the salmon into 4 portions and serve each portion with sauce.

Salmon Stuffed with Smoked Salmon Mashed Potatoes

This recipe is delicious on so many levels, I don't know where to start. There are the mashed potatoes, a near perfect food that is brought closer to gastro nirvana by the addition of smoked salmon, dill, and roasted garlic. The potatoes are wrapped with a slice of salmon and roasted until they have a thin crust. Cut into the fish, and you'll encounter three distinct layers: flinty skin; soft, moist flesh; and a molten core of creamy, salty, smoky, dilly, garlicky potatoes that ooze like mousse and act like a sauce.

Makes 4 servings

1 tablespoon olive oil
¼ cup chopped onion, frozen or fresh
1⅓ cups refrigerated, prepared mashed
   potatoes
1 ounce smoked salmon, finely chopped
¼ teaspoon dried dill weed
⅛ teaspoon minced roasted garlic, jarred
   or fresh
Black pepper to taste
2 salmon fillets, each about 8 ounces,
   skin removed

Preheat the oven to 450°F. Heat 1 teaspoon of the oil in a small skillet or saucepan. Add the onion and sauté until soft but not brown. Mix with the mashed potatoes, smoked salmon, dill, garlic, and pepper. Slice each salmon fillet in half horizontally. Place the salmon pieces on a clean surface, darker side up, and mound a quarter of the potato mixture at one end of each piece. Roll the fillet around the potatoes and secure the end with a toothpick. Coat each roll with some of the remaining oil.

Place the fish rolls on a rack set on a sheet pan and roast in the oven for 15 minutes. The salmon will have a crusty brown surface and will flake to gentle pressure. Remove from the oven, remove the toothpicks, and serve.

Southwest Blackened Salmon with Escabeche

Blackening creates a spicy, bitter crust on the surface of salmon that contrasts nicely with its soft, sweet meat. This recipe adds a third contrast: An escabeche, or pickled sauce, is spooned over the finished fish. Simply constructed from a jar of green salsa and some sweet vinegar, the tartness of the sauce heightens the flavor of the fish.

Makes 4 servings

2½ tablespoons Southwest seasoning
½ teaspoon kosher salt
Four 1-inch-thick salmon fillets (about 6 ounces each)
Nonstick oil spray
⅔ cup salsa verde
¼ cup apple cider vinegar

Place a large iron skillet over high heat for 5 minutes. While the pan is heating, combine the seasoning and salt, and rub 2 teaspoons of the mixture into each piece of salmon.

Liberally coat the skillet with oil spray and carefully place the fish in the skillet. Cook until the salmon is blackened and crusty on both sides, about 3 to 4 minutes per side. While the fish is cooking, combine the salsa verde and vinegar. Remove the salmon from the pan, top each piece of fish with some of the salsa mixture, and serve.

Caribbean Salmon Couscous

Couscous is tiny pasta. The most commonly available type is so small that it can be cooked through by just soaking it in boiling water. This recipe uses a larger couscous that is toasted and then boiled briefly with browned slices of salmon, until it becomes an upscale, spicy salmon and couscous hash.

Makes 4 servings

1 pound salmon fillet, skin removed, cut in ½-inch-thick slices
1 tablespoon Jamaican jerk seasoning
1 tablespoon vegetable oil
⅔ cup chopped onion, frozen or fresh
1½ cups (6 ounces) Israeli couscous
1 can (about 14 ounces) chicken broth
1 tablespoon Jamaican jerk sauce

Season the salmon slices with the jerk seasoning. Heat the oil in a large skillet over medium heat, add the onion, and sauté until soft. Add the salmon slices and cook on each side until the fish loses its raw look, about 30 seconds per side. Add the couscous and stir gently until lightly toasted, about 1 minute. As you stir, the salmon pieces will begin to break; that's fine. Add the broth, stir once, cover, and simmer for 10 to 12 minutes, until the couscous is tender and the broth is mostly absorbed. Stir in the jerk sauce and serve.

Mexican Monkfish

The elaborate flavor and appearance of this stew belies its simplicity. It uses red tomato salsa as the base for the broth and green tomatillo salsa as a finish. Monkfish is a very firm white-flesh fish, but if you wish, any firm seafood can take its place. Shrimp, scallops, salmon, catfish, or cod would all work well.

Makes 4 servings

1½ pounds monkfish fillet, cut in 8
   chunks
3 tablespoons lemon juice
Salt and black pepper to taste
½ teaspoon minced garlic, jarred or fresh
1 jar (16 ounces) salsa, medium hot
1 cup water
1 large (9 grams) seafood bouillon cube
2 tablespoons extra-virgin olive oil
1 cup salsa verde, any heat level
1 avocado, peeled and diced (optional)

Season the fish with the lemon juice, salt, pepper, and garlic. In a large saucepan combine the salsa and water, and bring to a boil. Stir in the bouillon until dissolved and stir in the oil. Add the monkfish and its juices, and simmer for 10 minutes, until the fish is firm and opaque. Just before serving, swirl the salsa verde into the stew, but do not mix too thoroughly. The green of the tomatillo mixture and the red of the sauce should form a marble pattern. Garnish with diced avocado if desired.

Escabeche of Sole

Escabeche is a Spanish preparation in which fish is seared and then marinated in citrus juice until it is opaque and firm. This recipe is served warm, but it is equally good cold.

Makes 4 servings

1½ pounds sole or flounder fillet
Salt and black pepper to taste
Baker's Joy No Stick Spray with Flour
3 tablespoons extra-virgin olive oil
½ cup chopped onion, frozen or fresh
2 tablespoons minced garlic, jarred or
   fresh
2 tablespoons chili powder
1 cup orange juice
¼ cup lemon juice, organic bottled or
   fresh
¼ cup lime juice, organic bottled or fresh
2 teaspoons cilantro pesto or chutney, or
   2 tablespoons chopped fresh cilantro

Season the fish with salt and pepper and coat with flour spray. Heat a large skillet. Brown the fish on both sides and transfer to a platter. Do not cook the fish through. Add the oil to the pan and sauté the onion until it starts to brown. Add the garlic, chili powder, and orange, lemon, and lime juices. Heat until simmering and stir in the cilantro. Return the fish to the pan and cover. Turn off the heat and let rest for 5 to 10 minutes, until the fish flakes when gently pressed. Serve the fish with the sauce.

Flounder in Orange-Tomato Marinara

The very name "marinara" leads us toward the origins of this fresh, light tomato sauce, originally intended for cooking seafood. This recipe also has its origins in the sea. A fish is sautéed and a citrus-scented tomato sauce is quickly assembled in the same pan.

Makes 4 servings

4 flounder fillets, about 1½ pounds total
½ teaspoon Old Bay seasoning
2 tablespoons olive oil
4 ounces sliced crimini mushrooms
1 teaspoon minced garlic, jarred or fresh
1 teaspoon dried or freshly grated orange peel
½ cup orange juice
1½ cups chunky marinara sauce

Sprinkle the fish fillets with the seasoning. Heat the oil in a large skillet over medium-high heat and sauté the flounder on both sides until well browned, about 3 minutes per side. Transfer to a platter and keep warm. Sauté the mushrooms over medium heat in the remaining oil until lightly browned. Add the garlic, orange peel, orange juice, and marinara sauce. Heat until simmering and spoon over the fish.

Parmesan Flounder with Caesar Sauce

Caesar came, it sauced, it conquered. Once a salad dressing so refined that we believed it could be made only by tuxedoed waiters, Caesar has been bottled into ubiquity. Here its flavors have been deconstructed and reformed. The fish is breaded with crushed Caesar croutons, and sauced with Caesar dressing.

Makes 4 servings

½ cup Caesar croutons, crushed
2 tablespoons grated imported Parmesan cheese
1 teaspoon garlic powder
¼ cup mayonnaise
¼ cup Caesar salad dressing
4 flounder fillets, about 1½ pounds
1 tablespoon olive oil
2 tablespoons lemon juice, organic bottled or fresh

Mix the crushed croutons, Parmesan, and garlic powder on a sheet of foil. Combine the mayonnaise and 1 tablespoon of the salad dressing. Brush the fish fillets with the dressing mixture and coat thoroughly with the Parmesan crumbs.

Heat the oil in a large skillet. Sauté the fillets, without crowding, until they are browned on both sides and cooked through. While the fish is cooking, combine the remaining salad dressing and the lemon juice. Top each fish fillet with about 1 tablespoon of sauce.

Wok-Seared Tuna on Thai Noodles

Sushi-grade tuna is pale rose in color and evenly grained with a clean, fresh aroma. It is available in good fish stores or in supermarkets with a significant Japanese clientele. In this recipe the tuna is simply spiced and seared, and is served still raw at the center on a mound of noodles, drizzled with peanut sauce. You will find noodle salads at your market prepackaged in the refrigerator case or freshly made in the salad bar.

Makes 4 servings

*1 tuna steak, preferably sushi-grade,
    about 1½ pounds and 1 inch thick*
1 teaspoon Szechwan seasoning
Baker's Joy No Stick Spray with Flour
½ cup Thai peanut sauce
2 tablespoons rice vinegar
1 teaspoon vegetable oil
1 pound Asian noodle salad
2 scallions, thinly sliced

Season the tuna with the Szechwan seasoning, coat on both sides with flour spray, and set aside. Combine the peanut sauce and vinegar, and set aside. Place a large wok or iron skillet over high heat until very hot. Pour the oil into the hot pan and place the tuna steak in the smoking oil. Be careful of splattering. When one side of the tuna is browned, about 2 minutes, turn and cook the same way on the other side. When the tuna is done, it will have a crisp surface but will still be rare in the center.

While the tuna is browning, warm the noodle salad in a microwave at full power for 90 seconds. Mound it on a serving platter. When the tuna is cooked, slice it against the grain in ¼-inch-thick slices and arrange the slices on top of the noodles. Drizzle the peanut sauce over the top and scatter with sliced scallions.

Tuna Seared in a Wasabi Crust

Wasabi and tuna are so closely tied to Japanese cooking that the appearance of one immediately triggers an expectation of the other. When I wanted to create a crusty seared tuna steak, wasabi seemed the natural flavor choice, and crushed wasabi peas, the snack food of freeze-dried sweet green peas, proved to be the perfect breading: crunchy, wasabi-hot, and vegetable sweet.

Makes 4 servings

½ cup wasabi peas
One 1½-pound tuna steak, trimmed of dark flesh and cut in 4 equal slices
4 teaspoons mayonnaise
Nonstick oil spray
¼ cup ponzu sauce
¼ cup sake

Grind the wasabi peas in a food processor into a fine meal and pour onto a sheet of foil. Brush the tuna pieces with the mayonnaise and dredge in the ground wasabi peas until they are thoroughly coated.

Place an iron skillet over high heat for 5 minutes and coat with oil spray. Brown the tuna pieces on both sides for 2 to 4 minutes per side, depending on the thickness of the tuna and how you like your fish cooked. While the tuna is cooking, combine the ponzu sauce and sake. Serve each portion of tuna with sauce for dipping or slice and fan the slices and drizzle with the sauce.

Maki Tuna Burgers

Tuna burgers are available freshly made at many fish markets, supermarket fish counters, and specialty food stores. The burgers are grilled and glazed with a Japanese barbecue sauce called roasted eel sauce. Relax; there's no eel in it. It's just the tangy, sweet sauce used to glaze the eel that goes into sushi. The burgers are served on—what else?—rice cakes.

Makes 4 servings

4 tuna burgers, about 4 ounces each
Nonstick oil spray
2 tablespoons roasted eel sauce or teriyaki sauce
4 teaspoons prepared wasabi sauce in a tube
1 sheet toasted Nori seaweed, cut in four 2-inch-wide strips
4 rice cakes, salted or unsalted
2 tablespoons pickled ginger for garnish

Preheat a broiler. Coat the burgers and broiler rack with oil spray. Broil the burgers 2 inches from the fire until browned on both sides and still slightly soft in the center, about 2 minutes per side. Brush each side of the burger with eel sauce after it is cooked. To serve, spread ½ teaspoon of the wasabi sauce on each burger and wrap a strip of seaweed around each burger. Spread another ½ teaspoon of wasabi sauce on each rice cake. Top each with a burger and garnish with portions of pickled ginger.

Bluefish Baked with Lemon and Mustard

Bluefish is meaty and rich, and has a creamy flesh that flakes into soft curds when cooked. But its flavor is strong, so it needs assertive ingredients to tame it. A glaze of mustard and lemon juice will meet the bluefish head-on, and the resulting flavor is balanced and robust. If you don't like bluefish, substitute another dark-meated fish such as swordfish, salmon, or mackerel.

Makes 4 servings

1½ pounds bluefish fillets
2 teaspoons olive oil
Salt and black pepper to taste
2 tablespoons honey mustard
1 tablespoon lemon juice, organic bottled or fresh

Preheat the oven to 400°F. Rub the fish with the oil and place, skin side down, in a single layer in a large baking dish. Season with salt and pepper. Bake for 10 minutes. While the fish is baking, combine the mustard and lemon juice. Brush the fish with the mixture and bake 5 to 8 minutes more, until the fish flakes when gently pressed.

Caramelized Catfish

Catfish is the poster child for aquaculture. Not long ago, catfish were ugly, bottom-feeding scavengers. Now they are mainstream. Even though their flavor is mild, they go very well with sweet, spicy glazes. This one is made from concentrated apple juice, available frozen or pourable. Pourable is much more convenient.

Makes 4 servings

1 container (11½ ounces) apple juice concentrate
1 tablespoon spicy brown mustard
¼ teaspoon cayenne pepper
4 catfish fillets, 5 to 6 ounces each (about 1½ pounds total)
Salt and black pepper to taste
Nonstick oil spray
1 teaspoon apple cider vinegar

Combine the apple juice concentrate, mustard, and cayenne pepper in a bowl. Season the fish with salt and pepper and dip in the apple-juice mixture. Heat a nonstick skillet and coat it with oil spray. Remove the fish fillets from the glaze and sauté in the hot skillet until the fish is browned on both sides and flakes when gently pressed, about 4 minutes per side, basting with glaze several times during cooking. Transfer to a platter and sprinkle with the vinegar.

Catfish Corn Burgoo

A burgoo is a southern country stew; it is usually made with a variety of game meats, beans, and a tangy tomato sauce. This one starts by breading catfish in graham cracker crumbs. Not your usual breading, but the crackers become a rich, caramelized crust.

Makes 4 servings

½ cup graham cracker crumbs
Pinch of cayenne pepper
½ teaspoon salt
4 catfish fillets, 6 ounces each (about 1½ pounds total)
2 tablespoons vegetable oil
1 jar (16 ounces) chipotle salsa
3 slices ready-to-serve bacon, finely chopped
½ cup chicken broth
½ box (5 ounces) frozen succotash
½ teaspoon cider vinegar

Combine the graham cracker crumbs, cayenne pepper, and salt on a sheet of foil. Coat the fish with the crumbs. Heat the oil in a large skillet and brown the fish on both sides. Spoon off any excess oil. Add the salsa, bacon, and broth, and simmer until the fish flakes when gently pressed, about 3 minutes. Remove the fish with a slotted spatula and place on a platter. Add the succotash and vinegar to the pan and simmer until the succotash is cooked through, about 4 minutes. Adjust the salt and pepper, and pour the sauce over the fish.

Fish Steaks with Sesame Rouille

Baking fish in a pouch of foil cooks a delicate ingredient without scorching it or drying it out. Although the cooking is done in the oven, it's really steamed, because the liquids in the fish bubble in the pouch, creating a closed package of steam. The fish is served with rouille, flavored with sesame paste.

Makes 4 servings

Nonstick olive oil spray
4 fish steaks (such as halibut, salmon, or cod), 5 to 6 ounces each (about 1½ pounds total)
1 teaspoon lemon pepper
¼ cup roasted red pepper spread
½ teaspoon minced roasted garlic, jarred or fresh
2 tablespoons tahini (sesame paste)

Preheat the oven to 450°F. Coat a large sheet of heavy-duty foil with oil spray. Place the fish in the center of the foil in a single layer and sprinkle with lemon pepper. Fold the foil over the fish and seal tightly by crimping the edges. Bake on a baking pan for 15 to 20 minutes, until you hear juices bubbling inside the foil.

While the fillets bake, combine the roasted red pepper spread, garlic, and tahini. When the fish is done, slit open the foil and fold back to expose the fish. Spoon the rouille on the fish and serve.

Pesto Fish Stew

This basic stew of fish and potatoes, swirled with herbs and enough garlic to perk one's interest, is so straightforward in its construction, so homespun and simple, that it makes one regret dinner ever has to end. Serve it with crusty black bread.

Makes 4 servings

1 tablespoon olive oil
½ cup chopped onion, frozen or fresh
1 teaspoon chopped garlic, jarred or fresh
½ cup white wine
2 cups water
1 large (9 grams) seafood bouillon cube
½ package (9 ounces) refrigerated diced or sliced potatoes
6 tablespoons pesto, jarred or fresh
1½ pounds fish fillets (salmon, cod, or other mild fish), skinned and cut into 1-inch pieces

Heat the oil in a large, heavy saucepan and sauté the onion until it begins to soften. Add the garlic and cook for 10 seconds. Add the wine and boil for 1 minute. Add the water and return to a boil. Add the bouillon and stir until dissolved. Add the potatoes, cover the pan, and simmer for 5 to 8 minutes, until the potatoes are tender. Stir in the pesto and fish, and simmer until the fish is cooked through, about 3 minutes.

Fish in Green Curry

This simple stew sparks from the pairing of fragrant, spicy green curry and the exotic sweetness of coconut milk. Do not use light coconut milk, it is too watery and will not emulsify the sauce properly.

Makes 4 servings

1½ pounds fish fillets (salmon, flounder, or other mild fish)
Salt and black pepper to taste
1 tablespoon olive oil
1 teaspoon chopped garlic, jarred or fresh
1 package (18 ounces) refrigerated diced or sliced potatoes
1 can (about 14 ounces) chicken broth
2 teaspoons Thai green curry paste
1 cup regular coconut milk
1 teaspoon cilantro pesto or chutney, or 1 tablespoon chopped cilantro

Season the fish fillets with salt and pepper. Heat the oil in a large skillet and brown the fish on both sides. Transfer to a platter. Add the garlic, potatoes, and broth to the skillet, and simmer until the potatoes are tender, about 5 minutes.

Return the fish to the pan and simmer until it flakes when gently pressed, about 3 minutes. Transfer the fish and potatoes to a warm platter. Over high heat, reduce the liquid in the pan by about half. Stir in the curry and coconut milk and simmer until slightly thickened. Stir in the cilantro and pour over the fish and potatoes.

Fried Fish in Chickpea Batter with Citrus Dressing

This batter-fried fish is a bit more complex than those in the other fish recipes in this chapter. But the combination of moist fish morsels in a skin of crispy chickpeas and sesame drizzled with a cilantro-tinged citrus garlic dressing is absolutely spectacular. The batter is made from falafel mix, a seasoned dehydrated chickpea powder that is usually found next to the dried and canned beans in the supermarket.

Makes 4 servings

DRESSING:
3 tablespoons olive oil
3 tablespoons orange juice
1 tablespoon lemon or lime juice,
*   organic bottled or fresh*
¼ teaspoon minced garlic, jarred or fresh
1 teaspoon cilantro chutney or pesto, or
*   1 tablespoon chopped cilantro*

FISH:
¾ cup falafel mix
1 large or extra-large egg
¾ cup buttermilk
1 tablespoon olive oil
Oil for frying
1 pound fish fillets (salmon, flounder, or
*   other mild fish)*
Salt and black pepper to taste

Whisk together all the dressing ingredients. Make the batter for the fish breading by combining the falafel mix, egg, buttermilk, and olive oil. Set up a strainer in a bowl or pan. Heat 1 inch of oil in a deep skillet or large saucepan. Trim the fish so that the pieces are no more than ½ inch thick. Pat them dry and season with salt and pepper.

Test the oil temperature by dropping a small bit of batter in the oil. It should brown within 30 seconds. When the oil is hot, dip the fish, a piece at a time, in the batter and slip the fish into the hot oil. Do not crowd the pan. As each piece browns and crisps, remove it with a slotted spoon and place it in the strainer to drain.

Place the drained fish pieces on serving plates. Whisk the dressing so that it comes together and drizzle it over the fish. Serve the remaining dressing on the side.

Fish Stick Fajitas

This one's for the kids—and for me, too, I confess. I love fish sticks. It is a passion that started before I knew what passion was, and it has never waned. I love their crunch. I love their bland flaky fishiness. I love the crispy fried skin. Here they are used to make fajitas, a variation on the fish tacos that have become so popular in southern California.

Makes 2 servings

1 small package (6.2 ounces) frozen fish sticks (11 fish sticks)
½ cup ranch dressing
2 teaspoons lime juice, organic bottled or fresh
1 tablespoon mild hot pepper sauce
Four 8-inch flour tortillas
1 cup shredded lettuce
½ cup diced tomato

Preheat the oven to 375°F. Bake the fish sticks in a single layer on a sheet pan for 12 to 15 minutes. While the fish sticks are baking, combine the ranch dressing, lime juice, and hot pepper sauce, and wrap the tortillas in a tea towel. When the fish sticks are done, microwave the tortillas at full power for 30 seconds. To assemble a fajita, place 2 or 3 fish sticks on a tortilla. Top with about 2 tablespoons of sauce, about ¼ cup of lettuce, and about 2 tablespoons of diced tomato. Fold up each tortilla and serve.

Tuna Enchiladas Verde

These throw-together enchiladas are the perfect quick family dinner. Almost all the ingredients can be pulled from your pantry.

Makes 4 servings

2 cans (about 6 ounces each) tuna in water, drained and flaked
1 teaspoon chopped garlic, jarred or fresh
¼ teaspoon dried marjoram
1 jar (12 ounces) corn and black bean salsa
1 can (10 ounces) green enchilada sauce
1 cup sour cream
8 corn tortillas
8 ounces (2 cups) shredded Monterey Jack cheese

Preheat the oven to 375°F. Combine the tuna, garlic, marjoram, and salsa. Combine the enchilada sauce and sour cream. Add ½ cup to the tuna mixture and pour the rest into a pie plate. Warm the tortillas in a microwave at full power for 30 seconds. Dip the tortillas in the enchilada sauce. Top each tortilla with ⅓ cup of the tuna mixture and 2 tablespoons of cheese, roll it up, and place seam-side down in a 7 × 11-inch baking dish. Cover with the remaining sauce and top with the remaining cheese. Bake for 25 minutes, until the cheese is melted and the sauce is bubbling.

CHAPTER 7

COMPLETELY MEATLESS

Roasted "Chicken" and Sweet Potatoes
Sopa de Tortilla
Black Bean Burritos
Roasted Vegetable Chili
Mystery Quiche
Black-Bottom Tarte Niçoise
Russian Cabbage Pie
Meatless Lovers' Pizza
Pissaladière Pie
Pizza Rustica
Feta Artichoke Pizza
Roasted Caponata
Roasted Vegetable Mole
Couscous with Artichoke, Feta, and Walnuts
Asian Roasted Vegetables
Peppers Stuffed with Spinach and Polenta
Aztec Pie
Eggplant Marseilles
Veggie "Moussaka"
Lemon Chickpea Stew
Curried Potatoes, Spinach, and Chickpeas

Baked Tofu Teriyaki with Ginger Slaw
Cannellini Orzo Pilaf
Sweet Ricotta Bread Pudding with Warm Vanilla Pear Sauce
White and Black Bean Salad
Spaghetti Squash Primavera
Vegetable Pakoras
Fettuccine with Tofu Vodka "Cream" Sauce
Udon Noodles with Peanut Sauce
Eggplant and Soba
Vegetables with Thai Fried Noodles
White Bean Tabbouleh
Warm Rice, Pepper, and Lentil Salad
Polenta and Rabe
Garlic Potato Cakes with Horseradish Sour Cream
Veggie Burger Falafel
Eggplant Falafel
Antipasto Pita Pocket
Slavic Egg Salad
Artichoke Edamame Frittata
Olive, Potato, and Sun-Dried Tomato Frittata

Roasted "Chicken" and Sweet Potatoes

Vegetarian entrées either look, taste, and act like vegetables or they look, taste, and act like meat. This recipe is in the latter category. Imitation chicken and sweet potato fries are roasted until sticky with caramelized juices. I use frozen sweet potato fries for their ease, but if you can't find them (I have had trouble), cut fresh sweet potatoes into thin strips, and they'll cook in the same amount of time.

Makes 4 servings

Nonstick olive oil spray
2 medium onions, peeled and cut in
    wedges
1 box (10 ounces) frozen imitation
    grilled chicken, cut in ½-inch-wide
    strips
1 bag (20 ounces) frozen sweet potato
    fries
1 tablespoon chopped roasted garlic,
    jarred or fresh
1 tablespoon extra-virgin olive oil
2 tablespoons honey
¼ teaspoon dried crushed rosemary
1 to 2 teaspoons hot pepper sauce
Salt and black pepper to taste

Preheat the oven to 450°F. Coat a sheet pan with olive oil spray and scatter the onions, "chicken," and sweet potatoes on the pan in a single layer. Roast for 20 minutes, until the vegetables are browned and crisp on the edges. Meanwhile, whisk together the garlic, oil, honey, rosemary, hot pepper sauce, salt, and pepper. Toss the roasted ingredients with the sauce.

Sopa de Tortilla

This soupy Mexican-style stew combines vibrant flavors, bold colors, and contrasting textures into a hearty vegan main dish that could also be the festive centerpiece of a casual dinner party. Its main protein is seitan, which comes ready for seasoning and a quick turn on the grill.

Makes 4 servings

1 package (8 ounces) seitan
¼ teaspoon Southwest seasoning
Nonstick olive oil spray
1 jar (12 ounces) corn and black bean
    salsa
1 container (32 ounces) vegetable broth
1 teaspoon ground cumin
2 teaspoons cilantro pesto or chutney, or
    2 tablespoons chopped cilantro
¼ cup tabbouleh
48 tortilla chips

Preheat the grill. Sprinkle the seitan with the seasoning and coat with oil spray. Grill until the seitan is marked on both sides, about 2 minutes per side. Cut into 1-inch pieces. Combine the salsa, broth, and cumin in a saucepan, bring to a boil, and stir in the cilantro. Place 1 tablespoon of the tabbouleh in each of 4 shallow soup bowls. Ladle 1¼ cups of broth in each bowl and stir to soften the tabbouleh. Divide the seitan among the bowls. Arrange 12 chips around each bowl.

Black Bean Burritos

Prepackaged burritos abound, but they never taste very good. The refrigerated ones get cardboardlike and cracked, and frozen burritos are too often furred with ice. But with bean spread, fresh tortillas, salsa, cheese, and cilantro readily available, you can make your own fresh burritos anytime the urge hits.

Makes 4 servings

1 box (7 ounces) instant black beans
  (page 25)
1¾ cups boiling water
Nonstick oil spray
4 teaspoons cilantro pesto or chutney, or
  about 3 tablespoons chopped fresh
  cilantro
8 flour tortillas for burritos
½ cup salsa, any heat level
1 cup (4 ounces) shredded Monterey Jack
  or mild cheddar cheese

Combine the instant black beans and boiling water, and set aside for 10 minutes to thicken. Preheat the oven to 375°F and coat a 9 × 13-inch baking dish with oil spray.

Spread ½ teaspoon of the cilantro pesto or sprinkle about 1 teaspoon of chopped cilantro on each tortilla. Top with ¼ cup of the black beans and 1 tablespoon of the salsa. Roll up the tortillas, folding in the ends to enclose the filling completely. Place them side by side, seam side down, in the dish. Sprinkle with the cheese and bake for 10 minutes, until the filling is steaming and the cheese has melted.

Roasted Vegetable Chili

Somewhere in your supermarket sits a pile of roasted fresh vegetables. They might be in the refrigerated, prepared-foods case in the deli, or they are part of a party tray. But you aren't going to use them for either of those things. You're going to make chili, and it's going to take you about five minutes.

Makes 4 servings

2 cups V8 vegetable juice
1 tablespoon extra-virgin olive oil
1 tablespoon ground cumin
2 teaspoons chili powder
1 pound roasted vegetables, store-
  bought or homemade
1 can (about 15 ounces) white cannellini
  beans, rinsed and drained
Salt and black pepper to taste
2 tablespoons instant refried beans or
  black beans (page 25)

Combine the V8 juice, oil, cumin, and chili powder in a large saucepan and bring to a boil. Add the roasted vegetables, cannellini beans, salt, and pepper, and simmer for 3 minutes. Add the instant refried beans and stir until the broth thickens, about 1 minute more.

Mystery Quiche

This vegetable quiche is utterly delicious and completely unidentifiable. No one knows what's in it, and no one cares. Don't let the ingredient list deter you. Most of it gets mixed up in a bowl and then goes directly into a premade refrigerated pastry shell on its way to the oven.

Makes 6 servings

4 large or extra-large eggs, or 1 cup liquid egg substitute
½ cup milk, any fat content
Salt and black pepper to taste
2 tablespoons spicy brown mustard or Dijon mustard
Nonstick olive oil spray
1 cup chopped onions, frozen or fresh
1 teaspoon chopped garlic, jarred or fresh
2 tablespoons jarred sun-dried tomato pesto
6 ounces (about 1 cup) cauliflower florets, fresh or frozen
1 round refrigerated 9-inch piecrust (see Note)
½ cup grated imported Parmesan cheese
⅓ cup shredded mozzarella cheese

Preheat the oven to 375°F. Beat the eggs until blended and mix in the milk, salt, pepper, and mustard. Coat the skillet with oil spray, add the onions, and sauté until soft. Stir in the garlic, remove from the heat, and stir in the sun-dried tomato.

Boil the cauliflower until tender, about 5 minutes, or microwave with a tablespoon of water in a covered dish at full power until tender, about 4 minutes. Drain and crumble or thoroughly chop the cooked cauliflower. Toss the cauliflower with the onion mixture.

Unfold the piecrust and fit it into a 9-inch pie plate. Turn under the edges and crimp if desired. Sprinkle half of the Parmesan over the bottom of the pie and spread the cauliflower in an even layer. Top with the remaining Parmesan and mozzarella, and pour the egg-milk mixture over the top. Bake for 35 minutes, until the top is browned and the filling is set. (The center should still be a bit wobbly.)

NOTE: The package contains two pastry shells, so as long as you're baking one, you might want to double the filling ingredients and bake two. The second quiche will freeze well.

Black-Bottom Tarte Niçoise

The aromas of the south of France bloom in this easy quiche, which starts with a veneer of black olive tapenade topped with wedges of breaded eggplant, chunky tomato bruschetta, and lots of mozzarella—all layered in a Parmesan custard. If your market doesn't carry frozen breaded eggplant, ask about it. Trader Joe's carries a very good and very inexpensive brand.

Makes 6 servings

4 large or extra-large eggs, or 1 cup liq-
    uid egg substitute
½ cup milk, any fat content
½ teaspoon salt
¼ teaspoon pepper
½ cup grated imported Parmesan cheese
1 round refrigerated 9-inch piecrust (see
    Note)
2 tablespoons tapenade (black olive
    spread)
1 cup shredded mozzarella cheese
3 slices frozen breaded eggplant cutlets,
    cut in quarters
¾ cup (half of a 12-ounce jar) bruschetta

Preheat the oven to 375°F. Beat the eggs until blended and mix in the milk, salt, pepper, and Parmesan. Unfold the piecrust and fit it into a 9-inch pie plate, turning under the edges and crimping if desired.

Spread the tapenade on the crust, sprinkle with the mozzarella, and arrange the eggplant over the cheese.

Spread with the bruschetta and pour the milk-egg mixture over the top. Bake for 35 minutes, until the top is browned and the filling is set. (The center should still be a bit wobbly.)

NOTE: The package contains two pastry shells, so as long as you're baking one, you might want to double the filling ingredients and bake two. The second one will freeze well.

Russian Cabbage Pie

This Slavic-style pie is loaded with all the ingredients its heritage suggests. It's quite hearty.

Makes 6 servings

Nonstick oil spray
½ cup onion, frozen or fresh
8 ounces sliced mushrooms
Salt and black pepper to taste
1 package (2 rounds) refrigerated 9-inch
*   piecrust*
4 ounces softened cream cheese
3 hard-cooked eggs, sliced
1 jar (16 ounces) pickled red cabbage,
*   drained*
1 can (14 ounces) sliced new potatoes,
*   drained*

Preheat the oven to 400°F. Heat a large skillet and coat with oil spray. Add the onion and mushrooms, and sauté until lightly browned. Season with salt and pepper.

Fit a piecrust into a 9-inch pie plate, allowing the edges to hang over the rim. Dot the bottom with the cream cheese. Top with layers of egg slices, drained red cabbage, sliced potatoes, and sautéed onions and mushrooms.

Drape the second piecrust over the top, and crimp the edges of the top and bottom crusts together Cut a few slits in the top for steam to vent. Bake for 30 minutes, until the crust is browned and the interior is steaming. Cool for 10 minutes before cutting.

Meatless Lovers' Pizza

The ability of soy and TVP (textured vegetable protein) to imitate the flavor and texture of ground meat is remarkable. Here, the two meet atop a prebaked pizza round to create the meatiest meatless pizza ever. It is quick enough to make for a snack (taking longer to preheat the oven than to build the pizza) but hearty enough to serve for dinner.

Makes 3 or 4 servings

1 large (12-inch) already baked pizza
*   round with a thin crust, such as Boboli*
½ cup pasta or pizza sauce
4 ounces soy sausage, crumbled
4 ounces textured vegetable protein,
*   such as Veggie Ground Round, crum-*
*   bled*
1 cup shredded mozzarella cheese

Preheat the oven to 400°F. Place the pizza round on a baking sheet. Spread the sauce to 1 inch from the edge and scatter the crumbled soy sausage and meatless ground meat over the sauce. Top with the cheese. Bake for 10 minutes, until the cheese has melted and the pizza is hot. Let rest for 3 minutes. Cut into 6 or 8 wedges.

Pissaladière Pie

The Provençal pizza, pissaladière, is the inspiration for this quiche. Note that the pastry is coated with grated Parmesan before the custard is added, which helps to keep the crust from becoming soggy during baking.

Makes 6 servings

4 large or extra-large eggs, or 1 cup liquid egg substitute
½ cup milk, any fat content
Salt and black pepper to taste
¼ cup grated imported Parmesan cheese
Nonstick olive oil spray
1 cup chopped onions, frozen or fresh
1 tablespoon chopped garlic, jarred or fresh
2 tablespoons jarred basil pesto
1 round refrigerated 9-inch piecrust (see Note)
1 cup (4 ounces) shredded mozzarella cheese
2 plum tomatoes, sliced
¼ cup chopped olives or green olive tapenade

Preheat the oven to 375°F. Beat the eggs, milk, salt, pepper, and half of the Parmesan until blended. Heat a large skillet, and coat with oil spray. Add the onions, and sauté until soft. Stir in the garlic, remove from the heat, and stir in the pesto.

Unfold the piecrust and fit it into a 9-inch pie plate, turning under the edges and crimping if desired. Sprinkle the remaining Parmesan over the crust. Top with an even layer of half of the onion mixture, half of the mozzarella, half of the tomatoes, and half of the olives. Repeat with the remaining onion mixture, mozzarella, tomatoes, and olives. Pour the milk-egg mixture on top.

Bake for 35 minutes, until the top is browned and the filling is set. (The center should still be a bit wobbly.)

NOTE: The package contains two pastry shells, so as long as you're baking one, you might want to double the filling ingredients and bake two. The second one will freeze well.

Pizza Rustica

Pizza Rustica shares nothing with a true pizza except a name. In southern Italy it is a deep-dish cheese pie made with several types of meat in a ricotta custard. This version substitutes spinach and roasted peppers for the meat, and the pie is baked in a single crust. The finished dish is a cross between a quiche, a savory cheesecake, and a white veggie pizza deluxe.

Makes 6 servings

2 large or extra-large eggs, or ½ cup liquid egg substitute
¾ cup ricotta cheese
Salt and black pepper to taste
Nonstick olive oil spray
1½ cups diced onions, frozen or fresh
1 teaspoon chopped garlic, jarred or fresh
1 package (10 ounces) frozen spinach, thawed and squeezed dry
4 ounces sliced roasted red peppers, jarred or fresh
1 round refrigerated 9-inch piecrust (see Note)
1 cup shredded mozzarella cheese

Preheat the oven to 375°F. Beat the eggs, ricotta, salt, and pepper until blended. Heat a large skillet and coat with oil spray. Add the onions and sauté until soft. Stir in the garlic, spinach, and peppers. Remove from the heat and add salt and pepper.

Unfold a piecrust and fit into a 9 inch-pie plate, turning under the edges and crimping if desired. Sprinkle half of the mozzarella over the bottom of the pie. Spread half of the spinach mixture in an even layer, followed by half of the ricotta mixture. Top with the remaining spinach mixture, the remaining mozzarella, and the remaining ricotta mixture. Bake for 35 minutes, until the top is browned and the filling is set. (The center should still be a bit wobbly.)

NOTE: The package contains two pastry shells, so as long as you're baking one, you might want to double the filling ingredients and bake two. The second one will freeze well.

Feta Artichoke Pizza

The prebaked pizza round may be the ultimate vehicle for culinary self-expression. Top it with anything and have a complete meal in no time. For this pizza I've combined marinated artichoke hearts, flavored feta, pitted black olives, and walnuts. If the walnuts strike you as an odd addition, I beg you not to reject them outright. They toast as the pizza cooks, giving it a roasted sweetness that's a wonderful counterpoint to the saltiness of the olives and cheese.

Makes 3 or 4 servings

1 jar (12 ounces) marinated quartered
   artichoke hearts
1 package (7 ounces) herbed feta cheese,
   crumbled
1 large (12-inch) pizza round, such as
   Boboli
¼ medium red onion, thinly sliced
12 black olives, pitted and coarsely
   chopped
1 cup walnut pieces

Preheat the oven to 400°F. Combine the artichoke hearts and the cheese. Spread the mixture on the pizza round and scatter the onion, olives, and walnuts over the top. Bake for 10 minutes, until the cheese is melted, and let rest for 3 minutes. Cut in 6 or 8 wedges.

Roasted Caponata

Caponata is a sautéed Sicilian salad of garden vegetables that is multicolored, multitextured, and multiflavored. In this recipe the cooking technique is simplified by roasting all of the vegetables together.

Makes 4 servings

1 medium eggplant, cut in 1-inch cubes
1 medium zucchini, cut in ¾-inch slices
1 cup diced red bell pepper
1 cup chopped onions, frozen or fresh
1½ cups sliced mushrooms
8 peeled cloves garlic, jarred or fresh
Salt and black pepper to taste
¼ cup extra-virgin olive oil
1 can (about 15 ounces) Italian-style
   diced or stewed tomatoes
2 tablespoons capers
2 tablespoons red wine vinegar

Preheat the oven to 425°F. Toss the eggplant, zucchini, bell pepper, onions, mushrooms, garlic, salt, and pepper on a sheet pan with 2 tablespoons of the oil. Spread in an even layer and then roast for 30 minutes, until most of the vegetables have browned.

Combine the tomatoes, capers, remaining oil, and vinegar, and toss the roasted vegetables with the mixture. Adjust the seasoning with more salt and pepper if needed.

Roasted Vegetable Mole

The lushness of mole is not usually associated with vegetables. Vegetables are acid-bright, light, and fresh, while mole is rich and dark. But roast those vegetables, and the relationship is transformed. Now the caramelized tips of the onions, the burnt sugar of the sweet potatoes, and the smoky char on the peppers find a soulmate in mole.

Makes 4 to 6 servings

Nonstick olive oil spray
1 medium onion, halved and cut in ½-inch-thick slices
1 large sweet potato, peeled, halved, and cut in wedges
2 medium zucchini, cut in 1-inch slices
1 medium red bell pepper, cut in 1-inch-wide strips
2 tablespoons jarred mole (page 23)
1 can (about 14 ounces) vegetable broth
1 jar (16 ounces) chipotle salsa
1 can (about 15 ounces) white beans, rinsed and drained
1 tablespoon cilantro pesto or chutney, or 3 tablespoons chopped cilantro
Salt and black pepper to taste
Sour cream for garnish

Preheat the oven to 425°F. Coat a rimmed sheet pan with olive oil spray and toss the onion, sweet potato, zucchini, and bell pepper together on the pan. Coat with more oil spray and roast for 30 minutes, until most of the vegetables are browned.

While the vegetables are roasting, mix the mole with enough broth to thin it to the consistency of heavy cream. Combine the softened mole, remaining broth, salsa, and beans in a saucepan. Bring to a boil and stir in the cilantro. When the vegetables are roasted, add to the mole sauce and heat through. Adjust the seasoning with salt and pepper. Serve with sour cream.

Couscous with Artichoke, Feta, and Walnuts

This vibrant entrée is ready in about five minutes, and it is as easy as boiling water.

Makes 4 servings

2½ cups water
Salt and black pepper to taste
1 box (12 ounces) couscous
1 jar (12 ounces) marinated quartered artichoke hearts
8 ounces crumbled feta cheese
1 cup walnut pieces
2 tablespoons chopped Italian (flat-leaf) parsley

Heat the water until boiling and season liberally with salt and pepper. Add the couscous, stir, remove from the heat, cover, and set aside for 5 minutes. When the couscous is tender add the artichoke hearts, cheese, walnuts, and parsley, and toss well.

Asian Roasted Vegetables

Asian vegetables are usually stir-fried, but this recipe moves the stir-fry into the oven. The vegetables get more time to caramelize, their flavors become more concentrated and sweeter, their fibers relax, and the typical hoisin-ginger-garlic seasoning trio assumes a new role as a complement to the vegetables rather than as the whole flavor package. Roasting takes a little longer than stir-frying, but you don't have to stand at the stove.

Makes 4 servings

Nonstick oil spray
1 medium sweet potato, peeled and cut in 1-inch cubes
2 medium onions, peeled and cut in wedges
3 cups (about 10 ounces) precut fresh broccoli and cauliflower mix
8 peeled cloves garlic, jarred or fresh
Salt and black pepper to taste
2 jarred roasted red peppers, cut in strips
1 can (about 15 ounces) straw mushrooms, drained
2 tablespoons stir-fry sauce
Rice or noodles (optional)

Preheat the oven to 425°F. Coat a rimmed sheet pan with oil spray. Toss the sweet potato, onions, broccoli, cauliflower, garlic, salt, and pepper on the sheet pan and coat with more oil spray. Roast for 15 minutes, until most of the edges have browned and the vegetables are barely tender. Remove from the oven, add the roasted peppers, mushrooms, and stir-fry sauce, toss to combine, and roast for another 15 minutes. Adjust the seasoning with salt and pepper if needed. Serve with rice or noodles if desired.

Peppers Stuffed with Spinach and Polenta

These cups of lipstick-red peppers mounded with golden polenta, bright green spinach, and a glistening glaze of cheese are so cheerful that on sight they erase the flabby olive-drab image associated with the words "stuffed pepper." As the polenta gets warm, it relaxes into a creamy smooth mass.

Makes 4 servings

Nonstick olive oil spray
¼ cup chopped onion, frozen or fresh
1 package (10 ounces) frozen spinach, thawed and squeezed dry
1 teaspoon minced garlic, jarred or fresh
Salt and black pepper to taste
1 package (16 to 18 ounces) prepared polenta, chopped
⅓ cup grated imported Parmesan cheese
2 cups shredded mozzarella cheese
4 medium-size red bell peppers, halved lengthwise, and seeds, membranes, and stems removed
¾ cup vegetable broth

Preheat the oven to 450°F. Heat a large saucepan and coat it with oil spray. Add the onion and sauté until tender. Add the spinach, garlic, salt, and pepper, and heat through. Remove from the heat. Mix in the chopped polenta and the cheeses.

Mound the polenta filling in the pepper halves and place, filled side up, in a square 9-inch baking pan. Pour the broth around the peppers. Bake for 45 minutes, until the peppers are tender and the filling has browned.

Aztec Pie

Aztec Pie (Boudin Azteca) is a homey casserole of tortillas, salsa, crema (Mexican sour cream), and cheese. I've added beans to this rendition for protein, and used sour cream in place of crema.

Makes 4 servings

Nonstick oil spray
10 corn tortillas, cut in wedges
2 jars (16 ounces each) salsa verde
1 can (19 ounces) black beans or white beans, rinsed and drained
1 cup sour cream
1½ cups shredded Monterey Jack cheese

Preheat the oven to 350°F. Coat a sheet pan with oil spray, place the tortilla wedges on the pan in a single layer, and coat with more oil spray. Bake about 5 minutes, until slightly toasted.

Place half of 1 jar of the salsa in the bottom of a 3-quart casserole. Top with one-third of the tortilla wedges arranged in an even layer. Place half of the beans on top, another half jar of the salsa, ⅓ cup of the sour cream, and one-third of the cheese. Repeat the layers, finishing with the remaining tortilla wedges, half jar of salsa, and cheese. Bake, uncovered, about 20 minutes, until browned and bubbly.

Eggplant Marseilles

No one who tastes this upscale rendition of eggplant parmigiana will believe that it is assembled from three jars, one box, and a log of cheese. There is no chopping, no beating, and no sautéing, and you don't even need a can opener. Best of all, the ingredients are all the real thing.

Makes 6 servings

Nonstick olive oil spray
1 jar (16 ounces) bruschetta
1 jar (8 ounces) olive salad or tapenade,
1 jar (6 ounces) roasted pepper strips
1 box (16 ounces) frozen breaded egg-
plant cutlets, thawed
1 log (10 or 11 ounces) fresh chèvre, cut
in 12 disks
¼ cup grated imported Parmesan cheese

Preheat the oven to 375°F. Coat a 2-quart baking dish with olive oil spray. Combine the bruschetta, olive salad, and roasted pepper, and spread 1 cup of the mixture over the bottom of the dish. Top with half of the eggplant cutlets (about 7). Place the disks of chèvre evenly over the eggplant and top each disk with 1 tablespoon of the tomato mixture. Add the remaining eggplant slices and the remaining tomato mixture. Sprinkle with Parmesan. Bake for 40 minutes, until the sauce is bubbling and the cheese is soft.

Veggie "Moussaka"

I know moussaka is usually made with lamb, but this one isn't. Couscous is substituted for the lamb, and because the most commonly available couscous is instant, you can layer it into the moussaka without rehydrating it.

Makes 6 servings

1 box (16 ounces) frozen breaded egg-
plant cutlets
1 cup chunky marinara sauce
¼ cup water
1 tablespoon chopped fresh dill leaves
⅛ teaspoon ground cinnamon
1 can (about 10 ounces) Campbell's
condensed cream of mushroom soup
½ cup milk
1 large or extra-large egg, or ¼ cup liq-
uid egg substitute
4 ounces crumbled feta cheese
Nonstick olive oil spray
½ cup uncooked couscous
3 tablespoons grated Parmesan cheese

Preheat the oven to 400°F. Bake the eggplant slices on a sheet pan for 10 minutes. Combine the marinara sauce, water, dill, and cinnamon in one bowl, and the soup, milk, egg, and cheese in another bowl.

Coat an 8-inch square pan with oil spray. Pour ⅓ cup of the marinara sauce into the pan and top with ⅓ of the couscous and 5 eggplant slices. Spread ¾ cup of the cheese sauce over the eggplant. Repeat twice and sprinkle the Parmesan on top. Bake for 35 minutes, until bubbling and brown.

Lemon Chickpea Stew

This creamy bean stew is brightened with lemon juice and inundated with the flavors of an Arab market: coriander, olive oil, peppers, parsley, and garlic.

Makes 4 servings

2 tablespoons extra-virgin olive oil
1 cup chopped onions, frozen or fresh
2 tablespoons chopped garlic, jarred or fresh
2 teaspoons ground coriander
1 container (32 ounces) vegetable broth
Salt and black pepper to taste
1 can (about 19 ounces) chickpeas, rinsed and drained
1 large or extra-large egg
¼ cup couscous
3 tablespoons lemon juice, organic bottled or fresh
2 tablespoons chopped Italian (flat-leaf) parsley
1 bag (7 ounces) cleaned baby spinach

Heat the oil in a large saucepan. Add the onions and sauté until tender. Add the garlic, coriander, broth, salt, pepper, and chickpeas, and simmer for 5 minutes. Meanwhile, beat the egg, couscous, and lemon juice together. Whisk the mixture into the stew and continue stirring until slightly thickened. Do not allow to boil. Stir in the parsley and spinach, and cook just until wilted, about 1 minute. Adjust the seasoning with additional salt and pepper.

Curried Potatoes, Spinach, and Chickpeas

In northern India, *Aloo Sak,* potatoes and spinach cooked together with spices, is homespun fare. This recipe uses modern convenience ingredients to save time while maintaining the full flavors and silken textures that make this combination so pleasing.

Makes 4 servings

2 tablespoons olive oil
2 cups chopped onions, frozen or fresh
1 package (20 ounces) refrigerated diced potatoes
1 can (about 19 ounces) chickpeas, rinsed and drained
1 cup salsa, any heat level
1 jar (16 ounces) curry sauce
Salt and black pepper to taste
1 bag (7 ounces) cleaned baby spinach
1 teaspoon cilantro pesto or chutney, or 1 tablespoon chopped cilantro

Heat the oil in a large skillet and sauté the onions until they lose their raw look. Add the potatoes and sauté until the onions and potatoes are uniformly browned, about 10 minutes. Add the chickpeas, salsa, and curry sauce, and simmer for 5 minutes. Season with salt and pepper. Add the spinach and cook just until the spinach wilts, about 2 minutes. Stir in the cilantro.

Baked Tofu Teriyaki with Ginger Slaw

This simple tofu cutlet is marinated and baked until it develops the thinnest caramelized veneer. It is served with a slaw made from finely shredded pickled ginger, spring onion, and slivers of almond. The effect is bright, spare, and lean.

Makes 4 servings

Nonstick oil spray
¼ cup teriyaki sauce
2 tablespoons rice wine vinegar
½ teaspoon Chinese chili purée
1 pound firm or extra-firm tofu, cut in 8 slices
¼ cup pickled sushi ginger, cut in fine strips
2 scallions, roots trimmed and finely sliced
1 tablespoon sliced almonds

Preheat the oven to 400°F. Coat a small-rimmed sheet pan with oil spray. Combine the teriyaki sauce, vinegar, and chili purée, and dip the tofu slices in their marinade. Arrange the slices in a single layer evenly spaced on the pan. Pour the remaining marinade over the top and bake for 15 minutes.

While the tofu is baking, combine the ginger, scallions, and almonds. Transfer the baked tofu to a serving platter with a small spatula and place a small mound of the ginger slaw on each tofu slice.

Cannellini Orzo Pilaf

In Italian, "orzo" means barley, but the long, oval pasta looks much more like grains of rice. Because it is small, it cooks fairly quickly and, like all pastas, lends itself to a myriad of flavor manipulations. The flavors in this pilaf cross Mediterranean cultures: a little Greek, a little Moroccan, and a little Tunisian. The cannellini beans are my own addition to help boost the protein level.

Makes 4 servings

1 medium zucchini, cut in ½-inch dice
½ cup shredded carrot
1 teaspoon minced garlic, jarred or fresh
1 teaspoon dried dill weed
1 teaspoon dried marjoram
1 jar (about 6 ounces) marinated quartered artichoke hearts, drained
½ cup canned diced tomato, drained, or fresh
2½ cups vegetable broth
1 cup dried orzo
1 cup cannellini beans, drained
2 teaspoons apple cider vinegar
Salt and black pepper to taste
1 tablespoon chopped fresh mint leaves

In a saucepan, combine the zucchini, carrot, garlic, dill, marjoram, artichoke hearts, tomato, and broth, and bring to a boil. Stir in the orzo and beans, and simmer for 10 minutes, until the orzo is tender and most of the broth is absorbed. Stir in the vinegar, salt, pepper, and mint.

Sweet Ricotta Bread Pudding with Warm Vanilla Pear Sauce

This slightly sweet, vanilla-scented pudding, reminiscent of a cannoli and French toast, could be served for an outrageous breakfast or a homey dinner. The pudding can be made a day ahead and rewarmed in a 375°F oven for twenty minutes.

Makes 12 servings

4 tablespoons (½ stick) unsalted butter, melted
1 pound (about half a large loaf) challah, cut in 1-inch cubes
1 cup golden raisins
2 cups milk, whole or 2%
2 containers (15 ounces each) ricotta cheese
1 cup sugar
4 large or extra-large eggs, or 1 cup liquid egg substitute
1 large container (16 ounces) sour cream
2 teaspoons dried lemon rind, or 1 tablespoon freshly grated lemon zest
1 teaspoon vanilla extract
¼ teaspoon cinnamon
Warm Vanilla Pear Sauce (page 374)

Preheat the oven to 350°F. Pour half of the melted butter in a 9 × 13-inch baking dish, add the bread cubes and raisins, and toss to coat. Pour the milk over the top and toss until all the bread has been moistened. Gently distribute the bread evenly in the baking dish.

Combine the ricotta, sugar, eggs, sour cream, lemon rind, and vanilla. Pour over the bread and mix lightly. Drizzle the remaining butter over the top, sprinkle with the cinnamon, and bake for 1 hour. Let cool for 10 minutes before serving. Serve warm with Warm Vanilla Pear Sauce.

White and Black Bean Salad

Bean salads are easy to assemble, and they keep perfectly well in the refrigerator for days. This one is colorful and delicious, flavored simply with Italian dressing and lemon.

Makes 4 servings

1 can (about 19 ounces) white beans, rinsed and drained
1 can (about 19 ounces) black beans, rinsed and drained
1 cup chunky salsa, any heat level
1 roasted red or yellow pepper, jarred or fresh, chopped
¼ cup chopped Italian (flat-leaf) parsley
½ cup garlic herb salad dressing
1 tablespoon lemon juice, organic jarred or fresh
Salt and black pepper to taste

Combine the white and black beans, salsa, pepper, and parsley. Add the dressing, lemon juice, salt, and pepper, and toss.

Spaghetti Squash Primavera

Like its pasta namesake, the flavor impact of spaghetti squash is in its sauce. The primavera stir-fry in this recipe fulfills the role admirably. A variety of vegetables (I've made a selection, but be guided by what's best and brightest at your market) is sautéed with garlic and finished with an ample handful of Parmesan. To boost the protein, I've included some tofu.

Makes 4 servings

2 spaghetti squash, stems removed, seeds discarded, and split in half lengthwise
¾ cup water
3 tablespoons extra-virgin olive oil
8 ounces firm tofu, cubed
½ cup chopped onion, frozen or fresh
1 red bell pepper, cut in strips
1 cup sliced white mushrooms or diced Portobello mushrooms
½ teaspoon minced garlic, jarred or fresh
8 ounces asparagus, trimmed and cut in 1-inch pieces
1 cup frozen peas
Salt and black pepper to taste
5 tablespoons grated imported Parmesan cheese

Preheat the oven to 350°F. Place the squash, cut sides down, on a rimmed sheet pan. Pour the water over the top, cover loosely with foil, and bake until soft, about 30 minutes. While the squash is cooking, heat 1 tablespoon of the oil in a large nonstick skillet. When the oil is smoking, add the tofu cubes and brown on all sides. Remove the tofu.

Add another tablespoon of oil to the pan and sauté the onion, bell pepper, and mushrooms until tender. Add the garlic, asparagus, and peas, and sauté just until the asparagus is bright green, about 2 minutes. Season liberally with salt and pepper. Add the tofu and toss to combine.

When the spaghetti squash is tender, scrape the strands of flesh from the skin with the tines of a fork. Toss with the warm sautéed vegetables, remaining olive oil, Parmesan, and more salt and pepper.

Vegetable Pakoras

Pakoras are Indian fritters made by frying vegetables coated in chickpea batter. Here the batter is streamlined with falafel mix and spiced yogurt. Pakoras can be served as an entrée, a snack, or an appetizer.

Makes 4 servings

16 ounces plain yogurt
2 tablespoons ground cumin
2 teaspoons curry powder
2 pounds vegetables: a mixture of broc-
*   coli and cauliflower florets, mush-*
*   rooms, pepper strips, and zucchini*
*   slices*
¼ cup sesame tahini
Oil for frying
1 box (10 ounces) instant falafel mix

Combine the yogurt, cumin, and curry powder. Place the vegetables in half of this mixture for 30 minutes. Stir the tahini in the remaining mixture and set aside.

Heat 2 inches of oil in a deep skillet, to 350°F. Place a strainer in a large bowl and set near the fryer.

Place the falafel mix on a sheet of foil. Remove the vegetable from the yogurt and coat with falafel mix. Cook several pieces at a time in the hot oil until browned and cooked through, about 3 to 4 minutes per batch. Transfer each batch with a slotted spoon to the strainer to drain. Serve with the reserved sauce as a dip.

Fettuccine with Tofu Vodka "Cream" Sauce

Blush pasta sauces spiked with vodka became de rigueur in fine restaurants in the early '80s. Casual dining picked up the trend a decade later, and now these sauces are available jarred on your supermarket shelves. Ready for the next generation? Here's a vegan version.

Makes 4 servings

12 ounces fettuccine
6 ounces silken tofu
1 jar (26 ounces) marinara sauce
¾ cup water
1 tablespoon extra-virgin olive oil
¾ cup chopped onion, frozen or fresh
1 teaspoon minced garlic, jarred or fresh
Pinch of crushed red pepper flakes
½ cup vegetable broth (optional)
Salt and black pepper to taste
¼ cup vodka

Boil the pasta in a large pot of lightly salted water until al dente, about 8 minutes.

Meanwhile, purée the tofu, marinara sauce, and water in a food processor. Heat the oil in a large skillet, sauté the onion until tender, add the garlic and pepper flakes, and stir briefly. Add the marinara mixture and heat until simmering. If too thick, add the broth until it reaches the desired consistency. Season with salt and pepper. Add the vodka to the sauce and heat through. Toss with the cooked pasta.

Udon Noodles with Peanut Sauce

"Udon" is the word for any plain Asian noodle made from wheat flour. They are similar to spaghetti or linguine, either of which can be used in this simple stir-fry.

Makes 4 servings

8 ounces udon noodles or linguine
¼ cup peanut butter, chunky or smooth
2 tablespoons rice wine vinegar
2 tablespoons soy sauce
½ teaspoon Chinese chili purée
¼ cup vegetable broth
Nonstick oil spray
1½ cups shredded carrots
6 ounces baked tofu, halved and cut in
    ¼-inch-thick slices
3 scallions, roots trimmed, thinly sliced
Salt and black pepper to taste

Boil the noodles in a large pot of lightly salted water until tender, and drain.

While the noodles are cooking, combine the peanut butter, vinegar, soy sauce, chili purée, and vegetable broth. Set aside. Place a large wok over high heat and coat with oil spray. Stir-fry the carrots for 1 minute. Add the cooked noodles and stir-fry until heated through. Add the peanut mixture, tofu, and scallions, and stir-fry until the noodles are coated with sauce and everything is heated through. Adjust the seasoning with salt and pepper if needed.

Eggplant and Soba

The nutty whole-grain flavor of buckwheat soba mingles exotically with a barbecued eggplant sauce. Asian eggplants are slimmer, paler, and milder than their European counterpart.

Makes 4 servings

½ cup hoisin sauce
¾ cup salsa, medium or hot
½ cup vegetable broth
2 tablespoons extra-virgin olive oil
1 pound Asian eggplant (Japanese or
    Chinese), halved lengthwise and cut in
    1-inch slices
4 ounces soy sausage, cut in 4 slices
1 package (about 8 ounces) soba noodles
Salt and black pepper to taste

Preheat the broiler and bring a large pot of lightly salted water to a boil.

Combine the hoisin sauce, salsa, broth, and 1 teaspoon of the oil. Toss ½ cup of this sauce with the eggplant. Place the eggplant and sausage slices on a broiler tray and broil about 4 minutes per side, until the eggplant and sausage are browned.

Boil the soba noodles until tender, about 6 minutes. Bring the remaining sauce to a simmer in a small saucepan. When the eggplant and sausage are done, add the eggplant to the sauce and crumble in the sausage. Drain the noodles and toss with the sauce and the remaining oil. Season with salt and pepper.

Vegetables with Thai Fried Noodles

Cellophane noodles look cloudy when they're dry, but they turn clear after cooking. Thin cellophane noodles are ready to eat after a quick soaking in boiling water, and wide ones (sold as Pad Thai noodles) need only a second or two of heat after they are soaked.

Makes 4 servings

2 cups boiling water
1 package (about 5 ounces) Pad Thai noodles or wide cellophane noodles
2 teaspoons basil pesto, jarred or fresh
2 teaspoons jarred cilantro pesto or chutney, or 2 tablespoons chopped cilantro
3 tablespoons stir-fry sauce
1 cup regular coconut milk
2 tablespoons vegetable oil
½ cup diced red bell pepper
1½ cups shredded carrots
2 scallions, roots trimmed, thinly sliced
20 snow pea pods, stems removed

Pour the water over the noodles, let soften about 5 minutes, and drain. Meanwhile, combine the basil pesto, cilantro, stir-fry sauce, and coconut milk. Heat the oil in a large skillet or wok and sauté the pepper and carrots until barely tender, about 1 minute. Add the scallions and snow peas, and toss to coat with oil. Add the noodles and sauce, and heat until the sauce is boiling and the noodles are heated through, about 1 minute.

White Bean Tabbouleh

This entrée salad is perfect for either a summer dinner (you hardly have to turn on the stove) or a winter lunch (the combination of whole grain, almonds, and beans makes for a substantial meal). Tabbouleh mixes are common in the supermarket's grain section.

Makes 4 servings

1 package (about 5 ounces) tabbouleh
1 cup boiling water
¼ cup vinaigrette salad dressing
½ cup diced roasted peppers, jarred or fresh
1 plum tomato, diced
1 scallion, roots trimmed, thinly sliced
½ medium cucumber, peeled and diced
½ cup sliced almonds
¼ cup sliced black olives
1 can (about 15 ounces) small white beans, rinsed and drained
2 tablespoons chopped fresh mint leaves
Salt and black pepper to taste

Mix the tabbouleh and 1 tablespoon of the salad dressing in the boiling water. Set aside 15 minutes, until the water has been absorbed. Add the roasted peppers, tomato, scallion, cucumber, almonds, olives, beans, remaining dressing, mint leaves, salt, and pepper.

Warm Rice, Pepper, and Lentil Salad

A vast array of rice awaits at your market: white, brown, red, black, wild, basmati, and blends of any and all of them. Many are quite good—chewy and nutty, as hearty as roasted meat, or as pale and perfumed as an herb garden.

Makes 4 servings

1 cup brown rice blend
½ cup red lentils
3 cups water
1 tablespoon soy sauce
½ cup red wine vinaigrette salad dressing
2 tablespoons lime juice, organic bottled or fresh
1 jar (12 ounces) roasted red peppers, diced
1 bunch scallions, roots trimmed, thinly sliced
¼ cup chopped Italian (flat-leaf) parsley
Salt and black pepper to taste

Place the rice and lentils in a strainer and rinse under cold water for several minutes. Combine in a medium saucepan with the water and soy sauce. Bring to a boil over high heat, stir once, lower the heat, and simmer until the water has been absorbed and the rice and lentils are tender, about 45 minutes. Toss the cooked rice and lentils in the serving bowl with the dressing, lime juice, peppers, scallions, and parsley. Season with salt and pepper. Serve warm or at room temperature.

Polenta and Rabe

Broccoli rabe may be bitter at first bite, but its robust character could make you a convert for life. It can invigorate bland foods such as pasta and potatoes, and is complemented by strong flavors like garlic and pungent cheese. In this recipe it transforms baked polenta into a full-bodied main dish.

Makes 4 servings

Nonstick olive oil spray
1 package (16 to 18 ounces) prepared polenta, sliced into 12 rounds
Kosher salt and freshly ground black pepper
2 bunches (about 1 pound each) broccoli rabe, stalk ends removed, cut into 2-inch lengths, and thoroughly cleaned
2 tablespoons olive oil
Pinch of crushed red pepper flakes
2 teaspoons chopped garlic, jarred or fresh
¾ cup shredded Parmesan cheese

Preheat the oven to 400°F. Coat a sheet pan with oil spray, arrange the polenta slices on the pan, and season with salt and pepper. Coat with more oil spray and bake for 15 minutes, until lightly toasted.

Boil the broccoli rabe in a large pot of water until tender, about 5 minutes, and drain. Heat the oil in a large skillet. Add the rabe and season with salt, pepper, and pepper flakes. Sauté until dry. Stir in the garlic and adjust the salt and pepper if necessary.

To serve, top each polenta round with a large pinch of cheese. Pile the rabe on the polenta and top with the remaining cheese.

Garlic Potato Cakes with Horseradish Sour Cream

In years past, potato cakes would have been a lot of work, with lots of shredding, rinsing, and wringing of potatoes, but now, with the ready availability of refrigerated preshredded potatoes, preparations like this have been simplified. Just assemble a few ingredients and bake. They are served with a cold creamy horseradish sauce.

Makes 4 servings

Baker's Joy No Stick Spray with Flour
1 package (20 ounces) refrigerated
   shredded hash brown potatoes
1 teaspoon minced garlic, jarred or fresh
6 large or extra-large eggs, or 1½ cups
   liquid egg substitute
Salt and black pepper to taste
1 cup sour cream
¼ cup prepared horseradish

Preheat the oven to 375°F. Coat a 12-cup muffin tin with flour spray. Combine the potatoes, garlic, eggs, salt, and pepper, scoop into the muffin tin, and bake for 30 minutes, until browned and set. While the cakes are baking, combine the sour cream and horseradish. Loosen the edges of the potato cakes with a small knife, remove them from the tin, and serve with the horseradish sour cream.

Veggie Burger Falafel

I use the term "falafel" loosely. This sandwich isn't actually made with falafel, the Arab croquettes of chickpeas and bulgur seasoned with garlic. Rather, it takes its form from the way falafel is traditionally served—in a split flatbread with vegetables and a tangy yogurt sauce. Prepared veggie burgers conveniently and nutritionally take the place of traditional falafels.

Makes 4 servings

Nonstick oil spray
4 veggie burgers
1 cup Garlic Yogurt Dressing (page 265)
4 pita breads, halved and pockets
   opened
1 cup shredded lettuce
½ cup diced tomato

Place a nonstick skillet over medium-high heat until the pan is hot. Coat with oil spray and brown the veggie burgers on both sides, about 3 to 4 minutes per side. Cut each burger into quarters. Assemble the sandwiches by spreading about 2 teaspoons of the yogurt sauce on the interior of each pita half. Place 2 veggie burger quarters in each pita half and top with a little more sauce, lettuce, and tomato.

Eggplant Falafel

This variation on falafel uses prepared breaded eggplant slices that you bake and stuff warm into pita pockets with a lemony, garlicky yogurt sauce, a tangle of baby spinach leaves, and a shimmer of diced tomato.

Makes 4 servings

Nonstick oil spray
8 slices (about 8 ounces) frozen breaded
   eggplant cutlets
1 cup Garlic Yogurt Dressing (page 265)
4 pita breads, halved and pockets
   opened
3 ounces baby spinach leaves
½ cup diced tomato

Preheat the oven to 425°F. Coat a sheet pan with oil spray. Place the eggplant slices on the pan, bake for 15 minutes, until crisp and browned, and cut the slices in half. Assemble the sandwiches by spreading about 1 tablespoon of the sauce on the interior of each pita half, placing 2 half-slices of eggplant in each pita half, and topping with a little more sauce, spinach, and tomato.

Antipasto Pita Pocket

Jars of gardiniera, the Italian mixed vegetable pickle, have been stacked on supermarket shelves for the better part of a century. It has become so familiar that I had completely forgotten about it until I went to make this sandwich, for which gardiniera is a natural centerpiece. It is accompanied by other classic Italian flavors: fresh mozzarella, olives, and olive oil. Pita is the only interloper.

Makes 4 servings

1 jar (about 19 ounces) gardiniera,
   drained
½ cup quartered black or green pitted
   olives
4 ounces mozzarella cheese, preferably
   fresh, cut in bite-size pieces
2 tablespoons extra-virgin olive oil
½ teaspoon minced garlic, jarred or fresh
Salt and black pepper to taste
4 pita breads, halved and pockets
   opened

Combine the gardiniera, olives, mozzarella, oil, garlic, salt, and pepper. Spoon into the pita pockets and serve.

Slavic Egg Salad

I'm not a fan of traditional egg salad, but toss in some beets, a red onion, a few potatoes, and a chopped dill pickle, and that's a whole other story. This salad is a vivid magenta, pungent with dill and an ebullience of pickle juice, and it has a creamy sauce of mayonnaise inundated with hard-cooked egg yolk. For ovo-vegetarians it is not just packed with protein; it is a vibrant, highly flavorful, complete meal in a bowl.

Makes 6 servings

½ cup mayonnaise
2 tablespoons lemon juice, organic bottled or fresh
4 ounces kosher dill pickles, cut in small dice, and ⅓ cup pickle juice
1 teaspoon dried dill weed
12 hard-cooked eggs, peeled and chopped
1 can (about 14 ounces) whole baby beets, drained and diced
1 can (about 14 ounces) whole baby potatoes, drained and diced
½ cup diced red onion

Combine the mayonnaise, lemon juice, pickle juice, and dill weed. Add the eggs, beets, potatoes, pickles, and onion, and toss to combine.

Artichoke Edamame Frittata

Edamame are green soybeans. They are sold frozen in most supermarkets and in all Asian markets, shelled and unshelled. You want shelled for this recipe.

Makes 4 servings

¾ cup frozen shelled edamame
6 large or extra-large eggs
½ cup milk
¼ teaspoon Tabasco sauce
1 tablespoon grated imported Parmesan cheese
Nonstick oil spray
1 scallion, roots trimmed, thinly sliced
1 jar (6 ounces) marinated artichoke heart quarters, drained

Preheat the broiler. Boil the edamame in lightly salted water until tender, about 4 minutes, and drain. Meanwhile, beat the eggs with the milk, Tabasco, and Parmesan. Heat a nonstick 12-inch skillet with a metal handle and coat with oil spray. Add the scallion, edamame, and artichoke hearts, and warm through.

Add the egg mixture and cook until the bottom sets. Lift the edges and tilt the skillet, so that some egg runs under the omelet. Cook until a little more than half set. Place the pan under the broiler and cook until the egg is fully set and the top is browned and puffed, about 1 to 2 minutes. Remove using a heavy potholder. Cut in wedges and serve.

Olive, Potato, and Sun-Dried Tomato Frittata

Frittatas are open-faced omelets that, because they are not folded, have the ability to house a small arsenal of flavorful ingredients. This one boasts a combination of potatoes, olives, and goat cheese. To make this recipe or any frittata, use a large skillet (preferably nonstick) with a metal handle so that you can start cooking on a stovetop and finish under a broiler. I think you should serve frittatas immediately, but if you want to hold them longer, refrigerate them and then return them to room temperature before serving.

Makes 4 servings

6 large or extra-large eggs
½ cup milk
½ cup crumbled fresh chèvre
½ teaspoon salt
¼ teaspoon black pepper
1 tablespoon olive oil
¾ cup refrigerated shredded hash brown potatoes
¼ cup sliced black olives
2 tablespoons chopped sun-dried tomato in oil

Preheat the broiler. Beat the eggs, milk, cheese, salt, and pepper together. Heat a 12-inch nonstick skillet with a metal handle. Add the oil and swirl over the bottom of the pan. Sauté the potatoes until browned, about 8 minutes. Add the olives and tomato, and toss with the potatoes. Spread all the ingredients evenly over the bottom of the pan.

Add the egg mixture and cook until the bottom is set. Lift the edges of the set egg, tilt the skillet, and allow some egg to run to the underside of the omelet. Cook until the egg is a little more than half set. Place the pan under the broiler and cook until the egg is fully set and the top is browned and puffed, about 1 to 2 minutes. Remove from the broiler using a heavy potholder. Cut in wedges and serve.

CHAPTER 8

INCREDIBLE VEGETABLES FOR EVERY MEAL

Roasted Garlic Parmesan Mashed Potatoes
Blue Cheese Whipped Potatoes
Shrimp Mashed Potatoes
Potatoes Mashed with Almost Anything
Pesto Potato Pancakes
Buffalo Fries
New Potatoes Nuked with Bacon
Black Pepper Parmesan Fries
Smoked Salmon Hashed Potatoes
Potatoes Hashed with Spinach
Twice-"Baked" Potatoes with Cheese
Smoky Sweet Potato Hash
Pickled Roasted Peppers
Roasted Ratatouille
Spinach Gratin
Spinach with Feta and Olives
Easy Cheesy Herbed Creamed Spinach
Curried Spinach
Broccoli and Apples with Bacon
Broccoli Rabe with Roasted Grapes
Cabbage Flowers with Raisins and Capers

Orange Mustard Cauliflower
Curried Cauliflower
Parmesan Dijon Cauliflower
Black Pepper Cabbage
Ginger-Roasted Brussels Sprouts
Green Beans in Almond Butter
Sweet Tomato Green Beans
Pesto-Painted Green Beans
Peas, Prosciutto, and Sweet Peppers
Peas with Anchovies and Mint
Very Ginger Glazed Carrots
Carrots Stir-Fried with Capers
Carrots Glazed with Red Pepper
Cumin Corn with Almonds
Corn with Guacamole
Sweet and Spicy Corn Pudding
Baked Plantains with Mustard Fruit
Sautéed Grape Tomatoes with Pesto
Tomatoes Sautéed with Chipotles
Apple Squash Purée
Asparagus with Lemon and Smoked Salmon
Eggplant Mousse with Orange Tomato Butter
Sicilian Artichokes
Artichoke Hearts Braised with Peppers
Balsamic Beets
Leeks Braised in Onion Soup
Caramelized Onions with Blue Cheese
Roasted Fennel Provençal
Fennel Parmesan
Braised Celery with Orange and Olives
Roasted Mushrooms with Roasted Garlic and Cheese
Broiled Portobello Mushrooms
Mushrooms Broiled with Sweet Onions
Exotic Mushroom Stew

Roasted Garlic Parmesan Mashed Potatoes

Roasted garlic products abound, but, alas, most have nothing to do with the creamy spread that starts out with such an off-putting smell. The only jarred brand that I think comes close to the taste of oven-roasted garlic is Christopher Ranch. At this writing it is sold only as whole cloves, which is slightly inconvenient since most of what I use is chopped. So I keep one jar of whole cloves and chop the contents of the other. Then I freeze teaspoon-size mounds so that I always have some on hand.

Makes 4 servings

1 tablespoon extra-virgin olive oil
2 tablespoons chopped roasted garlic, jarred or fresh
1 package (16 ounces) refrigerated mashed potatoes
¼ cup grated imported Parmesan cheese
Salt and black pepper to taste

Heat the oil in a saucepan, add the garlic and potatoes, and heat through, stirring often. Stir in the Parmesan and add salt and pepper if needed.

Blue Cheese Whipped Potatoes

Dressed-up mashed potatoes, hijacked by roasted garlic, lobster, wasabi, and most often blue cheese, are all the fashion in trendy restaurants. In this easy recipe the blue cheese comes in the form of salad dressing, which contributes a provocative tang. The potatoes are prediced. The same companies that make refrigerated mashed potatoes sell shredded and diced potato products, too. Although they require some cooking, they've already been peeled and chopped for you. If you don't mind the prep work, chop your own; the cooking time is the same either way.

Makes 4 servings

1 package (20 ounces) refrigerated diced potatoes, or 1½ pounds baking potatoes, peeled and cut in small chunks
¾ cup creamy blue cheese dressing
½ teaspoon minced garlic
Salt and black pepper to taste

Place the potatoes in a large saucepan, cover with water, and bring to a boil over high heat. Boil until tender, about 15 minutes. Drain and mash the potatoes right in the pot using a potato masher or fork. When they're almost smooth, whisk in the dressing, garlic, salt, and pepper.

Shrimp Mashed Potatoes

Seafood mashed potatoes emerged in restaurants several years ago, but there is no need for you to dine out to indulge in your own extrava*mash* when the mood hits. This recipe for shrimp mashed potatoes can be made with any size shrimp (you're going to chop them, so don't pay extra for jumbo) and refrigerated or thawed frozen mashed potatoes.

Makes 4 servings

1 tablespoon extra-virgin olive oil
8 ounces shrimp (any size), peeled, cleaned, and chopped, thawed if frozen
½ large fish-flavored bouillon cube, crushed
½ teaspoon minced garlic, jarred or fresh
½ teaspoon dried dill weed, or 2 teaspoons chopped fresh dill
1 package (16 ounces) refrigerated mashed potatoes
Black pepper to taste

Heat the oil in a medium saucepan, add the shrimp, bouillon, and garlic, and cook until the shrimp are opaque, about 30 seconds. Stir in the dill and potatoes, and heat through, stirring often. Add the pepper. You probably won't need more salt.

Potatoes Mashed with Almost Anything

Mashed potatoes are almost perfect in and of themselves—fluffy potato fattened with butter and indulged with cream. I never understood why we messed with them. Then I added parsnips. The mashed potato perfection remained, but it became sweeter and a little tangy. So I tried turnip. Mashed potatoes still, but with a peppery twist. What about sweet potato? They glowed with a pale peachy tint and a hint of caramel.

Makes 4 servings

2 parsnips or 1 turnip or 1 sweet potato or ½ small celeriac or 2 carrots, peeled and finely chopped
1 package (20 ounces) refrigerated diced potatoes, or 1½ pounds baking potatoes, peeled and cut in small chunks
½ cup light cream, yogurt, or sour cream
2 tablespoons butter
Salt and black pepper to taste

Place the parsnip or other vegetable in a large saucepan half-filled with water. Bring to a boil and boil until barely tender, about 5 minutes. Add the diced potatoes and boil 15 minutes more, until all the vegetables are soft. Drain and mash the vegetables right in the pot using a potato masher or fork. When they're almost smooth, stir in the cream, butter, salt, and pepper.

Pesto Potato Pancakes

Preparing potato pancakes—with so much shredding, washing, and frying—is messy at best. I can't help you with the frying (although oil spray does cut down on splattering), but shredding and washing can be eliminated by using refrigerated preshredded potatoes.

Makes 4 to 6 servings

1 package (20 ounces) refrigerated hash brown potatoes
2 large or extra-large eggs, or ½ cup liquid egg substitute
2 tablespoons flour
2 tablespoons chopped onion, frozen or fresh
2 teaspoons anchovy paste
2 tablespoons plus 1 teaspoon pesto, jarred or fresh
Salt and black pepper to taste
Nonstick oil spray
1 teaspoon extra-virgin olive oil
1 teaspoon lemon juice, organic bottled or fresh

Combine the potatoes, eggs, flour, onion, 1 teaspoon of the anchovy paste, 1 tablespoon of the pesto, salt, and pepper. Heat a large skillet and coat with oil spray. Place heaping soupspoons of the mixture on the hot pan and flatten lightly into pancakes that are ¼ inch thick and 3 inches in diameter. Brown well on both sides and keep warm in a low oven while you cook the remaining pancakes.

While the pancakes are cooking, combine the remaining pesto and anchovy paste with the oil and lemon juice. Serve 2 to 3 pancakes per person, topping each with a small amount of the pesto sauce.

Buffalo Fries

The cosmic pairing of hot sauce and butter known as "Buffalo" is legendary. The flavor has been adopted endlessly, and nowhere is it better suited than with fried potatoes.

Makes 6 servings

Nonstick oil spray
1 package (about 28 ounces) frozen French fries or other shaped potato
1 tablespoon butter
3 tablespoons Frank's Red Hot Sauce or other mild hot pepper sauce

Coat the potatoes with oil spray and bake or broil them according to package directions. (This usually means baking on a sheet pan at 450°F for 15 minutes or broiling on a broiler pan for 10 minutes.) While the potatoes are cooking, melt the butter and mix in the hot sauce. Drizzle the sauce over the potatoes and toss to coat.

New Potatoes Nuked with Bacon

Your microwave is a steamer, not an oven, and it's the best tool in your kitchen for steaming vegetables. It requires so little additional liquid that flavors are not diluted, and water-soluble vitamins and minerals don't get washed away. New potatoes are so young that their sugars have not yet been stored as starch, which means they can be served al dente without tasting starchy—perfect for microwaving.

Makes 4 servings

2 strips ready-to-serve bacon, finely chopped
⅓ cup chopped onion, frozen or fresh
1 bag (28 ounces) new (baby) potatoes, red or white, washed and halved
Salt and black pepper to taste
⅛ teaspoon dried crushed rosemary

Scatter the bacon and onion in a 9-inch glass pie plate or microwave-safe baking dish and microwave at full power for 2 minutes. Add the potatoes and season with the salt, pepper, and rosemary. Cover with plastic wrap and microwave at full power for 6 to 7 minutes, until the potatoes are tender.

Black Pepper Parmesan Fries

There is nothing revolutionary about salt and pepper on potatoes. Yeah, right.

Makes 6 servings

1 package (about 28 ounces) frozen shoestring French-fried potatoes
Nonstick olive oil spray
2 tablespoons grated imported Parmesan cheese
¼ teaspoon kosher salt or other coarse salt
½ teaspoon freshly ground black pepper
½ teaspoon dried granulated garlic, or ¼ teaspoon garlic powder

Bake, broil, or fry the potatoes according to package directions. (This usually means baking on a sheet pan at 450°F for 15 minutes, broiling on a broiler pan for 10 minutes, or deep-frying at 400°F for 5 minutes.) As soon as the fries are finished, coat them with oil spray and toss with the Parmesan, salt, pepper, and garlic.

Smoked Salmon Hashed Potatoes

Hash, a chopped mélange of meat and vegetables, has been synonymous with low-class dining (hence the terms "hash house" and "hash slinger") since the middle of the nineteenth century. All that is about to change. Here's a hash so wonderfully decadent that it redefines the name, and all it took was a few ounces of smoked salmon.

Makes 4 servings

3 tablespoons olive oil
1 package (20 ounces) shredded hashed
    potatoes
Salt and black pepper to taste
½ teaspoon dried dill weed, or 2 tea-
    spoons chopped fresh dill
2 ounces smoked salmon, finely chopped

Heat the oil in a large skillet over medium heat. When the oil is hot, add the potatoes and flatten to fill the pan with a firmly packed layer. Brown well, about 5 minutes. Cut into pieces with a spatula and turn over. Season with salt, pepper, and dill. Continue cutting the potatoes into a hash and turning every few minutes, until they are uniformly browned. Add the salmon, hash one more time, and adjust the seasoning with additional salt and pepper.

Potatoes Hashed with Spinach

Long live fresh spinach in all its prewashed glory! Now that fresh spinach comes prewashed and trimmed, and can be microwaved right in its bag, the convenience crown has passed. Frozen spinach used to be the height of spinach simplicity, needing no washing or trimming and coming whole or chopped. But it did need thawing. No more. Here, fresh spinach adds nutrition, flavor, and color to a simple hashed potato.

Makes 4 servings

3 tablespoons olive oil
1 package (20 ounces) shredded hashed
    potatoes
Salt and black pepper to taste
½ teaspoon chopped garlic, jarred or
    fresh
1 package (8 ounces) cleaned baby
    spinach, chopped

Heat the oil in a large skillet over medium heat. When the oil is hot, add the potatoes and flatten to fill the pan in a firmly packed layer. Brown well, about 5 minutes. Cut into pieces with a spatula and turn over. Season with salt, pepper, and garlic. Continue cutting the potatoes into a hash and turning every few minutes, until they are uniformly browned. Add the spinach and hash one more time, until the spinach is wilted, and adjust the seasoning with additional salt and pepper.

Twice-"Baked" Potatoes with Cheese

Maybe it's the gratinéed peak or the craggy crust masking a mountain of mashed potato fluff. Maybe it's the way it bulges over the lip of its potato-skin sarcophagus. I don't know, but I surely am a sucker for twice-baked potatoes. In their honor, I propose this simple casserole of prepared mashed potatoes, sour cream, and cheese. Though it misses the visual impact of the classic twice-baked, it gives you twice the amount of crust.

Makes 4 servings

Nonstick oil spray
1 package (about 1 pound) refrigerated mashed potatoes
½ cup sour cream
½ cup shredded sharp cheddar cheese
Salt and black pepper to taste

Preheat the oven to 400°F. Coat an 8-inch square baking pan or other 2-quart casserole with oil spray. Combine the potatoes, sour cream, cheese, salt, and pepper, and spoon the mixture into the prepared baking dish. Smooth the top and bake for 35 to 40 minutes, until the top has browned and the edges are bubbling.

Smoky Sweet Potato Hash

All vegetables suffer from canning, but some do better than others. The fact is that a canned sweet potato is not much different from one that has been baked and chilled. This recipe for sweet potato hash is fragrant with roasted garlic, sautéed onions, smoked meat, and chipotle pepper. No one will guess that it came from a can.

Makes 4 servings

1 can (19 ounces) yams or sweet potatoes in syrup, drained
4 cloves roasted garlic, jarred or fresh
8 ounces smoked turkey or ham, finely chopped
½ cup chopped onion, frozen or fresh
½ teaspoon chipotle pepper
Salt to taste
Nonstick oil spray

Mash the yams and roasted garlic with a fork (the mixture doesn't have to be completely smooth). Mix in the turkey, onion, chipotle pepper, and salt. Place a large nonstick skillet over medium-high heat and coat the skillet with oil spray. Spoon the potato mixture into the hot pan in 5 or 6 mounds and flatten the mounds with the back of a spatula. Brown on one side, then flip and brown on the second side. Chop each "pancake" into a few pieces and serve.

Pickled Roasted Peppers

I can't believe I lived so long without frozen roasted peppers. Seeded and stemmed but not cut, and with their charred skin still attached, they are firmer than jarred peppers and a little softer than freshly roasted. I think they're better than jarred for this preparation, although jarred will yield acceptable results.

Makes 6 servings

1 pound roasted peppers, frozen or jarred, cut in strips
⅓ cup oil and vinegar salad dressing
½ teaspoon minced roasted garlic, jarred or fresh
Salt and black pepper to taste
2 tablespoons chopped Italian (flat-leaf) parsley

Preheat the oven to 450°F. Place the frozen peppers on a sheet pan in a single layer and bake for 10 to 15 minutes, until the peppers are steaming. (If using jarred peppers, bake for 5 to 10 minutes.) While the peppers are still hot, toss them with the salad dressing, garlic, salt, pepper, and parsley. Let cool to room temperature or serve warm. Serve as an appetizer or as a side dish with sandwiches, grilled meats, or fried seafood.

Roasted Ratatouille

Ratatouille recipes abound. They usually note exact times for sautéing each component and then combine them to braise briefly in vinaigrette. Forget all that. This twist on ratatouille is very easy, and a caramelized richness is added from the roasted vegetables.

Makes 6 servings

Nonstick olive oil spray
1 medium zucchini, cut in ½-inch slices
1 medium eggplant, cut in 1-inch chunks
1 package (8 ounces) sliced mushrooms
1 cup chopped onions, frozen or fresh
1 jar (12 ounces) tomato bruschetta, or fresh
1 tablespoon basil pesto, jarred or fresh
1 teaspoon chopped garlic, jarred or fresh
Salt and black pepper to taste

Preheat the oven to 425°F. Coat a rimmed sheet pan with olive oil spray. Toss the zucchini, eggplant, mushrooms, and onions together on the sheet pan. Coat with more oil spray and roast for 20 minutes, until most of the edges have browned and the vegetables are tender but not mushy. While the vegetables are roasting, combine the bruschetta, pesto, and garlic. Pour the mixture over the roasted vegetables, toss to coat, and season with salt and pepper.

Spinach Gratin

Gratins—baked dishes that are brown and crusty on the surface and bubbling and creamy inside—used to be the height of gastro-fashion. Then along came al dente everything—grilled artichokes, and raw food. Everyone forgot how soul-satisfyingly good a vegetable casserole could be. Let this hearty baked dish bring back the memory.

Makes 6 servings

3 tablespoons butter
1 package (8 ounces) sliced mushrooms
½ teaspoon minced garlic, jarred or fresh
4 bags (7 ounces each) cleaned baby spinach
½ cup ricotta cheese
1 large or extra-large egg, or ¼ cup liquid egg substitute
6 tablespoons grated imported Parmesan cheese
Salt and black pepper to taste
2 tablespoons seasoned bread crumbs

Preheat the oven to 375°F. Melt the butter in a large, deep skillet and sauté the mushrooms until they lose their raw look. Add the garlic and toss to combine. Add the spinach and sauté until dry. Combine the spinach mixture, ricotta, egg, and ¼ cup of the Parmesan, and season with salt and pepper. Mound the mixture in a 2-quart baking dish. Combine the remaining Parmesan and bread crumbs, and sprinkle over the top. Bake for 35 to 45 minutes, until browned and bubbling.

Spinach with Feta and Olives

The combination of spinach, feta cheese, and olives defines Greek cuisine, and this convenient recipe modernizes it as well. Prewashed spinach is microwaved right in its bag and is tossed with the other ingredients in a serving bowl. There is nothing to chop, no stove to turn on, and no pots to wash. It's a classic.

Makes 6 servings

2 packages (10 ounces each) washed fresh spinach
½ cup crumbled feta cheese
¼ cup olive salad
1 tablespoon extra-virgin olive oil
Salt and black pepper to taste

Poke a few holes in the spinach bags and microwave them on high for 4 minutes, until the spinach is wilted. While the spinach is cooking, toss the cheese, olive salad, and oil in a serving bowl. Add the spinach and toss to coat. Season with salt and pepper.

Easy Cheesy Herbed Creamed Spinach

Creamed spinach is usually a big deal, requiring a separate white sauce and a long list of ingredients. Here the creaminess evolves instantly as a dollop of herbed cream cheese and a scattering of Parmesan turn into a sauce so lush it would seem to have simmered for hours.

Makes 4 servings

1 tablespoon extra-virgin olive oil
¼ cup chopped onion, frozen or fresh
2 bags (10 ounces each) cleaned spinach
¼ cup (2 ounces) soft garlic-and-herb cheese, such as Boursin
Salt and black pepper to taste
1 tablespoon grated imported Parmesan cheese

Heat the oil in a large nonstick skillet over medium heat and sauté the onion until tender but not brown, about 2 minutes. Sauté the spinach until wilted and almost dry, about 3 minutes. Remove from the heat and stir in the herb cheese, salt, pepper, and Parmesan.

Curried Spinach

The combination of spinach, curry, and potatoes is common in India, but *Aloo Sak* (potatoes and spinach) typically simmers for a while, because although the spinach cooks quickly, the potatoes, as the longest-cooking ingredient, dictate the timing. Not here. In this recipe the spinach sets the pace. As soon as it softens, a precooked curry sauce is added with a handful of instant potato flakes. The flakes lend the recipe the flavor of potato while preserving the integrity of the spinach.

Makes 4 servings

2 teaspoons olive oil
3 bags (7 ounces each) baby spinach
⅔ cup jarred curry sauce
½ cup instant mashed potato flakes
Salt and black pepper to taste

Place a large skillet over medium-high heat. Add the oil, and when it is hot add the spinach and stir until the spinach leaves wilt. Add the curry sauce and bring to a boil. Stir in the potato flakes, salt, and pepper, and remove from the heat. Set aside for 2 minutes before serving.

Broccoli and Apples with Bacon

Broccoli and apple is one of my favorite wacky flavor pairings. The acrid pungency of the broccoli and the mild sweetness of the apple are culinary soulmates. Here they are enhanced with a smoky hit of bacon and the piney scent of rosemary.

Makes 4 servings

2 strips ready-to-serve bacon, finely
   chopped
¼ cup chopped onion, frozen or fresh
⅛ teaspoon dried crushed rosemary
1 pound fresh broccoli florets
1 tart apple, peeled, cored, and cut into
   bite-size chunks
Salt and black pepper to taste
1 teaspoon lemon juice, organic bottled
   or fresh

Combine the bacon, onion, and rosemary in a 2-quart microwave-safe baking dish or casserole. Microwave, uncovered, at high power for 3 minutes. Add the broccoli and apple, toss to combine, cover, and microwave at high power for 3 minutes. Uncover, toss to redistribute the contents, and microwave, uncovered, at high power for 1 minute more, until the broccoli is bright green and the broccoli and apple are tender. Season with salt, pepper, and lemon juice.

Broccoli Rabe with Roasted Grapes

Of the basic four flavors we taste on the tongue, bitterness is the hardest to love. No wonder broccoli rabe has such a tough time. This pungent green is decidedly bitter. That quality may challenge newcomers, but for seasoned rabe-o-philes, it's what elevates rabe above the ordinary. In this recipe the rabe's bitterness is turned to bittersweet with the addition of roasted grapes and garlic.

Makes 6 servings

8 ounces seedless red grapes
3 tablespoons extra-virgin olive oil
2 bunches broccoli rabe, ends trimmed,
   washed
Pinch of crushed red pepper flakes
Kosher salt to taste
1 teaspoon chopped garlic, jarred or
   fresh

Preheat the oven to 400°F. Toss the grapes with 1 tablespoon of the oil in a pie pan and bake for 15 minutes, until the grapes are shiny and puffed.

Meanwhile, boil the broccoli rabe in water until tender and drain. Heat the remaining oil in a large, heavy skillet. Add the rabe to the pot. Sprinkle with pepper flakes and salt. Sauté until dry. Toss with the grapes and serve.

Cabbage Flowers with Raisins and Capers

Broccoli and cauliflower, both flowers of the cabbage, have an acrid aroma (as do all members of the cabbage family). That aroma is balanced in this recipe by the sweetness of raisins and the salty brine of capers. The sauce gets its creaminess from mayonnaise. Do not use fat-free or reduced-fat mayonnaise, which can separate when warmed.

Makes 4 servings

1 package (10 ounces) fresh broccoli florets
1 package (10 ounces) fresh cauliflower
florets
⅓ cup jarred caponata or antipasto
3 tablespoons regular mayonnaise
⅓ cup golden raisins
2 tablespoons nonpareil capers

Combine the broccoli and cauliflower in a microwave-safe bowl, cover with plastic wrap, and microwave at full power for 4 to 5 minutes, until heated through. Meanwhile, combine the caponata, mayonnaise, raisins, and capers. When the broccoli and cauliflower are hot, drain off any excess water and toss with the sauce.

Orange Mustard Cauliflower

The humble cauliflower is just spry enough to stand up to assertive flavors such as olives, capers, mustard, and blue cheese. In this recipe steamed cauliflower is tossed with a sweet and pungent glaze of bitter orange marmalade, spicy brown mustard, and garlic, transforming the sallow wallflower into a gastronomic diva.

Makes 4 servings

1½ pounds fresh cauliflower florets
¼ cup bitter orange marmalade
2 tablespoons spicy brown mustard
½ teaspoon minced garlic, jarred or fresh
1 teaspoon olive oil
1 tablespoon freshly chopped Italian
(flat-leaf) parsley
Salt and black pepper to taste

Cook the cauliflower in a large pot of boiling water until tender, about 4 to 5 minutes, or in a covered microwave-safe bowl for 4 minutes at full power. Meanwhile, combine the marmalade, mustard, garlic, oil, parsley, salt, and pepper. Toss the mixture with the cooked cauliflower.

Curried Cauliflower

No one would guess that this exotic side dish, laden with spices, golden raisins, and flecks of toasted coconut, is made completely in a microwave oven. A microwave can only steam, but if an ingredient contains enough oil (coconut, for example), the microwave can toast it with no additional fat.

Makes 6 servings

½ cup shredded unsweetened coconut
  (see Note)
½ cup golden raisins
1½ pounds fresh cauliflower florets
1 jar (16 ounces) curry simmer sauce
Salt and black pepper to taste

Place the coconut in a large microwave-safe bowl and microwave at full power for 3 minutes, stirring halfway through, until the coconut is lightly toasted. Add the raisins, cauliflower, and curry sauce, and toss to coat the ingredients evenly. Cover and microwave on high for 7 minutes, until the cauliflower is tender. Season with salt and pepper.

NOTE: Sweetened coconut can be substituted, but you must check it every 30 seconds or so to make sure it doesn't burn. Stop cooking it as soon as it is lightly browned.

Parmesan Dijon Cauliflower

Cauliflower has a tendency to release sulfur as it cooks. Most people find the smell unpleasant, and there are many ways to minimize this phenomenon. One of the most foolproof methods is to add a dairy product to the cooking liquid. In this recipe cauliflower is steamed with milk and sauced with a creamy salad dressing and Parmesan cheese.

Makes 6 servings

1½ pounds fresh cauliflower florets
¼ cup milk
3 tablespoons Dijon mustard salad dress-
  ing
1 tablespoon grated imported Parmesan
  cheese

Place the cauliflower and milk in a large microwave-safe bowl, cover, and microwave at full power for 7 minutes, until the cauliflower is tender. Uncover, toss with the dressing, and sprinkle with the cheese.

Black Pepper Cabbage

Cabbage is pleasantly peppery, and this recipe exploits that property by adding a fair amount of cracked black pepper. But, unfortunately, cabbage is also unpleasantly sulfurous. Years ago cooks dealt with the sulfur by boiling cabbage until the fumes evaporated. Here's a better way: Stop the cooking before the cabbage releases its sulfur in the first place. This recipe utilizes the ready availability of preshredded cabbage (sold as coleslaw mix) to yield slightly crunchy cabbage with hardly a whiff of sulfur.

Makes 4 servings

1 tablespoon extra-virgin olive oil
½ cup chopped onion, frozen or fresh
1 package (16 ounces) coleslaw mix
1 teaspoon minced garlic, jarred or fresh
Salt to taste
1 teaspoon cracked black pepper
1 tablespoon butter

Heat the oil in a large, deep skillet and sauté the onion until soft, about 1 minute. Add the coleslaw, garlic, and salt, and cook about 3 minutes, stirring until the cabbage is barely tender. Add the pepper and cook 1 minute more. Stir in the butter.

Ginger-Roasted Brussels Sprouts

Brussels sprouts are yet another vegetable in the diverse cabbage family. They are, in essence, miniature heads of cabbage that grow in several places up the cabbage stem. Although they are typically boiled, this recipe gives them a wonderfully sweet, nutty flavor by roasting them in a super-hot oven just until they are soft.

Makes 6 servings

Nonstick olive oil spray
2 pints Brussels sprouts, outer leaves and
*   stems trimmed, cut in half lengthwise*
1 tablespoon chopped ginger, jarred or
*   fresh*
1 teaspoon chopped garlic, jarred or
*   fresh*
Kosher salt and freshly ground pepper to
*   taste*

Preheat the oven to 400°F. Coat a rimmed sheet pan with oil spray. Toss the sprouts, ginger, and garlic together, and place on the sheet pan in an even layer. Season liberally with salt and pepper, add more oil spray, and roast about 15 minutes, until the sprouts are browned and barely tender. Adjust the seasoning if needed.

Green Beans in Almond Butter

Green beans amandine has come to typify the pretension of fine food rather than the artful blend of toasted nuts and buttery beans that it is. By substituting almond butter for the almonds, this recipe simplifies the preparation and modernizes the dish, recapturing its buttery, nutty culinary roots. Note that almond butter is available salted or unsalted in health food stores and some upscale groceries.

Makes 4 servings

1½ pounds green beans, ends removed
1 tablespoon almond butter
1 tablespoon butter, preferably unsalted
¼ teaspoon minced garlic, jarred or fresh
Salt and black pepper to taste

Cook the green beans about 4 minutes in a large pot of boiling water, until the beans are bright green. Drain the beans and toss them with the almond butter, butter, garlic, salt, and pepper until they are well coated.

Sweet Tomato Green Beans

Green beans go great with tomato, except that you can't cook them together. If you do, the beans turn olive drab and the tomato ever so slightly gray. This recipe gets around that problem by never cooking the two together. The tomato is part of a sweet, spicy dressing that is tossed with the steamed beans just before they're served.

Makes 4 servings

1 pound frozen green beans, whole or cut
⅓ cup water
4 teaspoons hot jalapeño jelly
2 teaspoons tomato paste in a tube
1 teaspoon minced garlic, jarred or fresh
¼ teaspoon hot pepper sauce
Salt and black pepper to taste

Cook the green beans in the water, either in a saucepan or at full power in a microwave, until heated through, about 4 minutes. Combine the jelly, tomato paste, garlic, and hot pepper sauce in a serving bowl. Drain the beans, toss them with the sauce, and season with salt and pepper.

Pesto-Painted Green Beans

Pesto is Instant Riviera. Brush it on green beans, toss it with tomatoes, drizzle it over mushrooms, or implant it in eggplant, and the vegetables are immediately transported to the beaches of Provence or the shores of Liguria. And best of all, high-quality pesto is now readily available, fresh as a refrigerated prepared sauce or jarred as a condiment. In this recipe it is fortified with additional garlic and olive oil, and enhanced with lemon peel before it glazes steamed green beans.

Makes 4 servings

1 pound frozen green beans
⅓ cup water
3 tablespoons basil pesto, jarred or fresh
2 teaspoons grated imported Parmesan cheese
½ teaspoon dried lemon peel
1 teaspoon minced garlic, jarred or fresh
2 tablespoons extra-virgin olive oil
Salt and black pepper to taste

Cook the green beans in the water, either in a saucepan or at full power in a microwave, until heated through, about 4 minutes. Combine the pesto, Parmesan, lemon peel, garlic, and oil in a serving bowl. Drain the beans, toss them with the sauce, and season with salt and pepper.

Peas, Prosciutto, and Sweet Peppers

This colorful confetti of peas, finely chopped ham, and roasted peppers is made with a frozen vegetable. Usually, fresh vegetables exceed frozen in color, flavor, and consistency, but not peas. Too often, fresh peas are old, woody, and bland or immature, tiny, and pale. They must be shelled, and the yield is only a fraction of what you paid for. On the other hand, frozen peas are consistent in size, sweetness, and color. Sometimes quality and convenience go hand in hand.

Makes 4 servings

1 tablespoon olive oil
1 pound frozen peas
4 slices (1½ ounces) prosciutto, finely chopped
¼ cup chopped roasted red bell pepper, jarred or fresh
1 tablespoon butter
Salt and black pepper to taste

Heat the oil in a medium skillet over medium heat. Add the peas and prosciutto, and cook until the peas are thawed, stirring occasionally. Stir in the bell pepper and butter, and season with salt and pepper.

Peas with Anchovies and Mint

Like other strong, assertive ingredients, anchovies are best thought of as a seasoning. Their olive oil richness, seawater salinity, and subtle fermented flavors underscore less complex flavors the same way that truffles transform scrambled eggs or Parmesan cheese perfects pasta. Here they add depth to one of my favorite flavor combinations, green peas and mint.

Makes 4 servings

1 pound frozen baby peas
2 teaspoons anchovy paste
1 teaspoon extra-virgin olive oil
1 tablespoon dried mint leaves
Freshly ground black pepper to taste

Heat the peas in a medium saucepan with a few tablespoons of water or in a covered microwave-safe bowl in a microwave at full power for 4 minutes. While the peas are cooking, combine the anchovy paste and oil in a serving bowl. Add the peas, mint, and pepper, and toss to coat. Cover and let rest for 1 minute to help the flavors mingle.

Very Ginger Glazed Carrots

Ginger has multiple personalities. It is hot on grilled meats, cooling in a curry, sweet in a cake, and fragrantly floral in ice cream. Here it is all things all at once. Baby carrots are sautéed with chopped gingerroot, braised in ginger beer, sweetened with ginger preserves, and brightened with vinegared sushi ginger.

Makes 4 servings

Nonstick oil spray
1 package (16 ounces) baby carrots
1 tablespoon chopped ginger, jarred or
  fresh
½ teaspoon chopped garlic, jarred or
  fresh
1 can or bottle (12 ounces) ginger beer,
  such as Reed's
2 tablespoons ginger preserves
Salt and black pepper to taste
2 tablespoons pickled sushi ginger, finely
  chopped

Heat a large nonstick skillet and coat with oil spray. Add the carrots and sauté until lightly browned, about 3 minutes. Add the ginger and garlic, and toss to combine. Add the ginger beer and ginger preserves, and stir to combine. Boil gently until the liquid has reduced to a glaze and the carrots are tender, stirring often. Season with salt and pepper. Stir in the pickled ginger.

Carrots Stir-Fried with Capers

Carrots get sweeter as they cook, and that sweetness skyrockets when they brown. In this recipe the super-high heat of stir-frying is used to maximize a caramelized sweetness. It is offset simply and elegantly with the addition of slightly salty, lightly pickled capers.

Makes 4 servings

1 tablespoon olive oil
1 package (16 ounces) baby carrots
1 teaspoon minced garlic, jarred or fresh
¾ cup chicken or vegetable broth
2 tablespoons capers
1 tablespoon chopped Italian (flat-leaf)
    parsley
Salt and black pepper to taste

Place a wok over high heat until very hot. Add the oil and stir-fry the carrots until they are lightly speckled with brown. Add the garlic and stir-fry for 1 or 2 seconds, until the garlic aroma is apparent. Add the broth, cover, and cook until the carrots are barely tender, about 2 minutes. Uncover, add the capers, and stir-fry until the remaining liquid is reduced to a glaze. Sprinkle the parsley over the carrots and season with salt and pepper.

Carrots Glazed with Red Pepper

Carrots and red bell pepper make a stunningly attractive couple. They create a color combo that vibrates like a pop art silk screen—and they taste pretty good together, too. Both are naturally sweet, but the carrot is a little earthy while the red pepper is fruitier and more floral. Here their differences are bridged with a combination of ginger, garlic, honey, and butter.

Makes 4 servings

1 teaspoon olive oil
1 pound sliced carrots
1 teaspoon minced ginger, jarred or
    fresh
1 teaspoon minced garlic, jarred or fresh
½ cup water
¼ cup jarred roasted red pepper spread
1 teaspoon butter, preferably unsalted
1 tablespoon honey
Salt and black pepper to taste

Heat the oil in a large skillet and sauté the carrots until they begin to soften, about 3 minutes. Add the ginger and garlic, and toss to combine. Add the water, cover, and simmer until the carrots are tender and the water has mostly evaporated, about 5 minutes. Stir in the pepper spread, butter, honey, salt, and pepper, and simmer for 1 to 2 minutes to blend the flavors.

Cumin Corn with Almonds

Cumin is closely associated with Mexican food, where it is paired inextricably with corn and cornmeal products. In this recipe panfried almonds further intensify the toasted, nutty character of the cumin.

Makes 4 servings

2 tablespoons butter
½ cup (about 2 ounces) sliced almonds
2 teaspoons ground cumin
Pinch of cayenne pepper
1 package (16 ounces) frozen corn kernels
Salt and black pepper to taste

Melt 1 tablespoon of the butter in a large skillet and sauté the almonds over medium heat until they are toasted, about 3 minutes. Transfer the almonds to a dish with a slotted spoon. Add the cumin and cayenne to the skillet, and stir briefly. Add the corn and sauté until the corn is heated through and the water has evaporated. Add the almonds, remaining butter, salt, and pepper.

Corn with Guacamole

In this novel version of creamed corn, guacamole replaces the cream and butter, and redirects the flavor south of the border. In place of dairy there are piquant chiles, sweet bell peppers, lush puréed avocado, and a spark of cider vinegar and lime.

Makes 4 servings

1 pound frozen corn kernels
¼ cup water
½ cup refrigerated guacamole
2 tablespoons finely chopped roasted red bell peppers, jarred or fresh
1 tablespoon canned diced green chiles, any heat level
¼ teaspoon apple cider vinegar
Salt and black pepper to taste

Cook the corn in the water, either in a saucepan or at full power in a microwave, until heated through, about 4 minutes. Combine the guacamole, peppers, chiles, and vinegar in a serving bowl. Drain the corn, toss with the sauce, and season with salt and pepper.

Sweet and Spicy Corn Pudding

Part corn bread, part soufflé, and part casserole, this lightly sweetened, mildly piquant corn pudding is wonderfully addictive and incredibly easy to prepare.

Makes 12 servings

2 cans (15 ounces each) corn kernels, drained
2 cans (15 ounces each) cream-style corn
2 cups (16 ounces) sour cream
3 eggs, large or extra-large, separated
2 teaspoons hot pepper sauce
2 tablespoons butter, melted
1 package (8.5 ounces) corn muffin mix
Nonstick oil spray

Preheat the oven to 375°F. Combine the corn, cream corn, sour cream, egg yolks, hot pepper sauce, butter, and corn muffin mix. Spray a 9 × 13-inch baking dish with oil. Beat the egg whites to a soft peak and fold into the batter. Pour into the baking dish and bake for 45 minutes, until browned and springy in the center.

Baked Plantains with Mustard Fruit

Plantains are savory bananas that taste like a cross between a potato and an underripe banana. If you want a little more banana flavor, look for plantains that are more yellow and have brown spots along their ridges. In this recipe the plantains are baked like potatoes but are seasoned to enhance their bananalike tropical personality.

Makes 4 servings

4 ripe plantains, yellow to black in color
½ cup mango or pineapple salsa
1 tablespoon spicy brown mustard

Preheat the oven to 375°F. Poke the plantains in several places with a skewer or fork. Place them in a single layer in a baking dish and bake for 45 minutes, until the skins are slightly puffed and crisp, and the fruit is easily pierced with a fork. While the plantains are baking, mix the salsa with the mustard.

When done baking, slit the skin of the plantains from end to end and push open like a baked potato. Spoon some of the mustard fruit into each opened plantain and serve with the remaining sauce on the side.

Sautéed Grape Tomatoes with Pesto

Grape tomatoes are relatively new, but in no time they took over the produce aisle—all but shutting out sales of their main competition, the cherry tomato. They are sweeter than cherry tomatoes and easier to eat in a single bite. They have become the darling of crudités platters and the poster vegetable for healthy snacks. In this recipe they are sautéed for a few minutes and tossed with pesto and Parmesan.

Makes 4 servings

1 tablespoon extra-virgin olive oil
¼ cup chopped onion, frozen or fresh
1 pint (12 ounces) grape tomatoes
1 teaspoon minced garlic, jarred or fresh
2 tablespoons basil pesto, jarred or fresh
1 teaspoon grated imported Parmesan cheese
Salt and black pepper to taste

Heat the oil in a large skillet and sauté the onion until tender. Add the tomatoes and sauté until they blister and burst, about 3 minutes. Stir in the garlic, remove from the heat, and stir in the pesto, Parmesan, salt, and pepper.

Tomatoes Sautéed with Chipotles

The intoxicating smoke of chipotle peppers enlivens a skillet of plain stewed tomatoes with a spicy wallop, transforming the geriatric of side dishes into a hip and trendy accompaniment to seafood, chicken, or meat.

Makes 4 servings

2 cans (14½ ounces) stewed tomatoes
1 teaspoon chopped roasted garlic, jarred or fresh
1 tablespoon chipotle hot pepper sauce
2 teaspoons lime juice, organic bottled or fresh
2 teaspoons cilantro pesto or chutney, or 2 tablespoons chopped cilantro (optional)

Combine the stewed tomatoes, garlic, and hot pepper sauce in a medium skillet or saucepan. Bring to a simmer and stir in the lime juice and cilantro if desired.

Apple Squash Purée

Creamy, buttery puréed vegetables continue to hover in and out of vogue on restaurant menus. But regardless of fashion, this one will always be delicious and decidedly simple. Frozen winter squash purée is sweetened with applesauce and enriched with butter. No food processor, no sieving, no whipping, no mess. Something this good doesn't deserve to be this easy.

Makes 4 servings

6 tablespoons unsalted butter
½ cup minced onion
2 packages (10 ounces each) puréed winter squash, thawed
½ cup applesauce
½ teaspoon pumpkin pie spice
Salt and black pepper to taste

Melt 2 tablespoons of the butter in a medium skillet or saucepan and sauté the onion until tender. Add the squash, applesauce, and pumpkin pie spice, and heat through, stirring often. Stir in the remaining butter until it has melted and is fully incorporated, and season with salt and pepper.

Asparagus with Lemon and Smoked Salmon

The brilliant green and deep salmon pink colors of this dish are spectacular, and its flavor is a takeoff on a classic poached salmon and asparagus. Although it could accompany any light meat, poultry, or seafood, it is perfect served with an omelet or scrambled eggs.

Makes 4 servings

1 pound asparagus, trimmed of hard ends
1 tablespoon extra-virgin olive oil
1 tablespoon lemon juice, organic bottled or fresh
Salt and black pepper to taste
1 ounce smoked salmon, cut in thin strips

In a large skillet with enough simmering water to cover the spears, poach the asparagus until they are bright green, about 1 to 2 minutes for thin to medium asparagus. Use tongs to transfer to a platter. (Or to microwave, place the asparagus in a single layer on a platter, sprinkle with 1 tablespoon of water, cover, and microwave at full power for 1 to 2 minutes. Uncover and drain the excess water.) Combine the oil and lemon juice, drizzle over the asparagus, season with salt and pepper, and scatter the smoked salmon over the top.

Eggplant Mousse with Orange Tomato Butter

Vegetable custards and mousses are in the highest echelon of haute cuisine, mostly because they take so much work—chopping, cooking, puréeing, and sieving. But commercially prepared baba ghanouj (Middle Eastern eggplant and tahini dip) changes all that. This eggplant mousse is seasoned with garlic and ginger, and is accompanied by a fragrant composed butter. Serve it as an accompaniment to roasted meats or grilled fish, or as an appetizer with pieces of toasted pita.

Makes 4 servings

Nonstick oil spray
1 container (8 ounces) baba ghanouj
1 large or extra-large egg
⅓ cup heavy cream
½ teaspoon minced garlic, jarred or fresh
½ teaspoon minced ginger, jarred or fresh
Salt and black pepper to taste
1 tablespoon sun-dried tomato pesto
⅓ cup orange juice
3 tablespoons unsalted butter

Preheat the oven to 350°F. Coat four 4-ounce ramekins or 4 cups of a muffin tin with oil spray. Whisk together the baba ghanouj, egg, heavy cream, garlic, ginger, salt, and pepper. Divide the mixture among the ramekins. Cover with plastic wrap, place in a shallow pan of hot water, and cover with foil. Bake for 40 minutes, until the mousse is set.

Meanwhile, in a small skillet, combine the pesto and orange juice, bring to a boil, and boil until the juice is reduced by half. Remove from the heat and mix in the butter.

To serve, uncover the mousses and run a knife around the edge of each ramekin. Invert each one onto a small plate and top with 1 tablespoon of the sauce.

Sicilian Artichokes

This simple sauté of artichoke hearts and tomatoes, seasoned with garlic, lemon, and parsley, is the quintessential Mediterranean antipasto, but it is also the perfect side dish for a plate of pasta, a seafood stew, or grilled chicken. In this recipe I call for frozen artichoke hearts, but if you have only canned, they will work almost as well.

Makes 4 servings

⅓ cup extra-virgin olive oil
1 cup chopped onions, frozen or fresh
1 tablespoon minced garlic, jarred or fresh
2 boxes (8 ounces each) frozen artichoke hearts, thawed
1 can (about 14 ounces) diced tomatoes, drained
Salt and black pepper to taste
3 tablespoons lemon juice, organic bottled or fresh
¼ cup chopped Italian (flat-leaf) parsley

Heat 2 tablespoons of the oil in a large skillet over medium-high heat. Sauté the onions until tender, about 3 minutes. Add the garlic and artichoke hearts, and sauté until the artichokes are dry on the surface. Add the tomatoes, salt, and pepper, and simmer for 5 minutes. Remove from the heat and stir in the remaining oil, the lemon juice, and parsley. Adjust the seasoning with salt and pepper if necessary.

Artichoke Hearts Braised with Peppers

Marinated artichoke hearts emerge from their jar fully prepared, so if you're going to cook with them, all they really need is a little dressing up. In this recipe the preparation involves little more than opening up another jar or two: some roasted peppers, a little chopped garlic, and a can of chicken broth.

Makes 6 servings

1 tablespoon extra-virgin olive oil
½ cup chopped onion, frozen or fresh
1 teaspoon chopped garlic, jarred or fresh
18 ounces marinated artichoke heart quarters (three 6-ounce jars or a 12-ounce jar plus a 6-ounce jar)
½ cup chicken or vegetable broth
½ cup chopped roasted red bell pepper, jarred or fresh
1 teaspoon balsamic vinegar
Salt and black pepper to taste

Heat the oil in a skillet and sauté the onion until soft. Add the garlic, stir to combine, and add the artichoke hearts, their marinade, the broth, and bell pepper. Heat until simmering and stir in the vinegar, salt, and pepper.

Balsamic Beets

Beets get a bum rap for being earthy and coarse, but blame the boiling, not the beets. Beets are naturally sweet. If you boil them, their sugars dissolve in the liquid and leave behind a reddened root that tastes mostly, well, earthy and coarse. But *bake* beet, and the sugars stay inside, with fabulously sweet results. Because the baking can take several hours, the perfect compromise is to use a microwave oven. It will steam the beets with a minimum of extra water. The beets cook quickly, but their sugars don't get washed away. In this recipe the beet flavor is enhanced with a syrup of honey and balsamic vinegar.

Makes 4 servings

1 pound fresh beets
1 tablespoon honey
1 tablespoon balsamic vinegar
Salt and black pepper to taste

Cut the leaves and stems from the beets, leaving about 1 inch of stems. Wash the beets to remove any loose surface dirt; leave wet. Snap off the "tail." Place in a microwave-safe bowl, cover with plastic wrap, and microwave on high for 12 to 15 minutes, until the beets are tender. Meanwhile, combine the honey, balsamic vinegar, salt, and pepper in a bowl.

When the beets are cooked, run them under cold water just until they are cool enough to handle. Cut the stem end from each beet, slip off the skins, quarter the beets, and toss with the honey-balsamic mixture.

Leeks Braised in Onion Soup

Leeks are underused. They are sweeter than shallots and more elegant than onions, but the way they are grown makes them very sandy. Although leek producers get rid of most of the sand, you have to finish the job by washing them well before cooking. But once cleaned, they can be sautéed, roasted, or deliciously braised. In this recipe leeks are braised in red wine and French onion soup.

Makes 4 servings

4 leeks, about 1 inch thick
1 tablespoon olive oil
1 package (1.4 ounces) Knorr French Onion Soup and Recipe Mix, or 1 can (10¾ ounces) Campbell's Condensed French Onion Soup
2 cups water
3 tablespoons balsamic vinegar
½ cup red wine

Preheat the oven to 425°F. Trim the root and dark green parts of the leeks. Slice the leeks in half lengthwise and run water within the layers to wash out any collected sand and soil. Shake off the excess water. Rub the leeks with oil, place them in a roasting pan in a single layer cut side up, and bake until browned, about 20 minutes. Meanwhile, combine the onion soup, water, vinegar, and wine. Pour the mixture over the leeks and bake until tender, about 20 minutes more.

Caramelized Onions with Blue Cheese

These roasted onions are the perfect side dish for a charcoal-grilled pepper-crusted steak and a baked potato. Be sure to make extra; they keep very well and make a great omelet filling or pasta topping.

Makes 4 servings

3 large onions, peeled and cut in 8
    wedges with root end attached
Nonstick olive oil spray
Salt and black pepper to taste
1 tablespoon extra-virgin olive oil
1 tablespoon minced roasted garlic,
    jarred or fresh
⅓ cup crumbled blue cheese
2 tablespoons chopped Italian (flat-leaf)
    parsley

Preheat the oven to 400°F. Coat the onion wedges with oil spray, spread out in a baking dish, and season with salt and pepper. Roast for 30 minutes, until golden brown and tender. Scrape into a bowl. Pour the oil into the baking dish, and use a spatula to scrape any brown bits clinging to the pan into the oil. Add the oil to the onions. Add the garlic and blue cheese, and toss to combine. Adjust the seasoning with salt and pepper, and sprinkle with parsley.

Roasted Fennel Provençal

Fennel is a bulbous vegetable that looks somewhat like celery but has a swollen base and feathery leaves. Fennel tastes like licorice, but that flavor becomes more subtle as the vegetable cooks. Here it is tossed with tomato bruschetta, olives, and pesto for an instant Provençal taste.

Makes 4 servings

Nonstick olive oil spray
2 fennel bulbs, trimmed of stems and
    leaves, sliced lengthwise ¼ inch thick
Salt and black pepper to taste
1 jar (12 ounces) tomato bruschetta
1 jar (8 ounces) olive salad
1 tablespoon pesto, jarred or fresh
1 teaspoon minced roasted garlic, jarred
    or fresh

Preheat the oven to 425°F. Coat a sheet pan with oil spray, arrange the fennel slices on the pan in a single layer, add more oil spray, and season liberally with salt and pepper. Roast for 15 minutes. Turn the fennel pieces and roast for another 5 minutes. While the fennel is roasting, combine the bruschetta, olive salad, pesto, and roasted garlic. Pour over the fennel, toss to mix, and roast 10 minutes more. Serve immediately or let cool to room temperature before serving.

Fennel Parmesan

The light licorice aroma of fennel sweetens the marinara sauce in which it is braised. Choose a light, chunky marinara product. If you have a very thick sauce, thin it with some broth or water.

Makes 4 servings

2 fennel bulbs, trimmed of stems and
   leaves
1 tablespoon extra-virgin olive oil
1 teaspoon chopped garlic, jarred or
   fresh
Salt and black pepper to taste
½ cup white wine
1½ cups light marinara sauce
2 tablespoons grated imported Parmesan
   cheese

Break the fennel bulbs into individual ribs and cut the wide ribs in half lengthwise. Heat the oil in a large skillet, add the fennel pieces, and sear them. Add the garlic, salt, pepper, and white wine, and bring to a boil. Add the marinara and heat to simmering. Cover and simmer until the fennel is tender, about 15 minutes. Scatter the Parmesan on top.

Braised Celery with Orange and Olives

Celery goes without notice. Simmering in soup, browning beneath a roast, adding crunch to a stuffing or bulk to a salad, it's everywhere—yet it is virtually ignored. That is odd for a vegetable of such distinctive flavor and crispness. This recipe gives celery its due by braising it simply and by enhancing its aromatic qualities with the perfume of orange peel, the sweetness of white wine, and the salty punch of fermented olives.

Makes 4 servings

2 celery hearts, trimmed of leaves and
   tops
2 tablespoons olive oil
1 cup chopped onions, frozen or fresh
1 teaspoon minced garlic, jarred or fresh
1 tablespoon dried orange peel
½ cup white wine
½ cup orange juice
Salt and black pepper to taste
½ cup olive salad

Cut each celery heart lengthwise into 4 or 5 wedges. Heat the oil in a large skillet, brown the celery on both sides, and transfer to a platter. Add the onions to the hot pan and cook for 1 minute, stirring constantly. Add the garlic, orange peel, wine, orange juice, salt, and pepper. Return the celery to the pan, cover, and simmer over medium heat for 30 minutes, until the celery is soft. Toss in the olive salad and serve.

Roasted Mushrooms with Roasted Garlic and Cheese

Mushrooms are largely water. As they roast the water evaporates, which intensifies their flavor and gives them a rich meaty texture.

Makes 4 servings

1 pound cleaned mushrooms
1 tablespoon olive oil
Salt and black pepper to taste
1 tablespoon minced roasted garlic, jarred or fresh
½ teaspoon good-quality balsamic vinegar
2 tablespoons grated imported Parmesan cheese

Preheat the oven to 450°F. Toss the mushrooms with the oil, salt, and pepper in a pie plate or on a baking sheet. Bake about 15 minutes, until the mushrooms just begin to brown and release their juices. Remove from the oven and toss with the roasted garlic and vinegar. Sprinkle with the Parmesan and serve.

Broiled Portobello Mushrooms

Portobello mushrooms, the prime rib of fungi, are essentially white mushrooms gone to spore. As white mushrooms mature, they darken from pale cream to woodland brown. Their caps spread, their flesh becomes spongier, and their flavor grows more intense. In other words, they become Portobellos. Portobellos are often grilled or broiled because of their size. In this recipe they are glazed with a bit of balsamic vinegar and a dusting of Parmesan for flavoring.

Makes 4 servings

1 pound (about 4) large Portobello mushroom caps, wiped clean
¼ cup oil and vinegar salad dressing
4 teaspoons balsamic vinegar
2 teaspoons grated imported Parmesan cheese
Kosher salt and coarsely ground black pepper to taste

Preheat the broiler and place a rack about 4 inches from the flame. Arrange the mushroom caps upside down on a broiler pan and drizzle 2 tablespoons of the dressing over them. Broil until the surface of the caps is moist and starting to brown. Turn them over and coat with the remaining dressing. Broil 5 minutes more, until the caps are thoroughly browned. Remove to a cutting board and cut into thick slices. Drizzle with the vinegar and sprinkle with the Parmesan, salt, and pepper.

Mushrooms Broiled with Sweet Onions

Vidalia, Maui, and other varieties that we call "sweet onions" are not higher in sugar than other onions. In fact, they have less sugar. What makes them sweet is that they have less volatile onion flavor, so when eaten raw, they seem less pungent or sweeter. Other onions actually have more sugar than "sweet" varieties. For that reason they caramelize much better when grilled or broiled.

Makes 4 servings

1 pound cleaned white mushrooms
2 medium-size onions, cut in 8 wedges
3 tablespoons balsamic salad dressing
Kosher salt and freshly ground black
*   pepper to taste*

Preheat the broiler and set a rack 4 inches from the flame. Toss the mushrooms, onion wedges, and dressing together. Spread out in a single layer on a broiler pan and season with salt and pepper. Broil for 15 minutes, tossing halfway through, until the mushrooms are well browned and the onions are tender and browned on their edges.

Exotic Mushroom Stew

This mushroom dish is so richly exotic and so fragrant with lush mushroom flavor that no one will guess you prepared it without even using a knife. White mushrooms have been available presliced for years, and Portobellos have followed suit. Now crimini and shiitakes are available fully washed, fully trimmed, and sliced. Using mushroom broth for the braising liquid intensifies the mushroom flavor.

Makes 6 servings

2 tablespoons butter
1 cup chopped onions, frozen or fresh
1 pound sliced crimini, Portobello, or
*   other exotic mushrooms*
1 pound sliced white mushrooms
1 teaspoon dried crushed rosemary
1½ cups mushroom or beef broth
1 can (about 14 ounces) diced tomatoes,
*   drained*
2 tablespoons chopped Italian (flat-leaf)
*   parsley*
Salt and black pepper to taste

Melt the butter in a large, deep skillet over medium-high heat and sauté the onions until softened. Add the mushrooms and rosemary, and cook until the mushrooms begin to release their moisture. Add the broth and tomatoes, and simmer for 5 minutes. Stir in the parsley and season with salt and pepper.

CHAPTER 9

DISTINCTIVE GRAINS

Sweet Curried Rice with Pistachios
Dirty Rice
Basmati Rice with Tobiko and Capers
Simple Rice Pilaf with Vegetables
Vanilla Rice
Coconut Rice
Curried Rice and Lentils
Lemon Basmati Rice
Fruity Brown Rice
Shrimp and Basil Pilaf
Rice and Chickpea Pilaf
Spinach Pilaf
Variations on Wild Rice Pilaf
Pilaf with Hazelnuts and Currants
Artichoke Tomato Pilaf
Mushroom and Chicken Liver Risotto
Broccoli Confetti Risotto
Winter Garden Risotto
Herbed Risotto
Tuna and White Bean Risotto
Pumpkin Seed Risotto

Paella Risotto
Fried Rice Niçoise
Rice Fried with Orzo
Savory Rice Pudding
Sweet and Spicy Rice Pudding
Mint Couscous with Tart Cherries
Porcini Quinoa
Quinoa with Smoked Salmon and Dill
Kasha and Tortellini
Tuna and Basil Tabbouleh
Black Bean Bulgur Salad
Mushroom Barley Pilaf
Creamy Goat Cheese Polenta
Scallion Polenta
Polenta Cakes with Tapenade Butter
Chorizo Polenta
Hominy Nachos
Posole Succotash
Chili Corn Bread
Corn Bread Blini with Cilantro Sour Cream

Sweet Curried Rice with Pistachios

Thai green curry is made from coconut milk, green chiles, lemongrass, cilantro, and a mixture of curry spices. It is available jarred as a sauce, but if you can't find it, you can mix your own by whisking a packet of Thai green curry paste or powder into a can of coconut milk. In this recipe the piquant curry is sweetened with golden raisins and pistachio nuts.

Makes 4 servings

1 tablespoon butter
½ cup diced onion, frozen or fresh
1 cup long-grain rice
½ teaspoon cinnamon sugar
1 cup Thai green curry sauce
1¼ cups chicken broth
¼ cup golden raisins
¼ cup shelled pistachio nuts

Melt the butter in a medium saucepan and sauté the onion until tender. Add the rice and cinnamon sugar, and toss to coat. Add the curry sauce and broth, and stir to combine. Cover and simmer for 10 minutes. Add the raisins, cover again, and simmer 5 minutes more, until all the liquid has been absorbed. Add the pistachios, and fluff with a fork to incorporate the pistachios and separate the rice grains.

Dirty Rice

Dirty rice is a southern country specialty made by cooking rice with chopped-up chicken giblets. But substituting a container of chopped chicken liver from the deli gets rid of the mess, the chopping, and the chicken without sacrificing any of the flavor.

Makes 4 servings

1 teaspoon oil
1 cup diced bell peppers, frozen or fresh
8 ounces chopped chicken liver
1 cup long-grain rice
2½ cups chicken broth
Salt and crushed red pepper flakes to taste

Heat the oil in medium saucepan and sauté the peppers until tender. Add the chicken liver and break it up into small pieces. Add the rice and broth, and stir to combine. Season with the salt and pepper flakes. Cover and simmer over low heat for 15 minutes, until all the liquid has been absorbed. Fluff with a fork to separate the rice grains.

Basmati Rice with Tobiko and Capers

Tobiko is flying fish roe, which is frequently used in making sushi. It is bright orange, lightly crunchy, and a little sweet. It is available in Asian markets and is often found with the sushi in large supermarkets. In this recipe the tobiko flavors basmati rice, a fragrant long-grain rice from Asia. For the best results rinse the basmati rice before cooking to wash away surface starch and soften the rice so that it cooks more evenly and more quickly.

Makes 4 servings

1½ cups basmati rice, rinsed and drained
3 cups water
1 teaspoon salt
¼ cup tobiko or masago (Japanese fish roe)
1 tablespoon nonpareil capers

Combine the rice, water, and salt in a small saucepan. Bring to a boil, cover, and simmer over low heat until the rice is tender and the liquid has been absorbed, about 15 minutes. Take the pot off the heat and remove the lid. Add the tobiko and capers, cover with a clean, folded dish towel, and replace the lid. Let rest for 5 minutes. Fluff with a fork to incorporate the tobiko and separate the rice grains.

Simple Rice Pilaf with Vegetables

Pilaf is a method of cooking rice, in which the rice is sautéed to coat it with fat before the liquid is added to ensure that the rice grains stay separate as they soften. In this straightforward recipe, vegetables are added to the pilaf in sequence so that each one reaches tenderness at the moment the rice is done cooking.

Makes 4 servings

1 tablespoon vegetable oil
½ cup chopped onion, frozen or fresh
1⅓ cups long-grain rice
3 cups chicken or vegetable broth
Salt and pepper to taste
1 cup shredded carrots
6 to 8 ounces (about 2 cups) precut fresh vegetables (such as broccoli or cauliflower florets; asparagus cut in 1-inch lengths; green beans cut in half; diced bell pepper)

Heat the oil in a large saucepan and sauté the onion until tender. Add the rice and coat with oil. Add the broth, salt, and pepper, stir the rice once, and heat until boiling. Lower the heat so that the broth simmers gently, cover, and cook for 10 minutes.

Add the carrots and other vegetables, cover, and simmer 5 minutes more, until the rice is tender, the broth has been absorbed, and the vegetables are al dente. Fluff the rice with a fork to separate the grains.

Vanilla Rice

The combination of vanilla and rice may seem strange, but I assure you that once you take a bite, it will become your new comfort food. The rice is ever so slightly sweet, with a hint of cayenne fire and a floral fragrance that lingers on the palate long after the last swallow is gone.

Makes 4 servings

2 cups water
½ teaspoon salt
1 teaspoon sugar
Dash of cayenne pepper
1 cup long-grain or basmati rice
½ teaspoon vanilla extract

Bring the water to a boil in a small saucepan. Add the salt, sugar, cayenne pepper, and rice, and stir. Heat until simmering, cover, and simmer about 15 minutes, until the rice is tender and the liquid has been absorbed. Take the pot off the heat and remove the lid. Sprinkle with vanilla and fluff the rice with a fork to separate the grains.

Coconut Rice

Simmering rice in coconut milk is common in Southeast Asian cuisines. This recipe embellishes the tradition by adding minced gingerroot and toasted coconut.

Makes 4 servings

1½ cups long-grain rice
1 can (14 ounces) coconut milk, regular or light
1 cup water
1 teaspoon chopped ginger, jarred or fresh
Salt and pepper to taste
¼ cup shredded unsweetened coconut

Combine the rice, coconut milk, water, ginger, salt, and pepper in a small saucepan and simmer for 15 minutes, until the liquid has been absorbed and the coconut is tender. While the rice is cooking, place the coconut on a microwave-safe plate and microwave at full power for 2 to 3 minutes, until lightly toasted. Take the rice off the heat, remove the lid, scatter the coconut on top, cover with a clean, folded dish towel, and replace the lid. Let rest for 5 minutes. Fluff the rice with a fork to separate the grains and mix in the coconut.

Curried Rice and Lentils

Cooked and eaten together, rice and lentils form a complete protein. Although ancient cultures were not aware of the nutrition behind it, they must have admired the combination, for beans and rice have been served together in almost every culture for as long as recipes have been recorded. This one follows a favorite Indian flavor combination, matching rice, dal (lentils), and masala (curry).

Makes 4 servings

2 cups chicken broth
1 cup long-grain rice
1 can (about 15 ounces) lentils, rinsed
   and drained
¼ cup curry sauce
2 tablespoons chopped Italian (flat-leaf)
   parsley
Salt and black pepper to taste

Heat the broth to a boil in a medium saucepan. Add the rice, stir, and bring to a simmer. Cover and cook until the rice is tender and the broth has been absorbed, about 15 minutes. Take off the heat, remove the lid, and add the lentils, curry sauce, and parsley. Do not mix. Cover the pan with a clean, folded dish towel and replace the lid. Let rest for 5 minutes. Fluff the rice with a fork to separate the grains and mix in the lentils, curry sauce, and parsley.

Lemon Basmati Rice

Florally fragrant and subtly sweet, basmati rice is delicious when steamed plain, but the cooks of India and Pakistan, where most basmati is still grown, are never ones to refrain from embellishment. Citrus is a traditional basmati seasoning, and this recipe features lemon flavor twice. Lemon peel is added to the rice as it simmers, so the oil in the peel has adequate time to be released. Lemon juice goes in at the end because its lemon flavor is more volatile and will disperse quickly when exposed to heat.

Makes 4 servings

1 can (about 14 ounces) chicken or vegetable broth
1 teaspoon dried lemon peel
1 cup basmati rice
1 tablespoon lemon juice, organic bottled or fresh
1 tablespoon chopped Italian (flat-leaf)
   parsley, or 1 teaspoon dried chives
Salt and black pepper to taste

Simmer the broth in a small saucepan and stir in the lemon peel and rice. Return to a simmer, cover, and cook until the broth has been absorbed, about 15 minutes. Take off the heat, remove the lid, and add the lemon juice, parsley, salt, and pepper. Do not mix. Cover with a clean, folded dish towel and replace the lid. Let rest for 5 minutes. Fluff the rice with a fork to separate the grains and mix in the lemon juice and parsley.

Fruity Brown Rice

The growing popularity of basmati rice has brought about a field of spin-offs. American-grown basmati is marketed under the names Kasmati and Texmati. Texmati is available in whole-grain brown rice, too, as are many brands of Indian and Pakistani basmati rices. Although the American basmatis are not as fragrant as the imports, the brown Texmati is quite aromatic. It is my choice when making a sweet brown rice, such as this one that is simmered with dried fruit and spices.

Makes 6 servings

2 cups Rice Select Texmati Brown Rice
4 cups chicken or vegetable broth
½ teaspoon garlic powder
½ teaspoon onion powder
1 teaspoon salt
¼ teaspoon black ground pepper
½ cup coarsely chopped mixed dried fruit
2 scallions, roots trimmed, thinly sliced

Combine the rice, broth, garlic powder, onion powder, salt, pepper, and fruit in a large saucepan. Simmer, covered, for 45 minutes, until the rice is tender and all the liquid has been absorbed. Take the pot off the heat, remove the lid, and add the scallions. Fluff with a fork to separate the rice grains and incorporate the scallions.

Shrimp and Basil Pilaf

Rice cooked in water is rice. Rice cooked in broth is a meal. As rice simmers, it absorbs liquid, and if that liquid is flavored, the rice will be, too. In this recipe, rice is cooked in chicken broth and then tossed with shrimp and basil pesto. You'll enhance the shrimp flavor by using a fish bouillon cube dissolved in water instead of chicken broth.

Makes 4 servings

1 tablespoon vegetable oil
½ cup chopped onion, frozen or fresh
1½ cups long-grain rice
3 cups chicken broth
Salt and black pepper to taste
8 ounces shelled and cleaned shrimp, thawed if frozen, cut in bite-size pieces
3 tablespoons pesto, jarred or fresh

Heat the oil in a heavy saucepan and sauté the onion until lightly browned. Add the rice and stir to coat it with the oil. Add the broth, salt, and pepper, and simmer until the rice is tender and the liquid has been absorbed, about 15 minutes. Take the pot off the heat and remove the lid. Add the shrimp, cover with a clean, folded dish towel, and replace the lid. Let rest for 5 minutes to allow the shrimp to heat through. Add the pesto and fluff the rice with a fork to separate the grains and mix in the shrimp and pesto.

Rice and Chickpea Pilaf

Chickpeas circle the globe. They appear in almost all warm-climate cuisines, where they are frequently paired with rice (to make a complete protein). Here they are part of a simple pilaf, seasoned with garlic, lemon, and parsley.

Makes 4 servings

1 tablespoon olive oil
1 cup chopped onions, frozen or fresh
1 cup long-grain rice
½ teaspoon chopped garlic, jarred or fresh
1 can (about 19 ounces) chickpeas, rinsed and drained
2½ cups chicken or vegetable broth
Salt and black pepper to taste
½ teaspoon dried lemon peel, or 1 teaspoon freshly grated lemon zest
1 tablespoon lemon juice, organic bottled or fresh
1 tablespoon chopped Italian (flat-leaf) parsley

Heat the oil in a medium skillet and sauté the onions until tender, about 2 minutes. Add the rice and garlic, and toss to coat with the oil. Add the chickpeas, broth, salt, and pepper, and bring to a simmer. Cover and simmer until the rice is tender and the broth has been absorbed, about 15 minutes. Take the skillet off the heat and add the lemon peel, lemon juice, and parsley. Fluff with a fork.

Spinach Pilaf

Any pilaf can be made more beautiful, more flavorful, and more nutritious by adding a vegetable near the end of cooking. In this recipe baby spinach is added to the pot and is steamed by the residual heat from the rice. The steamed (and very shrunken) spinach is then combined with the rice and finished with a touch of lemon juice.

Makes 4 servings

1 tablespoon olive oil
½ cup chopped onion, frozen or fresh
1 cup long-grain rice
½ teaspoon chopped garlic, jarred or fresh
2 cups chicken or vegetable broth
Salt and black pepper to taste
1 bag (7 ounces) cleaned baby spinach, coarsely chopped
½ teaspoon lemon juice, organic bottled or fresh

Heat the oil in a large skillet and sauté the onion until tender, about 2 minutes. Add the rice and garlic, and toss to coat with the oil. Add the broth, salt, and pepper, and simmer until the rice is tender and the broth has been absorbed, about 15 minutes. Take the skillet off the heat, remove the lid, and add the spinach. Do not mix. Cover with a clean dish towel and replace the lid. Let rest for 5 minutes. Add the lemon juice and fluff the rice with a fork to separate the grains and mix in the spinach.

Variations on Wild Rice Pilaf

Wild rice is native to the northern Great Lakes, where the bulk of the world's supply is still grown and harvested. The cost of wild rice is high, which is why wild rice is often mixed with white or brown rice. The following recipes provide five distinctly different wild rice presentations. Serve the basic wild rice pilaf with any fish, meat, or poultry; the pistachio ginger wild rice pilaf with salmon or chicken; the sweet walnut wild rice pilaf with roasted lamb or beef; and the cilantro white bean wild rice pilaf with pork or roasted vegetables. Use the creamy garlic wild rice pilaf for stuffing a roasted turkey breast or accompanying sautéed veal.

Makes 4 servings

FOR BASIC WILD RICE PILAF:
1 tablespoon vegetable oil
1 cup chopped onions, frozen or fresh
1 cup long-grain and wild rice blend
2½ cups chicken broth
Salt and black pepper to taste

FOR PISTACHIO GINGER PILAF:
1 ounce pistachio nuts, coarsely chopped
    (about ¼ cup)
1 ounce crystallized ginger, chopped
    (about 3 tablespoons)

FOR SWEET WALNUT PILAF:
¾ ounce glazed walnuts, such as
    Diamond brand, coarsely chopped
    (about ¼ cup)
¾ teaspoon soy sauce

FOR CILANTRO WHITE BEAN PILAF:
8 ounces canned small white beans,
    rinsed and drained
2 teaspoons cilantro pesto or chutney, or
    2 tablespoons chopped cilantro

FOR CREAMY GARLIC PILAF:
1 ounce (¼ cup) herbed cream cheese,
    such as Boursin
1 teaspoon minced roasted garlic, jarred
    or fresh

Heat the oil in a large skillet and sauté the onions until tender, about 2 minutes. Add the rice and toss to coat with the oil. Add the broth, salt, and pepper, and simmer until the rice is tender and the broth has been absorbed, about 15 minutes.

Take the skillet off the heat and remove the lid. Add the ingredients for whichever variation you choose, cover the skillet with a clean dish towel, and replace the lid. Let rest for 5 minutes. Fluff the rice with a fork to separate the grains and mix in the ingredients added for your variation.

Pilaf with Hazelnuts and Currants

This raucous rice pilaf is plush with the crunch of hazelnuts and the winey flavor of currants. The hazelnuts taste richer if you roast them. Roasted hazelnuts are available in more and more places, although they're still not as common as the raw nuts.

Makes 4 servings

1 tablespoon olive oil
¾ cup chopped onion, frozen or fresh
1 teaspoon minced roasted garlic, jarred or fresh
1½ cups long-grain rice
3 cups chicken broth
⅓ cup dried currants
¾ cup chopped toasted hazelnuts (see Note)
1 tablespoon Italian (flat-leaf) parsley, or 1 teaspoon dried parsley flakes

Heat the oil in a heavy saucepan and sauté the onion until lightly browned. Add the garlic and rice, and stir until the rice is coated with the oil. Add the broth and simmer until the rice is tender and the liquid has been absorbed, about 15 minutes.

Take the pan off the heat and remove the lid. Add the currants, nuts, and parsley. Do not mix. Cover with a clean, folded dish towel and replace the lid. Let rest for 5 minutes. Fluff the rice with a fork to separate the grains and mix in the currants and nuts.

NOTE: Roast your own hazelnuts on a sheet pan in a preheated 375°F oven for about 15 minutes, until the nuts are golden brown. As they toast, their skins will loosen. You can remove the skins by enclosing the warm nuts in a dish towel and rubbing them vigorously.

Artichoke Tomato Pilaf

This Mediterranean-style pilaf owes its instant Riviera chic to what should by now be your two best friends: marinated artichoke hearts and tomato bruschetta.

Makes 4 to 6 servings

1 jar (6 ounces) marinated artichoke hearts
1¼ cups long-grain or basmati rice
2 cups chicken broth
1 cup tomato bruschetta, jarred or refrigerated
Salt and black pepper to taste

Heat the artichoke hearts and their marinade in a medium saucepan. Add the rice and stir to coat. Add the broth and simmer for 15 minutes, until the liquid has been absorbed and the rice is tender. Take the pan off the heat, remove the lid, and add the bruschetta, salt, and pepper. Fluff with a fork.

Mushroom and Chicken Liver Risotto

This recipe could be called Dirty Risotto, for it combines the flavors of Dirty Rice (page 241) with the ethereal creaminess of risotto. Since most of the flavor comes from a box of mushroom risotto, just add the chicken livers. You can choose among several brands and varieties of mushroom risotto (porcini, shiitake, Portobello, or plain old white). I've tried about half a dozen, and all have yielded good results. Unlike risotto from scratch, boxed risottos do not need to be mixed and attended to.

Makes 4 servings

1 tablespoon extra-virgin olive oil
8 ounces chicken livers, trimmed of fat
    and tendon, coarsely chopped
1 package (8 ounces) mushroom risotto,
    any type
2½ cups boiling water
Pinch of cayenne pepper

Heat the oil in a medium, heavy saucepan and sauté the livers until well browned. Add the rice from the risotto mix and toss until the grains are coated with oil. Add the water, cayenne pepper, and (if there is one) the seasoning packet from the risotto mix. Cover and simmer until the rice is tender and the liquid has become a creamy sauce, about 15 to 20 minutes.

Broccoli Confetti Risotto

Allow me to introduce you to broccoli coleslaw. You'll find it near the other preshredded slaws in your market's produce section. It looks a lot like coleslaw except that the main ingredient is shredded broccoli stem. Broccoli stems are crunchy, sweet, and mild, especially when julienned into slivers. They make a great salad and add instant panache and nutrition to this garden-fresh risotto.

Makes 4 servings

1 tablespoon olive oil
½ cup chopped red onion
1 box (5½ ounces) creamy Parmesan or
    Italian herb risotto
2½ cups water
2 cups broccoli coleslaw mix
Salt and black pepper to taste

Heat the oil in a heavy saucepan and sauté the onion until tender, about 1 minute. Add the rice from the risotto mix and toss until it is coated with oil. Add the water and seasoning packet from the risotto mix (if there is one), cover, and simmer until the rice is tender and the liquid has become a creamy sauce, about 15 minutes. Stir in the broccoli slaw and cook another few minutes, until the vegetables become tender. Adjust the seasoning with salt and pepper.

Winter Garden Risotto

This complex-tasting risotto is filled with vegetables, and its unusual sauce takes on a glorious auburn glow from butternut squash purée. In Modena they serve a festive tortelli filled with pumpkin purée and crushed bitter almond cookies. This risotto, made from the most modern convenience ingredients, finds its inspiration there.

Makes 6 servings

2 tablespoons olive oil
1 bag (16 ounces) coleslaw mix
1 teaspoon minced gingerroot, jarred or fresh
1 teaspoon minced garlic, jarred or fresh
1¼ cups arborio rice
1 container (32 ounces) chicken broth
1 box (10 ounces) frozen winter squash purée, thawed
1 tablespoon pesto, jarred or fresh
⅓ cup grated Parmesan cheese
¼ cup sliced roasted almonds
Salt and black pepper to taste

Heat the oil in a large skillet over medium heat and sauté the coleslaw mix until wilted. Stir in the gingerroot, garlic, and rice, and cook until the rice is well coated with oil. Add half of the broth, cover, and simmer, stirring often, until the broth has been almost completely absorbed. Add the remaining broth, cover, and continue cooking, stirring frequently, until the broth has been mostly absorbed and the rice is tender. The entire cooking process will take about 15 minutes.

Stir in the squash and heat through. Take the pot off the heat and stir in the pesto, Parmesan, almonds, salt, and pepper.

Herbed Risotto

Risotto is a creamy rice dish in which the rice is stirred to break down its starch. As the starch migrates from the rice into the broth, the broth thickens into a sauce. The trick is to stir constantly and to add just enough broth so that the rice reaches al dente perfection at the exact same moment that a silken creamy sauce develops. It isn't easy, but if you start with a cream soup, the sauce is there to begin with. There is no stirring, and when the rice is cooked, the dish is done.

Makes 4 servings

1 cup arborio rice
1 can (10¾ ounces) Campbell's Condensed Cream of Chicken with Herbs Soup
2 cans water
½ cup grated Parmesan cheese
Salt and black pepper to taste

Combine the rice, soup, and water in a large saucepan and bring to a simmer over medium heat, stirring often. Cover and simmer, stirring occasionally, until the liquid has reduced to a sauce and the rice is tender, about 15 minutes. Stir in the Parmesan and season with salt and pepper.

Tuna and White Bean Risotto

The tuna and white beans make this risotto hearty and nutritious enough to serve as a main course, which can be accompanied by a salad.

Makes 4 servings

1 tablespoon olive oil
1 box (5½ ounces) creamy Parmesan or Italian herb risotto
½ teaspoon chopped garlic, jarred or fresh
2½ cups water
1 can (about 6 ounces) white tuna in water, drained and flaked
1 small can (about 10 ounces) white beans, any size, rinsed and drained
2 tablespoons grated imported Parmesan cheese
2 tablespoons chopped Italian (flat-leaf) parsley
Salt and black pepper to taste

Heat the oil in a heavy saucepan. Add the rice from the risotto mix and the garlic, and toss until the rice is coated with oil. Add the water and seasoning packet from the rice mix (if there is one), cover, and simmer until the rice is tender and the liquid has become a creamy sauce, about 15 minutes. Stir in the tuna and beans, and cook another few minutes, until heated through. Add the Parmesan, parsley, salt, and pepper.

Pumpkin Seed Risotto

This risotto mingles the flavors of the Old and New Worlds with a topsy-turvy spin. Toasted pumpkin seeds, cilantro, and posole from Mexico unite with a Venetian risotto enriched with Italian Parmesan and Asian toasted sesame oil. I know it sounds wacky, like fusion run amok, but it tastes great.

Makes 4 servings

1 tablespoon olive oil
¼ cup raw pumpkin seeds
1 box (5½ ounces) Italian herb risotto
2½ cups water
1 can (about 15 ounces) posole, rinsed and drained
1 teaspoon cilantro pesto or chutney, or 1 tablespoon chopped cilantro
2 tablespoons grated imported Parmesan cheese
½ teaspoon Asian toasted sesame oil
Salt and black pepper to taste

Heat the olive oil in a medium, heavy saucepan and sauté the pumpkin seeds until they toast slightly, about 1 minute. Add the rice from the risotto mix and stir until the rice is coated with oil. Add the water, posole, and seasoning packet from the rice mix (if there is one), and bring to a boil. Lower the heat, cover, and simmer until the rice is tender and the liquid has become a creamy sauce, about 15 minutes. Stir in the cilantro, Parmesan, and sesame oil, and adjust the seasoning with salt and pepper.

Paella Risotto

This rice combines the flavors of paella with the creamy affluence of risotto. Because it is meant as a side dish, I have used just enough meat to flavor the rice and I have eliminated the seafood. But you can turn this risotto into an entrée by doubling the recipe and adding seafood near the end of the cooking. The Milanese risotto mix contains saffron, which will give you the characteristic golden glow of paella.

Makes 4 servings

1 tablespoon olive oil
2 ounces smoked ham or turkey breast, chopped (about ¼ cup)
1 pound chicken sausage, sliced ¼ inch thick
1 teaspoon chopped garlic, jarred or fresh
1 box (about 5 ounces) Milanese risotto
2½ cups boiling water
1 jar (16 ounces) salsa, any heat level
1 cup frozen small peas
Salt and black pepper to taste

Heat the oil in a large skillet, add the ham and sausage, and sauté until the meats are lightly browned. Add the garlic and rice mix, and stir until the rice is coated with oil. Add the water and seasoning packet from the rice mix (if there is one) and simmer, covered, until the rice is tender and the liquid has become a creamy sauce, about 15 minutes. Stir in the salsa and peas, and cook until heated through. Adjust the seasoning with salt and pepper.

Fried Rice Niçoise

There is a stigma to the word "leftover." Leftovers are unnecessary, unwanted, unused. I prefer to think of them as homemade convenience ingredients. Consider fried rice; if you had to boil rice every time you made fried rice at home, no one would ever do it. But start with leftover rice, and the dish is almost instantaneous. Just add the flavor—and it need not be Chinese. The flavor providers for this very un-Asian fried rice are Provençal.

Makes 4 servings

2 tablespoons extra-virgin olive oil
3 cups leftover cooked rice, or 1 cup raw rice cooked fresh
¼ cup olive salad
1 can (about 6 ounces) tuna packed in water, drained and flaked
1 tablespoon jarred chopped sun-dried tomatoes in olive oil
1 tablespoon basil pesto, jarred or fresh

Heat 1 tablespoon of the oil in a large skillet and sauté the rice until lightly browned. Add the olive salad, tuna, sun-dried tomatoes, and pesto, and stir to coat the rice. Remove from the heat and mix in the remaining oil.

Rice Fried with Orzo

This Rice-a-Roni wannabe is a combination of toasted pasta and garlicky, broth-infused rice. The only difference is the pasta. Here it is orzo, a noodle shaped like a rice grain that blends perfectly with the rice.

Makes 4 servings

1 tablespoon olive oil
½ cup orzo
1 cup long-grain rice
¼ teaspoon minced garlic, jarred or fresh
2 cups chicken broth
Salt and black pepper to taste

Heat the oil in a saucepan and sauté the orzo until lightly browned. Add the rice and toss to coat with the oil. Stir in the garlic, broth, salt, and pepper, and simmer, covered, until the rice is tender and the broth has been absorbed, about 15 minutes. Fluff with a fork to separate the rice grains. Adjust the seasoning if needed.

Savory Rice Pudding

Must a pudding be sweet? This one isn't. In the place of sugar, vanilla, and raisins, it is packed with onions, capers, pesto, and Parmesan cheese. The creamy results are similar to risotto, but this is saucier. And because it starts with leftover rice, it is ready in 5 minutes.

Makes 4 servings

1 tablespoon olive oil
½ cup chopped onion, frozen or fresh
1 tablespoon nonpareil capers
¼ teaspoon minced garlic, jarred or fresh
1 cup milk, 2% or whole
1 cup chicken or vegetable broth
2 cups leftover cooked rice, or ⅔ cup raw
    rice cooked fresh
⅓ cup grated imported Parmesan cheese
2 tablespoons basil pesto, jarred or fresh
¾ teaspoon salt

Heat the oil in a large saucepan and sauté the onion until tender. Add the capers and garlic, and stir briefly. Add the milk, broth, and rice, and simmer for 5 minutes. Add the Parmesan and stir until the mixture is creamy and thickened to a pudding consistency. Stir in the pesto and salt.

Sweet and Spicy Rice Pudding

This piquant rice pudding has the flavors of a Mexican mole. If you can't find chipotle salsa, substitute any spicy salsa, boosted with a pinch of ground chipotle pepper or a splash of chipotle hot sauce.

Makes 4 servings

1 tablespoon vegetable oil
½ cup chopped onion, frozen or fresh
¼ cup sliced almonds
½ cup raisins
¼ teaspoon ground cinnamon
¾ teaspoon salt
2 cups leftover cooked rice, or ⅔ cup raw rice cooked fresh
1½ cups chicken or vegetable broth
½ cup chipotle salsa
¼ cup sour cream

Heat the oil in a large saucepan and sauté the onion until tender. Add the almonds and raisins, and sauté 1 minute more. Stir in the cinnamon and salt. Add the rice, broth, and salsa, and simmer until thickened to a pudding consistency. Stir in the sour cream.

Mint Couscous with Tart Cherries

In Morocco, mint and couscous are *bon amis*. And in my house, mint and cherries, especially tart cherries, are a favorite combination. So it was inevitable that they would all meet. A couscous disclaimer: I know that couscous is really pasta, not a grain, but in this kind of preparation, it looks like a grain, acts like a grain, and tastes like a grain.

Makes 4 servings

1 cup water
2 teaspoons olive oil
½ cup packed coarsely chopped dried tart cherries, such as Montmorency
1 cup couscous
1 teaspoon crumbled dried mint leaves, or 2 tablespoons chopped fresh mint leaves
Salt and black pepper to taste

Boil the water, take the pot off the heat, and add the oil, cherries, couscous, mint, salt, and pepper. Cover and let rest for 5 minutes. Fluff with a fork and adjust the seasoning.

Porcini Quinoa

Quinoa (pronounced *keen*-wah) was the sacred grain of the Incas. Now it's an American wonder grain. It has a mild flavor and a light, crunchy texture, and it cooks in about the same time as white rice. Unless you wash it before cooking, it will taste very bitter. Here, quinoa is cooked with dried porcini, Italy's most common wild mushroom. If you have trouble finding them, you can substitute any dried wild mushroom.

Makes 4 servings

1 tablespoon vegetable oil
½ cup chopped onion, frozen or fresh
1¾ cups mushroom broth
2 ounces dried porcini mushrooms, broken in pieces
1 cup uncooked quinoa, washed thoroughly under running water
Salt and black pepper to taste
1 tablespoon chopped Italian (flat-leaf) parsley

Heat the oil in a small saucepan and sauté the onion until tender. Add the broth and dried mushrooms, and bring to a boil. Take the pot off the heat, cover, and let stand for 5 minutes. Add the washed quinoa and salt and pepper to the pot and simmer about 15 minutes, until the broth has been absorbed and the quinoa is tender. A curly white tail on the side of each quinoa grain indicates that it is cooked through. Add the parsley and fluff with a fork.

Quinoa with Smoked Salmon and Dill

The slightly nutty flavor and crunchy texture of quinoa is enhanced by the rich smoothness of smoked salmon. This recipe calls for vegetable broth, but you can intensify the flavor of the salmon by substituting a fish bouillon cube (such as Knorr) dissolved in boiling water.

Makes 4 servings

1 tablespoon olive oil
1 small onion, quartered and thinly sliced
1 cup uncooked quinoa, washed thoroughly under running water
1 can (about 15 ounces) vegetable broth
1 teaspoon dried dill weed, or 1 tablespoon chopped fresh dill
Salt and black pepper to taste
2 ounces smoked salmon, chopped
½ teaspoon lemon juice, organic bottled or fresh

Heat the oil in a medium-size skillet and sauté the onion until lightly browned. Add the washed quinoa, broth, dill, salt, and pepper. Simmer, covered, about 15 minutes, until the broth has been absorbed and the quinoa is tender. A curly white tail on the side of each quinoa grain indicates that it is cooked through. Add the salmon and lemon juice, fluff with a fork, and adjust the seasoning.

Kasha and Tortellini

Kasha (buckwheat groats) are quite soft and will become mushy if they are not coated with egg before simmering. In this recipe liquid egg substitute simplifies the process. The cooked kasha is tossed with tortellini as a variation on the traditional Jewish dish, kasha and bowties.

Makes 4 servings

1 package (9 ounces) refrigerated or
    frozen spinach or cheese tortellini
2 tablespoons liquid egg substitute or
    egg whites
1 cup whole-groat kasha
1 tablespoon minced roasted garlic,
    jarred or fresh
1 can (about 15 ounces) chicken broth
1 tablespoon jarred sun-dried tomato
    pesto
2 tablespoons chopped Italian (flat-leaf)
    parsley

Boil about 3 quarts of lightly salted water and cook the tortellini according to package directions until tender. Drain. Meanwhile, combine the egg and kasha, and sauté in a large heated skillet until the kasha separates into individual grains. Add the garlic, broth, and sun-dried tomato, and simmer about 10 minutes, until the kasha is puffed and the liquid has been absorbed. Stir in the tortellini and parsley, fluff with a fork, and adjust the seasoning.

Tuna and Basil Tabbouleh

Bulgur is whole wheat that is steamed, dried, and cracked, resulting in a grain that needs only to be soaked, not boiled, to make it edible. Soaked grains retain more flavor than those that are cooked, and their texture is chewy instead of soft. Because the grain is not fully expanded during soaking, it can better absorb the flavors of a sauce or a salad dressing—and this grainy entrée salad takes full advantage of that quality.

Makes 4 servings

1 package (about 5 ounces) tabbouleh
    (discard seasoning pack)
1 cup boiling water
1 can (about 6 ounces) tuna in water,
    drained and flaked
¾ cup tomato bruschetta, jarred or fresh
1 tablespoon basil pesto, jarred or fresh
1 teaspoon lemon juice, organic bottled
    or fresh
Salt and black pepper to taste

Combine the tabbouleh (without its seasoning pack) and boiling water. Cover loosely and set aside until the water has been absorbed, about 5 minutes. Add the tuna, bruschetta, pesto, lemon juice, salt, and pepper. Toss to distribute the ingredients evenly.

Black Bean Bulgur Salad

The combination of black beans and bulgur makes this southwestern-style grain salad a complete protein. The recipe is strictly vegan, but you can boost the protein by adding poultry, seafood, or a smoked meat.

Makes 4 servings

1 package (about 5 ounces) tabbouleh
1 cup boiling water
1 cup canned black beans, rinsed and
   drained
1 medium tomato, finely chopped
1 tablespoon cilantro pesto or chutney,
   or 3 tablespoons chopped cilantro
¼ cup chopped roasted red pepper,
   jarred or fresh
½ teaspoon chili powder
1 tablespoon lime juice, organic bottled
   or fresh
Salt and black pepper to taste

Combine the tabbouleh (without its seasoning pack) and boiling water. Cover loosely and set aside until the water has been absorbed, about 5 minutes. Add the beans, tomato, cilantro, pepper, chili powder, lime juice, salt, and pepper. Toss to distribute the ingredients evenly.

Mushroom Barley Pilaf

Although barley is available as a whole grain (groats) or as grits, it is most commonly found skinned, when it is called pearl barley. Pearl barley cooks faster than whole groats, and its flavor is much milder. In this recipe the barley is combined with sautéed mushrooms and the beefy sweet flavor of French onion soup, an addition that gives the grain incredible richness with minimum work.

Makes 4 servings

1 tablespoon vegetable oil
1 package (8 ounces) sliced mushrooms
1 cup pearl barley
½ cup white wine
½ cup water
2 cans (10¾ ounces each) Campbell's
   Condensed French Onion Soup
1 teaspoon tomato paste in a tube
1 tablespoon chopped Italian (flat-leaf)
   parsley
Black pepper to taste

Heat the oil in a large saucepan and sauté the mushrooms until they are lightly browned. Add the barley and toss to coat with the oil. Add the wine and bring to a boil. Add the water and soup, and stir to combine. Simmer, covered, for 30 minutes, or until the barley is tender. Stir in the tomato paste and parsley. Season with pepper; it should not need salt.

Creamy Goat Cheese Polenta

Recipes for polenta are fraught with warnings. Stir constantly! Watch out for splattering! Beware of scorching! It's amazing that such a simple food needs such a complex technique. But manufacturers have taken away the pitfalls without much sacrifice in quality. Prepared polentas are available refrigerated or vacuum-packed on the shelf. Most are intended to be sliced and sautéed, but you can chop them to make excellent creamy polenta as well.

Makes 4 servings

1 package (about 16 ounces) prepared polenta, chopped
1 teaspoon minced garlic, jarred or fresh
2 teaspoons basil pesto, jarred or fresh
2 ounces (½ cup) fresh goat cheese
Salt and black pepper to taste

Combine the polenta and garlic in a microwave-safe bowl, cover, and microwave at full power for 4 to 5 minutes, until steamy. Carefully remove the cover and stir in the pesto, cheese, salt, and pepper until smooth and creamy.

Scallion Polenta

When I was growing up, our neighbors, who I think were Lithuanian, made the most wondrously soft cornmeal mush. They called it "mamaliga," and it was loaded with chopped scallions and topped with great dollops of homemade sour cream. Only decades later did my repressed mamaliga memory resurface. Here it is, updated and slimmed down.

Makes 4 servings

1 package (about 16 ounces) refrigerated prepared polenta, chopped
1 teaspoon minced garlic, jarred or fresh
1 teaspoon minced ginger, jarred or fresh
1 bunch scallions, roots trimmed, finely chopped
Salt and black pepper to taste
1 cup sour cream or yogurt

Combine the polenta, garlic, and ginger in a microwave-safe bowl, cover, and microwave at full power for 4 to 5 minutes, until steamy. Carefully remove the cover and stir in the scallions, salt, and pepper until creamy. Serve with sour cream.

Polenta Cakes with Tapenade Butter

Tapenade, the pungent black olive paste of Provence, is the flavoring for a simple composed butter that glazes the crisped skin of these sautéed polenta cakes. The butter can be made days ahead and is great tossed with rice or pasta or plopped atop a baked potato.

Makes 4 servings

4 tablespoons (½ stick) butter, softened
1 tablespoon tapenade (black olive spread)
½ teaspoon minced garlic, jarred or fresh
2 teaspoons extra-virgin olive oil
2 teaspoons tomato paste in a tube
Salt and black pepper to taste
1 package (about 16 ounces) refriger-ated prepared polenta, cut in 12 slices
Nonstick olive oil spray

Combine the butter, tapenade, garlic, olive oil, and tomato paste, and season with salt and pepper. Place a large non-stick skillet over high heat, coat with olive oil spray, and brown the polenta slices on both sides. Add more oil spray as needed. Serve the polenta slices topped with the composed butter.

Chorizo Polenta

Chorizo, the highly spiced, coarsely ground Mexican sausage, is traditionally made with pork, but now you can find lower-fat versions made from chicken and turkey. Although this nouvelle chorizo can't compete in a side-by-side tasting with the real thing, when chopped up in a soup or paella or this creamy polenta, it lends the appropriate jolt of chili and a smoky tang that tastes quite authentic.

Makes 4 servings

Nonstick oil spray
8 ounces chorizo, chopped
1 package (about 16 ounces) refriger-ated prepared polenta, chopped
1 cup salsa, any heat level
Salt and black pepper to taste

Place a large nonstick skillet over high heat and coat with oil spray. Add the chorizo and sauté until lightly browned. Add the polenta and continue to sauté until the polenta and chorizo are both well browned. Stir in the salsa and season with salt and pepper.

Hominy Nachos

A laid-back presentation and vibrant flavors make this raucous vegetable side dish a perfect accompaniment for outdoor grilling or a casual meal of sandwiches. Assembled like nachos, the white kernels of hominy set off the red kidney beans and golden cheddar in a blaze of color and savor.

Makes 4 servings

1 can (19 ounces) whole hominy (or posole), rinsed and drained
1 cup canned red kidney beans, rinsed and drained
½ cup shredded sharp cheddar cheese, preferably yellow
1 cup salsa, any heat level

Arrange the hominy, beans, and cheese in layers on a microwave-safe platter. Heat in the microwave at full power for 2½ minutes, or until the cheese has melted. Spoon the salsa over the top.

Posole Succotash

Substituting posole for sweet yellow corn makes all the difference in this succotash. The textures are softer and creamier than traditional succotash, and the addition of salsa and cilantro gives this Native American staple a decided Latin flare.

Makes 4 servings

1 package (14 ounces) frozen lima beans
1 can (19 ounces) posole (or whole hominy), rinsed and drained
½ cup chicken or vegetable broth
½ cup salsa, any heat level
1 teaspoon cilantro pesto or chutney, or 1 tablespoon chopped cilantro

Combine the lima beans, posole, broth, and salsa in a medium saucepan. Heat through, stirring often. Stir in the cilantro.

Chili Corn Bread

Chili spices and beans transform this boxed corn bread from a standard bread accompaniment to a nutritious side dish. The beans modify the traditional crumbly consistency of corn bread, giving it a decidedly creamier texture.

Makes 8 servings

1 box (15 ounces) corn bread mix
1 teaspoon chili powder
1 teaspoon ground cumin
1 large or extra-large egg
½ cup vegetable oil
¾ cup milk, any fat content
1 can (15 ounces) red kidney beans, rinsed and drained
Nonstick oil spray

Preheat the oven to 375°F and place a 9-inch iron skillet or a 9-inch round cake pan in the oven as it preheats. Combine the corn bread mix, chili powder, and cumin. Add the egg, oil, and milk, and mix until the batter is smooth. Stir in the beans.

Remove the hot pan from the oven and coat the interior with oil spray. Pour the batter into the pan, return the pan to the oven, and bake for 45 minutes, or until a tester inserted in the center comes out clean. Cool on a rack for 5 minutes and cut into 8 wedges.

Corn Bread Blini with Cilantro Sour Cream

These savory corn pancakes are made with a box of corn bread mix, crowned with pale green cilantro cream.

Makes 24 pancakes, 6 to 8 servings

1 package (15 ounces) corn bread mix
2 teaspoons ground cumin
½ teaspoon ground chipotle pepper
2 cups milk, 2% or whole
2 large or extra-large eggs
1 cup corn kernels, frozen and thawed, or canned and drained
2 scallions, roots trimmed, thinly sliced
½ cup diced roasted red pepper, jarred or fresh
Nonstick oil spray
1 cup sour cream
2 tablespoons cilantro pesto or chutney, or ¼ cup chopped cilantro

Combine the corn bread mix, cumin, and chipotle pepper. Add the milk and eggs, and stir until smooth. Stir in the corn, scallions, and red pepper.

Heat a large skillet over high heat and coat with oil spray. Spoon the batter onto the hot pan, forming pancakes about 3 to 4 inches in diameter. Brown on both sides, and repeat with the remaining batter.

Combine the sour cream and cilantro. Serve with the pancakes.

CHAPTER 10

SALADS AND DRESSINGS IN AND OUT OF THE BOTTLE

Garlic Yogurt Dressing
Sweet Bacon Dressing
Niçoise Salad Dressing
Green Olive Vinaigrette
Salsa Vinaigrette
Chipotle Mayo
Hot Pepper Ranch Dressing
Caesar Tonnato Dressing
Tomato and Olive Oil Dressing
Pesto Dressing
Sesame Rice Wine Vinaigrette
Guacamole Ranch Dressing
Warm Endive Salad
Four-Can Salad
Shrimp and Spinach Salad with Grapefruit Vinaigrette
Chicken Corn Salad with Pinto Bean Vinaigrette
Spinach Salad with Red Pepper Vinaigrette
Salmon and Field Greens with French Fry Croutons
Cranberry Horseradish Turkey Salad

Barbecued Chicken Salad
Tuna and White Bean Salad
Tuna Salad with Coconut Green Curry
Shrimp and Cucumber Salad with Guacamole Dressing
Ginger Carrot Slaw
Sesame Cabbage Slaw
Sweet-and-Sour Coleslaw
Broccoli Cranberry Slaw
Broccoli Sprout Slaw
Crab and Corn Slaw
Potato Salad Niçoise
Maple Bacon Potato Salad
Potato Salad with Brown Butter Vinaigrette
Waldorf Potato Salad
Pastrami Potato Salad
Soba Noodle Salad with Balsamic Glaze
Crab, Lime, and Black Bean Salad
Corn Chili Salad
Red and Yellow Tomato Salad
Broccoli and Cauliflower Salad with Caper Dressing
Roasted Pepper and Mozzarella Salad
Roasted Pepper and Warm Goat Cheese Salad
Thai Shredded Pork Salad
Shrimp Caponata

Garlic Yogurt Dressing

Yogurt is one of the original convenience foods; it probably originated when nomadic Balkan tribes left raw milk to sour, first by accident and then as a means of preserving it. Yogurt is a readily available source of protein, B vitamins, and calcium. Its creaminess and tartness also make it a low-calorie base for salad dressing, especially if you use fat-free yogurt. Here is a recipe for a basic dressing, flavored simply with garlic, salt, and pepper. Toss it with any leafy green or use it in place of mayonnaise in tuna or chicken salad.

Makes 1 cup, enough for about 8 servings

1 container (8 ounces) plain yogurt, any
    fat content
1 tablespoon minced garlic, jarred or
    fresh
1 tablespoon red or white wine vinegar
1 tablespoon extra-virgin olive oil
Salt and black pepper to taste
2 tablespoons chopped Italian (flat-leaf)
    parsley

Whisk all the ingredients together until smooth. Refrigerate up to 1 week.

Sweet Bacon Dressing

Bacon dressings are smoky-sweet, rich, and usually overrun with saturated fat. Here I bypass a potential bypass by substituting vegetable oil for bacon fat, and ready-to-serve bacon for raw. Precooked bacon is more convenient than frying your own, and most of the fat has been rendered away before you buy it. Because bacon fat solidifies at room temperature, bacon dressings are usually served warm, but since the oil in this recipe is unsaturated, it will not solidify even when cold. You can therefore use the dressing warmed or straight from the refrigerator. Toss it with any green salad, potato salad, or seafood salad.

Makes ¾ cup (6 servings)

3 slices ready-to-serve bacon, finely
    chopped
2 tablespoons minced onion
¼ cup apple cider vinegar
¼ cup ketchup
¼ cup vegetable oil
Salt and black pepper to taste

Place the bacon and onion in a microwave-safe bowl and microwave at full power for 1½ minutes, until the bacon is crisp and the onion is tender. Stir in the vinegar, ketchup, oil, salt, and pepper. Refrigerate up to 1 week.

Niçoise Salad Dressing

This dressing encompasses all the flavors of Provence in just three ingredients. Olive oil, garlic, and cheese come from bottled Caesar dressing, basil and sun-dried tomato from the pesto, and olives from the tapenade. Use it on romaine or spinach salads, or with tuna or shrimp. It is also a great marinade for grilled chicken.

Makes ¾ cup, enough for 6 servings

½ cup Caesar salad dressing
1 teaspoon sun-dried tomato pesto
3 tablespoons tapenade (black olive spread)

Whisk all the ingredients together until smooth. Refrigerate up to 1 week.

Green Olive Vinaigrette

All olives start out green, hard, fibrous, and bitter, and must be coaxed to an edible state through soaking and brining, which is why green olives are often chopped up with sweet vegetables into a raucous condiment called olive salad. This recipe stretches the flavors of olive salad into a lively dressing that can be tossed with greens and garden vegetables, or used to dress a pasta or meat salad.

Makes about ¾ cup, enough for 6 servings

¼ cup green olive salad
¼ cup extra-virgin olive oil
3 tablespoons red wine vinegar
1 teaspoon chopped garlic, jarred or fresh
Salt and black pepper to taste

Combine all the ingredients. Refrigerate up to 1 week.

Salsa Vinaigrette

Think Italian dressing. Now make it salsafied with chunks of tomato, onions, peppers, a whiff of cilantro, and a spark of chili fire. Salsa vinaigrette can be as piquant or as laid-back as you want, but I wouldn't use mild salsa in this recipe; it is too plain to add much beyond color and a few vegetables. Salsa vinaigrette is delicious on any type of salad—seafood, meat, chicken, potato, pasta, rice, vegetable, or green. (Any salad but fruit, that is.)

Makes 2 cups, enough for 8 servings

½ cup salsa, medium or hot
½ cup Italian salad dressing

Combine the salsa and dressing. Refrigerate up to 1 week.

Chipotle Mayo

All it takes is a hint of cumin and a jolt of chipotle to send your run-of-the-mill Russian dressing scurrying toward Mexico. Chipotle peppers (smoked jalapeños) can be quite fiery, so adjust the amount according to your taste. If you can't find chipotle hot sauce, substitute half the amount of ground chipotle or half a canned chipotle pepper in adobo sauce.

Makes about ¾ cup, enough for 6 servings

½ cup mayonnaise
2 teaspoons ground cumin seed
3 tablespoons ketchup
2 teaspoons chipotle hot pepper sauce

Combine all the ingredients. Refrigerate up to 2 weeks.

Hot Pepper Ranch Dressing

If the flavor of Buffalo wings was to land on a salad, it would taste like this. Don't be shy with the hot sauce; you need to balance the creamy tang of the ranch. The dressing is ready when it turns a peachy pink—if, that is, you use a hot sauce on the mild side, as this recipe does. In the amount called for, hotter-'n-hell-kick-yo'-butt-four-alarm hot sauce will combust your taste buds, and I can't be responsible for the consequences. It is a great dressing for chicken or seafood salad, potato or tomato salad, or a salad of hearty greens.

Makes about ¾ cup, enough for 6 servings

½ cup ranch dressing
3 tablespoons mild hot pepper sauce

Combine the ranch dressing and hot sauce. Refrigerate up to 2 weeks.

Caesar Tonnato Dressing

This simple vinaigrette is inspired by an Italian classic, Vitello Tonnato, a sultry dish of braised and chilled veal finished with a creamy tuna sauce. Although any canned tuna will work, the sauce is best when made with tuna that has been packed in oil, preferably olive oil. Use the whole can, oil and all. The dressing is spectacular on a pasta or potato salad, or tossed with hearty greens such as romaine or endive.

Makes 3 cups, enough for 12 servings

1 can (about 6 ounces) tuna packed in olive oil
1 bottle (16 ounces) Caesar salad dressing
2 teaspoons minced garlic, jarred or fresh
1 tablespoon lemon juice, organic bottled or fresh

Purée all the ingredients in a blender or food processor. Refrigerate up to 1 week.

Tomato and Olive Oil Dressing

Oil gives consistency and volume to a salad dressing. In this very flavorful vinaigrette, tomato purée takes the place of much of the oil, creating a dressing that is very versatile and extremely low in fat. Use it with fresh greens or as a sauce with grilled meats or poached fish. It is especially good warm, as in Warm Endive Salad (page 271).

Makes about ¾ cup,
enough for 6 servings

½ cup tomato purée
2 tablespoons extra-virgin olive oil
1 tablespoon red wine vinegar
½ teaspoon minced garlic, jarred or fresh
1 tablespoon chopped Italian (flat-leaf)
   parsley
Salt and black pepper to taste

Whisk all the ingredients together until smooth. Use warm or at room temperature, or store in the refrigerator up to 2 weeks.

Pesto Dressing

Pesto dressing can make almost anything (except maybe a dessert) taste better, so I recommend you use it wherever and as often as you can. It is especially good as dressing for potato salad.

Makes about 1 cup,
enough for 8 servings

½ cup jarred pesto
3 tablespoons white or red wine vinegar
¼ cup extra-virgin olive oil

Whisk all the ingredients together until smooth. Refrigerate up to 1 week.

Sesame Rice Wine Vinaigrette

This unusual Japanese-style dressing uses tahini (sesame butter) for its oil, which gives the finished vinaigrette a rich, nutty, lightly creamy finish. If you would like even more sesame flavor, add a teaspoon of toasted sesame oil, but I think the dressing is more versatile without it. Use it to coat noodle salads, fish salads, or any green salad.

Makes ¾ cup, enough for 6 servings

¼ cup sesame tahini (sesame butter)
1 teaspoon minced garlic, jarred or fresh
2 teaspoons minced ginger, jarred or fresh
¼ cup rice wine vinegar
¼ cup water
Salt to taste

Whisk all the ingredients together until smooth. Refrigerate up to 1 week.

Guacamole Ranch Dressing

If you find guacamole too rich and ranch dressing too spare, this is the dressing for you. It is very creamy, slightly tangy, and a beautiful pale green. It is delicious as a dip for vegetables or shrimp, and a great sauce on grilled chicken. It makes an innovative potato salad, and it's a fine alternative to Caesar on romaine lettuce.

Makes 2 cups, enough for 8 servings

1 cup refrigerated guacamole
1 cup buttermilk
1 teaspoon chopped or minced garlic, jarred or fresh
Salt and pepper to taste

Combine all the ingredients. Refrigerate up to 3 days.

Warm Endive Salad

Hearty lettuce—especially those in the endive family, such as escarole, chicory, and radicchio—is improved by an assertive dressing and a little heat to soften its tough fibers. This recipe's ingredients are for an elegant small salad, but it would make an excellent entrée if the ingredients were doubled and fortified with some diced smoked meat, grilled poultry, or steamed shrimp.

Makes 6 appetizer servings

2 bags (8 ounces each) Mediterranean
    salad blend or other blend of hearty
    lettuce
Kosher salt and freshly ground black
    pepper to taste
1 tablespoon extra-virgin olive oil
1½ cups (about 4 ounces) sliced mush-
    rooms
1 teaspoon chopped garlic, jarred or
    fresh
2 scallions, roots trimmed, thinly sliced
1 cup diced roasted bell pepper, jarred or
    fresh
¼ cup water
⅓ cup Tomato and Olive Oil Dressing
    (page 269)
¼ cup toasted walnut pieces

Place the lettuce in a salad bowl and season with the salt and pepper. Heat the oil in a medium skillet and sauté the mushrooms until they just begin to lose their raw look, about 1 minute. Stir in the garlic, scallions, and bell pepper. Add the water and dressing, and bring to a boil. Pour over the greens and toss until well coated and lightly wilted. Divide among 6 plates and scatter the nuts over each.

Four-Can Salad

The recipe for this Russian-style beet and herring salad came to me via my mother-in-law. It is a vivid magenta, and hearty enough to serve as a light entrée. Best of all you can make the whole recipe with little more than a can opener.

Makes 4 to 6 servings

1 jar (about 12 ounces) pickled herring
    fillet in wine sauce, drained
1 can (about 16 ounces) sliced beets,
    drained and quartered
¾ cup chopped dill pickle
1 can (about 15 ounces) small whole
    potatoes, drained and cut in eighths
2 cups walnut pieces
1 cup sour cream
Salt and black pepper to taste

Cut the herring into bite-size pieces and place in a medium serving bowl with any onions that were in the jar. Add the beets, pickles, potatoes, walnuts, sour cream, salt, and pepper. Toss together. Refrigerate for at least 1 hour.

Shrimp and Spinach Salad with Grapefruit Vinaigrette

With its pearl pink shrimp, magenta red onion shards, and shiny auburn-glazed walnuts glistening in a tangle of forest-dark spinach, this is a beautiful salad. It is subtly flavored with grapefruit juice, ginger, and garlic.

Makes 4 entrée servings

½ cup grapefruit juice
½ teaspoon chopped ginger, jarred or fresh
½ teaspoon chopped garlic, jarred or fresh
2 tablespoons extra-virgin olive oil
Salt and black pepper to taste
2 bags (7 ounces each) baby spinach
½ small red onion, halved and thinly sliced
1 pound large shrimp, thawed if frozen, peeled, cleaned, and cooked
½ cup glazed walnuts, or toasted walnuts

Combine the grapefruit juice, ginger, garlic, oil, salt, and pepper. Layer the spinach, onion, shrimp, and walnuts in a salad bowl. Pour the dressing over and toss to combine. Adjust the salt and pepper.

Chicken Corn Salad with Pinto Bean Vinaigrette

The dressing for this salad is oil-free. Bean dip replaces the richness of mayonnaise, and salsa provides an acidic spark, a tomato sweetness, and a buzz of hot pepper. It is tossed with chicken breasts that you can buy roasted or grilled, and finished with diced roasted pepper, corn kernels, and fresh avocado.

Makes 4 entrée servings

⅓ cup jarred pinto bean dip
⅓ cup salsa, any heat level
1 tablespoon red wine vinegar
½ teaspoon minced garlic, jarred or fresh
Salt and black pepper to taste
1 can (11 ounces) corn kernels, drained, or 1 box (10 ounces) frozen corn kernels, thawed
1 pound grilled or roasted chicken breast, cut in cubes
1 bunch scallions, roots trimmed, thinly sliced
8 ounces roasted red bell peppers, jarred or fresh, diced
2 cleaned celery ribs, thinly sliced
1 avocado, peeled, pitted, and diced

Whisk together in a salad bowl the bean dip, salsa, vinegar, garlic, salt, and pepper. Add the corn, chicken, scallions, bell peppers, and celery, and toss with the dressing. Add the avocado at the last minute and toss briefly.

Spinach Salad with Red Pepper Vinaigrette

This vivid red dressing blooms with the fragrance of honey and the concentrated essence of roasted red peppers. It is a succulent sauce that blends provocatively with the smoky cured meat and fresh spinach. Serve the salad before or after a roasted chicken or braised beef.

Makes 4 appetizer servings

4 ounces roasted red peppers, jarred or
   fresh, finely chopped
1 teaspoon minced garlic, jarred or fresh
2 tablespoons extra-virgin olive oil
2 tablespoons red wine vinegar
1 tablespoon honey
Salt and black pepper to taste
1 bag (7 ounces) cleaned baby spinach
4 ounces sliced mushrooms
4 ounces smoked turkey breast or ham,
   diced

Combine the peppers, garlic, oil, vinegar, honey, salt, and pepper in a large salad bowl. Add the spinach, mushrooms, and turkey breast. Toss to coat.

Salmon and Field Greens with French Fry Croutons

This salad combines all the elements of a restaurant meal in a single bowl: roasted salmon, crisp French fries, and a medley of tender greens, all sauced with a sweet and tangy balsamic vinaigrette. Although you can turn any fried potato into a crouton, thin ones like shoestrings get crispiest.

Makes 4 entrée servings

Nonstick olive oil spray
1 pound salmon fillet, skin removed, cut
   in ½-inch-thick slices and the slices cut
   in 1-inch lengths
6 ounces frozen shoestring French fries
   (about 60 fries)
1 bag (8 ounces) field greens or other
   European lettuce blend
2 packages (5 ounces each) spring mix
   salad blend
½ cup bottled balsamic vinaigrette

Preheat the oven to 450°F. Coat a sheet pan with oil spray. Arrange the salmon in a single layer on one end of the sheet pan and coat with more oil spray. Place the potatoes on the other end, also in a single layer. Bake for 8 minutes. Remove the fish and set aside. Return the potatoes to the oven for 10 minutes more, until crisp and well browned, and cut them into bite-size pieces. Toss the lettuce with half of the dressing and place the fish and potatoes on top. Pour the remaining dressing over the top and toss lightly.

Cranberry Horseradish Turkey Salad

If your image of turkey salad is mayonnaise punctuated by an occasional speck of pallid celery, take a taste of its gastropolar opposite. Here is a turkey salad with hardly a speck of extra fat and flaring with flavor and flaming red. Its pizzazz comes from cranberry sauce mixed with horseradish and thinned to vinaigrette consistency with orange juice. You can make it with leftover roasted turkey or from fully prepared roasted turkey breast.

Makes 4 servings

1 cup whole-cranberry sauce
2 tablespoons white horseradish
½ cup orange juice
Salt and black pepper to taste
8 ounces roast turkey, cut in ½-inch pieces
2 ribs celery, cut in ¼-inch slices
½ cup walnut pieces
2 scallions, roots trimmed, thinly sliced, or ¼ cup finely chopped red onion

Combine the cranberry sauce, horseradish, orange juice, salt, and pepper in a salad bowl. Add the turkey, celery, walnuts, and scallions. Toss to combine. Chill before serving.

Barbecued Chicken Salad

This salad emerges from the inspired blending of barbecued chicken and sweet-and-sour bacon dressing. The barbecue sauce is thinned with sweet vinegar and tossed with prepared barbecued chicken, ready-to-serve bacon, and romaine lettuce, and becomes a powerfully flavored, effortless entrée salad.

Makes 4 servings

1 package (8 ounces) romaine lettuce
1 package (1 pound) sliced barbecued chicken
1 red bell pepper, diced
5 ounces sliced mushrooms
2 scallions, roots removed, thinly sliced
3 slices ready-to-serve bacon, chopped
½ cup chopped onion, frozen or fresh
1 teaspoon chopped garlic, jarred or fresh
¼ cup spicy barbecue sauce
2 tablespoons apple cider vinegar
Salt and black pepper to taste

Toss the lettuce, chicken, bell pepper, mushrooms, and scallions in a salad bowl. Cook the bacon and onion in a nonstick skillet until the onion is lightly browned. Add the garlic, barbecue sauce, and vinegar, and bring to a simmer. Remove from the heat and season with salt and pepper. Pour over the salad in the bowl and toss until uniformly dressed.

Tuna and White Bean Salad

The combination of tuna, beans, garlic, and olive oil is pure Provençal. This recipe provides you with a classic French salad, and all you have to do is artfully open five jars.

Makes 4 servings

2 cans (about 6 ounces each) solid-pack white tuna in water, drained and flaked
½ teaspoon chopped garlic, jarred or fresh
4 scallions, roots removed, thinly sliced
1 can (about 15 ounces) small white beans
½ cup olive salad
⅓ cup vinaigrette or Caesar dressing

Combine all the ingredients. Refrigerate up to 3 days. Serve on a bed of lettuce or on sliced tomatoes, or serve as a sandwich filling.

Tuna Salad with Coconut Green Curry

Thai green curry paste is a complex combination of chiles, spices, herbs, ginger, and citrus. To make it yourself would require more than a dozen ingredients, but fortunately there are several widely available products that do all the work for you. This salad combines the flavor of green curry with the richness of canned coconut milk into an exotic dressing for tuna salad. If you are unsure about spices, start with half the amount of curry paste and add more to taste.

Makes 4 servings

1 teaspoon Thai green curry paste
½ cup light or regular coconut milk
1 tablespoon rice wine vinegar
Salt and black pepper to taste
2 cans (about 6 ounces each) solid-packed white tuna, drained and flaked
3 scallions, roots trimmed, thinly sliced

Whisk the curry paste with the coconut milk until smooth. Add the vinegar, salt, pepper, tuna, and scallions, and toss to combine. Use as a sandwich spread or serve wrapped in lettuce leaves.

Shrimp and Cucumber Salad with Guacamole Dressing

This sparkling shrimp salad juxtaposes three high-quality convenience ingredients: cooked shrimp, refrigerated guacamole, and deli-prepared cucumber salad. Fully cooked, peeled, and cleaned shrimp is now available freshly steamed or frozen. Frozen is often the better buy and can be just as good as those marked fresh. Buying guacamole is a little trickier. There are several brands, and some are not very good. Look for products that have as few gums or preservatives as possible.

Makes 4 servings

½ cup refrigerated guacamole
2 tablespoons lemon juice, organic bottled or fresh
2 tablespoons olive oil
Salt and black pepper to taste
1 pound cooked, peeled, and cleaned large shrimp, thawed if frozen
1 container (16 ounces) vinaigrette-style cucumber salad, drained

Combine the guacamole, lemon juice, oil, salt, and pepper. Add the shrimp and cucumber salad, and toss to combine.

Ginger Carrot Slaw

This sophisticated slaw owes its fragrance to pickled ginger. These paper-thin slices of ginger, usually associated with Japanese sushi and sashimi, are pale pink and permeated with sweet rice wine vinegar. They are lovely tangled with shredded carrot and tiny disks of green onion. I serve this slaw with grilled fish or as a cleansing side dish for a stir-fry.

Makes 4 servings

¼ cup pickled sushi ginger
2 tablespoons soy sauce
1 bag (10 ounces) shredded carrots
2 scallions, roots trimmed, thinly sliced

Chop the ginger and mix with the soy sauce, carrots, and scallions. Refrigerate until cold, up to 3 days.

Sesame Cabbage Slaw

This very easy, intensely flavored dressing shows the hidden Asian potential in a bag of seemingly all-American coleslaw.

Makes 4 servings

1 tablespoon Asian dark sesame oil
2 tablespoons honey
2 tablespoons rice vinegar
1 tablespoon soy sauce
1 package (8 ounces) coleslaw mix
1 tablespoon toasted sesame seeds

Whisk together the oil, honey, vinegar, and soy sauce. Add the coleslaw mix and sesame seeds, toss to coat, and refrigerate until cold, up to 3 days.

Sweet-and-Sour Coleslaw

This tangy coleslaw is a good partner for barbecued ribs or a grilled steak.

Makes 4 servings

2 tablespoons apricot or peach preserves
2 tablespoons apple cider vinegar
1 tablespoon ketchup
3 tablespoons olive oil
1 teaspoon spicy brown mustard
½ teaspoon salt
1 package (8 ounces) coleslaw mix

Combine the preserves, vinegar, ketchup, oil, mustard, and salt. Add the coleslaw mix, toss to coat, and refrigerate until cold, up to 3 days.

Broccoli Cranberry Slaw

The sweet-tart chewy jewels known as dried cranberries are an intriguing foil to the acrid nuance and watery crunch of the shredded broccoli stem in broccoli slaw. Serve it with pork chops, grilled salmon, or roast turkey.

Makes 4 servings

½ cup coleslaw dressing
⅓ cup dried cranberries
½ cup walnut pieces
1 package (8 ounces) broccoli slaw mix

Combine all the ingredients and refrigerate until cold, up to 3 days.

Broccoli Sprout Slaw

Broccoli sprouts are destined for slaw. They're the perfect size and are crisp enough to hold their own in a dressing. In this salad they are coupled with shredded apple and tossed in a fat-free sweet-and-sour vinaigrette. Here's a shredding tip: The easiest way to shred an apple is to set your shredder in or over a serving bowl. Shred one side of the apple until you reach the core, then turn the fruit a quarter turn and shred that side in the same way. Continue shredding until all that's left is the core.

Makes 4 small servings

1 tablespoon apple cider vinegar
1 teaspoon honey
¾ teaspoon salt
1 tablespoon pickled sushi ginger, finely chopped
1 large tart apple, such as Granny Smith
1 package (4 ounces) broccoli sprouts or other green bean sprout

Whisk together the vinegar and honey until the honey dissolves. Mix in the salt and pickled ginger. Shred the apple against the largest teeth of a grater. Let the shreds fall directly into the dressing. Toss them with the dressing, toss in the sprouts, and serve.

Crab and Corn Slaw

This casually elegant crab salad is a slaw in appearance only. It is not raw, nor does it predominantly contain vegetables. To the contrary, it is a complex counterpoint of crab and corn, black beans and bits of tomato, lime juice and chiles, and is punctuated with dabs of avocado.

Makes 4 entrée servings

1 pound crabmeat, any grade, pasteurized or fresh, picked clean (see Note)
1 jar (12 ounces) black bean corn salsa
2 tablespoons lime juice, organic bottled or fresh
1 avocado, peeled, pitted, and diced

Combine the crabmeat, salsa, lime juice, and avocado. Refrigerate up to 1 day.

NOTE: The only hard part about using crab is picking the shell from the crab. If you buy a container of crabmeat, most of the shell will be gone, but there can still be tiny shards that are hard to spot. Try this: Spread the crab in a pie plate in a thin layer and bake in a preheated 350°F oven for 5 minutes. Any pieces of shell will become hard and opaque, and will be more visible and easier to feel.

Potato Salad Niçoise

Salad Niçoise, the ubiquitous assemblage of potatoes, hard-cooked egg, black olives, and green beans, appears on diner menus from coast to coast. This rendition leans more heavily on potato than the diner version, and is tossed together rather than composed on a platter. Almost all the ingredients come already prepared; all you have to do is finish cooking the potatoes and toss.

Makes 4 entrée servings

1 bag (2 pounds) refrigerated red potato wedges
1 cup garlic-flavored salad dressing
6 tablespoons basil pesto, jarred or fresh
1 teaspoon chopped garlic, jarred or fresh
Pinch of crushed red pepper flakes
1 tablespoon anchovy paste
Salt and black pepper to taste
2 cans (about 6 ounces each) solid-packed white tuna, drained and flaked
¾ cup olive salad
¼ cup chopped Italian (flat-leaf) parsley
1 ripe tomato, cut in 16 wedges

Boil the potato wedges in lightly salted water until tender, about 5 to 10 minutes. Drain. Meanwhile, whisk together the salad dressing, pesto, garlic, pepper flakes, anchovy paste, salt, and pepper until smooth. Add the potatoes (while they're still warm), tuna, olive salad, and parsley, and toss to coat. Serve garnished with tomato wedges.

Maple Bacon Potato Salad

Maple syrup means New England, instantly evoking falling leaves and cider every time bacon is maple-cured or ham is maple-glazed. This recipe is no exception. In it, maple syrup, apple cider vinegar, and bacon join forces in a sweet, tangy, smoky vinaigrette for potato salad that is equally good warm or chilled.

Makes 6 servings

¼ cup apple cider vinegar
¼ cup maple syrup
8 slices ready-to-serve precooked bacon, chopped
1 teaspoon chopped garlic, jarred or fresh
1 teaspoon kosher salt
1 bag (2 pounds) refrigerated freshly diced potatoes with onion
½ cup shredded carrot

Combine the vinegar, syrup, bacon, garlic, salt, and potatoes in a microwave-safe mixing bowl, cover, and microwave at full power for 4 minutes, until the potatoes are tender. Or, alternatively, place in a large saucepan and simmer for 5 minutes, until the potatoes are tender. Add the carrot and serve warm or chilled.

Potato Salad with Brown Butter Vinaigrette

Sometimes all it takes to reinvent a dish is a subtle shift, a change of ingredient, a slimmer slice, or a hotter oven. In this potato salad, the oil in the dressing is replaced with browned butter, creating a cross-culinary hybrid: half vinaigrette, half butter sauce.

Makes 4 servings

¼ cup olive oil
1 package (2 pounds) refrigerated diced potatoes with onion
1 teaspoon salt
½ teaspoon black pepper
1 package (8 ounces) romaine lettuce
4 tablespoons (½ stick) lightly salted butter
½ cup red wine vinegar
¼ cup capers

Heat the oil in a large skillet, add the potatoes, and sauté until browned, about 8 minutes. Season with salt and pepper. Meanwhile, place the lettuce in a large salad bowl. When the potatoes are done, spoon them over the lettuce, leaving any excess oil in the pan. Return the skillet to high heat. Add the butter and cook until it begins to brown slightly. Remove from the heat, stir in the vinegar and capers, pour over the salad, and toss well. Serve warm.

Waldorf Potato Salad

The flavors of a Waldorf salad—apples, celery, and walnuts in a slightly sweet, lightly tangy creamy dressing—is the inspiration for this surprising potato salad that is inundated with fruits and nuts. When the potatoes are roasted, their crunchy skin and flaky flesh form a textural counterpoint to the crisper Waldorf ingredients.

Makes 6 servings

1 package (2 pounds) refrigerated diced
   potatoes with onion
⅓ cup apple cider vinegar
2 tablespoons honey
2 tablespoons sour cream
2 tablespoons mayonnaise
Salt and black pepper to taste
2 ribs celery, peeled and sliced
4 ounces smoked ham, finely diced
2 ounces (½ cup) walnut pieces
1 large tart apple, such as Granny Smith,
   cored and diced

Preheat the oven to 450°F. Spread the potato pieces on a sheet pan and bake until tender, about 15 minutes. While the potatoes are baking, whisk together the vinegar, honey, sour cream, mayonnaise, salt, and pepper in a serving bowl. Add the potatoes (while still hot), celery, ham, walnuts, and apple. Toss to combine, and chill.

Pastrami Potato Salad

Pastrami is designer corned beef—same cut and same cure, but permeated with smoke and crusted with cracked pepper, coriander, and clove. Pastrami acts as the spice in this full-flavored roasted potato salad.

Makes 6 servings

1 package (2 pounds) refrigerated diced
   potatoes with onion
1 tablespoon whole-grain brown mustard
2 tablespoons apple cider vinegar
½ cup mayonnaise
Salt and pepper to taste
4 ounces pastrami, diced
¼ cup chopped onion, frozen or fresh
2 tablespoons chopped Italian (flat-leaf)
   parsley

Preheat the oven to 450°F. Spread the potato pieces on a sheet pan and bake until tender, about 15 minutes. While the potatoes are baking, whisk together the mustard, vinegar, mayonnaise, salt, and pepper in a serving bowl. Add the potatoes (while still hot), pastrami, onion, and parsley. Toss to combine, and serve warm or chilled.

Soba Noodle Salad with Balsamic Glaze

Aficionados of soba, Japanese buckwheat noodles, insist on serving the delicately flavored ribbons as plainly as possible, either in a clear broth (*kake-soba*) or cold with a sweet and pungent dipping sauce (*zaru soba*). This salad is inspired by the latter, substituting the sweet-tart syrup of balsamic vinegar for the traditional dipping sauce.

Makes 4 servings

1 package (about 8 ounces) soba noodles, broken in half
1½ cups shredded carrots
½ cup balsamic vinegar
1 teaspoon minced roasted garlic, jarred or fresh
¼ cup chicken broth
Salt and black pepper to taste
3 scallions, roots trimmed, thinly sliced

Bring a large pot of generously salted water to a boil and boil the soba noodles for 5 minutes. Add the carrots and boil 1 minute more. Meanwhile, combine the vinegar, garlic, and broth in a large skillet and boil until reduced by half. Season liberally with salt and pepper. Drain the noodles and carrots, and toss with the sauce in the skillet. Stir in the scallions and, if needed, additional salt and pepper. Serve warm or at room temperature.

Crab, Lime, and Black Bean Salad

This colorful citrus-bright crab salad can be casual or opulent, depending on the grade of crab you use. The highest (and most expensive) grade is jumbo lump, which is large sections of meat taken from the body of the crab. It is followed by lump, made from smaller whole chunks; backfin, made up of small pieces and shreds of body meat; and special, mostly shredded claw meat. All are pure crab and taste good, so choose according to the size of your purse and the effect you want to create.

Makes 4 servings

¼ cup garlic vinaigrette
2 tablespoons lime juice, organic bottled or fresh
½ teaspoon minced garlic, jarred or fresh
2 tablespoons chopped Italian (flat-leaf) parsley
1 pound crabmeat, any grade, pasteurized or fresh (see Note on cleaning crab, page 279)
1 can (about 15 ounces) black beans, rinsed and drained
3 scallions, roots trimmed, thinly sliced
12 black olives, chopped
1 small red onion, chopped

Combine the vinaigrette, lime juice, garlic, and parsley in a serving bowl. Add the cleaned crabmeat, beans, scallions, olives, and red onion. Toss to combine.

Corn Chili Salad

This spirited salad is redolent with smoky jalapeños, the fragrance of cumin, sweet corn, and caramelized roasted peppers. It's hearty enough to serve as a luncheon or light supper entrée, and it's flavorful enough to turn a burger or sandwich into a meal.

Makes 4 servings

½ cup Chipotle Mayo (page 267)
1 tablespoon cilantro pesto or chutney,
    or 2 tablespoons chopped cilantro
1 can (11 ounces) corn kernels, drained,
    or 1 box (10 ounces) frozen corn ker-
    nels, thawed
1 can (about 15 ounces) kidney beans,
    rinsed and drained
½ cup chopped roasted red pepper,
    jarred or fresh
1 bunch scallions, roots trimmed, sliced
1 avocado, peeled, pitted, and diced
    (optional)

Whisk the Chipotle Mayo with the cilantro in a serving bowl. Add the corn, beans, red pepper, and scallions, and toss to combine. Stir in the avocado if desired.

Red and Yellow Tomato Salad

The best thing to do with a perfectly ripe tomato is as little as possible—which is exactly what this recipe does. But don't let its simplicity mislead you. Its flavors are complex and sensual, and the juxta-position of crimson and gold tomato slices drizzled with emerald pesto is eye-popping.

Makes 4 servings

¼ cup Caesar dressing
1 tablespoon jarred basil pesto
2 large ripe red tomatoes, cored and cut
    in large dice
1 large ripe yellow tomato, cored and
    cut in large dice

Combine the dressing and pesto, add the tomatoes, and toss to coat. Refrigerate for 10 minutes.

Broccoli and Cauliflower with Caper Dressing

This is a salad of buds. Broccoli and cauliflower are both the budding heads of cabbage but have different flavor profiles because of the presence (broccoli) or the absence (cauliflower) of chlorophyll. They are tossed in a creamy sauce that tames the sulfurous element in the cabbage flowers and creates a backdrop against which the salty buds of capers pop and spark.

Makes 4 servings

1 package (10 ounces) fresh broccoli florets
1 package (10 ounces) fresh cauliflower florets
¼ cup mayonnaise
1 tablespoon orange marmalade
2 tablespoons nonpareil capers

Combine the broccoli and cauliflower in a microwave-safe bowl, cover with plastic wrap, and microwave at full power for 4 to 5 minutes, until heated through. Meanwhile, combine the mayonnaise, marmalade, and capers. When the broccoli and cauliflower are hot, drain off any excess water and toss with the dressing. Serve warm or chilled.

Roasted Pepper and Mozzarella Salad

The slightly bitter char and caramelized sweetness of roasted peppers are the perfect foil for the creamy blandness of fresh mozzarella cheese. Fresh mozzarella used to be a rarity, but it is now available in any above-average cheese department. It is usually formed into a lopsided ball that is sold in a tub of water. It's very white and much softer than the brick mozzarella used for lasagna and pizza. The peppers and cheese are glazed with pesto and olive oil for an effortless and beautiful first course or luncheon entrée. Serve it with plenty of crusty bread.

Makes 4 servings

8 ounces fresh mozzarella, cut in ¼-inch-thick slices
¾ cup chopped roasted red peppers, jarred or fresh
Salt and black pepper to taste
1 tablespoon extra-virgin olive oil
1 teaspoon basil pesto, jarred or fresh

Alternate the cheese and red peppers on a serving plate, and season with salt and pepper. Combine the oil and pesto, and drizzle the mixture over the cheese and red peppers. Serve immediately or refrigerate up to 1 hour before serving.

Roasted Pepper and Warm Goat Cheese Salad

This pungent marinated salad of tomato bruschetta and roasted peppers tossed in a garlic and balsamic vinaigrette lasts up to a week in the refrigerator. Keep it on hand for mounding atop a bed of greens, or tossing with pasta.

Makes 4 servings

1 teaspoon chopped garlic, jarred or fresh
½ cup balsamic vinaigrette or oil and vinegar dressing
1 tablespoon extra-virgin olive oil
Pinch of crushed red pepper flakes
2 cups tomato bruschetta, jarred or fresh
8 ounces roasted red peppers, jarred or fresh, cut in chunks (about 1 cup)
Salt and black pepper to taste
8 ounces fresh goat cheese, cut in 8 rounds
8 slices French bread

Preheat the broiler. Combine the garlic, dressing, oil, and pepper flakes in a medium-large bowl. Add the bruschetta and red peppers, toss to coat, and adjust the seasoning with salt and pepper. Place a round of cheese on each slice of bread and heat about 2 inches from the broiler flame for 1 minute, until the cheese is soft and the edges of the bread are toasted. Serve each person a portion of the salad topped with 2 cheese toasts.

Thai Shredded Pork Salad

Thai fish sauce (*nam pla*), which flavors this exotic meat salad, is an ancient and important flavoring in Southeast Asian dishes. There are many brands and a range of quality. The one I use most often is Tiparos from Thailand. Serve this salad as a main course or as a first course in an elaborate meal.

Makes 4 entrée servings

3 tablespoons Thai fish sauce (*nam pla*)
¼ cup light brown sugar
1 teaspoon chopped roasted garlic, jarred or fresh
1 teaspoon hot pepper sauce
⅓ cup lime juice, organic bottled or fresh
1 pound prepared pork roasted with gravy, drained
3 tablespoons chopped peanuts
4 scallions, roots trimmed, sliced
1 cup diced mango, frozen and thawed or fresh

Simmer the fish sauce, brown sugar, and garlic in a small saucepan, stirring until the sugar dissolves. Stir in the hot pepper sauce and lime juice, and let cool. While the dressing is cooling, pull the pork apart with your fingers until it is shredded into fine strands. Toss the shredded pork with the dressing. Add the peanuts, scallions, and diced mango, and toss to combine. Serve at room temperature or chilled. Store in the refrigerator up to 3 days.

Shrimp Caponata

Caponata is a popular marinated vegetable salad from Sicily. It is easy to make
fresh, but it also keeps well and has been
a staple jarred ingredient in Italian markets for decades. This recipe uses jarred
caponata as a base for a dressing for
shrimp salad. Serve it as an appetizer or
luncheon entrée.

Makes 4 servings

1 pound cooked, peeled and cleaned
   shrimp, thawed if frozen
1 jar (about 16 ounces) caponata
3 tablespoons nonpareil capers
1 tablespoon extra-virgin olive oil
1 tablespoon basil pesto, jarred or fresh
1 tablespoon lime juice, organic bottled
   or fresh
Salt and black pepper to taste

Cut the shrimp into bite-size pieces and
toss with the caponata, capers, oil, pesto,
lime juice, salt, and pepper.

CHAPTER 11

PASTABILITIES

Fettuccine with Artichoke Marinara
Ribbon Noodles with "Sweet" Meat Ragù
Spaghetti with Eggplant Tomato Sauce
Pasta with Three Pestos
Cavatappi with Tomatoes and Cream
Fettuccine with Spinach and Roasted Peppers
Soba with Roasted Onions and Garlic
Capelli with Herbed Chèvre and Greens
Angel Hair with Arugula Pesto
Ziti with Cheddar and Broccoli
Ziti with Asparagus
Ziti with Tomato and Olive Relish
Ziti with Garlic and White Beans
Bayou Spaghetti
Creamy Fettuccine Primavera
Farfalle with Feta and Cracked Olives
Fettuccine with Roasted Pepper and Anchovy Rouille
Green Fettuccine with Greens and Green Olive Tapenade
Pappardelle with Roasted Peppers and Ricotta
Lemon Pepper Shrimp with Pasta Shmatas
Broken Lasagna with Tahini, Sage, and Asiago

Farfalle, Smoked Salmon, and Cucumber
Farfalle with Wild Mushroom Ragù
Penne with Tomato, Artichoke, and Feta
Penne with Lemon Pesto
Tricolored Rotelle with Lemon Artichoke Purée
Orrechiette with Prosciutto and Peas
Fusilli with Spinach, Potatoes, and Lots of Garlic
Strozzapretti with Rosemary Roasted Chicken and Forest Mushrooms
Ditalini with Tomatoes and Roasted Corn
Radiatore with Blue Cheese and Toasted Walnuts
Conchiglie with Tuna and Hazelnuts
Conchiglie and Sea Scallops in Ginger Broth
Orzo with Sausage and Clam Sauce
Orzo Parmesan Pilaf
Moroccan Carrot Couscous
Mediterranean Vegetable Lasagna
White Pesto Lasagna
Tuna Noodle Lasagna
Ravioli Lasagna
Spinach Ravioli with Sun-Dried Tomato Oil
Pumpkin Ravioli in Ginger Tomato Sauce
Baked Tortellini with Spring Peas
Curried Tortellini with Lentils
Sesame Garlic Potstickers
Dutch Country Chicken and Potato Dumplings
Gnocchi in Gorgonzola Cream
Gnocchi with Anchovy Aioli

Fettuccine with Artichoke Marinara

This pasta sauce takes advantage of the artichoke avalanche that has been taking place on the shelves of your supermarket. There are artichoke marinades, condiments, dressings, and pestos. In this recipe, marinara sauce is spiked with jarred artichoke spread and lemon juice. One quirk of artichokes is that they stimulate many people's taste buds, causing foods eaten with artichoke, or immediately after it, to taste sweet, a phenomenon that transforms the flavor of the marinara sauce.

Makes 4 servings

1 pound fettuccine
1 jar (26 ounces) marinara sauce
1 jar (12 ounces) artichoke spread
1 tablespoon lemon juice, organic bottled or fresh
Salt and black pepper to taste

Heat a large pot of lightly salted water to a boil. Add the pasta, stir to separate, and cook until al dente, about 10 minutes. Meanwhile, heat the marinara sauce in a large saucepan. Add the artichoke, lemon juice, salt, and pepper, and heat through. Drain the pasta and toss it with the sauce.

Ribbon Noodles with "Sweet" Meat Ragù

The "sweet" in this sauce doesn't come from sugar or fruit. Pork creates the mellow, slightly sweet character. Its consistency and flavor imitate a slow-simmered ragù even though the sauce comes together in the time it takes to boil the fettuccine; the secret is prepared pork roast available in your supermarket's meat case.

Makes 4 servings

1 pound fettuccine
1 jar (26 ounces) traditional pasta sauce
1 cup shredded carrots
1 package (17 ounces) preroasted pork roast in gravy, finely chopped
¼ teaspoon dried crushed rosemary
¼ cup tomato paste, preferably in a tube
Salt and black pepper to taste

Heat a large pot of lightly salted water to a boil. Add the pasta and cook until al dente, about 10 minutes. Meanwhile, heat the sauce in a large saucepan. Add the carrots and simmer for 5 minutes. Add the pork, ¼ cup gravy, rosemary, and tomato paste, and simmer 5 minutes more. Season with salt and pepper. Drain the pasta and toss with the sauce.

Spaghetti with Eggplant Tomato Sauce

Marinara is made from tomatoes, onion, and garlic. It is light and fluid, requiring just enough cooking for the vegetables to melt into a sauce. For this recipe use the lightest, freshest, and thinnest jarred marinara you can find, and just before it is served, add baked breaded eggplant, which thickens and flavors the sauce.

Makes 4 servings

8 ounces frozen breaded eggplant slices
 (about 7 slices)
1 pound spaghetti
1 jar (26 ounces) marinara sauce
2 ounces feta cheese, crumbled (about ½
 cup)
Salt and black pepper to taste

Preheat the oven to 425°F and bake the frozen eggplant slices on a sheet pan for 15 minutes. Cut the eggplant slices into 1-inch pieces.

    Meanwhile, cook the pasta in a large pot of lightly salted boiling water until al dente, about 10 minutes. While the pasta is cooking, simmer the marinara sauce in a large saucepan or microwave at full power for 2 to 3 minutes in a microwave-safe serving bowl. Stir in the cheese, then toss the eggplant pieces with the sauce. Drain the pasta, season with salt and pepper, and toss it with the sauce.

Pasta with Three Pestos

The marriage of pasta and pesto began on the shores of Genoa where the basil is small-leaved and fragrant. The Genoese insist that real pesto can be made only with their basil in a marble mortar. But in reality the ancient mixture of herbs, olive oil, garlic, nuts, and cheese is so inspired that its flavor blooms whether it emerges puréed from a blender, stored in a refrigerator, or processed in a jar. This recipe triples the impact with three highly flavored jarred pestos: basil, red pepper, and olive (tapenade).

Makes 4 servings

1 pound pasta, any shape
¼ cup basil pesto, jarred or fresh
¼ cup red pepper pesto, jarred or fresh
¼ cup black olive tapenade (olive
 spread), jarred or fresh
¼ cup grated imported Parmesan cheese
1 tablespoon grated imported Romano
 cheese
2 tablespoons chopped Italian (flat-leaf)
 parsley
Salt and black pepper to taste

Heat a large pot of lightly salted water to a boil. Add the pasta, stir to separate, and cook until al dente, about 10 minutes. Meanwhile, combine the three pestos, Parmesan, Romano, and parsley in a serving bowl. Drain the pasta, season with salt and pepper, and toss with the sauce.

Cavatappi with Tomatoes and Cream

This rich, creamy tomato sauce is assembled in seconds. Toss it with a wide, sleek pasta so that its richness spreads evenly over the surface of the noodle. I recommend either cavatappi (some brands call the same shape "cellentani"), which are double-twisted ziti, or farfalle, which is shaped like large bow ties or butterflies.

Makes 4 servings

1 pound cavatappi or large farfalle pasta
1 can (10¾ ounces) Campbell's condensed
    tomato soup
1 cup half-and-half
1 can (14½ ounces) Italian-style stewed
    tomatoes, coarsely chopped
2 tablespoons chopped Italian (flat-leaf)
    parsley
Salt and black pepper to taste

Heat a large pot of lightly salted water to a boil. Add the pasta, stir to separate, and cook until al dente, about 10 minutes. Meanwhile, in a large skillet or saucepan, combine the soup, half-and-half, and tomatoes. Bring to a boil and stir in the parsley. Drain the pasta, season with salt and pepper, and toss it with the sauce.

Fettuccine with Spinach and Roasted Peppers

This brightly colored pasta sauce takes so little time to prepare that I suggest you make it with a fresh noodle, which will cook far more quickly than dried. Cleaned baby spinach leaves come prepackaged, need no washing, and the roasted pepper cream cheese melts effortlessly into a pale pink silken sauce.

Makes 4 servings

1 pound fresh fettuccine
1 tablespoon olive oil
¼ cup chopped onion, frozen or fresh
1 bag (7 ounces) cleaned baby spinach
1 package (6 ounces) roasted pepper
    cream cheese
¼ cup milk
Salt and black pepper to taste
2 tablespoons grated imported Parmesan
    cheese

Heat a large pot of lightly salted water to a boil. Add the pasta, stir to separate, and cook until al dente, about 3 minutes. Meanwhile, heat the oil in a skillet and sauté the onion until tender. Add the spinach and stir about 45 seconds, until the spinach is wilted. Mix in the cream cheese and milk, stir until smooth, and season with salt and pepper. Drain the pasta, season with additional salt and pepper if needed, and toss with the sauce and Parmesan.

Soba with Roasted Onions and Garlic

Soba, buckwheat noodles, have a subtle purple-gray-brown stony hue and a slick surface that slides between the lips like silk. The flavor is hearty and nutty, tinged with the fragrance of molasses and toast. It is glorious reinforced by caramelized onions and roasted garlic.

Makes 4 servings

4 medium onions, peeled and cut in 8
  wedges
Nonstick olive oil spray
Salt and black pepper to taste
1 package (about 9 ounces) buckwheat
  soba noodles
1 tablespoon minced roasted garlic,
  jarred or fresh
2 tablespoons extra-virgin olive oil
2 tablespoons chopped Italian (flat-leaf)
  parsley

Preheat the oven to 400°F. Coat the onion wedges with oil spray and spread them on a baking dish. Season with salt and pepper, and roast for 30 minutes. (This preparation can be done several days in advance and reheated.)

Heat a large pot of lightly salted water to a boil. Add the pasta, stir to separate, and cook until al dente, about 5 minutes. Meanwhile, toss the onions, garlic, and oil in a serving bowl. Drain the pasta, season with additional salt and pepper, and toss it with the onion mixture and parsley.

Capelli with Herbed Chèvre and Greens

If you were given the choice between a plate of capelli d'angelo or extra-thin spaghetti, which would you pick? English may be easier to understand, but it sure sounds better in Italian. Capelli d'angelo, or angel hair pasta, is the thinnest of all noodles. Because it is so fine, it cooks in a few minutes. As soon as the pasta is done, add baby spinach leaves, which wilt instantly. Sauce it with olive oil and goat cheese, and serve it immediately; it will get pasty if it sits.

Makes 4 servings

1 pound capelli d'angelo (angel hair
  pasta) or extra-thin spaghetti
1 bag (7 ounces) cleaned baby spinach
¼ cup extra-virgin olive oil
1 teaspoon minced garlic, jarred or fresh
Salt and black pepper to taste
1 package (about 5 ounces) herbed
  chèvre cheese, crumbled

Heat a large pot of lightly salted water to a boil. Add the pasta, stir to separate, and cook until al dente, about 3 to 4 minutes. Stir in the spinach and drain; leave wet. Toss with the oil, garlic, salt, pepper, and chèvre in a warm bowl.

Angel Hair with Arugula Pesto

Arugula is a dark green leaf that resembles a large version of radish tops. It is quite pungent, peppery, and sharp, and it can be full of grit, so wash it very well. When mixed with basil pesto, its bite is tamed by the sweetness of the basil while it lends a garden-fresh spiciness to the sauce. Arugula is sold in bunches in your supermarket alongside smaller lettuce, watercress, and leafy herbs. If you can't find it, watercress makes a fine substitute.

Makes 4 servings

1 pound angel hair pasta (capelli d'angelo) or extra-thin spaghetti
¼ cup basil pesto, jarred or fresh
1 teaspoon minced garlic, jarred or fresh
2 tablespoons extra-virgin olive oil
1 large bunch arugula leaves, washed well and shaken dry
Pinch of crushed red pepper flakes
Salt and black pepper to taste
6 tablespoons grated imported Parmesan cheese

Heat a large pot of lightly salted water to a boil. Add the pasta, stir to separate, and cook until al dente, about 3 minutes. Meanwhile, in a food processor, purée the pesto, garlic, oil, arugula, pepper flakes, and salt. Transfer to a serving bowl and stir in the Parmesan. Drain the pasta, leave wet, season with salt and pepper, and toss it with the sauce.

Ziti with Cheddar and Broccoli

Sometimes convenience can go too far. When it comes to macaroni and cheese, home cooking was never simpler or so good. This recipe attempts to bridge the gap between the endangered cheese-encrusted baked macaroni casserole and the ubiquitous box of blue. It uses cheddar spread for the creaminess we have come to expect, plus real cheddar for a flavor that we long to remember.

Makes 4 servings

1 pound ziti
1 bag (12 ounces) fresh precut broccoli florets
1 container (8 ounces) crock-style cheddar cheese spread
Salt and black pepper to taste
2 cups shredded cheddar cheese

Heat a large pot of lightly salted water to a boil. Add the pasta, stir to separate, and cook until al dente, about 10 minutes. Add the broccoli for the last 3 minutes of cooking. Drain the pasta and broccoli, toss with the cheddar spread in a microwave-safe serving bowl, and season with salt and pepper. Microwave at full power, covered, for 2 minutes. Uncover and top with the shredded cheddar. Microwave 1 minute at full power. Stir together and serve.

Ziti with Asparagus

In this recipe, asparagus is tossed with pasta just before it is done. That way, vegetable and pasta emerge together, perfectly cooked, from a single pot. When trimming the asparagus, try to keep the pieces a little longer than the ziti. The finished dish will be more attractive and easier to eat.

Makes 4 servings

1 pound ziti or penne
8 ounces thin asparagus, trimmed, cut in
   1½-inch lengths
1 tablespoon olive oil
¼ cup chopped onion, frozen or fresh
1 package (6 ounces) garlic and herb
   cream cheese
¼ cup milk
Salt and black pepper to taste
2 tablespoons grated imported Parmesan
   cheese

Heat a large pot of lightly salted water to a boil. Add the pasta, stir to separate, and cook until al dente, 8 minutes. Add the asparagus and cook 2 minutes more, until the ziti and asparagus are both tender. Meanwhile, heat the oil in a small skillet and sauté the onion until translucent. Turn the heat to low. Add the cream cheese and milk, stir until the cream cheese is melted, and season with salt and pepper. Drain the pasta and asparagus, and toss with the sauce and Parmesan.

Ziti with Tomato and Olive Relish

You first taste this pasta with your eyes as you take in the brilliant red of a ripe tomato, oil-slicked black olives, and a peppering of emerald green parsley flecks. Right away you know it is packed with flavor. Because the tomatoes aren't cooked, you can be assured of garden-fresh results only if your tomatoes are perfectly ripe. Don't even bother making this sauce with tepid, genetically engineered hothouse tomatoes.

Makes 4 servings

1 pound ziti or penne
8 very ripe plum tomatoes, finely
   chopped
1 teaspoon minced garlic, jarred or fresh
1 cup olive salad
Pinch of crushed red pepper flakes
¼ cup chopped Italian (flat-leaf) parsley
6 tablespoons extra-virgin olive oil
Kosher salt and freshly ground black
   pepper to taste
5 tablespoons grated imported Parmesan
   cheese

Heat a large pot of lightly salted water to a boil. Add the pasta, stir to separate, and cook until al dente, about 10 minutes. Meanwhile, toss the tomatoes, garlic, olive salad, pepper flakes, parsley, and oil in a serving bowl. Drain the pasta, season with salt and pepper, and toss it with the sauce and Parmesan.

Ziti with Garlic and White Beans

Not all pasta sauces are liquid. Many are just flavorful ingredients chopped fine enough to spread their flavor over a whole bowl of pasta. Getting rid of excess water is why traditional pasta sauces take so long to cook. But in a dry sauce, there's nothing to dilute; just a few seconds over a flame releases the aroma of onion, garlic, and herbs.

Makes 4 servings

1 pound ziti or penne
¼ cup extra-virgin olive oil
¼ cup chopped onion, frozen or fresh
1 teaspoon chopped garlic, jarred or fresh
1 teaspoon ground sage
½ teaspoon dried crumbled rosemary
1 can (about 15 ounces) white beans, rinsed and drained
¼ cup chopped Italian (flat-leaf) parsley
Salt and black pepper to taste
2 tablespoons grated Romano cheese

Heat a large pot of lightly salted water to a boil. Add the pasta, stir to separate, and cook until al dente, about 10 minutes. Meanwhile, heat 1 tablespoon of the oil in a skillet and sauté the onion until tender but not brown. Add the garlic, sage, rosemary, and beans, and heat through. Stir in the parsley and season with salt and pepper. Remove from the heat and stir a small ladleful (about ½ cup) of the pasta water into the skillet. Drain the pasta, season with additional salt and pepper, and toss it with the sauce, the remaining olive oil, and Romano cheese.

Bayou Spaghetti

This sauce is brimming with the flavors of the Acadian bayou: bell peppers, hot peppers, tomatoes, onions, garlic, and smoked pork. If you were assembling it from scratch, your shopping list would be very long, but in this rendition, most of the ingredients are found in two staples: marinara sauce and hot salsa.

Makes 4 servings

1 pound spaghetti, any thickness
1 jar (26 ounces) marinara sauce
1 jar (16 ounces) chunky salsa, hot
4 slices ready-to-serve bacon, finely chopped
1 tablespoon chopped garlic, jarred or fresh
½ teaspoon dried thyme
1 tablespoon Worcestershire sauce
¼ cup chopped Italian (flat-leaf) parsley
Salt and black pepper to taste

Heat a large pot of lightly salted water to a boil. Add the pasta, stir to separate, and cook until al dente, about 10 minutes. Meanwhile, combine the marinara sauce, salsa, bacon, garlic, thyme, and Worcestershire sauce. Simmer, stirring often, for 3 minutes, until slightly thickened. Drain the pasta, season with salt and pepper, and toss it with the sauce.

Creamy Fettuccine Primavera

This vegetable-laden pasta sauce is a mini-primer in convenience produce. The carrots have been peeled, the mushrooms have been sliced, the peas are frozen, and the peppers are jarred. Each vegetable has been processed to its own limits and enters the recipe in its own time so that all are done simultaneously. At the end, everything is combined into a rainbow of colors and flavors.

Makes 4 servings

1 pound fettuccine
4 ounces baby carrots, each cut in 8 strips
2 tablespoons olive oil
¼ cup chopped onion, frozen or fresh
4 ounces mushrooms, sliced
8 ounces thin asparagus, trimmed and cut in 1½-inch lengths
½ cup frozen peas
Salt and black pepper to taste
1 jar (16 ounces) Alfredo pasta sauce
4 ounces roasted red bell pepper, jarred or fresh, cut in thin strips

Heat a large pot of lightly salted water to a boil. Add the pasta, stir to separate, and cook until al dente. Add the carrots and cook 5 minutes more, until the pasta and carrots are tender. Meanwhile, heat the oil in a large, deep skillet over medium-high heat and sauté the onion until barely softened, about 1 minute. Add the mushrooms, asparagus, peas, salt, and pepper, and cook until the mushrooms lose their raw look and the asparagus is bright green, about 1 minute. Add the Alfredo sauce and heat to simmering. Stir in the bell pepper. Adjust the seasoning with additional salt and pepper. Drain the pasta and carrots, and toss them with the sauce.

Farfalle with Feta and Cracked Olives

Chunky sauces need nooks in which to nestle. Farfalle, pasta that is pinched in the center, like tiny bow ties, are just right for trapping bits of olive salad and crumbled feta that are the beginning and end of this simple sauce.

Makes 4 servings

1 package (12 ounces) large bow tie noodles
1 jar (8 ounces) olive salad
6 ounces feta cheese, crumbled (about 1½ cups)
Salt and black pepper to taste

Heat a large pot of lightly salted water to a boil. Add the pasta, stir to separate, and cook until al dente, about 10 minutes. Drain and toss with the olive salad, cheese, salt, and pepper in a serving bowl.

Fettuccine with Roasted Pepper and Anchovy Rouille

The acrid char and sweet fruit of roasted red peppers is the natural mate for the salt-drenched succulence of anchovies. Both ingredients are cut into thin strips to match the ribbon shape of the pasta. A simple basil vinaigrette enhances the flavors of both and helps them disperse evenly over the noodles.

Makes 4 servings

1 pound fettuccine or linguine
1 jar (7 ounces) roasted red peppers, cut in strips
½ teaspoon minced garlic, jarred or fresh
1 can (2 ounces) anchovy fillets packed in olive oil, cut in thin strips
3 tablespoons extra-virgin olive oil
1 tablespoon lemon juice, organic bottled or fresh
Salt and black pepper to taste
¼ cup chopped basil leaves or Italian (flat-leaf) parsley
¼ cup grated imported Parmesan or Romano cheese

Heat a large pot of lightly salted water to a boil. Add the pasta, stir to separate, and cook until al dente, about 10 minutes. Meanwhile, combine the red peppers, garlic, anchovies and the oil from the can, olive oil, and lemon juice in a large serving bowl. Drain the pasta, season with salt and pepper, and toss it with the sauce, basil or parsley, and cheese.

Green Fettuccine with Greens and Green Olive Tapenade

Most flavored pastas aren't truly flavored; they're colored. Let's face it, a pile of spinach noodles contains less than a thimble of vegetable and tastes nothing like spinach. Only very assertive additions, such as garlic, basil, or squid ink, will affect the flavor. In this recipe the spinach in the fettuccine is augmented by more spinach in the sauce, a hefty dose of garlic and olive oil, and a sheath of briny, earthy green olive paste.

Makes 4 servings

1 pound spinach fettuccine
1 bag (7 ounces) baby spinach
¼ cup extra-virgin olive oil
1 teaspoon minced garlic, jarred or fresh
Salt and black pepper to taste
¼ cup green olive tapenade
1 tablespoon grated imported Romano cheese

Heat a large pot of lightly salted water to a boil. Add the pasta, stir to separate, and cook until al dente, about 10 minutes. Stir in the spinach just before the pasta is finished. Drain the pasta and toss with the oil, garlic, salt, pepper, tapenade, and Romano in a warm serving bowl.

Pappardelle with Roasted Peppers and Ricotta

Pappardelle, or wide egg noodles, are the broadest of Italian-cut noodles that go well with velvety, flavorful sauces. Here, pappardelle are coated with a creamy sauce made from whole-milk ricotta and an abundance of roasted peppers. I would not use part-skim ricotta here; it tends to get grainy and lacks the dairy sweetness of the full-fat product.

Makes 4 servings

12 ounces pappardelle noodles
1 jar (12 ounces) roasted red peppers, or 1 bag (1 pound) frozen roasted peppers, thawed
½ teaspoon minced garlic, jarred or fresh
1 container (15 ounces) whole-milk ricotta cheese (not part-skim)
1 tablespoon extra-virgin olive oil
Salt and black pepper to taste
2 tablespoons chopped Italian (flat-leaf) parsley

Heat a large pot of lightly salted water to a boil. Add the pasta, stir to separate, and cook until al dente, about 10 minutes. Meanwhile, cut the peppers into strips and place the strips in a microwave-safe serving bowl with the garlic, ricotta, and oil. Microwave at full power for 1 minute to remove the chill and season liberally with salt and pepper. Drain the pasta and toss it with the sauce and parsley.

Lemon Pepper Shrimp with Pasta Shmatas

These noodle "rags," made by breaking lasagna noodles into random pieces, are hearty and fun. They are tossed in a chunky tomato sauce filled with shrimp and flavored with lemon and garlic.

Makes 4 servings

8 ounces lasagna noodles (about 10), each broken in 3 or 4 pieces
1 pound medium shrimp, peeled and cleaned
1½ teaspoons lemon pepper
1 tablespoon extra-virgin olive oil
1½ cups jarred bruschetta
½ teaspoon minced garlic, jarred or fresh
1 tablespoon lemon juice, organic bottled or fresh
1 tablespoon chopped Italian (flat-leaf) parsley
Salt and black pepper to taste

Heat a large pot of lightly salted water to a boil. Add the pasta, stir to separate, and cook until al dente, about 10 minutes. Meanwhile, toss the shrimp with the lemon pepper. Just before the pasta is done, heat the oil in a large skillet and sauté the shrimp until they lose their raw look. Add the bruschetta, garlic, and lemon juice. Heat to a boil, stirring often. The shrimp should be firm and opaque. Stir in the parsley. Drain the pasta, season with salt and pepper, and toss it with the sauce.

Broken Lasagna with Tahini, Sage, and Asiago

I'll admit it: This recipe is deliciously odd. The pasta is broken and cooked in a skillet, the sauce is made from sesame paste and sage, and the pasta never gets drained. The reason the pasta is cooked in a precise amount of water is that the liquid remaining in the skillet once the pasta is tender becomes the base for the sauce.

Makes 4 servings

4 cups water
8 ounces lasagna noodles (about 10), each broken in 3 or 4 pieces
½ cup sesame tahini
¾ cup milk
1 tablespoon extra-virgin olive oil
1 tablespoon minced garlic
10 fresh sage leaves, torn into small pieces
Salt and black pepper to taste
2 tablespoons grated Asiago cheese

Heat the water in a large covered skillet to a boil. Add the noodles, stir, and cover and cook until tender, about 12 minutes. Stir often. There should be about 1 cup of water left in the pan. Stir in the tahini, milk, oil, garlic, sage, and plenty of salt and pepper until a smooth sauce forms. Add more water if needed to make a sauce the consistency of cream. Stir in the Asiago and serve.

Farfalle, Smoked Salmon, and Cucumber

A prepared cucumber salad from your supermarket's deli case streamlines this sophisticated spring pasta sauce. It is combined with bits of smoked salmon into a pale pastel sauce that is tossed with bow tie noodles.

Makes 4 servings

1 package (12 ounces) large bow tie noodles
2 tablespoons butter
2 tablespoons extra-virgin olive oil
½ teaspoon minced garlic, jarred or fresh
1 cup heavy cream
1 tablespoon chopped dill, or 1 teaspoon dried dill weed
1 container (8 ounces) prepared deli cucumber salad, drained and coarsely chopped
4 ounces smoked salmon, cut in thin strips
Salt and black pepper to taste

Heat a large pot of lightly salted water to a boil. Add the pasta, stir to separate, and cook until al dente, about 10 minutes. Meanwhile, melt the butter in a medium skillet and add the olive oil, garlic, cream, and dill. Simmer until the cream is slightly thickened. Remove from the heat and stir in the cucumber salad, salmon, salt, and pepper. Drain the pasta, season with more salt and pepper, and toss it with the sauce.

Farfalle with Wild Mushroom Ragù

Cèpes, shiitake, crimini, or morels—any of the commonly available cleaned and sliced wild mushrooms—will be celebrated in this elegantly simple sauce. The mushrooms are scented with garlic, and tinged with tomato, but it is the rich flavor of the mushrooms themselves that is the star.

Makes 4 servings

1 package (12 ounces) large bow tie noodles
3 tablespoons extra-virgin olive oil
1 cup chopped onions, frozen or fresh
1 pound sliced wild mushroom medley
1 teaspoon chopped garlic, jarred or fresh
1 cup white wine
1 can (15 ounces) diced tomatoes, drained
1 tablespoon chopped Italian (flat-leaf) parsley
Salt and black pepper to taste

Heat a large pot of lightly salted water to a boil. Add the pasta, stir to separate, and cook until al dente, about 10 minutes. Meanwhile, heat the oil in a large skillet and sauté the onions and mushrooms until lightly browned. Add the garlic and stir to combine. Add the wine and tomatoes and boil until reduced by half. Stir in the parsley, salt, and pepper. Drain the pasta and toss it with the sauce.

Penne with Tomato, Artichoke, and Feta

This sauce is completely uncooked. All it needs to set its flavors into motion is the warmth of freshly cooked pasta and a ladleful of pasta cooking water.

Makes 4 servings

1 pound penne pasta
1 large jar (12 ounces) marinated artichoke hearts
1 can (14.5 ounces) diced tomatoes with Italian herbs, drained
6 ounces feta cheese, crumbled (about 1½ cups)
2 tablespoons extra-virgin olive oil
¼ cup chopped Italian (flat-leaf) parsley
Salt and black pepper to taste

Heat a large pot of lightly salted water to a boil. Add the pasta, stir to separate, and cook until al dente, about 10 minutes. Meanwhile, chop the artichoke hearts and combine with the tomatoes, cheese, oil, parsley, salt, and pepper in a serving bowl. When the pasta is done, add a small ladleful (about ½ cup) of the pasta water to the sauce. Drain the pasta, season with additional salt and pepper, and toss it with the sauce.

Penne with Lemon Pesto

Lemon and basil are delicious together, but the pairing doesn't work in pesto. The problem is acid—citrus juice turns the basil drab, and its tartness makes Parmesan cheese taste spoiled. Enter zest. Lemon zest, the yellow skin of the peel, is bursting with lemon flavor. It contains lemon oil rather than citric acid, so it has all the flavor assets but causes none of the problems.

Makes 4 servings

1 pound penne pasta
¾ cup basil pesto, jarred or fresh
1 tablespoon dried lemon peel
1 tablespoon extra-virgin olive oil
½ teaspoon minced garlic, jarred or fresh
Salt and black pepper to taste
2 tablespoons grated imported Parmesan cheese

Heat a large pot of lightly salted water to a boil. Add the pasta, stir to separate, and cook until al dente, about 10 minutes. Meanwhile, combine the pesto, lemon peel, oil, and garlic in a serving bowl. Season liberally with salt and pepper. Drain the pasta and toss it with the sauce and Parmesan.

Tricolored Rotelle with Lemon Artichoke Purée

The combination of lemon, oregano, artichoke, and sheep's milk cheese is decidedly Greek. This recipe performs a slight twist by replacing the traditional feta, a fresh sheep's milk cheese from Greece, with pecorino Romano, a long-aged sheep's milk cheese from Italy.

Makes 4 servings

1 package (12 ounces) tricolored rotelle
1 jar (12 ounces) artichoke antipasto or artichoke relish
1 tablespoon lemon juice, organic bottled or fresh
1 teaspoon chopped fresh oregano, or ¼ teaspoon dried oregano leaves
2 tablespoons grated imported pecorino Romano cheese
Salt and black pepper to taste

Heat a large pot of lightly salted water to a boil. Add the pasta, stir to separate, and cook until al dente, about 10 minutes. Drain and toss with the artichoke, lemon juice, oregano, Romano, salt, and pepper in a serving bowl.

Orrechiette with Prosciutto and Peas

There is something magical about the combination of salty ham and sweet young peas accented with a breath of mint. In this recipe the three are tossed with orrechiette, whose tiny ears are cupped just enough to balance a pea and a tangle of prosciutto in every mouthful.

Makes 4 servings

1 pound orrechiette
2 tablespoons extra-virgin olive oil
½ cup chopped onion, frozen or fresh
2 ounces prosciutto, finely diced
1 box (10 ounces) frozen baby peas
2 tablespoons finely chopped mint leaves
1 can (about 15 ounces) diced tomatoes, drained
Salt and black pepper to taste
½ cup heavy cream

Heat a large pot of lightly salted water to a boil. Add the pasta, stir to separate, and cook until al dente, about 10 minutes. Meanwhile, heat the oil in a large skillet and sauté the onion until translucent, about 2 minutes. Add the prosciutto and peas, and cook until the peas are mostly defrosted. Add the mint and tomatoes, and cook until the tomatoes are bubbling, about 4 minutes. Season with salt and pepper. Turn the heat to low and stir in the cream until the sauce thickens slightly. Remove from the heat. Drain the pasta and toss it with the sauce. Adjust the seasoning with salt and pepper.

Fusilli with Spinach, Potatoes, and Lots of Garlic

This dish is unique in that it is simmered in a single pot. The pasta and potatoes, which take the same time to cook, are added together, and the spinach joins in at the end. It is all tossed with garlic, hot peppers, and cheese.

Makes 4 servings

1 pound fusilli
1 pound refrigerated red potato wedges
¼ cup extra-virgin olive oil
Pinch of crushed red pepper flakes
1 tablespoon chopped garlic, jarred or fresh
Salt and black pepper to taste
1 bag (7 ounces) baby spinach
⅓ cup grated imported Romano cheese

Heat a large pot of lightly salted water to a boil. Add the pasta and potatoes, stir to separate the pasta strands, and cook for 10 minutes, until the pasta is al dente and the potatoes are tender. Meanwhile, combine the oil, pepper flakes, garlic, salt, and pepper in a serving bowl. When the pasta and potatoes are tender, stir in the spinach until it wilts, about 10 seconds. Drain and toss the pasta, potatoes, and spinach with the sauce and cheese. Adjust the seasoning with salt and pepper.

Strozzapretti with Rosemary Roasted Chicken and Forest Mushrooms

Strozzapretti (it's pronounced stroh-sah-*pray*-tee, and it means "priest stranglers") are tiny twists of "rope" made from rough-hewn pasta. It is thicker than most machine-made pastas and quite twisted, allowing it to cradle gobs of sauce and wrap itself around chunky bits of meat or mushroom. The one drawback is that it can be difficult to find. If your market doesn't carry it, substitute another screwlike shape, such as gemelli, fusilli, or rotelle.

Makes 4 servings

1 package (12 ounces) strozzapretti or
   gemelli pasta
2 tablespoons olive oil
½ cup chopped onion, frozen or fresh
1 package (8 ounces) sliced mushroom
   medley
½ teaspoon chopped garlic, jarred or
   fresh
½ teaspoon dried crushed rosemary
½ cup white wine
1 cup chicken broth
1 package (1 pound) sliced roasted
   chicken cut in bite-size pieces
Salt and black pepper to taste

Heat a large pot of lightly salted water to a boil. Add the pasta, stir to separate, and cook until al dente, about 10 to 12 minutes. Meanwhile, heat the oil in a large skillet and sauté the onion and mushrooms until lightly browned. Add the garlic, rosemary, and wine, and bring to a boil. Add the broth and boil until reduced by half. Add the chicken and heat through. Season with salt and pepper. Drain the pasta and toss it with the sauce.

Ditalini with Tomatoes and Roasted Corn

As corn roasts, it becomes sweeter and meatier. The sugars caramelize, and the skin of each kernel toughens slightly into hundreds of leathery berries filled with molten sugar. Tossed with roasted onion, diced tomato, and a pile of tiny ditalini macaroni, it becomes a sweet and savory pasta confetti. The charm of this dish is that all its pieces are of similar size, so if you can't find petite cut diced tomato, chop what you have accordingly.

Makes 4 servings

Nonstick olive oil spray
1 box (10 ounces) frozen corn kernels
2 cups chopped onions, frozen or fresh
1 package (8 ounces) ditalini
1 can (about 14 ounces) petite cut diced
    tomatoes
½ teaspoon chopped garlic, jarred or
    fresh
Pinch of crushed red pepper flakes
Salt and black pepper to taste
2 tablespoons chopped Italian (flat-leaf)
    parsley

Preheat the oven to 400°F. Coat a sheet pan with olive oil spray. Break up the corn kernels, toss them with the onions on the sheet pan, and spread into as thin a layer as possible. Roast for 20 minutes, until the corn and onions are tipped with brown. Turn them halfway through. This step can be done ahead.

Meanwhile, heat a large pot of lightly salted water to a boil. Add the pasta, stir to separate, and cook until al dente, about 8 minutes. While the pasta is cooking, combine the corn and onions, diced tomatoes (including its liquid), and garlic in a large skillet. Heat until simmering and season with the pepper flakes, salt, and black pepper. Drain the pasta and toss it with the sauce and parsley in a serving bowl.

Radiatore with Blue Cheese and Toasted Walnuts

This pungent collage of ruffled pasta, toasted nuts, and blue cheese is far simpler than it tastes. Radiatore are embossed with rows of ruffles that trap the sauce—in this case, a fragrant combination of garlic and molten blue cheese. The walnuts are toasted, creating a textural and aromatic counterpoint to the lush softness of the pasta and cheese.

Makes 4 servings

12 ounces radiatore
¼ cup extra-virgin olive oil
1 cup walnut pieces
½ teaspoon chopped garlic, jarred or
    fresh
4 ounces blue cheese, crumbled
2 scallions, roots trimmed, thinly sliced
Salt and black pepper to taste

Heat a large pot of lightly salted water to a boil. Add the pasta, stir to separate, and cook until al dente, about 10 minutes. Meanwhile, heat 1 tablespoon of the oil in a medium skillet. Cook the walnuts, stirring, until you smell the aroma of toasted nuts and they have darkened a shade or two. Remove from the heat and stir in the remaining oil and garlic. Drain the pasta and toss it with the blue cheese, walnuts, oil, and scallions. Season with salt and pepper.

Conchiglie with Tuna and Hazelnuts

If you don't like canned tuna but have only tried it packed in water, you should try this pasta. The tuna here is oil-packed, which keeps it moist and full-flavored. Additional olive oil moistens the sauce, but you can omit this oil if you wish.

Makes 4 servings

1 pound conchiglie (shell-shaped) pasta
3 tablespoons extra-virgin olive oil
1 teaspoon chopped garlic, jarred or
    fresh
1 cup chopped toasted skinned hazel-
    nuts
1 can (about 6 ounces) tuna packed in
    olive oil
3 tablespoons chopped fresh dill
Salt and black pepper to taste

Heat a large pot of lightly salted water to a boil. Add the pasta, stir to separate, and cook until al dente, about 10 minutes. Meanwhile, heat the oil in a skillet and add the garlic. Remove the skillet from the heat and stir to warm the garlic through. Stir in the nuts, tuna and its oil, and dill, flaking the tuna into bite-size pieces as you stir. Drain the pasta, season with salt and pepper, and toss it with the sauce.

Conchiglie and Sea Scallops in Ginger Broth

A growing restaurant trend in these first years of the new millennium is for thinner and sparer sauces. Tomato waters, onion jus, and herb-scented broths abound. Here, conchiglie (shell-shaped pasta) are poached with sea scallops in a gingery, garlicky broth and served in a shallow bowl in a pool of the gingered seafood fumet.

Makes 4 servings

1 large container (32 ounces) chicken
    broth
1 teaspoon chopped garlic, jarred or
    fresh
1 teaspoon chopped ginger, jarred or
    fresh
Salt to taste
8 ounces conchiglie (shell-shaped) pasta
1 pound sea scallops, frozen or fresh, cut
    in half horizontally
4 scallions, roots removed, sliced
1 teaspoon Asian hot-pepper sesame oil

Heat the broth to boiling in a large saucepan. Add the garlic, ginger, salt, and pasta, and stir briefly. Boil gently for 12 minutes, until the pasta is tender. Add the scallops, cover, and simmer for 3 minutes, until the scallops are opaque but still slightly soft at their centers. Stir in the scallions and ladle into shallow soup bowls. Drizzle with the hot-pepper oil.

Orzo with Sausage and Clam Sauce

The combination of sausage and seafood is a tradition in Portugal and Spain. It's a natural—rich, meaty, and salty. Fresh clams are best, but you don't need to mess with shells. Fresh chopped clams are available at the seafood department of your supermarket. If you cannot find them, use canned baby clams.

Makes 4 servings

1 pound orzo
2 tablespoons olive oil
6 ounces mild Italian sausage, cut in
    small slices
½ teaspoon chopped garlic, jarred or
    fresh
1 cup white wine
1 can (about 15 ounces) clam sauce
1 container (about 16 ounces) chopped
    fresh clams, drained
Pinch of crushed red pepper flakes

Heat a large pot of lightly salted water to a boil. Add the pasta, stir to separate, and cook until al dente, about 8 minutes. Meanwhile, heat the oil in a large skillet. Sauté the sausage until it loses its raw look. Add the garlic and stir. Add the wine and boil for 2 minutes. Stir in the clam sauce, clams, and pepper flakes, and heat through. Drain the pasta and toss it with the sauce.

Orzo Parmesan Pilaf

Orzo is rice-shaped pasta. Pilaf is a cooking method usually used for rice in which the rice is sautéed in oil long enough to coat each grain with fat, sealing its surface and helping the grains stay separate as they simmer. But when you make a pilaf with orzo, just the opposite happens: It gets creamy and saucy, like a pasta risotto. When sautéing the orzo, allow it to cook long enough so that about a quarter of the "grains" toast. This slight browning will add richness and color to the finished dish.

Makes 4 entrée or 8 appetizer servings

1 tablespoon olive oil
½ cup chopped onion, frozen or fresh
1 pound orzo
1 large container (32 ounces) chicken broth
½ cup grated imported Parmesan cheese
1 tablespoon chopped Italian (flat-leaf) parsley
Salt and black pepper to taste

Heat the oil in a large skillet and sauté the onions until lightly browned. Sauté the orzo until a few grains are toasted. Stir in the broth and bring to a boil. Lower the heat, cover, and simmer for 12 minutes. Stir in the Parmesan, parsley, salt, and pepper.

Moroccan Carrot Couscous

This fragrant North African pasta preparation has a golden glow and incredible perfume. For a twist I've used large Israeli couscous, which must be toasted before it is simmered. If it isn't, it will collapse into a flaccid mound.

Makes 4 servings

1 tablespoon olive oil
1 package (about 8 ounces) Israeli couscous
1 bag (10 ounces) shredded carrots
3 cups water
1 teaspoon paprika
1 teaspoon minced garlic, jarred or fresh
1 teaspoon ground cumin
Salt and black pepper to taste
3 tablespoons chopped Italian (flat-leaf) parsley
2 tablespoons red wine vinegar

Heat the oil in a large skillet and sauté the couscous until it toasts slightly, about 3 minutes. Add the carrots and sauté until they begin to soften, about 2 minutes. Add the water, paprika, garlic, cumin, salt, and pepper. Cover and simmer for 10 minutes, until the couscous is tender and the liquid has been absorbed. Stir in the parsley and vinegar, and adjust the seasoning with salt and pepper.

Mediterranean Vegetable Lasagna

Lasagna is a lot of work—chopping, boiling, hot water splashing out of the sink. No more. Here is a flavor-packed hearty vegetable lasagna, in which you don't chop a single vegetable and don't boil a noodle. You've probably seen no-boil lasagna noodles in your market, but if you haven't tried them, I'm here to tell you that they work just fine. I'll also tell you that any noodle—uncooked, right out of the box—works just as well. Just add a little water to the sauce, and the noodles will rehydrate and soften as the lasagna bakes. (See the entry on pasta on page 26.)

Makes 8 servings

1 box (10 ounces) frozen creamed spinach, thawed
½ teaspoon chopped garlic, jarred or fresh
1 jar (about 8 ounces) roasted peppers, drained and diced
1 large jar (12 ounces) marinated artichoke heart quarters
½ cup olive salad
1 large container (2 pounds) whole-milk ricotta cheese
¼ cup grated imported Parmesan cheese
Salt and ground black pepper to taste
1 jar (26 ounces) chunky marinara sauce
1 cup water
16 (about three-fourths of a 1-pound box) lasagna noodles
1 pound shredded mozzarella cheese

Preheat the oven to 375°F. Combine the spinach, garlic, peppers, artichoke hearts and their marinade, olive salad, ricotta, Parmesan, salt, and pepper.

Pour one-fourth of the marinara sauce into a 9 × 13-inch baking dish, stir in ½ cup of the water, and spread evenly. Place 4 of the uncooked noodles in an even layer on the sauce. Spoon one-third of the vegetable-ricotta mix evenly over the noodles and then make layers as follows: one-fourth of the mozzarella, 4 more noodles, one-fourth of the marinara sauce, another one-third of the vegetable-ricotta mix, another one-fourth of the mozzarella, 4 more noodles, another one-fourth of the marinara, another one-third of the vegetable-ricotta mix, another one-fourth of the mozzarella, and the remaining 4 noodles.

Pour the remaining ½ cup of water into the marinara sauce left in the jar, seal with the lid, and shake to combine. Pour the sauce over the noodles and spread evenly. Cover with foil and place on a sheet pan to catch any drips.

Bake for 50 minutes. Remove the foil and sprinkle the top evenly with the remaining mozzarella. Bake 15 minutes more. Remove from the oven and set aside for 15 minutes. Cut into 8 or 10 servings and serve using a spatula. (The lasagna can be made a day ahead and reheated, after which it will cut more neatly.)

White Pesto Lasagna

The temptation when creating lasagna is to impress people with the number and diversity of ingredients. But some of the best lasagnas are wondrously plain, little more than pasta and sauce layered together and baked in a casserole. Here is a delicious example, combining the richness of Alfredo with the pungency of pesto.

Makes 6 servings

2 jars (16 ounces each) Alfredo sauce
1 cup water
9 (about half of a 1-pound box) lasagna noodles
½ cup basil pesto, jarred or fresh
12 ounces shredded mozzarella cheese

Preheat the oven to 375°F. Pour half a jar of Alfredo sauce in a 7 × 11-inch baking dish. Stir in ½ cup of the water and spread evenly. Place 3 uncooked noodles over the sauce in an even layer. Spread half of the pesto on the noodles, sprinkle with one-third of the mozzarella, and spread the rest of the first jar of Alfredo sauce. Top with 3 more noodles, the remaining pesto, another one-third of the mozzarella, and half of the second jar of sauce. Pour the remaining ½ cup of water into the rest of the second jar of sauce. Seal with the lid and shake to combine. Top with the remaining 3 noodles and pour the sauce-water mixture over the top. Cover with foil and bake for 30 minutes.

Remove the foil and bake for another 30 minutes. Top with the remaining mozzarella and bake 10 minutes more. Let rest for 15 minutes before cutting. (The lasagna can be made a day ahead and reheated, after which it will cut more neatly.)

Tuna Noodle Lasagna

This upscale version of tuna noodle casse-role attempts a tough three-way chal-lenge: being kid-friendly, adult-tempting, and an easy one-pot dinner. My family gave it a thumbs-up. Let's see what yours says.

Makes 6 servings

½ package (6 ounces) fresh precut broc-coli florets
2 jars (16 ounces each) Alfredo sauce
1 cup water
9 (about half of a 1-pound box) lasagna noodles
2 cans (about 6 ounces each) solid-packed white tuna in water or oil, drained and flaked
12 ounces shredded mozzarella cheese

Preheat the oven to 375°F. Cut the broc-coli into bite-size pieces and microwave in a covered microwave-safe container with a few tablespoons of water at full power until tender, about 3 minutes.

Pour half a jar of Alfredo sauce in a 7 × 11-inch baking dish. Stir in ½ cup of the water and spread evenly. Place 3 uncooked noodles in an even layer on the sauce and top with half the tuna, half the broccoli, one-third of the mozzarella, and the remaining half of the first jar of Alfredo sauce. Top with 3 more noodles, the rest of the tuna, the rest of the broc-coli, another one-third of the mozzarella, and half of the second jar of sauce.

Pour the remaining ½ cup of water into the remaining sauce, seal with the lid, and shake to combine. Top the lasagna with the remaining 3 noodles and pour the sauce-water mixture over the top. Cover with foil and bake for 30 minutes. Remove the foil and bake another 30 minutes. Top with the remaining moz-zarella and bake 10 minutes more. Let rest for 15 minutes before cutting into servings. (The lasagna can be made a day ahead and reheated.)

Ravioli Lasagna

What is a ravioli but layers of pasta with cheese in between? What is a lasagna but layers of pasta with cheese in between? Hmmm.

Makes 8 servings

1 box (10 ounces) frozen chopped
   spinach, thawed or cooked
1 jar (8 ounces) olive salad
1 jar (26 ounces) marinara sauce
1 cup water
1 large package (24 ounces) or 2 regular
   packages (19 ounces) square cheese
   ravioli, about 55 pieces
12 ounces shredded mozzarella
   cheese

Preheat the oven to 375°F. Combine the spinach and olive salad. Pour half of the marinara sauce in a 9 × 13-inch baking dish. Add ½ cup of the water and stir to combine. Make a layer of 20 ravioli (4 rows of 5 ravioli) on top of the sauce. Spoon half of the spinach-olive mixture over the ravioli and scatter one-third of the mozzarella over the top. Make a second layer of ravioli, this time using 15 ravioli (3 rows of 5). Top with the remaining spinach-olive mixture and another one-third of the mozzarella. Make a final layer of the remaining 20 ravioli (4 rows of 5 ravioli). Add the remaining water to the remaining sauce, seal with the lid, shake until combined, and pour over the ravioli.

Spread evenly and cover with foil. Bake for 1 hour. Uncover, scatter the remaining mozzarella over the top, and bake 10 minutes more. Remove from the oven and let rest for 10 minutes before cutting into servings.

Spinach Ravioli with Sun-Dried Tomato Oil

The luscious purses known as ravioli come to us already stuffed with flavor; our only challenge is to dress them for our guests. In this recipe spinach ravioli are glazed with a flavorful oil, crimson from sun-dried tomatoes and redolent with garlic and Parmesan.

Makes 4 servings

1 pound frozen spinach ravioli
2 tablespoons sun-dried tomato paste
1 teaspoon chopped garlic, jarred or fresh
Pinch of crushed red pepper flakes
¼ cup extra-virgin olive oil
Salt and black pepper to taste
⅓ cup grated imported Parmesan cheese

Heat a large pot of lightly salted water to a boil. Add the pasta, stir to separate, and cook until al dente, about 12 minutes. Meanwhile, combine the sun-dried tomato paste, garlic, pepper flakes, oil, salt, and pepper in a serving bowl. When the ravioli are done, transfer a few spoonfuls of the pasta water into the sauce to loosen it. Drain the pasta, toss it with the sauce and Parmesan, and adjust the seasoning with additional salt and pepper.

Pumpkin Ravioli in Ginger Tomato Sauce

This recipe was an accident, and it's all Bonny Barry's fault. Bonny worked with me testing recipes for this book. When I gave her this one, I neglected to note what pasta sauce I was using. I was thinking white, because a tomato sauce with pumpkin was not part of my culinary consciousness. Thank goodness Bonny is further evolved than I. When I saw what she had done, I didn't react well, but when I tasted it, I was thrilled. The marinara sauce lightened the ravioli, and the ginger romanced the pumpkin. We added some scallions, and a new dish was born.

Makes 4 servings

2 packages (about 10 ounces each) refrigerated or frozen pumpkin or squash ravioli
1 jar (26 ounces) marinara pasta sauce, not thick
3 tablespoons minced ginger, jarred or fresh
2 scallions, roots trimmed, thinly sliced
Salt and black pepper to taste

Heat a large pot of lightly salted water to a boil. Add the pasta, stir to separate, and cook until al dente, about 10 minutes. Meanwhile, bring the marinara sauce to a simmer in a small saucepan. Stir in the ginger and simmer for 3 minutes. Stir in the scallions. Drain the ravioli, toss with the sauce, and season with salt and pepper.

Baked Tortellini with Spring Peas

We live in the golden age of pasta engineering. Every year fanciful shapes come and go, but I have yet to see any of them surpass the elegance, function, and pudgy cuteness of a tortellini. I have always loved the way the navel of a tortellini (which means "belly button" in Italian) holds the perfect amount of sauce, but it is also a natural nesting spot for a chunk of tomato, a shard of shrimp, or, best of all, those sweet tiny peas that before the popularity of frozen food were the harbinger of spring.

Makes 4 servings

2 packages (9 ounces each) refrigerated
    or frozen tortellini, any variety
1 jar (16 ounces) Alfredo sauce
¼ cup grated imported Parmesan cheese
⅔ cup whole-milk ricotta cheese
1 cup frozen tiny peas

Preheat the oven to 375°F. Heat a large pot of lightly salted water to a boil. Add the pasta, stir to separate, and cook until al dente, about 8 minutes. Meanwhile, combine the Alfredo sauce, Parmesan, and ricotta in a small (1½-quart) casserole dish. Stir in the cooked tortellini and peas, and bake for 25 minutes, until browned and bubbling.

Curried Tortellini with Lentils

This tortellini stew is inspired by the vegetarian karhis of northern India, usually made with beans, vegetables, and at times pieces of dried dal wafers (called "pappadam"), which resemble cooked noodles when simmered in sauce. Because the pasta is simmered in the curry sauce, it becomes infused with exotic spices and a golden color as it softens. It is important to use fresh pasta for this preparation; dried pasta requires far more liquid to rehydrate.

Makes 4 servings

1 jar (15 ounces) curry sauce
1 can (14 ounces) lentil soup
1 cup water
2 packages (9 ounces each) refrigerated
    or frozen tortellini, any variety
1 box (10 ounces) frozen chopped
    spinach
½ cup plain yogurt, whole milk or low-fat

Combine the curry sauce, lentil soup, and water in a large skillet and bring to a simmer. Add the tortellini, stir to separate, and simmer until tender and the liquid has thickened slightly, about 10 minutes. Meanwhile, cook the spinach in a microwave at full power for 3 minutes. Squeeze out any excess water and stir into the finished tortellini, along with the yogurt. Heat through and serve.

Sesame Garlic Potstickers

The only hard part about making pot-stickers (Chinese dumplings) is assembling the dumplings themselves. Years ago high-quality dumpling wrappers made the job much easier, but you still had to make the filling and stuff the little buggers, which was fun but took time. Now more and more delicious prewrapped dumplings are sold frozen. The flavor selection and quality keep growing, and all you have to do is cook them.

Makes 4 servings

1 teaspoon minced garlic, jarred or fresh
1 tablespoon chopped ginger, jarred or fresh
½ cup teriyaki sauce, preferably Soy Vay Veri Veri Teriyaki Sauce
1 tablespoon vegetable oil
1 pound frozen Asian dumplings, any variety
¼ cup water

Combine the garlic, ginger, and teriyaki sauce. Heat the oil in a large skillet, place the dumplings in the oil in a single layer, flat side down, and sauté until the bottoms of the dumplings are uniformly browned. Add the teriyaki mixture and the water, cover, and boil until the dumplings are tender and the liquid has reduced to a glaze, about 5 minutes. Shake the pan to coat the dumplings with the glaze. Transfer to a platter and serve.

Dutch Country Chicken and Potato Dumplings

This classic Amish chicken-and-dumpling stew is modernized with precut fresh vegetables and frozen potato gnocchi. I'm sure gnocchi-loving Italians never thought they'd see their beloved dumplings floating in chicken gravy and dolloped with sour cream, but the transition works just fine.

Makes 4 servings

2 tablespoons butter
1 pound boneless, skinless chicken thighs, cut in eighths
2 cups chicken broth
1 package (16 ounces) blend of precut fresh broccoli, carrot, and cauliflower
1 package (16 ounces) frozen potato gnocchi
¼ teaspoon poultry seasoning
¼ cup instant mashed potato flakes
¼ cup sour cream

Melt the butter in a large skillet over medium heat. Sauté the chicken until lightly browned. Add the broth, bring to a boil, then simmer the vegetables, covered, for 5 minutes. Stir in the gnocchi, cover, and boil until the gnocchi are puffed and tender, about 3 minutes. Stir in the potato flakes and simmer for 1 minute, until the sauce is slightly thickened. Remove from the heat and stir in the sour cream.

Gnocchi in Gorgonzola Cream

Gorgonzola is lush and flavorful enough to be a sauce on its own; a little cream smooths its texture and softens its strong flavors.

Makes 4 servings

1 package (about 13 ounces) potato gnocchi
1 cup light cream
Pinch of dried crushed rosemary
2 ounces Gorgonzola or other blue cheese
Salt and black pepper to taste

Heat a large pot of salted water to a boil. Add the gnocchi and stir briefly. Once the gnocchi rise to the surface, boil for 3 minutes. Meanwhile, heat the cream in a small skillet until boiling. Add the rosemary and lower the heat until the cream is simmering. Stir in the Gorgonzola until a smooth sauce forms. Do not overcook. Season with salt and pepper. Drain the gnocchi and toss with the sauce.

Gnocchi with Anchovy Aioli

Gnocchi are usually served baked with butter and cheese or in a simple marinara sauce, or sometimes they are simmered in broth. Here they are glazed with aioli, the pungent garlic mayonnaise from Provence, and spiked with anchovy paste. The effect is intense and, if you love anchovies, luscious. If you don't love anchovies, turn the page.

Makes 4 servings

1 package (13 ounces) gnocchi, refrigerated or frozen
1 small tube (about 1½ ounces) anchovy paste
2 teaspoons minced garlic, jarred or fresh
¼ cup mayonnaise
2 tablespoons extra-virgin olive oil
1 teaspoon balsamic vinegar
2 tablespoons chopped Italian (flat-leaf) parsley
Black pepper to taste

Heat a large pot of salted water to a boil. Add the gnocchi and stir briefly. Once they rise to the surface, boil for 3 minutes. Meanwhile, combine the remaining ingredients in a warm serving bowl. Drain the gnocchi and toss with the anchovy sauce. Adjust the seasoning with pepper.

CHAPTER 12

GONE GRILLIN'

Doctored Barbecue Sauce
APPLE BARBECUE SAUCE
WASABI LIME BARBECUE SAUCE
MOLASSES MUSTARD BARBECUE SAUCE
RED CHILI BARBECUE SAUCE
ORANGE HOISIN BARBECUE SAUCE
ROASTED GARLIC BALSAMIC BARBECUE SAUCE
CHIPOTLE BARBECUE SAUCE
MOLE BARBECUE SAUCE
BLACK BEAN BARBECUE SAUCE
CARIBBEAN BARBECUE SAUCE
TZATZIKI BARBECUE SAUCE
Caesar Grilled Steak and Salad
Grilled Steaks with Olive "Butter"
Steak Sauce London Broil
Fajita London Broil with Chipotle Butter
Grilled Buffalo Burgers
Gorgonzola Burgers with Tarragon Mustard Sauce
Jerk Pork Ribs Grilled with Allspice Yams
Barbecued Chinese Pork Chops
Curried Pineapple Veal Chops

Tandoori Lamb Steaks with Apricot Chutney
Tandoori Chicken with Cucumber Raita
Red Tandoori Chicken Thighs
All-American Turkey Burger
Ginger Turkey Burgers with Teriyaki Glaze
Chicken Grilled with Roasted Pepper Rouille
Satay Spectacular
Smoked Turkey Breast Grilled with Spicy Maple Glaze
Grilled Chilied Shrimp
Grilled Salmon with Artichoke Aioli
Grilled Salmon with Olive Tomato Vinaigrette
Grilled Tuna with Tapenade, Pesto, and Bruschetta Relish
Grilled Escabeche
Grilled Ratatouille
Veggie Burger with the Works
Grilled Summer Squash Vinaigrette
Grilled Hoisin Eggplant
Grilled Asparagus Vinaigrette
Grilled Corn with Tomato Butter
Grilled Chicken Salad on Wilted Lettuce

Doctored Barbecue Sauce

Americans love to mess with barbecue sauce—a dash of hot sauce here, a spoon of marmalade there. The base is generally a sort of sweet, tart, spicy tomato purée designed for flavoring, not cooking. Try grilling with a barbecue sauce, and you'll end up with nothing but char. Use it instead as a sauce at the table or basted onto the surface of grilled ingredients in the last five minutes of cooking. The following sauces were tested with national brands of barbecue sauces, labeled either spicy or mild. They are suitable for almost anything you want to grill, although specific recommendations are given at the end of each recipe.

APPLE BARBECUE SAUCE

Makes 6 servings

1 bottle (about 18 ounces) tomato-based
   barbecue sauce, spicy if desired
1 jar (8 ounces) apple butter
2 teaspoons spicy brown mustard

Combine all the ingredients. Use as a sauce with grilled chicken or ribs.

WASABI LIME BARBECUE SAUCE

Makes 6 servings

1 bottle (about 18 ounces) tomato-based
   spicy barbecue sauce
2 tablespoons prepared wasabi in a tube
¼ cup lime juice, organic bottled or fresh

Combine all the ingredients. Use as a sauce with grilled seafood or vegetables.

MOLASSES MUSTARD BARBECUE SAUCE

Makes 6 servings

1 bottle (about 18 ounces) tomato-based
   barbecue sauce, spicy if desired
3 tablespoons spicy brown mustard
½ cup molasses

Combine all the ingredients. Use as a sauce with grilled poultry, pork, or burgers.

RED CHILI BARBECUE SAUCE

Makes 8 servings

1 bottle (about 18 ounces) tomato-based
    spicy barbecue sauce
1 tablespoon chili powder
2 teaspoons ground cumin
1 cup salsa

Combine all the ingredients. Use as a
sauce with grilled seafood, meat, poultry,
or vegetables.

ORANGE HOISIN BARBECUE SAUCE

Makes 6 servings

1 bottle (about 18 ounces) tomato-based
    barbecue sauce
½ cup orange juice
⅓ cup orange marmalade
⅓ cup hoisin sauce

Combine all the ingredients. Use as a
sauce with grilled seafood, meat, or poultry.

ROASTED GARLIC BALSAMIC BARBECUE SAUCE

Makes 6 servings

1 bottle (about 18 ounces) tomato-based
    barbecue sauce
3 tablespoons minced roasted garlic
5 tablespoons balsamic vinegar

Combine all the ingredients. Use as a
sauce with grilled seafood, meat, or poultry.

CHIPOTLE BARBECUE SAUCE

Makes 8 servings

1 bottle (about 18 ounces) tomato-based
    barbecue sauce, spicy if desired
1 teaspoon chipotle hot sauce
1 jar (12 ounces) salsa, any heat level

Combine all the ingredients. Use as a
sauce with grilled seafood, meat, or poultry.

MOLE BARBECUE SAUCE

Makes 6 servings

1 bottle (about 18 ounces) tomato-based
   spicy barbecue sauce
½ cup orange juice
2 tablespoons jarred mole (page 23)

Combine all the ingredients. Use as a
sauce with grilled meat or poultry.

BLACK BEAN BARBECUE SAUCE

Makes 6 servings

1 bottle (about 18 ounces) tomato-based
   barbecue sauce, spicy if desired
½ cup salsa, any heat level
1 cup black bean dip

Combine all the ingredients. Use as a
sauce with grilled meat, seafood, or poultry.

CARIBBEAN BARBECUE SAUCE

Makes 6 servings

1 bottle (about 18 ounces) tomato-based
   spicy barbecue sauce
1 can (14 ounces) coconut milk, light or
   regular
5 tablespoons jerk seasoning sauce

Combine all the ingredients. Use as a
sauce with grilled meat, seafood, or poultry.

TZATZIKI BARBECUE SAUCE

Makes 6 servings

1 teaspoon minced garlic, jarred or fresh
1 tablespoon dried mint leaves
1 tablespoon chopped Italian (flat-leaf)
   parsley
1 cup plain yogurt, whole or low-fat
2 tablespoons extra-virgin olive oil
2 tablespoons lemon juice, organic bottled or fresh

Combine all the ingredients. Use as a
sauce with grilled lamb, veal, seafood, or
poultry

Caesar Grilled Steak and Salad

Home cooks have known the multiple personalities of salad dressings for decades. One night it is tossed with romaine, the next night it is basting something on the grill, and the next it is saucing a steak. This recipe highlights all of them. It starts by marinating steaks in Caesar dressing. After grilling they are served with a Caesar-dressed salad and topped with a Caesar-based steak sauce.

Makes 4 servings

4 boneless steaks, sirloin or skirt, about 7 ounces each
½ cup plus 2 tablespoons Caesar salad dressing
½ teaspoon minced garlic, jarred or fresh
1 teaspoon mustard
2 teaspoons anchovy paste
1 bag (10 ounces) romaine lettuce

Marinate the steaks in ¼ cup of the Caesar dressing for 30 to 60 minutes. Preheat a grill. Combine another ¼ cup of dressing, the garlic, mustard, and anchovy paste. Grill the steaks about 2 inches from the flame to desired doneness. Just before they're done, toss the lettuce with the remaining dressing. Place a steak on a plate, top with a large spoonful of sauce, and mound the salad next to and overlapping the steak.

Grilled Steaks with Olive "Butter"

This simple sauce embodies the essence of Mediterranean eating. Tapenade is thinned to sauce consistency with olive oil, seasoned with garlic, and poured over a steak—any steak, grilled the way you want it—encrusted with rosemary, coarse salt, and black pepper.

Makes 4 servings

4 boneless steaks, such as sirloin strip, about 7 or 8 ounces each
1 teaspoon dried crushed rosemary leaves
Kosher salt and coarsely ground pepper to taste
Nonstick olive oil spray
3 tablespoons extra-virgin olive oil
2 tablespoons tapenade (black olive spread)
⅛ teaspoon minced garlic, jarred or fresh

Preheat a grill. Season each steak with ¼ teaspoon of rosemary, salt, and pepper. Coat with olive oil spray. Combine the oil, tapenade, and garlic. Grill the steaks over a hot fire to desired doneness and serve topped with the sauce.

Steak Sauce London Broil

My father believed in A.1. steak sauce, a faith that drove him to douse anything from hamburgers to eggs with its sweet, tangy, spicy syrup. Although my devotion does not compare to his, I have found it a great help with problematic cuts of meat such as London broil. I have also included five easily assembled steak sauces that start with A.1. Make one or more. Each yields enough for about six portions.

Makes 6 servings

FOR THE LONDON BROIL:
1½ pounds top round London broil or
   flank steak
½ cup A.1. steak sauce
Nonstick oil spray

FOR MUSTARD STEAK SAUCE:
¼ cup A.1. steak sauce
¼ cup spicy brown mustard

FOR HORSERADISH STEAK SAUCE:
¼ cup A.1. steak sauce
¼ cup prepared white horseradish
1 tablespoon tomato paste in a tube

FOR SAVORY HONEY STEAK SAUCE:
¼ cup A.1. steak sauce
¼ cup honey
Pinch of chopped garlic, jarred or fresh

FOR HOT PEPPER STEAK SAUCE:
¼ cup A.1. steak sauce
1 tablespoon Chinese chili purée

FOR SALSA STEAK SAUCE:
¼ cup A.1. steak sauce
½ cup salsa, any heat level

Marinate the London broil in the A.1. sauce for at least 1 hour or up to 8 hours. Preheat a grill. Make one or more of the sauces by combining the ingredients for that sauce. Coat the rack of the grill with oil spray and grill the London broil over a high fire to desired doneness. Transfer to a cutting board and slice against the grain in thin slices. Serve with the sauce(s).

Fajita London Broil with Chipotle Butter

In this recipe the tough fibers of a London broil are subjected to a pungent fajita-style marinade that permeates the meat quickly, giving it a bright flavor and increased tenderness. After a short stint on the grill, it is served with smoky spicy chipotle pepper butter.

Makes 6 servings

½ cup salsa, any heat level
½ teaspoon chopped garlic, jarred or fresh
2 tablespoons lime juice, organic bottled or fresh
1½ pounds top round London broil or flank steak
4 tablespoons (½ stick) butter
3 tablespoons chipotle hot pepper sauce
1 tablespoon Worcestershire sauce
1 tablespoon ketchup
Nonstick oil spray

Combine the salsa, garlic, and lime juice, and marinate the London broil in the sauce for at least 1 hour or up to 8 hours. Preheat a grill. Melt the butter and whisk in the chipotle hot pepper sauce, Worcestershire sauce, and ketchup. Keep warm. Coat the rack of the grill with oil spray and grill the London broil over a hot fire to desired doneness. Slice against the grain. Serve topped with the chipotle butter.

Grilled Buffalo Burgers

The recipe is simple: Grill perfectly seasoned burgers, slather them with butter and hot sauce, perch them on a toasted chewy roll, and top them with chunky blue cheese dressing.

Makes 4 servings

1½ pounds lean ground beef
½ teaspoon garlic powder
½ teaspoon onion powder
Salt and pepper to taste
Nonstick oil spray
2 tablespoons butter, melted
¼ cup Frank's RedHot Sauce
4 kaiser rolls, split
4 romaine lettuce leaves
3 tablespoons blue cheese salad dressing

Preheat a grill. Combine the ground beef, garlic powder, onion powder, salt, and pepper, and form into 4 burgers. Coat the rack of the grill with oil spray and grill the burgers over high heat to desired doneness. Meanwhile, combine the melted butter and hot sauce in a soup bowl. Toast the rolls, if desired, and place a lettuce leaf on the bottom half of each roll. When the burgers are done, dip them in the hot sauce mixture and turn to coat evenly. Place a burger on top of each lettuce leaf and top each burger with blue cheese dressing and the top half of the roll.

Gorgonzola Burgers with Tarragon Mustard Sauce

These novel cheeseburgers contain pieces of Gorgonzola that melt into the burgers as they grill, inundating them with flavor and pools of molten cheese. They are served with a simple mustard mayonnaise, fragrant with sweet tarragon, the perfect foil to the pungency of the Gorgonzola.

Makes 4 servings

1½ pounds lean ground beef
1 teaspoon onion salt
1 teaspoon ground black pepper
4 ounces Gorgonzola or other blue
   cheese, crumbled
Nonstick oil spray
1 tablespoon spicy brown mustard
3 tablespoons Dijonnaise dressing
1 teaspoon dried tarragon leaves
Toasted buns (optional)

Preheat a grill. Combine the ground beef, onion salt, and pepper. Mix in the Gorgonzola and distribute evenly through the meat. Form into 4 burgers. Coat the rack of the grill with oil spray and grill the burgers over a hot fire to desired doneness. Meanwhile, combine the mustard, dressing, and tarragon. When the burgers are done, top each one with 1 tablespoon of the sauce. Serve on toasted buns if desired.

Jerk Pork Ribs Grilled with Allspice Yams

In this recipe jerk-seasoned ribs are microwaved with yams until everything is tender. This is an important step; if the ingredients were placed raw on the grill, they would scorch and dry before they were cooked through.

Makes 4 servings

3 pounds pork spareribs
1 teaspoon jerk seasoning
2 large yams (about 12 ounces each),
   split lengthwise
1 bottle (about 18 ounces) Jamaican jerk
   sauce
Nonstick oil spray
¼ teaspoon ground allspice
Salt and black pepper to taste

Sprinkle the spareribs with jerk seasoning. Place the yams, cut side down, in a 9 × 13-inch microwave-safe baking dish. Place the ribs on top of the yams, pour the jerk sauce over all, cover with microwave-safe plastic wrap, and microwave at full power for 25 minutes. Meanwhile, preheat a grill and coat the rack with oil spray. Season the cut sides of the yams with allspice, salt, and pepper, and grill the yams and ribs until browned on both sides, about 5 minutes per side. Baste the ribs several times during cooking with liquid from the baking dish.

Barbecued Chinese Pork Chops

Modern pork is not well marbled, making it lean and dry, but brining can help. Soaking pork chops in a mixture of salt, water, and sugar slightly softens the proteins in the meat. Pork chops soaked in brine for only an hour absorb enough moisture to make fatter, juicier chops on the grill.

Makes 4 servings

½ cup kosher salt
¼ cup sugar
2 quarts water
4 boneless center-cut pork chops, each
  about ¾ inch thick
¼ cup Soy Vay Veri Veri Teriyaki Sauce
½ cup ketchup
1 teaspoon minced ginger, jarred or
  fresh
Small pinch of crushed red pepper flakes
Freshly ground pepper to taste
Nonstick oil spray

Mix the salt, sugar, and water until the sugar and salt dissolve. Add the pork chops and refrigerate for at least 1 hour or as long as 8 hours.

Preheat a grill. Combine the teriyaki sauce, ketchup, ginger, and pepper flakes. Remove the pork chops from the brine, pat dry, and season with pepper. Coat the grate of the grill with oil spray. Brown the chops on both sides, about 4 minutes per side. As you turn the chops, brush the browned sides with some of the sauce. Turn the chops so that they cook on their sauced sides briefly, just long enough to brown the sauce, about 1 minute per side. Turn and baste 2 or 3 more times. The chops will not be firm in the center when done and will register an internal temperature of 145°F on a meat thermometer inserted through the side of a chop

Curried Pineapple Veal Chops

Salsa is a surprisingly effective marinade, flavoring and tenderizing a veal chop in less than an hour. After grilling they are tossed with a sweet, pungent pairing of curry and fruit salsa.

Makes 4 servings

1 cup pineapple salsa
4 loin or rib veal chops, each about ¾ inch thick
Salt and black pepper to taste
Nonstick oil spray
1 cup curry sauce
1 teaspoon cilantro pesto or chutney, or 1 tablespoon chopped cilantro

Purée half of the salsa and pour it over the chops, turning the chops to coat them on both sides. Marinate for 30 minutes. Preheat a grill. Remove the chops from the salsa, wipe off the excess, and season with salt and pepper. Coat the grill rack with oil spray and grill the chops over a medium fire until browned on both sides and cooked through to desired doneness. When the chops are medium-rare, they will be not quite firm in the center and will register an internal temperature of 150°F on a meat thermometer inserted into the side of a chop.

While the chops are grilling, combine the remaining salsa and the curry sauce in a saucepan and heat to a simmer. Stir in the cilantro and pour over the grilled chops.

Tandoori Lamb Steaks with Apricot Chutney

Lamb shoulder steaks are a relatively inexpensive cut. They tend to be a bit tough, but the marinade should solve the problem. If you can find jarred apricot chutney, you can use it in place of the prepared chutney recipe given here.

Makes 4 servings

1 container (8 ounces) plain yogurt
½ cup curry simmer sauce
4 shoulder lamb chops
Salt and black pepper to taste
8 dried apricots, quartered
½ cup water
¾ cup fruit chutney (any fruit variety)
Nonstick oil spray

Combine the yogurt and curry sauce in a large zippered plastic bag. Season the lamb with salt and pepper, place in the bag, and seal. Massage the yogurt mixture into the meat until it is completely coated and refrigerate for at least 1 hour but no more than 8 hours. Meanwhile, combine the apricots and water in a small skillet and simmer until the apricots are tender and most of the water is gone. Stir in the chutney and heat through.

Preheat a grill and coat the grill rack with oil spray. Lift the chops from the marinade and grill until browned on both sides and cooked through to desired doneness. Serve with the apricot chutney on the side.

Tandoori Chicken with Cucumber Raita

This spicy grilled chicken is marinated in yogurt and served with a simple Indian yogurt salad, raita, a common accompaniment to spicy dishes.

Makes 4 servings

4 chicken breast halves, bone in, skinned
Salt and black pepper to taste
½ cup curry sauce
1 cup plain yogurt, any fat percentage
Nonstick oil spray
1 container (8 ounces) prepared deli cucumber salad
⅛ teaspoon ground cumin

Make 3 cuts almost to the bone in each chicken breast and season with salt and pepper. Combine the curry sauce and half of the yogurt, and pour into a large zippered plastic bag. Add the chicken and rub until the meat is fully coated. Refrigerate for at least 2 hours.

Preheat a grill and coat the grill rack with oil spray. Lift the chicken from the marinade and place on the rack. Grill the bone side about 10 minutes and the meat side about 5 minutes. Do not overcook. The chicken should be cooked through but still moist.

While the meat is cooking, make the raita by combining the cucumber salad, the remaining yogurt, and the cumin. Serve the chicken with the raita on the side.

Red Tandoori Chicken Thighs

Instead of using curry sauce for seasoning, this recipe gets its brick red color from paprika and the other red peppers in chili powder.

Makes 4 servings

⅓ cup yogurt
1 tablespoon lemon juice, organic bottled or fresh
1 teaspoon chili powder
1 teaspoon chopped garlic, jarred or fresh
½ teaspoon minced ginger, jarred or fresh
1 tablespoon sweet or hot paprika
Salt and pepper to taste
1½ pounds boneless, skinless chicken thighs
Nonstick oil spray
1 lime, cut in 8 wedges

Combine the yogurt, lemon juice, chili powder, garlic, ginger, paprika, salt, and pepper, and pour into a large zippered plastic bag. Place the chicken in the bag and rub it until the meat is fully coated. Refrigerate for at least 1 hour.

Preheat a grill and coat the grill rack with oil spray. Lift the chicken from the marinade, place on the rack, and grill about 10 minutes, turning once or twice, until the chicken is browned and firm to the touch. Serve each portion with 2 lime wedges to squeeze over the meat.

All-American Turkey Burger

Ground turkey is sweeter, milder, and drier than beef, characteristics that have given it a reputation for being bland. This recipe intends to change that image by boosting the flavor and moisture of the turkey. Mustard, ketchup, and Worcestershire sauce deepen the color and give the ground turkey something akin to the richer flavor of beef, while bread crumbs keep the meat moist.

Makes 4 servings

1½ pounds ground turkey
2 teaspoons ketchup
2 teaspoons spicy brown mustard
2 teaspoons Worcestershire sauce
¼ cup bread crumbs
Salt and black pepper to taste
Nonstick oil spray
Kaiser rolls or hamburger buns, split
Lettuce leaves, sliced tomatoes, and
    condiments (optional)

Combine the turkey, ketchup, mustard, Worcestershire sauce, bread crumbs, salt, and pepper. Form into 4 patties, each about ¾ inch thick. Preheat a grill, coat the grill rack with oil spray, and grill the burgers until browned on both sides and a thermometer inserted into the side of a burger registers an internal temperature of 165°F. Serve on buns with lettuce, tomatoes, and condiments if desired.

Ginger Turkey Burgers with Teriyaki Glaze

The mild character of ground turkey makes it a culinary chameleon, as able to assume a Mediterranean persona as an Indian one. This recipe heads farther east, with embedded bits of fresh ginger and garlic in the meat, and a glaze of sweet and salty teriyaki sauce. The finished burgers are topped with a few slices of pickled sushi ginger.

Makes 4 servings

1½ pounds ground turkey
1 teaspoon minced garlic, jarred or fresh
1 teaspoon ground gingerroot, jarred or
    fresh
1 teaspoon soy sauce
1 tablespoon ketchup
Nonstick oil spray
2 tablespoons teriyaki sauce
2 tablespoons pickled ginger for sushi

Combine the turkey, garlic, gingerroot, soy sauce, and ketchup, and form into 4 patties, each about ¾ inch thick. Preheat a grill, coat the grill rack with oil spray, and grill the burgers until browned on both sides, brushing with the teriyaki sauce before turning. The burgers are done when a thermometer inserted into the side of one registers an internal temperature of 165°F. Serve topped with pickled ginger.

Chicken Grilled with Roasted Pepper Rouille

Flayed, filleted, stripped of skin and bone, and defenseless against flames and caustic marinades, chicken breasts are routinely sacrificed on the grill, but there are some things you can do. Coat the meat with oil to lubricate the surface, where most drying occurs. As soon as the thickest part is almost firm, remove the chicken from the grill. It will set the rest of the way as it rests on the plate.

Makes 4 servings

4 slices crusty bread
Nonstick olive oil spray
4 boneless, skinless chicken breast halves
    (about 6 ounces each)
1 teaspoon Italian seasoning
1 tablespoon pesto, jarred or fresh
¼ cup roasted pepper spread
4 teaspoons grated imported Parmesan
    or Asiago cheese

Preheat a grill. Coat the slices of bread with olive oil spray and toast in a 400°F oven or toaster oven about 10 minutes. Coat the chicken breasts with olive oil spray and sprinkle with the Italian seasoning. Coat the rack of the grill with olive oil spray and grill the chicken until browned on both sides and firm to the touch.

While the chicken is grilling, combine the pesto and pepper spread, and sprinkle each slice of toasted bread with a tea-spoon of cheese. To serve, place a grilled chicken breast on each slice of toast and top each one with a tablespoon of the roasted pepper sauce.

Satay Spectacular

Satay, the popular Indonesian skewers of grilled meat served with spicy peanut dip, is typically served as a snack or hors d'oeuvre. This recipe elevates it to entrée status by removing the skewers, upping the portion, and transforming it into a mixed grill made with chicken, shrimp, and pineapple.

Makes 4 servings

1 pound chicken tenders
1 pound peeled and cleaned jumbo
  shrimp, thawed if frozen
1 can (20 ounces) sliced pineapple,
  drained, or 1 pineapple, peeled,
  cored, and cut in rings
⅓ cup garlic-flavored oil, or ⅓ cup olive
  oil mixed with ½ teaspoon minced garlic
1 jar (8 ounces) Thai peanut sauce
1 cup regular coconut milk
1 tablespoon cilantro pesto or chutney,
  or 3 tablespoons chopped cilantro
Nonstick oil spray

Preheat a grill. Coat the chicken, shrimp, and pineapple rings with the oil. Combine the peanut sauce, coconut milk, and cilantro. Coat the grill rack with oil spray.

Different ingredients take different amounts of time to cook. Therefore, to get everything done at the same time you must stagger their start times. Place the chicken and pineapple on the grill. As soon as the edges of the chicken look opaque and the edges of the pineapple are browned (about 2 minutes), add the shrimp and turn the chicken and pineapple. Turn the shrimp when they start to firm and curl. Remove everything when browned and cooked through. (It will take about 4 minutes total for the chicken and the pineapple, and 3 minutes for the shrimp.) Because the intensity of each grill is different, timing can only be approximate.

When done, toss the chicken and shrimp with half of the sauce and serve surrounded by grilled pineapple. Serve the remaining sauce on the side.

Smoked Turkey Breast Grilled with Spicy Maple Glaze

Like ham, a smoked turkey breast is fully cooked when you buy it. All you have to do is heat it through or, in the case of grilling, brand it with grill marks. The sauce in this recipe is predominantly maple syrup, and its high sugar content makes it vulnerable to easy scorching. To prevent burning, turn the turkey steaks frequently and don't leave them unattended for any length of time.

Makes 4 servings

⅓ cup maple syrup
3 tablespoons mild hot sauce
Nonstick oil spray
1½ pounds smoked turkey breast, cut into 4 thick slices

Preheat a grill. Combine the syrup and hot sauce. Coat the grill rack with oil spray, place the steaks on the rack, and grill for 2 minutes. Turn the steaks and brush with the syrup mixture. Grill for another 2 minutes, turn them over, and brush them again. Grill, turn, and brush in 1-minute intervals 4 more times—for 8 minutes of total grill time.

Grilled Chilied Shrimp

Chinese chili purée combines the heat of a hot sauce, the tang of ketchup, and the salty hit of fermented soy. It is available in the Asian section of every market, and it will last for years in the refrigerator. If you don't have any, this recipe is reason enough to buy some. In this recipe jumbo shrimp are marinated in the chili purée and grilled until the coating sets into a layer of fiery glaze.

Makes 4 servings

2 tablespoons olive oil
1 tablespoon Chinese chili purée
1 teaspoon soy sauce
1 pound peeled and cleaned jumbo shrimp, thawed if frozen
Nonstick oil spray
1 lime, cut in 8 wedges

Combine the oil, chili purée, and soy sauce. Coat the shrimp with the mixture and refrigerate for at least 1 hour but no longer than 8 hours. Preheat a grill and coat the grill rack with oil spray. Arrange the marinated shrimp on the rack and grill until firm and opaque, about 2 minutes per side. Serve with the lime wedges.

Grilled Salmon with Artichoke Aioli

There are many permutations of artichoke purée, from pesto to dip to relish. Any one of them would be suitable for the quick sauce in this recipe. While you're at it, make a double batch; any extra can be served with poached seafood, grilled or baked chicken, or as a sauce for tuna or chicken salad.

Makes 4 servings

4 pieces salmon fillet, 6 to 7 ounces each
2 teaspoons lemon pepper
1 tablespoon olive oil
½ cup artichoke dip or spread
2 tablespoons mayonnaise
1 tablespoon lemon juice
1 teaspoon minced garlic, jarred or fresh
Nonstick oil spray

Season the salmon with lemon pepper and rub each piece with oil. Combine the artichoke dip, mayonnaise, lemon juice, and garlic. Preheat a grill and coat the grill rack with oil spray. Grill the fish for 3 to 4 minutes per side, until it flakes to gentle pressure. Serve each piece of fish topped with a portion of the sauce.

Grilled Salmon with Olive Tomato Vinaigrette

This simple, straightforward grilled salmon explodes with flavor. The secret is a chunky Mediterranean sauce that is assembled in minutes from five prepared ingredients.

Makes 4 servings

½ cup olive salad
2 tablespoons tomato paste in a tube
2 tablespoons extra-virgin olive oil
2 tablespoons red wine vinegar
2 tablespoons lemon juice, organic bottled or fresh
2 tablespoons water
1½ pounds salmon fillet, or four 6-ounce salmon steaks
1 teaspoon Italian seasoning
Nonstick olive oil spray

Preheat a grill. Combine the olive salad, tomato paste, oil, vinegar, lemon juice, and water. Season the salmon with the Italian seasoning. Coat the fish and the grill rack with olive oil spray. Grill the fish on both sides, non-skin side first, until the flesh flakes to gentle pressure, about 5 minutes per side. Serve each portion of salmon with ¼ cup of the sauce.

Grilled Tuna with Tapenade, Pesto, and Bruschetta Relish

When buying tuna steaks, look for a smooth surface and a minimum of visible membrane and brown spots. The meat can be pale rose or mahogany red; personal taste will determine your preference. If you want your tuna moist, get steaks at least an inch thick; if they are thinner, the fish will cook through and become dry before a charred crust can form. In this recipe the grilled tuna is served with an Italian-style relish.

Makes 4 servings

1 jar (12 ounces) tomato bruschetta
¼ cup black or green tapenade (olive spread)
2 tablespoons basil pesto, jarred or fresh
4 boneless tuna steaks, about 6 ounces each and 1 inch thick
Salt and black pepper to taste
Nonstick olive oil spray

Combine the bruschetta, tapenade, and pesto. Preheat a grill. Season the tuna steaks with salt and pepper. Coat both sides of the fish and the grill rack with oil spray. Grill the tuna over the hottest fire possible to desired doneness. Serve each tuna steak topped with a portion of the bruschetta relish.

Grilled Escabeche

In this variation of escabeche the fish is grilled, a change that gives a smoky nuance to the finished dish. Escabeche can be served warm or chilled, and can be prepared days ahead.

Makes 4 to 6 servings

Nonstick olive oil spray
1½ pounds fish fillet, any type
½ teaspoon Southwest seasoning
2 medium onions, halved and cut in ¼-inch-thick slices
¼ cup extra-virgin olive oil
1 teaspoon Italian seasoning
¾ cup orange juice
2 tablespoons lemon juice, organic bottled or fresh
2 tablespoons lime juice, organic bottled or fresh
1 teaspoon to 1 tablespoon hot pepper sauce, to taste

Preheat a grill and coat the grill rack with oil spray. Sprinkle the fish with the seasoning. Coat the fish and onions with oil spray and grill until well browned on both sides. Transfer to a wide, deep serving dish.

Heat the oil, Italian seasoning, orange, lemon, and lime juices, and the hot pepper sauce until boiling. Add the onions and pour over the fish. Set aside and cover for 10 minutes until the fish flakes to gentle pressure.

Grilled Ratatouille

Ratatouille is a vegetable dish from the south of France in which vegetables and herbs are simmered in serious quantities of olive oil. This recipe augments tradition with the flavors of the grill and uses far less fat.

Makes 6 servings

Nonstick olive oil spray
1 medium eggplant, cut in ¾-inch-thick
    rounds
1 medium zucchini, cut lengthwise in ¾-
    inch slices
1 red bell pepper, cut in strips
1 large onion, cut in 8 wedges
1 package (6 ounces) sliced Portobello
    mushrooms
2 teaspoons chopped garlic, jarred or
    fresh
Salt and pepper to taste
1 container (about 15 ounces) Italian-
    style diced tomatoes
2 tablespoons basil pesto,
    jarred or fresh
Grated imported Parmesan cheese

Preheat a grill and coat the grill rack with oil spray. Coat the vegetables with oil spray. Toss them with half of the garlic and the salt and pepper. Grill the vegetables until they are browned on their surfaces and tender inside, about 5 minutes per side. (Watch carefully. Vegetables grill at different rates depending on the strength of the fire and how close the rack is to the flame. Turn as needed.)

Toss the grilled vegetables with the tomatoes and pesto, and adjust the salt and pepper if needed. Serve with the Parmesan.

Veggie Burger with the Works

There are two styles of veggie burgers: One tries to imitate the flavor and texture of meat, and the other is laden with shards of vegetables and lots of grain. Either is perfect for this preparation, which glorifies the veggie burger in classic hamburger style.

Makes 4 servings

Nonstick oil spray
¼ cup tartar sauce or mayonnaise
2 tablespoons mild salsa
2 teaspoons spicy brown mustard
4 "flame-grilled" veggie burgers
4 slices Monterey Jack cheese
4 hamburger buns, split
Lettuce leaves, sliced tomatoes, pickle
    slices, onion slices, or other burger
    toppings (optional)

Preheat a grill and coat the grill rack with oil spray. Combine the tartar sauce, salsa, and mustard. Brown the veggie burgers on both sides, about 3 to 4 minutes per side. Top each burger with a slice of cheese, cover the grill, and cook until the cheese melts, about 1 minute. Spread the sauce on the buns, place a burger on each bun, and add the desired toppings.

Grilled Summer Squash Vinaigrette

Summer squash grill effortlessly. They are porous enough to readily absorb the flavors of a marinade, soft enough to grill in minutes, and moist enough to keep from drying out. This recipe couldn't be simpler. The only aspect that may be unusual is that you must slice the squash lengthwise to get pieces long enough to rest across the rack of the grill without falling through its slots. Make your slices hefty, at least ¼ inch thick; otherwise they'll become overly soft before they brown.

Makes 4 servings

Nonstick oil spray
2 zucchini, stemmed and sliced lengthwise
2 yellow summer squash, stemmed and sliced lengthwise
½ cup Italian or garlic vinaigrette salad dressing

Preheat a grill and coat the grill rack with oil spray. Toss the zucchini and yellow squash with half of the vinaigrette. Grill over a hot fire for 2 to 4 minutes per side, until browned and barely softened. Transfer to a platter and dress with the remaining vinaigrette.

Grilled Hoisin Eggplant

Asian eggplants are smaller and sweeter than Mediterranean varieties. I prefer Chinese, which are thinner than the Japanese, and have a light purple skin and pale flesh.

Makes 4 servings

2 tablespoons hoisin sauce
2 tablespoons sake or vodka
½ teaspoon minced garlic, jarred or fresh
½ teaspoon minced ginger, jarred or fresh
1 teaspoon balsamic vinegar
1 pound Chinese or Japanese eggplants
Nonstick oil spray
¼ cup chunky salsa, any heat level

Combine the hoisin sauce, sake, garlic, ginger, and balsamic vinegar. Cut the stems from the eggplants, split them in half lengthwise, and cut the halves into 2-inch lengths. Toss them in the hoisin mixture. Preheat a grill and coat the grill rack with oil spray. Grill or broil the eggplant pieces 2 inches from the fire about 5 minutes per side, until they are browned and tender. While they are cooking, add the salsa to any marinade remaining in the bowl. When the eggplant is done, toss it with the sauce.

Grilled Asparagus Vinaigrette

Asparagus is one of the few tough vegetables that can be grilled without precooking. Even "asparaphobes" may accept their nemesis once its acrid elements are tamed with the flavor of the grill. Just lay them across the grill rack, and you should have no problem keeping the thin spears from falling through when you turn them.

Makes 4 servings

Nonstick olive oil spray
16 medium-thick asparagus
⅔ cup vinaigrette salad dressing

Preheat a grill and coat the rack of the grill with oil spray. Snap the tough ends from the asparagus, toss with half of the vinaigrette, and place the spears on the rack perpendicular to the rungs. Grill until browned on one side, about 2 minutes. Turn and brown on the other side, about 2 minutes more. By the time the asparagus is browned on both sides, it should be barely tender. Dress with the remaining vinaigrette.

Grilled Corn with Tomato Butter

Don't husk your corn before you grill it. Just lay the unpeeled ears right over a fire, close the lid of the grill, and cook. Although many recipes instruct you to soak the ears to keep the husk from igniting, I have never found that necessary. The silk flares a bit, but all that gets through to the corn is a delicious smokiness. When the ears are done, the husks will be scorched in spots, and you'll hear the corn bubbling inside its wrapper. Set it aside while you grill the rest of the meal. The corn will stay warm inside its leaves for at least twenty minutes. Peel it just before serving and slather it with some of the spicy tomato butter.

Makes 4 servings

4 ears unhusked corn
4 tablespoons (½ stick) unsalted butter
1 tablespoon tomato paste in a tube
¼ teaspoon Chinese chili purée
⅛ teaspoon garlic salt

Preheat a grill to medium. Place the corn on the rack of the grill and cook for 10 to 12 minutes, turning every 3 to 4 minutes. Let cool for 2 minutes and remove the husks and silks. While the corn is grilling, combine the butter, tomato paste, chili purée, and garlic salt. Serve the corn with the tomato butter on the side.

Grilled Chicken Salad on Wilted Lettuce

At some point anyone who grills chicken—and who doesn't?—is burdened with leftovers. This elegant, warm salad is the perfect solution, and you don't have to wait around until the leftovers arrive. Make it anytime with prepackaged grilled sliced chicken breast that is found in the meat case (often next to the cold cuts) in your neighborhood market.

Makes 4 servings

1 pound leftover grilled chicken, sliced, or 1 package (1 pound) sliced grilled chicken

1 package (8 ounces) escarole salad blend or other hearty lettuce blend

¼ cup finely diced red onion

1 roasted red pepper, jarred or fresh, diced

½ cup bottled oil and vinegar salad dressing

1 tablespoon chopped garlic, jarred or fresh

2 tablespoons sugar

Toss the chicken, lettuce, onion, and red pepper in a salad bowl. Combine the dressing, garlic, and sugar in a small saucepan and heat until the sugar dissolves. Pour over the salad and toss until it is uniformly dressed.

CHAPTER 13

STIR-FRIES FROM AROUND THE WORLD

Stir-Fried Shrimp with Candied Walnuts
Stir-Fried Shrimp with Feta and Honeydew
Stir-Fried Shrimp Thai Noodles
Stir-Fried Shrimp and Spicy Sausage
Stir-Fried Mussels Marinara
Stir-Fried Salmon with Potatoes and Dill
Stir-Fried Salmon with Greens
Wok-Seared Salmon with Pineapple Salsa
Wok-Seared Sesame Salmon
Stir-Fried Shrimp and Eggs with Oyster Sauce
Stir-Fried Hoisin Barbecued Chicken
Stir-Fried Chicken with Tomato Tapenade
Stir-Fried Chicken and Noodles in Garlic Sauce
Wok-Braised Chicken and Roasted Peppers
Stir-Fried Turkey with Corn and Peppers
Stir-Fried Turkey Mole
Stir-Fried Chinese Chicken Noodle Soup
Stir-Fried Wasabi Beef and Scallions
Stir-Fried Beef with Three Hot Sauces

Stir-Fried Short Rib Goulash
Stir-Fried Mango-Glazed Pork
Stir-Fried Peanut Butter Pork
Wok-Seared Ginger Ginger Ginger Ginger Spareribs
Stir-Fried Pork Ribs in Cider Syrup
Stir-Fried Lamb and Peaches with Cardamom
Stir-Fried Red Curry Lamb
Stir-Fried Chili
Stir-Fried Red Pepper, Artichokes, and White Beans
Stir-Fried Szechwan Brussels Sprouts
Stir-Fried Teriyaki Mushrooms
Stir-Fried Smoky Broccoli and Apples
Stir-Fried Apricot-Glazed Carrots
Stir-Fried Corn and Roasted Peppers
Stir-Fried Soy-Sauced Hashed Browns
Stir-Fried Curried Vegetables

Stir-Fried Shrimp with Candied Walnuts

A shrimp stir-fry finished with candied walnuts has been a Chinese restaurant favorite for years, but until recently it has been beyond the reach of any but the most adventurous home cooks. Glazed or candied walnuts are now readily available. The Diamond brand sells one coated with sesame seeds and an amber sugary shell that is especially suited to the Asian character of this dish. If you can't find glazed walnuts, toasted walnuts can be substituted.

Makes 4 servings

¼ cup teriyaki sauce
1 teaspoon chopped garlic, jarred or fresh
1 teaspoon Chinese chili purée
Nonstick oil spray
1 pound peeled and cleaned large shrimp, thawed if frozen
½ cup glazed walnuts
2 scallions, roots removed, thinly sliced
3 tablespoons lemon juice, organic bottled or fresh

Combine the teriyaki sauce, garlic, and chili purée. Heat a wok over high heat. Coat with oil spray, add the shrimp, and stir-fry until firm and opaque, about 1 minute. Add the teriyaki mixture and continue to stir-fry until the shrimp are glazed. Stir in the walnuts, scallions, and lemon juice.

Stir-Fried Shrimp with Feta and Honeydew

I know this dish sounds weird, but you must trust me. The combination of honeyed citrus-scented melon, garlicky sea-salty shrimp, and mildly fermented feta cheese is as satisfying as it is surprising.

Makes 4 servings

Nonstick oil spray
1 cup chopped onions, frozen or fresh
1 teaspoon minced garlic, jarred or fresh
½ teaspoon dried thyme leaves
1 pound peeled and cleaned shrimp, thawed if frozen
½ honeydew melon, seeds and rind removed, cut in short slices
Salt and black pepper to taste
½ cup crumbled feta cheese

Heat a wok and coat it with oil spray. Stir-fry the onions until lightly browned, about 1 minute. Add the garlic, thyme, and shrimp, and stir-fry until the shrimp are firm and opaque, about 1 minute. Add the melon and stir-fry until heated through, about 1 minute more. Season with salt and pepper, and serve topped with the crumbled cheese.

Stir-Fried Shrimp Thai Noodles

Don't let the length of the ingredient list disturb you, it's actually much shorter than a typical Pad Thai, the tangy stir-fried noodle dish that is very similar to this preparation. Here, apricot nectar combines with a pungent nam pla (Thai fish sauce) to form the common sweet-sour-salty cacophony of Thai cuisine. Precut vegetables keep chopping to a minimum, and once the noodles are soaked and the sauce ingredients are combined, the stir-fry takes less than ten minutes.

Makes 4 servings

1 package (about 5 ounces) wide cellophane (bean thread) noodles
1½ cups apricot nectar
⅓ cup honey
¼ cup Thai fish sauce
1 teaspoon Chinese chile purée
1½ tablespoons minced garlic, jarred or fresh
Nonstick oil spray
1 cup chopped onions, frozen or fresh
1 package (8 ounces) sliced mushrooms
1 package (8 ounces) broccoli slaw
1 pound peeled and cleaned shrimp, thawed if frozen
2 extra-large eggs, beaten
Salt and black pepper to taste
4 scallions, roots trimmed, sliced
½ cup unsalted roasted peanuts
1 lime, cut in 8 wedges

Cover the cellophane noodles with boiling water and soak until they soften, about 5 minutes. (They will not fully soften.) Drain and cover to keep moist. Combine the apricot nectar, honey, fish sauce, chile purée, and garlic in a microwave-safe dish. Microwave for 2 minutes and stir.

Heat a wok, coat with oil spray, and stir-fry the onions until lightly browned. Add the mushrooms and stir-fry until they brown. Add the broccoli slaw and stir-fry until the broccoli is barely tender, about 1 minute. Transfer the mixture to a bowl. Add more oil spray to the wok. Add the shrimp, stir-fry until firm and opaque, about 1 minute, and transfer to the bowl.

Place half of the apricot mixture in the wok and heat until boiling. Add the soaked noodles and stir-fry until the noodles are soft, about 30 seconds. Add the beaten eggs and stir-fry until the sauce thickens, not more than 1 minute. Season with salt and pepper.

Return the shrimp and vegetables to the wok, add the remaining apricot mixture, and stir-fry until the shrimp and vegetables are coated. Toss in the scallions and peanuts. Serve with lime wedges.

Stir-Fried Shrimp and Spicy Sausage

This stir-fry has a decided Mexican flavor, with spicy sausage leading the way. Although chorizo sausage will give you the most authentic flavor, any hot sausage will do.

Makes 4 servings

Nonstick oil spray
1 cup chopped onions, frozen or fresh
2 ounces spicy sausage, such as chorizo, chopped (about ⅓ cup)
½ teaspoon ground cumin
1 pound peeled and cleaned large shrimp, thawed if frozen
1 cup canned black beans, rinsed and drained
1 cup canned diced tomatoes, drained
1 cup orange juice
Salt and black pepper to taste

Heat a wok, coat with oil spray, and stir-fry the onions until lightly browned, about 1 minute. Add the sausage and cumin, and stir-fry until cooked through, about 3 minutes for Italian sausage, 1 to 2 minutes for chorizo or pepperoni. Add the shrimp and stir-fry until the shrimp are firm and opaque, about 1 minute more. Add the beans and tomatoes, and stir-fry until heated through, about 1 minute more. Stir in the orange juice and season with salt and pepper.

Stir-Fried Mussels Marinara

Steaming mussels in marinara sauce is nothing new, but using a wok is. It accelerates the cooking, and the fragrant, slightly charred nuance that ingredients get from a seasoned wok lends a subtle smokiness to the marinara sauce.

Makes 4 servings

4 dozen mussels, cleaned
¼ cup olive oil
1 cup chopped onions, frozen or fresh
1 tablespoon chopped garlic, jarred or fresh
1 cup white wine
2 cups marinara sauce
3 tablespoons pesto, jarred or home-made
3 tablespoons lemon juice, organic bottled or fresh
Salt and black pepper to taste

Discard any mussels that are not tightly closed.

Heat a wok, add half of the oil and stir-fry the onions until lightly browned, about 1 minute. Add the garlic and wine, and boil for 1 minute. Add the marinara sauce and pesto, and bring to a boil. Add the mussels, cover the wok, and simmer until the mussels open, about 4 minutes. Discard any unopened mussels, stir in the lemon juice and the remaining oil, and season with salt and pepper.

Stir-Fried Salmon with Potatoes and Dill

Most stir-fries are virtual one-dish meals, but each ingredient still needs individual attention. In typical stir-fries, the protein is sautéed first and then removed and the process is repeated with the vegetables. The sauce is added along with anything else that needs further simmering. At the end everything is combined and served. Here, the salmon cooks faster than the potatoes. Using precut refrigerated potatoes narrows that gap, but stir-frying in sequence is the real guarantee that each ingredient will shine in the finished recipe.

Makes 6 servings

2¼ pounds salmon fillets, cut in 1-inch
   cubes
Salt and black pepper to taste
3 tablespoons olive oil
1 package (20 ounces) refrigerated hash
   brown potatoes
¾ teaspoon dried dill
3 cups chicken broth
1 package (5 ounces) herbed cream
   cheese, such as Boursin

Season the salmon liberally with salt and pepper. Heat a wok, add the oil, and sear the salmon on all sides, gently turning the fish pieces to keep them whole as they brown. Do not cook through. Remove the browned salmon with a slotted spoon and set aside. Add the potatoes to the oil remaining in the wok and stir-fry until browned. Add the dill and broth, and simmer, uncovered, for 5 to 8 minutes, until the potatoes are tender.

Remove ½ cup of the broth from the wok and mix it with the cheese until smooth. Return the salmon and any juices that have collected around it to the wok and simmer, uncovered, for 2 minutes, until the salmon is cooked through. Transfer the salmon and potatoes with a slotted spoon to a serving platter. Boil the liquid in the wok over high heat until it reduces to about 1 cup and thickens slightly. Stir the cheese mixture into the liquid remaining in the wok and simmer until slightly thickened. Pour over the salmon and potatoes.

Stir-Fried Salmon with Greens

Seared salmon served on a bed of vinai-grette-splashed greens has become the luncheon standard in urban bistros. This recipe transforms the same elements into a lightning-quick stir-fry that is simple and sophisticated. If you have never stir-fried lettuce, you're in for a revelation; it gives the impression of a milder, sweeter form of spinach.

Makes 4 servings

1½ pounds salmon fillets, cut in pieces about 1-inch square
Salt and black pepper to taste
2 tablespoons extra-virgin olive oil
1 tablespoon chopped garlic, jarred or fresh
1 bag (8 ounces) baby lettuce or other tender greens
¼ cup lemon juice, organic bottled or fresh

Season the salmon liberally with salt and pepper. Heat a wok, add half of the oil, and sear the salmon on all sides, turning the fish pieces gently to keep them whole as they brown. Lower the heat, add the garlic, cover the wok, and cook until the salmon pieces are cooked through, about 2 minutes. Remove the cover, add the lettuce, and toss until the lettuce wilts, about 10 seconds. Transfer to a platter and drizzle the lemon juice and remaining olive oil over the top. Add more salt and pepper if needed.

Wok-Seared Salmon with Pineapple Salsa

An extremely hot wok surface is essential for browning ingredients in a stir-fry. In wok-searing, the same intense heat that sears meat in sautéing creates a thick, crispy crust on a single ingredient, such as fish or beef, without overcooking the interior. If you prefer salmon well cooked, let it rest for a few minutes so that the residual heat inside the fish cooks it through completely.

Makes 4 servings

4 pieces salmon fillet (about 1½ pounds total), each piece about 1 inch thick
1 teaspoon garlic spice blend
Salt and black pepper to taste
2 tablespoons extra-virgin olive oil
1 jar (about 16 ounces) pineapple salsa

Season the salmon with the spice blend, salt, and pepper. Heat a wok, add the oil, and sear the salmon until deeply browned on all sides. The surfaces of each piece will be lightly crispy, but the flesh will still be moist in the center of its thickest parts. Transfer the salmon with a slotted spatula to a platter. Add the salsa to the wok, bring to a boil, and spoon the salsa over the salmon.

Wok-Seared Sesame Salmon

This wok-seared salmon recipe uses the same technique described in the previous recipe, but it has a completely different result. This time the top surface of the salmon is dipped in egg, seasoned with garlic and ginger, and coated with a crust of sesame seeds. As the fish sears, the exposed surfaces develop a crispy browned veneer that contrasts dramatically with the caramelized sesame seeds on top. The finished fish is drizzled with toasted sesame oil and ponzu sauce.

Makes 4 servings

1 large egg, or ¼ cup liquid egg substitute
¼ teaspoon minced ginger, jarred or fresh
¼ teaspoon minced garlic, jarred or fresh
¼ teaspoon Asian toasted sesame oil
¼ cup raw sesame seeds
4 pieces salmon fillets (about 1½ pounds total), each piece about 1 inch thick
Salt and black pepper to taste
2 tablespoons ponzu sauce
2 tablespoons vegetable oil

Combine the egg, ginger, garlic, and half of the sesame oil in a pie pan or other rimmed plate. Place the sesame seeds on another plate or on a sheet of foil, plastic wrap, or waxed paper. Season the salmon with salt and pepper, and dip the top side in the egg mixture, then in the sesame seeds. The top surface of each piece of salmon should be encrusted with sesame seeds. Combine the remaining sesame oil and ponzu sauce.

Heat a wok, add the vegetable oil, and sear the salmon on all sides until deeply browned, being especially careful to keep the seeded side from scorching. When done, the surfaces of each piece will be lightly crispy and the flesh will still be moist in the center of its thickest parts. Drizzle the ponzu sauce mixture over the finished fish.

Stir-Fried Shrimp and Eggs with Oyster Sauce

Scrambling eggs in a wok is quick. As soon as they hit the surface, they are practically done. In this dish, eggs are combined with seared shrimp and scallions and then dressed with oyster sauce. The effect is both exotic and homey.

Makes 4 servings

12 large or extra-large eggs
¼ teaspoon hot pepper sauce
Salt to taste
Nonstick oil spray
1 pound shelled and cleaned medium
    shrimp, thawed if frozen
3 scallions, roots trimmed, sliced
¼ cup oyster sauce

Whisk together the eggs, hot pepper sauce, and salt. Heat a wok, coat it with oil spray, and stir-fry the shrimp until they are opaque and firm, about 1 minute. Add more oil spray. Add the eggs and stir-fry until the eggs are softly scrambled, about 1 minute. Stir in the scallions. Transfer to a platter and drizzle with oyster sauce.

Stir-Fried Hoisin Barbecued Chicken

A wok's heat is intense enough to imitate the searing effect of a grill, and by simmering the browned ingredient in barbecue sauce, you get the flavor of a traditional barbecue without having to stand guard basting.

Makes 4 servings

⅓ cup hoisin sauce
¼ cup honey
1 teaspoon minced garlic, jarred or fresh
1 teaspoon Chinese chili purée
3 pounds chicken parts, drumsticks and
    thighs separated, breasts halved
Salt and black pepper to taste
Nonstick oil spray

Combine the hoisin sauce, honey, garlic, and chili purée. Pat the chicken pieces dry and season them liberally with salt and pepper. Heat a wok, coat it with oil spray, and sear the chicken pieces on all sides. Lower the heat to medium-low, add the sauce, and toss the chicken to coat.

Cover the wok and cook until the chicken pieces are almost cooked through, about 15 minutes. Remove the cover and cook over high heat until the sauce has thickened and the chicken is thoroughly coated. Turn the chicken pieces frequently to make sure they don't burn.

Stir-Fried Chicken with Tomato Tapenade

The intense combination of sun-dried tomatoes and ripe black olives is the essence of sun-warmed Mediterranean flavor. Here they enhance an easy stir-fry of chicken tenders, onions, mushrooms, and lots of diced tomatoes. Serve it over rice or angel hair pasta.

Makes 4 servings

1½ pounds chicken tenders
Salt and black pepper to taste
Nonstick oil spray
1 medium onion, peeled and thinly sliced
1 package (8 ounces) sliced mushrooms
2 tomatoes, chopped, or about 1½ cups canned diced tomatoes, drained
½ cup sun-dried tomato pesto
2 tablespoons tapenade (black olive spread)

Season the chicken with salt and pepper. Heat a wok and coat it with oil spray. Stir-fry the chicken, onion, and mushrooms until all are browned and the chicken is cooked through, about 3 to 4 minutes. Add the tomatoes and stir-fry until they soften, about 2 minutes. Stir in the pesto and tapenade.

Stir-Fried Chicken and Noodles in Garlic Sauce

Light and spare, browned strips of chicken nestle in garlic-glazed linguine that is cooked in a syrup of parsley-flecked chicken broth.

Makes 4 servings

1½ pounds chicken tenders
Salt and black pepper to taste
Nonstick oil spray
2 cups chopped onions, frozen or fresh
1 tablespoon minced garlic, jarred or fresh
½ teaspoon minced ginger, jarred or fresh
Pinch of crushed red pepper flakes
1 can (about 15 ounces) chicken broth
1 package (9 ounces) fresh linguine, refrigerated
2 tablespoons chopped Italian (flat-leaf) parsley

Season the chicken with salt and pepper. Heat a wok, coat it with oil spray, and stir-fry the chicken and onions until all are browned, about 2 to 3 minutes. Transfer to a plate. Stir-fry the garlic, ginger, and pepper flakes for a few seconds. Add the broth and bring to a boil. Add the pasta and boil for 1 minute. Return the chicken to the wok and boil gently 2 minutes more, until the pasta is tender and the chicken is cooked through. Stir in the parsley.

Wok-Braised Chicken and Roasted Peppers

The flavor of this chicken stew depends on good-quality roasted peppers. They should be bright red and as whole as possible. Shards of charred skin don't guarantee excellence, but they often indicate bold roasted flavor.

Makes 4 servings

3 pounds chicken parts, drumsticks and thighs separated, breasts halved
Salt and black pepper to taste
2 tablespoons olive oil
1 medium onion, peeled and cut in 8 wedges
1 cup white wine
1 teaspoon garlic spice blend
1 jar (about 12 ounces) roasted red peppers, cut in strips
1 tablespoon basil pesto, jarred or fresh

Season the chicken with salt and pepper. Heat a wok and add the oil. Add the chicken, brown it in the hot oil, then push it toward the edges of the wok. Add the onion to the oil and stir-fry until the edges of the onion are dark brown. Return the chicken to the center of the wok, add the wine and spice blend, and cover. Simmer for 10 minutes. Turn the chicken, add the red peppers, and simmer 10 minutes more, until the chicken is cooked through.

Transfer the chicken to a platter, stir the pesto into the sauce, and adjust the seasoning with additional salt and pepper if needed. Pour the sauce over the chicken.

Stir-Fried Turkey with Corn and Peppers

This fragrant, colorful stir-fry is made almost entirely from native American ingredients. Turkey was the only animal domesticated by pre-Columbus Americans. Their main grain was corn, and they used both hot and sweet peppers as principal flavorings.

Makes 4 servings

1 pound boneless, skinless turkey breast, cut in 1-inch cubes
Salt and black pepper to taste
Nonstick oil spray
½ teaspoon ground cumin
1 package (10 ounces) frozen corn kernels, thawed
1 cup diced roasted bell pepper, jarred or fresh
3 scallions, roots removed, thickly sliced
2 tablespoons Worcestershire sauce

Season the turkey with salt and pepper. Heat a wok and coat it with oil spray. Stir-fry the turkey until browned and almost firm. Add the cumin and corn, and stir-fry until the corn browns on the edges. Add the roasted pepper and heat through. Stir in the scallions and Worcestershire sauce.

Stir-Fried Turkey Mole

Pay no attention to the wok, and you'll find that this dish is a traditional mole, redolent with Mexican seasonings, onions, and tomatoes. The long list of spices, fruits, and nuts typical of mole recipes has been simplified with the use of jarred mole sauce. Because the jarred sauce is precooked, it needs only to be warmed with the other ingredients.

Makes 4 servings

1½ pounds boneless, skinless turkey
　breast, cut into fingers
Salt and black pepper to taste
Nonstick oil spray
1 cup chopped onions, frozen or fresh
1 can (about 15 ounces) chicken broth
½ cup jarred mole sauce (page 23)
½ cup diced tomato, canned or fresh

Season the turkey with salt and pepper. Heat a wok and coat it with oil spray. Stir-fry the turkey and onions until both are browned. Add the broth and heat until simmering. Stir in the mole and tomato, and continue simmering until the turkey has cooked through and the sauce has thickened slightly. Adjust the seasoning with salt and pepper.

Stir-Fried Chinese Chicken Noodle Soup

The smoky flavor of the wok is the most distinctive ingredient in this nearly instant chicken soup. It is captured by quickly stir-frying chicken tenders. The chicken broth is flavored with ginger, garlic, and scallions, and the noodles are cooked right in the wok.

Makes 4 servings

Nonstick oil spray
12 ounces chicken tenders, cut in ½-inch
　pieces
1 teaspoon minced ginger, jarred or
　fresh
1 teaspoon chopped garlic, jarred or
　fresh
1 large can (49 ounces) chicken broth
8 ounces medium-thick egg noodles
2 scallions, roots trimmed, thinly sliced
Salt and black pepper to taste

Heat a wok and coat with oil spray. Stir-fry the chicken until lightly browned, then transfer to a platter. Place the ginger and garlic in the wok and stir briefly, about 10 seconds. Add the broth and bring to a boil. Add the noodles and boil gently about 5 minutes. Return the chicken to the wok and cook 5 minutes more, until the noodles are tender and the chicken is cooked through. Stir in the scallions and season with salt and pepper.

Stir-Fried Wasabi Beef and Scallions

Although wasabi, the incendiary pale green Japanese radish, is most often identified with sushi, I often pair it with beef for the same reason that I enjoy horseradish with roast beef or steak. Stand back when the wasabi hits the wok; the fumes can be quite pungent. Don't cook it too long after the wasabi is added; excess heat will cause its aromatics to dissipate.

Makes 4 servings

Nonstick oil spray
1 pound beef stir-fry strips
½ teaspoon chopped garlic, jarred or
    fresh
3 tablespoons prepared wasabi sauce in
    a tube
½ cup chunky salsa, any heat level
5 scallions, roots trimmed, thinly sliced

Heat a wok and coat with oil spray. Stir-fry the beef until browned but still rare. Add the garlic, wasabi sauce, and salsa, and bring to a boil. Stir in the scallions.

Stir-Fried Beef with Three Hot Sauces

This elegant three-tiered stir-fry ignites the palate with three sauces: a black pepper balsamic sauce that glazes the beef, a pool of salsa on which the beef is served, and a swirl of Tabasco butter that crowns the stir-fry and melts into a sweet, fiery sheen.

Makes 4 servings

4 tablespoons (½ stick) lightly salted but-
    ter, softened
1 tablespoon Tabasco sauce
1 cup salsa, any heat level
1¼ pounds beef stir-fry strips
½ teaspoon seasoning pepper
1 tablespoon vegetable oil
1 medium onion, halved and thinly sliced
2 teaspoons minced garlic, jarred or
    fresh
½ cup balsamic vinegar

Combine the butter and Tabasco, place the salsa in a microwave-safe bowl, and season the beef with the seasoning pepper. Heat a wok and add the oil. Stir-fry the onion until well browned. Add the beef and continue stir-frying until it is browned but still rare. Add the garlic and stir-fry another second or so. Add the vinegar, bring to a boil, and remove from the heat. Microwave the salsa at full power for 45 seconds. To serve, spoon some salsa onto a dinner plate, add a portion of beef, and top with a spoonful of Tabasco butter.

Stir-Fried Short Rib Goulash

Goulash, the legendary Slavic stew of beef, onions, and savory vegetables, usually simmers for hours while its ingredients meld. This stir-fry attempts the same melding but in a fraction of the time. Beef short ribs, frozen onions, and V8 juice dramatically reduce the time needed to reach tenderness and blend flavors. A true goulash is thickened by the bits of softened vegetables and meat that work their way into the sauce as the stew simmers. Since there is no time for that here, instant mashed potatoes do the thickening at the end. Serve the goulash with crusty bread to sop up the sauce, or ladle it over noodles.

Makes 4 servings

4 pieces (about 2 pounds) boneless beef
    short rib, sliced ½ inch thick
Salt and black pepper to taste
Nonstick oil spray
3 cups chopped onions, frozen or fresh
1 package (8 ounces) sliced mushrooms
1 teaspoon chopped garlic, jarred or
    fresh
1 can (about 14 ounces) beef broth
3 cups V8 vegetable juice
2 tablespoons Hungarian paprika
2 tablespoons instant mashed potato
    flakes
1 teaspoon balsamic vinegar

Season the beef with salt and pepper. Heat a wok and coat with oil spray. Add the beef and stir-fry until well browned.

Transfer the beef to a plate. Add more oil spray to the wok if needed and stir-fry the onions and mushrooms until well browned. Add the garlic and stir-fry for another second or so. Return the beef to the wok and add the broth, V8 juice, and paprika. Simmer for 5 to 10 minutes, until the beef is fork-tender. Stir in the potato flakes and simmer until the sauce is slightly thickened, about 1 minute. Add the vinegar and adjust the salt and pepper.

Stir-Fried Mango-Glazed Pork

Mangoes are as important to the food of Southeast Asia, the Caribbean, and Mexico as apples are to Europe and North America. In those cultures, mangoes are eaten daily and in countless ways. This recipe uses two of those ways in a pork stir-fry. Mango chutney, the most common type of chutney, is mixed with mango juice to form a sweet tropical sauce, while shredded carrots are added to increase sweetness and enhance the color.

Makes 4 servings

1½ pounds boneless pork chops, cut in ¼-inch-thick strips
Salt and black pepper to taste
Nonstick oil spray
1 small onion, halved and thinly sliced
2 cups shredded carrots
Pinch of crushed red pepper flakes
¼ cup mango chutney
¼ cup mango juice or apricot nectar
1 scallion, roots trimmed, thinly sliced

Season the pork with salt and pepper. Heat a wok and coat with oil spray. Stir-fry the onion until it browns lightly. Add the pork and stir-fry until it is barely cooked through, about 2 minutes. Add the carrots and pepper flakes, and stir-fry for 1 minute. Add the chutney and juice, and bring to a simmer. Stir in the scallion and adjust the salt and pepper.

Stir-Fried Peanut Butter Pork

In the United States, we think of peanut butter sweetly—with jelly, in a cookie, or filling a pie. But in Africa and Asia, where it is almost as popular, peanut butter means tangy and hot—enriching a stew or gilding grilled meat with a spicy glaze. Peanut butter's savory side is the inspiration for this pungent pork stir-fry.

Makes 4 servings

1 cup light or regular coconut milk
¼ cup chunky peanut butter
1 tablespoon Chinese chili purée
1 tablespoon lemon juice, organic bottled or fresh
1 teaspoon minced garlic, jarred or fresh
1 teaspoon minced ginger, jarred or fresh
1½ pounds boneless pork chops, cut in ¼-inch-thick strips
Salt and black pepper to taste
Nonstick oil spray
2 scallions, roots trimmed, thinly sliced

Combine the coconut milk, peanut butter, chili purée, lemon juice, garlic, and ginger. Season the pork with salt and pepper. Heat a wok and coat with oil spray. Stir-fry the pork until it is barely cooked through, about 2 minutes. Add the coconut milk mixture, bring to a boil, and stir-fry until the sauce coats the meat. Stir in the scallions and adjust the salt and pepper.

Wok-Seared Ginger Ginger Ginger Ginger Spareribs

Spareribs need time to melt into the richly marbled, slip-from-the-bone tenderness that we crave. Now that precooked spareribs are widely available in your market, you can prepare spareribs in no time. This recipe takes advantage of the saved time by searing the precooked ribs and playing with their flavor. The pork is simmered in ground dried ginger, jarred minced ginger, ginger preserves, and ginger beer.

Makes 4 servings

1 package (about 2 pounds) cooked ready-to-serve spareribs
Nonstick oil spray
1 bottle (12 ounces) ginger beer, such as Reed's
1 teaspoon ground ginger
1 tablespoon minced ginger, jarred or fresh
1 tablespoon ginger preserves
½ teaspoon minced garlic, jarred or fresh

Cut the rack of ribs into serving-size pieces of 1 or 2 ribs each. Heat a wok and coat it with oil spray. Sear the ribs on both sides until they are brown and a little crisp at the edges. Add the ginger beer, ground ginger, minced ginger, ginger preserves, and garlic. Simmer until the ribs are glazed with sauce, about 5 minutes. Turn the ribs every minute.

Stir-Fried Pork Ribs in Cider Syrup

Cider is liquefied fruit, complete with sweetness and tartness, big fruit flavor, and subtle floral aromatics. In this simple recipe, pork spareribs are rubbed with curry, seared in a wok, and braised in apple cider until the cider is transformed into a meaty, fruity, tart-sweet, curry-tinted syrup.

Makes 4 servings

3 pounds country-style pork ribs
1 teaspoon red curry powder
Salt and black pepper to taste
Nonstick oil spray
2 cups apple cider

Season the ribs with curry, salt, and pepper. Heat a wok and coat it with oil spray. Sear the ribs on both sides until well browned. Add the cider and scrape up any brown bits clinging to the pan. Simmer, covered, for 20 minutes, until the meat is fork-tender. Uncover, raise the heat, and boil until the cider sauce is syrupy and coats the pork in a thin glaze.

Stir-Fried Lamb and Peaches with Cardamom

The lamb and the peach. No, this is not an old Monty Python routine. The two ingredients play well off each other in texture, color, and flavor. The flavor of lamb can be pungent, which is why it is paired so often with other assertive flavors. But this easy stir-fry takes a different tack. The lamb is tamed by the subtle floral sweetness of peaches and cardamom, and is bolstered with a little spice and tang from the fruit salsa.

Makes 4 servings

1½ pounds boneless leg of lamb, cut in
    strips
Salt and black pepper to taste
Nonstick olive oil spray
2 cups (12 ounces) sliced peaches, frozen
    and thawed or fresh
1 teaspoon ground cardamom
⅓ cup fruit salsa, such as peach or mango
1 scallion, roots trimmed, thinly sliced
⅓ cup sliced almonds

Season the lamb with salt and pepper. Heat a wok and coat it with olive oil spray. Stir-fry the lamb until it is well browned. Add the peaches and cardamom, and stir-fry until they begin to soften, about 1 minute. Add the salsa and simmer to blend the flavors. Serve garnished with scallion and almonds.

Stir-Fried Red Curry Lamb

Thai red curry, a fragrant, fiery blend of spices and chilis, is used frequently in Thai cuisine. In this stir-fry, lamb and eggplant are simmered in a sauce made from V8 juice and red curry.

Makes 4 servings

1½ pounds boneless leg of lamb, cut into
    strips
Salt and black pepper to taste
Nonstick olive oil spray
1 onion, halved and thinly sliced
1 pound Chinese eggplant, halved
    lengthwise and cut in ½-inch-thick
    slices
1 teaspoon chopped garlic, jarred or
    fresh
1 tablespoon dried red curry powder, or
    2 tablespoons jarred red curry paste
1 cup V8 vegetable juice
1 tablespoon cilantro pesto or chutney,
    or 2 tablespoons chopped cilantro

Season the lamb with salt and pepper. Heat a wok and coat it with olive oil spray. Stir-fry the lamb until it is well browned and transfer it to a plate. Add more oil spray if needed and stir-fry the onion and eggplant until lightly browned. Add the garlic and red curry, and stir. Add the V8 juice and heat to a simmer. Return the lamb to the sauce and simmer for 5 to 8 minutes, until the lamb and eggplant are tender. Stir in the cilantro.

Stir-Fried Chili

Chili may be as easy to prepare and as down to earth as any stew, but it is still a complex, intriguing dish. This chili has been streamlined by stir-frying, but that doesn't mean its flavors have been compromised. Everything is there: the slow burn of jalapeño, the earthy perfume of cumin, and the balm of sweet pepper. This one is made with both ground beef and beans, but you can substitute beef stir-fry strips for the ground beef or eliminate the beans if you wish.

Makes 4 servings

Nonstick oil spray
2 pounds ground beef, any cut
2 tablespoons chili powder
1 tablespoon ground cumin
1 cup salsa, medium or hot
1 can (about 15 ounces) crushed tomatoes in purée
1 cup beef broth
Salt and black pepper to taste
1 can (about 20 ounces) red or dark red kidney beans, rinsed and drained

Heat a wok and coat it with oil spray. Stir-fry the beef until browned. Add the chili powder, cumin, salsa, tomatoes, broth, salt, and pepper. Stir to combine the ingredients and simmer for 20 minutes to blend the flavors. Stir in the beans and simmer 5 minutes more.

Stir-Fried Red Pepper, Artichokes, and White Beans

Brilliantly colored and artfully flavored, this Mediterranean vegetable mélange could be an antipasto, a side dish, or a vegetarian entrée. But however you serve it, it is virtually effortless. Because all the ingredients are precooked, they just need warming in the wok. If you don't like the flavor of olives, use basil pesto instead of tapenade.

Makes 4 servings

2 tablespoons extra-virgin olive oil
1 teaspoon chopped garlic, jarred or fresh
1 large jar (about 12 ounces) roasted red peppers, drained, cut in strips
1 jar (6 ounces) marinated artichoke hearts, drained
1 can (about 15 ounces) white beans, rinsed and drained
1 tablespoon tapenade (black olive spread)

Place a wok over high heat until very hot. Add the oil and stir-fry the garlic for a second or so. Add the peppers, artichoke hearts, and beans, and stir-fry until heated through. Stir in the tapenade.

Stir-Fried Szechwan Brussels Sprouts

Brussels sprouts have an odor problem, so many people dismiss them out of hand even though the aroma is not inevitable; it all depends on how they are cooked. In the old days, brussels sprouts were boiled interminably until their off-putting aroma literally cooked away. Sadly, so did all their flavor and texture. In this recipe the sprouts are shredded and stir-fried so quickly that their sulfur never gets released in the first place. The results are nutty and sweet, so good that most sprout haters never suspect that they are confronting their nemesis.

Makes 4 servings

1 tablespoon olive oil
1¼ pounds brussels sprouts, damaged
    leaves trimmed, halved lengthwise,
    and thinly sliced
4 teaspoons chopped garlic, jarred or
    fresh
2 teaspoons minced ginger, jarred or
    fresh
1 teaspoon Szechwan seasoning

Place a wok over high heat until very hot. Add the oil and stir-fry the brussels sprouts, garlic, ginger, and Szechwan seasoning until the slices of brussels sprouts are tender and browned on their edges.

Stir-Fried Teriyaki Mushrooms

Mushrooms are naturally high in umami, the savory quality now widely considered a fifth flavor perceived on the palate (the others are sweetness, saltiness, sourness, and bitterness). This explains why mushrooms enhance almost any stew or soup or stir-fry. This easy recipe combines presliced mushrooms with garlic, ginger, tomato, and teriyaki sauce. The mixture caramelizes on contact with the hot wok, glazing the mushrooms a deep mahogany. Serve them with roasted meats, poultry, or fish.

Makes 4 servings

2 tablespoons olive oil
1 large package (16 ounces) sliced mush-
    rooms
1 teaspoon chopped garlic, jarred or
    fresh
1 teaspoon minced ginger, jarred or
    fresh
2 teaspoons tomato paste
2 tablespoons teriyaki sauce

Heat a wok. Add the oil and stir-fry the mushrooms until browned. Add the garlic and ginger, and stir-fry for a second or so. Stir in the tomato paste and teriyaki sauce.

Stir-Fried Smoky Broccoli and Apples

Broccoli and apples have a natural affinity. Each brings out the best in the other. The apple flavor makes the broccoli sweeter and less bitter, while the broccoli lends cooked apple a greater depth of flavor. Here they are stir-fried with ginger, garlic, and bacon. The effect is a wonderful blend of sweet, tart, smoky, and savory flavors.

Makes 4 servings

Nonstick oil spray
2 strips ready-to-serve bacon
1 bag (10 ounces) fresh-cut broccoli florets
1 full-flavored apple, such as Braeburn, Winesap, or Granny Smith, peeled, cored, and diced
1 teaspoon minced ginger, jarred or fresh
1 teaspoon chopped or minced garlic, jarred or fresh
½ cup chicken broth
Salt and black pepper to taste

Heat a wok and coat it with oil spray. Stir-fry the bacon about 30 seconds, until crisp. Add the broccoli and apple, and stir-fry until the broccoli is bright green and the apple has lost its raw look, about 2 minutes. Add the ginger, garlic, broth, salt, and pepper. Cover and steam until the broccoli is tender, about 2 minutes.

Stir-Fried Apricot-Glazed Carrots

Baby carrots are adorable and convenient, but they frequently lack flavor when cooked. Not here. In this stir-fry they emerge shimmering and sweet, redolent with ginger, garlic, and a sweet tang of apricot—the perfect accompaniment to a roasted chicken.

Makes 4 servings

1 tablespoon vegetable oil
1 package (1 pound) baby carrots
½ teaspoon minced ginger, jarred or fresh
½ teaspoon minced garlic, jarred or fresh
¼ teaspoon salt
1⅓ cups water
1 tablespoon apricot preserves
¼ teaspoon ground cardamom
1 teaspoon butter

Heat a wok and add the oil. Stir-fry the carrots until they are lightly speckled with brown. Add the ginger and garlic, and stir-fry for a second or so. Add the salt and water, cover, and cook until the carrots are barely tender, about 2 minutes. Uncover, stir in the preserves and cardamom, and stir-fry until the liquid is reduced to a glaze. Stir in the butter.

Stir-Fried Corn and Roasted Peppers

The intense heat of stir-frying caramelizes the sugars in corn and crisps the edges of the kernels, giving them greater depth of flavor and more texture. Here the corn is seasoned with cumin and paired with the smoky flesh of sweet roasted peppers. Serve it with panfried pork or seafood.

Makes 4 servings

1 tablespoon vegetable oil
1 package (16 ounces) frozen corn kernels
1 cup diced roasted red peppers, jarred or fresh
¼ teaspoon dried cumin
Salt and black pepper to taste

Heat a wok and add the oil. Stir-fry the corn until some of the kernels start to brown. Add the roasted peppers, cumin, salt, and pepper, and stir-fry until heated through.

Stir-Fried Soy-Sauced Hashed Browns

Stir-frying is the fastest way to crisp hash brown potatoes. In this recipe beautifully crusty hash browns are seasoned with a sweet and salty glaze. They are a flavorful accompaniment to grilled or barbecued meats.

Makes 6 servings

¼ cup vegetable oil
1 cup chopped onions, frozen or fresh
1 bag (20 ounces) refrigerated shredded hash brown potatoes
3 tablespoons soy sauce
2 teaspoons honey
2 teaspoons chopped garlic, jarred or fresh
1 teaspoon minced ginger, jarred or fresh

Heat a wok. Add the oil and stir-fry the onion until golden brown, about 4 minutes. Add the potatoes and stir-fry until brown and crisp, about 8 minutes. Meanwhile, combine the soy sauce and honey. When the potatoes are cooked, add the garlic and ginger, and stir-fry for a few seconds. Add the soy-honey mixture and stir-fry another minute, until the liquid has been absorbed.

Stir-Fried Curried Vegetables

Recipes for curried vegetables usually call for a laundry list of ingredients and require you to precook each vegetable separately. In this simplified curry, the vegetables have been chosen so they cook at similar rates, allowing them to be stir-fried all at once and simmered to tenderness in a seasoned sauce. Serve it as a vegetarian entrée over rice or as a side dish for seafood or poultry.

Makes 4 servings

1 tablespoon vegetable oil
½ cup chopped onion, frozen or fresh
1 cup (about 4 ounces) frozen or refrigerated potato wedges
2 cups baby carrots
1 package (12 ounces) fresh-cut broccoli florets
1 jar (16 ounces) curry sauce
1 tablespoon cilantro pesto or chutney, or 2 tablespoons chopped cilantro
Salt and black pepper to taste

Heat a wok. Add the oil and stir-fry the onion, potatoes, carrots, and broccoli for 2 to 3 minutes, until the vegetables just start to brown. Lower the heat, add the curry sauce, cover, and simmer until the vegetables are tender, about 15 minutes. Stir in the cilantro and adjust the seasoning with salt and pepper.

CHAPTER 14

THERE'S ALWAYS TIME FOR DESSERT

Chocolate Layer Cake with Mint Chocolate Frosting
Coconut Mango Cake
Cherry Chocolate Pâté
Apple Sour Cream Coffee Cake
Blueberry Cornmeal Upside-Down Cake
Beta-Carrot Cake with Apricot Cream Cheese Drizzle
Bourbon Pecan Cake with Bourbon Sour Cream Topping
Fruited Chocolate Pudding Cake
Chipotle Chocolate Fruit Cake
Chocolate Rum Torte with Bitter Chocolate Glaze
Warm Rhubarb Crisp over Strawberries
Blueberry Crisp with Cardamom Custard
Ginger Peachy Cornmeal Crumble
Warm Baked Chocolate Mousse
Warm Vanilla Pear Sauce
Ricotta Apricot Mousse
Sweet Potato Coconut Pudding
Cinnamon Raisin Bread Pudding
Banoffee Bread Pudding

Fruitcake Cheesecake

No-Bake Mocha Cheesecake with Chocolate Pretzel Crust

Cookie Dough Cheesecake with Chocolate Chip Crust

Chèvre Cheesecake with Fig Coulis

Dark Chocolate Soufflé

Doctored Chocolate Pudding

Black-Bottom Espresso Walnut Pie

Chèvre Grape Tart

Sour Cream Peach Pie

Chocolate Peanut Butter Pie

Pecan Pie Cheesecake

Walnut Bran Biscotti

Cranberry Almond Corn Bread Biscotti

Halvah Shortbread

Brownie Shards

Linzer Chews

Peanut Butter Wheat Germ Brownies

Chocolate Truffle Pillows

White Chocolate Ginger Bark

Chocolate Coconut Brittle

Chocolate Brandy Pudgies

Grilled Honey-Glazed Pound Cake with Grilled Banana and Orange Chocolate

Tarragon Tea-Poached Pears

Stir-Fried Bananas in Chocolate Cream

Stir-Fried Caramelized Apple Pie

Stir-Fried Grapes and Walnuts with Gorgonzola Nubbins

Stir-Fried Vanilla Pears over Cardamom Shortcake

Ginger Lychee Sorbet

Orange Blossom Green Tea Sorbet

Frozen Ricotta Mousse

Apricot Sorbet

Balsamic Fig Sorbet

White Wine Granita

Chocolate Layer Cake with Mint Chocolate Frosting

I'm not a fan of cake mixes. Too often what you gain in ease you lose in flavor and consistency. This cake fixes those deficiencies elegantly. The applesauce adds moisture and a fruity background flavor, and the additional cocoa and coffee powder boost its chocolate essence. No one will ever know you used a mix. The applesauce has the added advantage of keeping the cake moist for up to a week. The layers are iced with the easiest frosting I know of.

Makes 12 servings

Baker's Joy No Stick Spray with Flour
1 box (about 18 ounces) devil's food cake mix
2 tablespoons cocoa powder
1 teaspoon instant coffee powder
½ cup vegetable oil
2 cups unsweetened applesauce
3 large eggs,

FOR THE FROSTING:
1 bag (12 ounces) semisweet mint-flavored chocolate chips, such as Hershey's (see Note)
1 cup sour cream or light sour cream

Preheat the oven to 350°F. Coat two 8- or 9-inch cake pans with flour spray. Combine the cake mix, cocoa powder, and coffee in a mixing bowl. Add the oil, applesauce, and eggs, and beat with a mixer on high or by hand for 2 minutes.

Divide between the prepared pans and bake for 25 minutes for 9-inch layers, 30 minutes for 8-inch layers. The layers are done when they are springy in the center. Let cool in the pans on racks for 15 minutes, then remove from the pans and cool completely on racks.

While the layers are cooling, make the frosting. Place the chocolate chips in a 2- to 3-quart microwave-safe mixing bowl. Cover with plastic wrap and microwave at full power until the chocolate is fully melted, about 2 minutes. While the chocolate is still warm, beat in the sour cream. When the cake layers are completely cool, spread the icing on top of one layer and top with the second layer. Ice the sides of the cake and then the top.

NOTE: If you can't find mint chocolate chips, use the same amount of regular semisweet chocolate chips and add ⅛ teaspoon of mint extract.

Coconut Mango Cake

This exotic island layer cake requires no baking. A prepackaged cake is layered with rum-laced mango purée and coconut cream into a moist rummy tropical confection.

Makes 12 servings

1 jar (14 ounces) marshmallow cream
1½ cups (about 4 ounces) shredded
  coconut
1 cup frozen mango purée or jarred
  mango sauce
1 tablespoon dark rum or bourbon
One 1-pound plain sponge cake or butter cake, in loaf form

Combine the marshmallow cream and coconut in one bowl and the mango and rum in another. Slice the cake horizontally into 4 layers. Place the bottom layer on a large sheet of plastic wrap. Spoon and spread about one-fourth of the mango mix on the layer. Top with one-third of the coconut marshmallow mix and spread over the mango. Continue stacking the layers in the same order—cake, mango, and coconut—twice more. Spoon and spread the remaining one-fourth of the mango mixture over the cut side of the top layer and place on top of the cake, mango-side down. Wrap the cake tightly in the plastic wrap to help it hold its shape and refrigerate for at least 1 hour or up to overnight.

Unwrap the cake. Don't worry about what the cake looks like whole. It will be redeemed when it is sliced. Slice off the ends and discard. Cut into 12 slices, each about ½ inch thick.

Cherry Chocolate Pâté

If you cross fudge, brownie, and a candy bar, you'll end up with something like this lush loaf, with its crispy crust, pudgy center, bursts of dried cherries, and abundance of chocolate chips.

Makes 12 servings

Baker's Joy No Stick Spray with Flour
¼ pound (1 stick) unsalted butter
2 large or extra-large eggs
1 package (16 ounces) brownie mix
1 cup (6 ounces) dried red (tart) cherries
2 cups (12 ounces) semisweet chocolate
  chips
⅓ cup cherry preserves

Preheat the oven to 350°F. Coat a loaf pan with flour spray. Melt the butter and mix in the eggs and brownie mix until smooth. Stir in the cherries and chocolate chips, and scrape the batter into the pan, spreading to fill the corners evenly. Drop the cherry preserves over the top in spoonfuls.

Bake for 45 to 50 minutes, until the edges are crisp, the center is crusted over, and a tester inserted in the center comes out with a bit of barely set batter still clinging to it. Let sit on a rack until the pan is cool enough to touch. Cover the pan with a cutting board, invert, and remove the pan after the cake drops. Cover the cake with a cooling rack and invert to cool the rest of the way right side up. Cut in thin slices.

Apple Sour Cream Coffee Cake

In the glitzy world of pastry, coffee cake remains puritanically plain. What makes it extravagant is the context in which it is served. It can turn a cup of coffee into a memorable meal, and served with a plate of scrambled eggs, even the humblest coffee cake can be the raison d'être for breakfast. In this recipe a box of coffee cake mix is enriched with sour cream and punctuated with morsels of dried apple and candied ginger. The aroma alone is worth waking up for.

Makes 9 servings

1 box (21 ounces) cinnamon
    crumb coffee cake mix
⅓ cup milk
⅓ cup sour cream
1 large or extra-large egg
½ cup chopped dried apple slices
¼ cup diced crystallized ginger
Baker's Joy No Stick Spray
    with Flour

Preheat the oven to 350°F. The box of cake mix will contain 2 packets—one with the cake mix itself, the other with the crumb mixture. Combine the cake mix, milk, sour cream, and egg until smooth. Stir in the dried apples and crystallized ginger. Coat an 8-inch square pan with flour spray. Scrape half of the batter into the pan and sprinkle half of the crumb mixture over the top. Add dollops of the remaining batter, swirl with a knife 2 or 3 times, and top with the remaining crumb mixture. Bake for 45 minutes, until a tester inserted in the center comes out clean. Let cool on a rack for 15 minutes. Cut into 9 squares.

Blueberry Cornmeal Upside-Down Cake

This corny, custardy, berry-bursting coffee cake is absolutely fabulous. Its surface is almost black with blueberries, and its interior is perfumed with a blend of maple and toasted corn. It mixes up in minutes and bakes in less than an hour, so it is certainly possible to throw it together for a special breakfast or for a decadent weeknight dessert. It bakes in a skillet, so you will need one with an ovenproof handle.

Makes 12 servings

¼ pound (1 stick) unsalted butter, melted
½ cup packed dark or light brown sugar
3 large or extra-large eggs
1 teaspoon vanilla extract
¾ cup maple syrup
¼ cup milk, 2% or whole
1 box (15 ounces) corn bread mix (not
  corn muffin mix)
1 pound (1½ pints) blueberries, thawed if
  frozen

Preheat the oven to 350°F. Spoon 2 tablespoons of the butter into a 10-inch non-stick skillet with a metal handle and warm over medium-high heat. Scatter the brown sugar in an even layer over the bottom of the pan and heat until the sugar melts, about 2 minutes. Swirl the pan to help the sugar melt evenly, and remove from the heat.

Combine the eggs, vanilla, maple syrup, milk, and remaining melted butter in a mixing bowl. Add the corn bread mix and stir until smooth. Mix in half of the blueberries. Scatter the remaining blueberries over the sugar in the skillet and spoon the batter on top. Bake for 45 minutes, until the center is set and the top is browned.

Let cool for 5 minutes on a rack. Loosen the edges with a knife. Cover the skillet with a platter and, using a potholder, grasp the handle of the skillet with one hand, the platter with the other, and invert. Remove the skillet and let cool at least 10 minutes more before slicing into 12 wedges.

Beta-Carrot Cake with Apricot Cream Cheese Drizzle

I usually don't believe in mixing dessert and health, but when it comes to carrot cake, the temptation is irresistible. Many people assume that carrot cake is good for them (as desserts go) when in truth it is as fatty and sugar-laden as any cake. The one thing it has is a little vitamin A, but in this recipe the beta-carotene has been supercharged with extra carrots, dried apricots, and apricot nectar to pack more than twice the recommended daily allowance of vitamin A for adults in each slice.

Makes about 12 servings

Nonstick oil spray
1 package (18 ounces) carrot cake mix
1 cup orange juice
½ cup vegetable oil
3 large or extra-large eggs, or ¾ cup liquid egg substitute
1½ cups shredded carrots
6 ounces dried apricots, diced (about 1 cup)
½ cup chopped nuts, any variety

FOR THE DRIZZLE:
4 ounces cream cheese
2 tablespoons powdered sugar
⅓ cup apricot nectar
½ teaspoon vanilla extract

Preheat the oven to 350°F. Coat a 10-inch Bundt pan or tube pan with the oil spray. Combine the cake mix, orange juice, oil, and eggs into a smooth batter. Fold in the carrots, apricots, and nuts, and scrape the batter into the pan. Bake for 35 minutes, or until a tester inserted in the crest of the risen cake comes out clean. Let cool in the pan for 30 minutes. Loosen the sides with a knife, cover with a rack, and invert. Remove the pan and let the cake cool the rest of the way.

TO MAKE THE DRIZZLE:

Mix the cream cheese until softened and whisk in the powdered sugar, apricot nectar, and vanilla until smooth. Spoon over the top of the cake, allowing rivulets to run down the sides.

Bourbon Pecan Cake with Bourbon Sour Cream Topping

Gingerbread is so versatile that even its manufactured mix can be turned into anything from cake to cookies by adding additional ingredients. But no manufacturer ever thought its gingerbread mix could become this nutty, boozy spice cake topped with bourbon and honey-flavored sour cream.

Makes 9 servings

Baker's Joy No Stick Spray with Flour
1 box (about 14 ounces) gingerbread
   cake and cookie mix
1 large or extra-large egg
1¼ cups milk, any type
¼ cup bourbon
1 teaspoon vanilla extract
2 cups (about 8 ounces) chopped pecans

FOR THE HONEY BOURBON SOUR
CREAM TOPPING:
¼ cup honey
2 teaspoons bourbon
¾ cup sour cream

Preheat the oven to 350°F. Coat an 8-inch square pan with flour spray and set it aside. Combine the gingerbread mix, egg, milk, bourbon, and vanilla until smooth, and stir in the pecans. Scrape the batter into the prepared pan and bake for 35 to 40 minutes, until the center is springy. Let cool in the pan on a rack for at least 15 minutes.

TO MAKE THE TOPPING:

While the cake is baking or cooling, combine the honey, bourbon, and sour cream until smooth. (The topping, which makes about 1 cup, can be refrigerated up to 3 days.)

Cut the cake into 9 squares and serve warm, topped with the honey bourbon sour cream.

Fruited Chocolate Pudding Cake

There are three types of pudding cake. The most common adds a packaged pudding to the batter producing a richer and moister, but still conventional, cake. Others are so creamy that they cross the line between pudding and cake. This recipe represents a third type, in which a standard cake batter is topped with a syrup. As it bakes, the cake rises up through the syrup—or maybe the syrup descends through the batter—resulting in a moist, brownielike cake that rests on a puddle of pudding. Serve it by scooping up some cake and its pudding-sauce. Eat it with a spoon.

Makes about 12 servings

Nonstick oil spray
1 box (about 1 pound) brownie mix
⅓ cup cocoa powder
1 cup milk
½ cup vegetable oil
1 jar (about 12 ounces) fruit preserves, any type
1 cup (approximately) boiling water

Preheat the oven to 350°F. Coat a 9 × 13-inch baking dish with oil spray. Combine the brownie mix and cocoa, and stir in the milk and oil until smooth. Scrape into the prepared baking dish and spread in an even layer.

Spoon the preserves into a 2-cup measuring cup and add enough boiling water to make a total of 2 cups. Spoon the preserves carefully over the top of the batter until it is evenly coated. Do not pour the preserves directly on the batter, or they will sink to the bottom. Bake for 30 minutes. The cake will be set around the sides, and the top will be very loose and bubbly. Let cool in the pan on a rack for 10 minutes or more. Slice or scoop to serve.

Chipotle Chocolate Fruit Cake

Chiles and chocolate have been titillating one another ever since Quetzalcoatl, the mythic plumed serpent god of the Toltecs, was praised for giving cocoa trees to the tropical forests of southern Mexico. In this raucous cake, chipotle chiles (smoked jalapeños) ignite a batter made in seconds from a chocolate cake mix, a bag of trail mix, and a jigger of prune juice.

Makes 12 servings

FOR THE CAKE:
Baker's Joy No Stick Spray with Flour
1 box (about 18 ounces) dark chocolate cake mix
2 tablespoons cocoa powder
½ teaspoon ground ginger
½ teaspoon ground allspice
2 cups fruit-and-nut trail mix
1 cup chocolate chips
⅓ cup vegetable oil
3 large or extra-large eggs
1¼ cups prune juice
1 teaspoon ground chipotle chiles or chipotle hot sauce

FOR THE GLAZE (OPTIONAL):
½ cup cocoa powder
⅓ cup honey
½ cup prune juice
1 tablespoon unsalted butter
¼ teaspoon vanilla extract

Preheat the oven to 350°F. Coat a 10-inch Bundt pan or tube pan with flour spray and set aside. Combine the cake mix, cocoa, ginger, allspice, trail mix, and chocolate chips in a large mixing bowl. Add the oil, eggs, and prune juice. Beat with a mixer on high or by hand for 2 minutes. Pour and scrape the batter into the prepared pan and bake for 45 minutes, until a tester inserted deep into the crack at the peak of the cake comes out with just a moist crumb clinging to it. Let cool in the pan on a rack for 15 minutes and then invert and let cool completely on the rack.

TO MAKE THE GLAZE:

Combine the cocoa, honey, and prune juice in a heavy saucepan until smooth. Place the pan over medium-high heat and bring to a boil, stirring constantly. Remove from the heat and stir in the butter and vanilla until the butter is melted. Cool until barely warm. Spoon over the top of the cake, allowing rivulets to run down the sides.

Chocolate Rum Torte with Bitter Chocolate Glaze

This elegant torte is nothing more than an aerated brownie. By adding a little rum, increasing the number of eggs, and beating the whites, you convert a box of brownie mix into a European-style mousse cake. Pour on a bittersweet chocolate glaze, and the transformation is complete.

Makes 12 servings

Baker's Joy No Stick Spray with Flour
12 tablespoons (1½ sticks) unsalted butter
4 extra-large eggs, separated
¼ cup dark rum
1 box (16 ounces) dark chocolate brownie mix
4 ounces bittersweet chocolate, broken in pieces
1 tablespoon honey

Preheat the oven to 350°F. Coat a 9-inch springform pan with flour spray and set aside.

Warm 1 stick of the butter in a large microwave-safe mixing bowl at full power for 45 seconds, until almost melted. Stir until smooth and mix in the egg yolks, rum, and brownie mix. In a clean bowl, beat the egg whites until they hold a soft shape. Do not overbeat. Stir half of the whites into the batter and then fold the remaining whites into the batter until completely incorporated. Pour and scrape into the pan. Bake for 22 minutes. Do not overbake. The cake will rise and still be soft in the center. Place on a rack to cool. (The cake will sink as it cools.)

While the cake cools, prepare the chocolate glaze: Melt the remaining half-stick of butter in a microwave-safe bowl at full power for 1 minute. Stir in the chocolate until fully melted and then stir in the honey. Set aside and let cool to a thick syrupy consistency.

When the cake is cool, remove the sides of the springform pan. Keep the cake on its bottom until after it is iced but place on a rack set over a drip pan. Pour half of the glaze over the top of the cake. Use an icing spatula or a wide knife, push the glaze toward the edge so that it runs down the side of the cake. Smooth the icing around the sides of the cake as you go. When the sides have a uniform coat of glaze, pour the rest of the glaze on top of the cake and smooth the top. Allow to cool until the glaze is set. Lift the cake from the springform bottom with a wide spatula and place on a serving plate.

Warm Rhubarb Crisp over Strawberries

I love strawberry rhubarb pie, but I hate that the strawberries always get overcooked by the time the rhubarb has softened. This recipe fixes the problem by baking the rhubarb with strawberry preserves and Grape-Nuts cereal to make the easiest fruit crisp ever. The warm crisp is served over freshly sliced strawberries. That way, its heat gently warms the berries without cooking them.

Makes 6 servings

1 pound frozen sliced rhubarb
½ to ¾ cup sugar (depending on the tartness of the rhubarb)
1 jar (12 ounces) strawberry preserves
2 cups Grape-Nuts cereal
1½ pints strawberries, stemmed and sliced
Vanilla ice cream (optional)

Preheat the oven to 350°F. Toss the rhubarb with the sugar and preserves in a 9-inch square baking pan and scatter the cereal over the surface. Bake for 1 hour. Arrange the strawberry slices on 6 plates and top with a portion of warm crisp. Serve with vanilla ice cream if desired.

Blueberry Crisp with Cardamom Custard

Similar to ginger but not as hot, cardamom is lightly floral and slightly peppery. It complements blueberries beautifully.

Makes 8 servings

1 package (about 6 ounces) cook-and-serve vanilla pudding mix
2 teaspoons ground cardamom
3 cups milk, 2% or whole
1 bag (20 ounces) frozen blueberries, thawed and drained
1 package (about 8 ounces) apple crisp mix, such as T. Marzetti's
1 cup oats (not instant)
1 cup (about 3 ounces) sliced almonds
5 tablespoons unsalted butter

Preheat the oven to 350°F. Combine the pudding mix and cardamom in a large saucepan and whisk in the milk until smooth. Cook over medium heat until the pudding comes to a full boil, stirring constantly. Remove from the heat and pour into a 9 × 13-inch baking pan. Scatter the blueberries over the pudding.

Combine the apple-crisp mix, oats, and almonds. Mix in the butter with your fingers until the mixture is crumbly, and scatter the mixture over the blueberries. Bake for 30 minutes, until the top is brown and crisp. Let cool on a rack for at least 15 minutes. Serve warm or at room temperature.

Ginger Peachy Cornmeal Crumble

This very easy dessert transforms a box of corn bread mix into a sweet ginger crumble that becomes both crust and streusel topping for a fruit-filled pastry. The filling is made from peach preserves and ginger preserves. Ginger preserves might be new to you. They are not the same as preserved ginger; rather, they are a kind of marmalade sold with the jellies and jams in your market. Finish the crumble with whipped cream or ice cream if you wish. I'm especially fond of it with *dolce de leche* or other caramel ice cream.

Makes 8 servings

Nonstick oil spray
1 box (15 ounces) corn bread mix
⅓ cup dark brown sugar
1 teaspoon ground ginger
4 tablespoons (½ stick) unsalted butter,
    cut in small pieces
1 egg
1 jar (12 ounces) ginger preserves
1 jar (10 ounces) peach preserves

Preheat the oven to 350°F. Coat a 9-inch square baking pan with oil spray. Combine the corn bread mix, brown sugar, and ginger in a mixing bowl or the bowl of a food processor. Add the butter and process or pinch with your fingers until the mixture has the texture of coarse oatmeal. Mix in the egg until the dough barely comes together. It should be moist but crumbly.

In a small saucepan or a microwave-safe bowl, combine the ginger and peach preserves, and heat or microwave at full power until the preserves liquefy, about 2 minutes. Press half of the crumble mixture on the bottom of the pan in an even, solid layer. Spread the preserves over the crumble mixture, and scatter the remaining crumble mixture evenly over the preserves.

Bake for 55 minutes, until the crumble is browned and the preserves are bubbling at the edges. Cool to room temperature on a wire rack.

Cut into 16 squares. Serve with whipped cream or ice cream. Caramel and peach ice cream are particularly good, especially if you mix minced candied ginger into them.

Warm Baked Chocolate Mousse

These individual baked puddings are utterly decadent. They start simply enough, as a box of cooked chocolate pudding; then they break loose. The pudding is inundated with butter and more chocolate, and is baked in muffin tins just until the exterior is set. When you crack the surface, warm, utterly lush chocolate pudding flows out.

Makes 12 servings

Nonstick oil spray
¾ cup sugar
2 packages (about 6 ounces each) cook-and-serve chocolate pudding mix
6 cups milk, 2% or whole
¾ pound (3 sticks) unsalted butter, cut in tablespoon-size pieces
2 cups (12 ounces) semisweet chocolate chips
8 large or extra-large eggs
Warm Vanilla Pear Sauce (recipe follows)

Preheat the oven to 400°F. Coat a 12-cup muffin tin with oil spray and dust the interior of each cup with 1 tablespoon of sugar.

Whisk the pudding mix and milk together in a saucepan until smooth. Cook over medium heat, stirring constantly, until the pudding is boiling. Stir in the butter and chocolate chips. When the butter and chips are half melted, remove from the heat and stir until they are fully melted and the batter is smooth. Mix in the eggs. Fill each cup of the muffin tin to its brim with the mousse mixture and bake for 15 minutes. The edges will be set, but there will be a puddle in the center of each mousse. Let cool on a rack for 10 minutes. Loosen the edges with a small knife and lift each pudding from its cup with a small spatula. Serve with pear sauce.

Warm Vanilla Pear Sauce

This pear sauce, similar to applesauce, can be served as is or as a sauce for pudding, cake, or fresh berries. It can be made ahead, refrigerated, and rewarmed in a microwave or on top of the stove over low heat.

Makes about 1 quart

3 cans (about 15 ounces each) pears in heavy syrup
½ cup white wine
Pinch of salt
1 tablespoon vanilla extract
4 tablespoons (½ stick) unsalted butter, at room temperature

Strain the syrup from the pears. Place the syrup, wine, and salt in a saucepan and simmer for 10 minutes, until reduced to about ⅓ cup. Purée the pears in a food processor or blender with the reduced syrup and the vanilla. When smooth, mix in the butter until incorporated.

Ricotta Apricot Mousse

Ricotta cheese, the Italian form of cottage cheese, is one of the most versatile ingredients in your kitchen. It's a filling, a spread, a custard, or a sauce—and in this recipe it's the ultimate convenience ingredient. With just a few flavorings and a whir of a food processor, it becomes the lightest, richest, fluffiest of mousses. And it takes less than five minutes to prepare.

Makes 4 servings

1 container (8 ounces) ricotta cheese,
   preferably whole-milk
⅔ cup apricot preserves
1 teaspoon vanilla extract
1 or 2 drops almond extract
2 teaspoons honey
Pinch of salt

Purée the ricotta in a food processor. Add the apricot preserves, vanilla and almond extracts, honey, and salt, and process until smooth. Pour into 4 dessert dishes, cover each dish with plastic wrap, and chill for at least 1 hour before serving.

Sweet Potato Coconut Pudding

Sweet potato puddings are among the homiest and best-loved sweets in Caribbean cooking. Because these puddings are typically made from potatoes that are cooked with sugar and spices, canned yams or sweet potatoes are a perfect labor-saving substitution. They jump-start this exotic island-style pudding, which requires no cooking and is assembled in seconds.

Makes 4 servings

1 can (15½ ounces) sweet potatoes or
   yams in syrup, drained
1 cup applesauce, any variety
⅓ cup honey
½ cup canned coconut milk

Purée all the ingredients in a food processor until creamy. Serve immediately or refrigerate in a tightly closed container for up to 3 days.

Cinnamon Raisin Bread Pudding

Bread pudding is bread, sugar, milk, and eggs. Everything else is just gilding. In this recipe three ingredients provide you with all the basics, plus some: raisin bread gives you fruit, spice, and filling; vanilla pudding provides sugar, vanilla, and thickener; and milk is your liquid. With these three alone you could get a perfectly edible dessert, but add a handful of golden raisins, additional vanilla, and a few extra spices, and you up the ante to spectacular.

Makes 12 servings

1 loaf (about 16 ounces) cinnamon raisin
    bread, cut in 1-inch pieces
1 cup golden raisins
6 cups milk, 2% or whole
1 box (about 6 ounces) cook-and-serve
    vanilla pudding mix
½ teaspoon ground ginger
¼ teaspoon ground cinnamon
1 teaspoon vanilla extract

Preheat the oven to 350°F. Toss the bread, raisins, and 2 cups of the milk in a 9 × 13-inch baking dish until all the bread pieces are moist. Set aside for 10 minutes. Combine the pudding, ginger, and cinnamon. Mix in the remaining milk and vanilla until smooth and pour over the bread. Bake for 1 hour, until the top is brown and the center is set. (It should still be soft in the center.) Let cool on a rack for at least 30 minutes and serve warm or chilled.

Banoffee Bread Pudding

This dark and sultry bread pudding is unusual on two fronts. The first is the flavor trio of banana, coffee, and butterscotch. The second is the use of cake. When you use cake instead of bread in a bread pudding, the doughy chunks in the custard disappear, and everything melds into a smooth, plush pudding.

Makes 12 servings

1 loaf (about 12 ounces) banana bread,
    cut in 1-inch pieces
1 cup coffee, brewed or instant
1 box (about 3 ounces) cook-and-serve
    butterscotch pudding mix
¼ teaspoon ground cinnamon
2 cups milk, 2% or whole
½ teaspoon vanilla extract
4 tablespoons (½ stick) unsalted butter,
    cut in pieces
2 bananas, peeled and sliced

Preheat the oven to 350°F. Combine the bread and coffee in a bowl until all the bread pieces are moist. Combine the pudding mix and cinnamon, and mix in the milk and vanilla until smooth. Add to the bowl with the bread. Grease an 8-inch square baking pan with half of the butter. Scatter the banana slices over the bottom of the dish, pour the pudding mixture into the pan, and press into an even layer. Dot with the remaining butter. Bake for 1 hour, until the top is brown and the center is set. Cool for at least 30 minutes. Serve warm or chilled.

Fruitcake Cheesecake

Loaded with fruit and nuts, brown-sugar clusters, and caramelized crunchies, this confection falls into the Italian tradition of cheesecake—fluffy and lean as opposed to the creamy New York deli version. The cheese is a blend of ricotta and cream cheese with a little sour cream thrown in for smoothness and lightness, and the fruit and nuts come from a bag of granola cereal and a package of dried fruit bits. The cake will keep well in the refrigerator for up to a week and can be frozen for months without ill effect.

Makes 12 servings

1 bag (16 ounces) granola, any variety
Nonstick oil spray
1 pound cream cheese, preferably
 Philadelphia brand, regular or
 reduced-fat
1 container (16 ounces) ricotta cheese,
 whole-milk or part-skim
1 cup sour cream, regular or reduced-fat
1½ cups sugar
1 teaspoon vanilla extract
¼ cup liqueur, rum, or brandy
5 extra-large eggs
1 cup dried fruit pieces or raisins

Preheat the oven to 350°F. Crush 1¼ cups (about one-fourth of the package) of the granola in a zippered plastic bag using a rolling pin, or finely grind in a food processor. Coat the interior of a 9-inch springform pan with nonstick spray and dust the bottom and sides of the pan with the crushed granola.

Beat the cream cheese by hand or with an electric mixer until it is soft and smooth. Mix in the ricotta, sour cream, sugar, vanilla, and liqueur until smooth. Mix in the eggs, dried fruit, and remaining granola. Pour and scrape the batter into the prepared pan and bake for 1 hour and 45 minutes, until a tester inserted in the center comes out clean.

Let cool until the pan is comfortable to touch. Remove the sides of the springform pan and refrigerate the cake for several hours, until firm. Lift the cake from the pan bottom, place it on a serving plate, cover, and refrigerate until serving, up to 7 days. Cut into 12 wedges with a thin-bladed knife dipped in water to keep the cake from sticking to the knife.

No-Bake Mocha Cheesecake with Chocolate Pretzel Crust

No-bake cheesecakes are just sweetened, flavored cream cheese. Kept cold, they will hold their shape, but because they contain no egg, their texture tends to be more like that of pudding than cake. Because they are not as sturdy as baked cheesecakes, they keep low profiles—more like cheese pies than cheesecakes. This recipe adds height, textural interest, and a salty-sweet vibration with a crumb crust made from ground chocolate-covered pretzels and a filling reinforced with extra cream cheese, espresso, and chocolate.

Makes 16 servings

1 bag (8 ounces) chocolate-covered pretzels
1 package (11 ounces) no-bake cheesecake mix
¼ pound (1 stick) unsalted butter, melted
1 tablespoon water
Nonstick oil spray
1 pound cream cheese, regular or reduced-fat
½ cup powdered sugar
¼ cup cocoa powder
1¾ cups milk
1 tablespoon instant espresso or instant coffee powder, dissolved in 1 tablespoon hot tap water

Coarsely crush the chocolate-covered pretzels with a rolling pin or in a food processor and set aside ½ cup. Finely grind the remaining pretzels and combine them with the contents of the crumb packet from the cheesecake mix. Add the melted butter and water, and mix until uniformly moist and a small amount pressed between your fingers sticks together. Coat a 9-inch springform pan with oil spray. Use the back of a large spoon to press the crust mixture against the sides of the pan and press the remaining crumbs over the bottom of the pan. Make sure the bottom crust is even, (at least ¼ inch thick) and has no buildup where the sides meet the bottom.

Beat the cream cheese with an electric mixer until it is smooth and soft. Beat in the powdered sugar, cocoa, and half of the milk. Add the dissolved espresso, the contents of the cheesecake filling packet, and the remaining milk, and beat until smooth. Scrape the batter into the crust and scatter the reserved chopped pretzels on top. Refrigerate for at least 2 hours to set the filling.

Cookie Dough Cheesecake with Chocolate Chip Crust

If you are one of the gazillion Americans trapped between your love of cookie dough and your need for home-baked cookies, then this recipe is for you. A cheesecake batter inundated with chunks of raw cookie dough is baked in a chocolate chip cookie crust. Because the interior of the cheesecake never gets hot enough to bake the dough, the chunks inside stay surprisingly moist and satisfyingly raw while the crust crisps.

Makes 16 servings

Nonstick oil spray
1 package (18 ounces, or 20 cookies) ready-to-bake chocolate chip cookies
1 tablespoon cocoa powder
2 pounds cream cheese, regular or reduced-fat
1 cup sugar
2 teaspoons vanilla extract
5 large or extra-large eggs
2 cups semisweet chocolate chips

Preheat the oven to 350°F. Coat a springform pan with oil spray, press half of the ready-to-bake cookies into the bottom, and dust the sides with cocoa. Don't worry if some cocoa gets on the cookie dough.

Beat the cream cheese with an electric mixer or by hand until it is soft and smooth. Beat in the sugar until completely incorporated. Beat in the vanilla and eggs until smooth, and stir in the chocolate chips. Pour the batter into the pan. Cut the remaining cookie dough into small pieces, scatter the pieces over the top of the cake, and swirl them into the batter, just until they are submerged.

Bake for 1 hour and 45 minutes, until the center is firm to the touch. Turn off the oven, open the oven door, and let the cake cool in the oven for 30 minutes. Transfer to a rack and let cool in the pan for another hour, until the pan is cool enough to touch. Remove the sides of the springform pan and refrigerate the cake on the springform bottom until firm, at least 2 more hours or overnight. Loosen the cake from the springform bottom with a long sharp knife and slide the cake onto a serving plate. Cut with the knife dipped in warm water.

Chèvre Cheesecake with Fig Coulis

I didn't know whether to put this in the appetizer or dessert chapter. It's here because I believe we are all longing for glorious, sophisticated desserts that are decidedly unsweet. But if I'm wrong, you may find this lightly tangy, creamy, wonderfully earthy cheesecake the perfect hors d'oeuvre to spread on black bread and nibble between sips of white wine.

Makes 12 servings

Baker's Joy No Stick Spray with Flour
2 packages (10 or 11 ounces each) fresh
   chèvre cheese
½ cup honey
1⅓ cups milk
4 large or extra-large eggs
1 teaspoon vanilla extract
1 jar (8 ounces) fig preserves
2 tablespoons balsamic vinegar

Preheat the oven to 300°F. Coat an 8-inch (1-quart) glass baking dish with flour spray. Combine the chèvre, honey, milk, eggs, and vanilla in a food processor and process until smooth, scraping the bowl as needed. Transfer the mixture to the baking dish, set the dish in a larger pan of water, and bake for about 1 hour, until a tester inserted in the center comes out clean. Remove the baking dish from the pan of water and let stand on a rack until the dish is cool enough to handle comfortably. Tilt to loosen the cheesecake from the edges of the pan. Invert onto a plate and remove the baking dish. Place the fig preserves in a microwave-safe dish and soften by microwaving at full power for 1 minute. Stir in the balsamic vinegar and spread the mixture over the top of the cake. Serve immediately or refrigerate up to 24 hours.

Dark Chocolate Soufflé

Are you afraid of dessert soufflés? Well, I have a cure for you: brownie mix. Unlike other cake starters, brownie mixes contain a minimal amount of flour and an abundance of chocolate. Just separate a few eggs, mix, and bake. When this soufflé is done, the top will be crusted and cracked, and the center will appear molten. Don't worry. Follow the directions and turn off the oven. That bubbling core is not underdone brownie—it's a rich chocolate sauce for the soufflé.

Makes 6 servings

Nonstick oil spray
2 tablespoons cocoa powder
1 box (about 16 ounces) dark chocolate
    brownie mix
½ cup vegetable oil
⅓ cup strong coffee
5 large eggs, separated

Preheat the oven to 375°F. Coat a 3-quart soufflé dish with oil spray and dust with cocoa. Set aside. Combine the brownie mix, oil, coffee, and egg yolks with a whisk in a large mixing bowl. In a separate bowl beat the egg whites with an electric mixer or a balloon whisk until they hold a soft shape. Do not beat until stiff. Whisk a few spoonfuls of the beaten whites into the chocolate mixture to lighten it. Fold in the remaining whites with a rubber spatula.

Pour the batter into the soufflé dish and bake for 45 minutes, until puffed and crisp on the surface and fully set around the edge but still wet in the center. Serve from the edge, dishing up sections of set soufflé along with some of the sauce that remains in the center.

Doctored Chocolate Pudding

Instant chocolate pudding needs help. It whips up in minutes, and it looks good enough—thick and rich and dark—but where's the flavor? It tastes more like sweet milk than chocolate. This recipe attempts to repair its deficiencies with an infusion of melted chocolate chips and brandy.

Makes 6 servings

3 cups milk, 2% or whole
⅔ cup semisweet chocolate chips
1 large package (about 6 ounces) instant
    chocolate pudding mix
2 tablespoons fruit-flavored liqueur or
    brandy

Combine 1 cup of the milk and the chocolate chips in a microwave-safe bowl. Microwave at full power for 2 minutes and stir until the mixture is smooth. Combine the pudding mix and the remaining milk, and beat until smooth and thick, about 1 minute. Mix in the melted chocolate mixture and the liqueur. Divide among 6 dessert dishes or stemmed glasses. Cover with plastic wrap and refrigerate until set, at least 1 hour.

Black-Bottom Espresso Walnut Pie

The nearly burnt bitterness of espresso is the perfect foil for the cloying sweetness of a nut pie. Here the pastry is lined with chocolate chips and filled with a gel of butterscotch, brown sugar, walnuts, and espresso. The results are incredibly rich and very intense.

Makes 12 servings

1 refrigerated 9-inch piecrust
½ cup semisweet chocolate chips
1½ cups (about 5 ounces) walnut halves
   and pieces
1 jar (about 19 ounces) butterscotch
   dessert topping
3 large or extra-large eggs
2 tablespoons instant espresso powder,
   dissolved in 2 tablespoons of hot
   water
½ cup dark brown sugar
1 teaspoon vanilla extract

Preheat the oven to 375°F. Unfold the piecrust in a 9-inch pie plate. Turn under the edges and crimp if desired. Scatter the chocolate chips across the bottom of the crust and the walnuts over the chips. Combine the butterscotch topping, eggs, espresso mixture, brown sugar, and vanilla until blended. Pour the mixture into the crust and bake for 45 to 50 minutes, until the top is set and browned and the filling is still soft in the center. Let cool on a rack for at least 30 minutes before slicing. Serve warm or at room temperature.

Chèvre Grape Tart

This tart of honeyed goat cheese and roasted grapes is not too sweet and decidedly adult.

Makes 12 servings

1½ cups Grape-Nuts cereal
¼ pound (1 stick) unsalted butter, melted
2 tablespoons sugar
1 log (about 10 ounces) fresh chèvre
   cheese
⅔ cup milk, 2% or whole
⅓ cup honey
2 large or extra-large eggs
1 teaspoon vanilla extract
1 pound seedless grapes, red and green
1 tablespoon extra-virgin olive oil

Preheat the oven to 375°F. Grind the cereal finely in a food processor. Add the melted butter and sugar, and combine until the mixture is uniformly moist. Use the back of a large spoon to press the crust mixture against the sides of a 9-inch pie pan. Press the remaining crumbs on the bottom of the pan. Bake for 5 minutes. Combine the chèvre, milk, honey, eggs, and vanilla until smooth. Pour into the crust and bake for 30 minutes, until the filling is set. Remove from the oven.

Raise the oven temperature to 400°F. Toss the grapes with the oil and arrange the grapes on top of the tart in tightly packed concentric circles of alternating colors. Bake about 10 minutes, until the grapes are swollen. Let cool to room temperature on a rack before slicing.

Sour Cream Peach Pie

In this simple pie, peaches and cream are baked in pastry with a flurry of cinnamon sugar caramelized on top.

Makes 8 servings

½ cup sour cream
½ cup powdered sugar
1 teaspoon vanilla extract
1 large or extra-large egg
2 packages (16 ounces each) frozen
    sliced peaches, thawed and drained
1 refrigerated 9-inch piecrust
2 tablespoons cinnamon sugar

Preheat the oven to 350°F. Combine the sour cream, powdered sugar, vanilla, and egg. Stir in the peaches. Unfold the piecrust in a 9-inch pie plate and turn under the edges and crimp. Pour the filling into the crust and bake for 45 minutes, until the crust is lightly browned and the filling is set.

Preheat a broiler. Sprinkle the cinnamon sugar over the top of the pie filling without getting it on the crust. Place the pie about 5 inches from broiler and broil until the cinnamon sugar caramelizes and the top is flecked with brown, about 1 to 2 minutes. Do not walk away while the top is browning. It takes only a few seconds for beautiful brown to become a burnt black. Let the pie cool on a rack for 20 minutes before slicing.

Chocolate Peanut Butter Pie

The secret to this confectionary marvel is peanut butter dessert topping. Sweeter and more fluid than peanut butter but not as cloying as corn syrup, it blends into the filling effortlessly and mixes well with other sweeteners. In this recipe the dessert topping gets a hint of molasses from dark brown sugar and a fleeting whiff of maple syrup. The flavor is complemented by chocolate, peanut butter's classic companion.

Makes 12 servings

1 refrigerated 9-inch piecrust
½ cup semisweet chocolate chips
¾ cup (about 4 ounces) roasted peanuts
1 jar (about 11 ounces) peanut butter
    dessert topping
⅔ cup dark brown sugar
1 cup maple syrup
3 large or extra-large eggs

Preheat the oven to 375°F. Unfold the piecrust in a 9-inch pie plate and turn under the edges and crimp if desired. Scatter the chocolate chips on the bottom of the crust and the peanuts over the chips. Combine the peanut butter topping, sugar, syrup, and eggs, and pour into the crust. Bake for 45 to 50 minutes, until the top is set and browned, and the filling is still soft in the center. Let cool on a rack for at least 30 minutes before slicing.

Pecan Pie Cheesecake

The inspiration for this elaborate cheese-cake is a prize winner (grand prize in a *Southern Living* recipe contest) whose construction has the simplicity of genius. You start by smashing a pecan pie in the bottom of a springform pan, then top it with cheesecake batter, and bake. The piecrust forms a base for the cake, which is an amalgam of pecan-pie goo and rich cheesecake custard.

Makes 12 servings

Nonstick spray oil
1 fully prepared 9-inch pecan pie, fresh or frozen and thawed
1 pound cream cheese, room temperature
1 cup light brown sugar
2 tablespoons bourbon
1 teaspoon vanilla extract
3 large or extra-large eggs

Preheat the oven to 325°F. Spray a 9-inch springform pan with oil. Place the pie in the pan and push it into the bottom of the pan so that its crust forms a solid base. Mix the cream cheese and sugar until smooth. Stir in the bourbon, vanilla, and egg, and pour over the pie. Bake for 1 hour, until browned and a little wobbly in the center. Cool to room temperature; loosen the edges of the cake from the sides of the pan and remove the sides. Refrigerate until firm before transferring to a serving plate.

Walnut Bran Biscotti

These are the perfect grab-and-go break-fast biscotti, more nutritious than toast (the bran and peanut butter combine to form a complete protein), satisfying, high in fiber, and relatively low in sugar. They are also not bad dunked in a cup of coffee at the end of the day.

Makes 22 cookies

1 box (15 ounces) bran muffin mix
⅓ cup dark brown sugar
3 extra-large eggs
⅓ cup peanut butter, preferably chunky
4 cups (about 1 pound) walnut halves and pieces
Nonstick oil spray

Preheat the oven to 350°F. Combine the muffin mix, sugar, eggs, peanut butter, and walnuts with a fork until all the dry ingredients have been moistened. (The batter will be crumbly.) Coat a sheet pan with oil spray and scrape the batter onto the sheet pan. Wet your hands with cold water and mold the batter into a loaf 11 inches long. If the batter starts sticking to your hands, wet them again.

Bake for 40 minutes, until the loaf is firm in the center. Remove from the oven and let cool for 5 minutes. Slice the loaf into 22 pieces, each about ½ inch thick. Place in a single layer on the sheet pan and return the pan to the oven for 15 minutes. Turn each piece over and bake 10 minutes more, until they are crisp and dry.

Cranberry Almond Corn Bread Biscotti

What is corn bread mix? Flour and corn-meal, some sugar, and a little salt and baking powder. To make it into corn bread, you mix in oil, milk, and an egg. But suppose you didn't? It could be a pan of muffins, and with a little more imagination it might be a flapjack or a frying batter. But who would ever guess that it could become the most sophisticated of biscotti, crisp and subtly sweet, punctuated by fruit, nuts, and the surprisingly pleasant grit of stone-ground corn?

Makes 24 to 28 cookies

1 box (15 ounces) corn bread mix (not corn muffin mix)
⅓ cup sugar
2 cups (about 10 ounces) whole roasted almonds, preferably unsalted
8 ounces (about 1½ cups) dried cranberries
4 large eggs
1 teaspoon vanilla extract
Baker's Joy No Stick Spray with Flour

Preheat the oven to 350°F. Combine the corn bread mix, sugar, almonds, and cranberries. Add the eggs and vanilla, and mix with a large fork until the dry ingredients have been moistened. Coat the interior of a 9 × 13-inch glass baking dish with flour spray. Scrape the batter into the dish and flatten into an even layer using a spatula or the back of a wide wooden spoon. Bake for 30 minutes, until a tester inserted in the center comes out clean.

Remove the pan from the oven. Cover with a cutting board, invert, and remove the pan. Cut the cake in half lengthwise with a serrated knife, then cut each half into 12 to 14 rectangular strips. Return the strips to the pan, setting each one on its narrow side, like dominoes. Return to the oven to bake 25 minutes more, until golden brown and crisp.

Halvah Shortbread

Halvah, the super-rich, oily sesame candy from the Middle East, is practically short-bread all by itself. Just add some flour to make it bakable and a little ginger to complement the flavor of sesame.

Makes 16 cookies

4 ounces halvah
4 tablespoons (½ stick) unsalted butter
1 teaspoon ground ginger
1 cup flour

Preheat the oven to 350°F. Purée the halvah, butter, ginger, and flour in a food processor until smooth. Pack the mixture into an 8-inch baking pan and bake for 20 minutes, until firm and dry. Let cool for 10 minutes and cut into 16 thin wedges. Lift the wedges from the pan with a spatula.

Brownie Shards

The crispiest, leanest, most buttery, and most decadent wafer ever devised, these super-thin brownies are also easy to make. They mix up in minutes and bake in ten. They are very delicate and will not hold a shape when warm, so make sure they are cooled to room temperature before you cut them. And most important, do *not* grease the baking sheet. If you do, the batter will not spread and the cookies will separate into a sheet of fried crumbs as they bake.

Makes 4 dozen cookies

½ pound (2 sticks) unsalted butter
1⅓ cups (about one-third of a 1-pound box) brownie mix
2 large or extra-large eggs
2 cups (6 ounces) sliced almonds

Preheat the oven to 375°F. Melt the butter in a saucepan over medium heat or in a microwave-safe bowl at full power for 2 minutes. Stir in the brownie mix and eggs, mixing just enough to make a smooth batter. Spread the batter in an even, thin layer on an ungreased 12 × 17-inch rimmed sheet pan. Scatter the sliced almonds over the top as evenly as possible.

Bake for 10 minutes, until the edges are crisp, the center is set, and the almonds are lightly toasted. Let cool on a rack for 20 minutes. Cut into 48 pieces; the pieces need not be regular. Remove with a small spatula to cool the rest of the way on a rack.

Linzer Chews

Linzertorte, a raspberry tart made with spiced nut-laden pastry, is the inspiration for these easy bar cookies. The crust, which is made like a crumb topping, is filled with raspberry preserves. As it bakes, the bottom sets into a solid pastry base, the raspberry preserves bubble and congeal into a chewy, gooey center, and the top browns and crisps into a spicy streusel topping.

Makes 16 cookies

1 package (about 8 ounces) apple-crisp mix, such as T. Marzetti's
1 tablespoon dried lemon peel
Pinch of ground clove
¼ teaspoon ground ginger
1 cup oats (not *instant*)
1 cup ground walnuts
5 tablespoons unsalted butter
¾ cup raspberry preserves

Preheat the oven to 350°F. Combine the apple-crisp mix, lemon peel, clove, ginger, oats, and walnuts. Add the butter and mix with your fingers until the mixture is uniformly crumbly. Press half of the crumbs into an 8-inch square baking dish until they form an even firm layer. Stir the preserves with a fork to loosen and spread the preserves evenly over the pressed crumbs. Sprinkle the remaining crumbs over the preserves in an even layer. Bake for 30 minutes, until evenly browned. Cool on a rack for 30 minutes, until firm, and cut into sixteen 2-inch squares.

Peanut Butter Wheat Germ Brownies

No one would guess that these chewy caramel-like squares are loaded with wheat germ, one of the most nutritious parts of wheat. They can be prepared by hand and are ready in less than half an hour.

Makes 16 brownies

Baker's Joy No Stick Spray with Flour
1 jar (14 ounces) chocolate peanut butter, such as Jiff Chocolate Silk
2 large or extra-large eggs
1 cup dark brown sugar
1 teaspoon vanilla extract
1 teaspoon baking powder
1 cup toasted wheat germ
1 cup whole wheat flour

Preheat the oven to 350°F. Coat an 8- or 9-inch square baking pan with flour spray. Combine the peanut butter, eggs, sugar, and vanilla until smooth. Add the baking powder and blend thoroughly. Mix in the wheat germ and flour just until blended. Scrape the batter into the pan and bake for 20 minutes, until a tester inserted in the center comes out moist but clean of batter and the cake at the edges of the pan has risen and become crusty. Let cool on a rack for at least 20 minutes. Cut into 16 squares.

Chocolate Truffle Pillows

These elegant puff-pastry pillows, lined with a very thin layer of chocolate ganache, are similar to what you would buy in an upscale French pastry shop. To make them from scratch would require lots of ingredients and professional technique, but with a box of frozen puff pastry and a dozen chocolate truffles, I guarantee you will triumph, regardless of your level of expertise.

Makes 12 cookies

1 box (about 1 pound) Pepperidge Farm Puff Pastry Sheets
1 egg, beaten, or ¼ cup liquid egg substitute
12 chocolate truffles

Thaw the pastry according to the package directions. Preheat the oven to 400°F. Cut 24 rounds from the pastry sheets using a 2-inch biscuit cutter, or cut each sheet into 12 squares. Brush 12 of the pastry pieces lightly with the beaten egg, place a truffle in the center of each piece, and cover with one of the remaining pastry pieces. Pinch the edges of the pastry together firmly to completely encase the truffle.

Place the pillows on an ungreased sheet pan and bake for 10 minutes, until browned, puffed, and crisp. Let cool for 3 minutes before removing from the sheet pan, and let cool completely on a rack.

White Chocolate Ginger Bark

I am not generally a fan of white chocolate, but when you pair it with crisp toasted almonds and the fragrant spiciness of crystallized ginger, I'm in line for seconds. This candy couldn't be easier. Just melt the chocolate, mix in the almonds and ginger, spread it on a sheet pan, and let it cool.

Makes about 1 pound or 24 pieces

8 ounces white chocolate, broken into pieces
1 cup (5 ounces) roasted whole almonds, skins on
1 cup (about 6 ounces) diced crystallized ginger

Melt the white chocolate in a covered microwave-safe bowl in a microwave oven at full power for 3 minutes. Stir in the almonds and ginger, and scrape onto a sheet pan. Spread to an even ½-inch-thick rectangle with the back of a wooden spoon or a stiff rubber spatula. Refrigerate at least 45 minutes, until firm. Cut into bite-size pieces.

Chocolate Coconut Brittle

This thin, crisp chocolate candy is very easy and has only two ingredients. Although you can toast the coconut in an oven, I highly recommend the microwave. It does a perfectly fine job, and you can melt the chocolate in the same bowl.

Makes about 1 pound or 24 pieces

8 ounces sweetened shredded coconut
8 ounces milk chocolate, broken into pieces

Place the coconut in an ample microwave-safe bowl and microwave at full power for 3 minutes. Toss with a fork and microwave 1 minute more, until the coconut is spotted with brown. It is normal for coconut to brown unevenly. Toss again. Add the chocolate pieces and microwave 1 minute more. Stir until the coconut is coated completely with the chocolate. Scrape onto a sheet pan and spread into a ¼-inch-thick layer using the back of a wooden spoon or a stiff rubber spatula. (Don't worry if there are thin spots or a few holes in the layer.) Refrigerate about 45 minutes, until firm. Run a spatula under the brittle to release it from the pan. It will naturally break into pieces along its weak points.

Chocolate Brandy Pudgies

Chock-full of fruit and nuts and redolent with brandy and chocolate, these chocolate candies are practically effortless and are made entirely in the microwave. A bag of dried fruit pieces are soaked in brandy, submerged in chocolate, combined with nuts, and cooled into squares. No tempering, no dipping, no molding, no fuss. In cool weather the candies can be stored at room temperature for several weeks, but it is best to keep them refrigerated in the summer. They can be frozen, tightly wrapped, for several months.

Makes 3 dozen candies, about 18 servings

1 package (7 ounces) dried fruit bits
3 tablespoons brandy
4 ounces semisweet chocolate, broken into pieces
1 tablespoon unsalted butter
1 cup (about 5 ounces) walnut, pecan, or cashew pieces

Line an 8-inch square baking dish with foil. Combine the fruit and brandy in a microwave-safe bowl, cover with plastic wrap, and microwave at full power for 2 minutes. Add the chocolate and butter, cover again, and microwave at full power for another minute, until both are melted. Add the nuts and mix to blend. Turn into the prepared baking dish and pack into an even layer. Refrigerate for 1 hour, until firm. Cover with a small cutting board and invert. Peel off the foil and cut into 36 squares.

Grilled Honey-Glazed Pound Cake with Grilled Banana and Orange Chocolate

When the steaks are all done and the grilled corn has been reduced to cobs, let the last dying embers enhance your dessert. In this recipe slices of pound cake and banana are toasted on the grill, infused with butter and honey, and peppered with bits of melting chocolate-covered orange peel. Heaven!

Makes 4 servings

4 tablespoons (½ stick) unsalted butter
¼ cup honey
8 slices pound cake
2 bananas, cut in half lengthwise
3 ounces chocolate-covered orange peel, chopped

Preheat a grill to medium. Melt the butter in a microwave-safe bowl at full power for 40 seconds. Add the honey and beat until blended. Brush the slices of pound cake lightly on both sides with half of the honey butter. Coat the bananas with the remaining honey butter. Grill the cake and bananas until lightly browned, about 90 seconds per side. Arrange on a platter and scatter the chopped chocolate-covered orange peel over the warm bananas and cake.

Tarragon Tea-Poached Pears

Tea lends an exotic floral fragrance and glowing amber hue to poached pears, but to create the effect you had to brew tea and simmer it with sugar and spices before the pears were added. Not anymore. Liquid concentrated iced teas (sold alongside the powdered ice tea mixes in the market) are a poaching liquid in a bottle. Here the tea is augmented with tarragon, a surprising twist that is perfect with pears.

Makes 4 servings

1 cup sweetened ice tea concentrate, lemon flavor
1½ cups water
¼ teaspoon dried tarragon leaves
4 pears, slightly underripe

Combine the tea concentrate, water, and tarragon in a medium-large saucepan and bring to a simmer. Meanwhile, peel the pears, cut them in half, and remove the core of seeds with a melon baller. As soon as the pears are prepared, submerge them in the simmering poaching liquid and simmer until tender, 10 to 20 minutes depending on their ripeness. When the pears are soft, remove them with a slotted spoon and boil the poaching liquid until slightly syrupy, about 5 minutes. Pour the syrup over the pears and let cool. Serve warm or chilled.

Stir-Fried Bananas in Chocolate Cream

Bananas are delicious warm, and they're even better warmed in a wok, where their edges caramelize as their flesh melts. For stir-frying it is best to use bananas that are not too ripe lest they lose their shape completely as they cook. Once they are done, a simple chocolate sauce is made in the wok and poured around the warm fruit.

Makes 4 servings

4 tablespoons (½ stick) unsalted butter
4 barely ripe bananas, peeled and sliced diagonally into ½-inch-thick pieces
⅔ cup light cream
1 ounce semisweet chocolate
¼ teaspoon vanilla extract

Melt the butter in a wok over medium heat. Add the bananas and stir-fry until the slices just begin to break at their edges, about 1 minute for medium-ripe bananas. Transfer the slices with a slotted spoon to a platter. Pour the cream into the wok and bring to a boil. Add the chocolate and stir until it melts. Turn off the heat and stir in the vanilla. Pour over the bananas.

Stir-Fried Caramelized Apple Pie

This is a great way to construct a pie. Start by parbaking a prepared piecrust. While it bakes, stir-fry the apples in butter and sugar, and prepare the streusel topping, sold as apple crisp topping in the produce aisles of your market. When the crust is baked, the three elements are layered together and returned to the oven.

Makes 8 servings

1 frozen piecrust, thawed
¼ pound (1 stick) unsalted butter
1½ pounds (about 6) apples, peeled, cored, and cut in 8 wedges
3 tablespoons brown sugar
1 package (8 ounces) apple crisp topping

Preheat the oven to 400°F. Bake the crust for 5 minutes.

Melt half of the butter in a wok over medium heat and stir-fry the apples until soft, about 5 minutes. Toss with the brown sugar. Combine the crisp topping and the remaining butter into a crumbly mass. Scatter about one-third of the crumbs across the bottom of the crust. Using a slotted spoon, fill the pie shell with the apples, leaving behind any excess liquid. Scatter the remaining crisp topping over the apples. Bake for 30 minutes, until the crust and crumbs on top are brown and crisp.

Stir-Fried Grapes and Walnuts with Gorgonzola Nubbins

Grapes, walnuts, and Gorgonzola are a glorious combination any way you can get it, but here it is glorified by toasting the walnuts, cooking the grapes until they swell almost to bursting, and adding the Gorgonzola while the grapes are still warm (but not hot). This way the cheese keeps its shape as it yields to the heat of the fruit. Serve it as an hors d'oeuvre or a savory dessert.

Makes 6 hors d'oeuvres or dessert servings

½ cup (2 ounces) walnut pieces
1 teaspoon extra-virgin olive oil
1 teaspoon minced garlic
¼ teaspoon crushed dried rosemary, or 1 teaspoon fresh rosemary leaves
1¼ cups red seedless grapes
1 tablespoon balsamic vinaigrette
2 ounces Gorgonzola cheese, broken in small pieces

Place the walnuts and oil in a cold wok and stir-fry over medium heat until the walnuts toast lightly. Add the garlic and rosemary, and toss. Raise the heat to high, add the grapes, and stir-fry until the grapes plump, about 30 to 45 seconds. Stop before they pop. Remove from the heat, add the vinaigrette, and spoon onto a serving plate. Scatter the Gorgonzola over the top.

Stir-Fried Vanilla Pears over Cardamom Shortcake

Get ready to swoon. This dessert starts with sweet cardamom-scented biscuits that are split and swathed with a warm stir-fry of pears in vanilla syrup, powdered sugar, and sour cream. If you are snobbish about using canned pears, you can poach your own, but good-quality canned pears are a great time-saver.

Makes 6 servings

2⅓ cups Original Bisquick
2 teaspoons ground cardamom
¼ cup sugar
5 tablespoons unsalted butter, melted
½ cup milk
2 cans (about 15 ounces each) sliced
    pears in heavy syrup
1 teaspoon vanilla extract
6 tablespoons sour cream
Powdered sugar (optional)

Preheat the oven to 425°F. Combine the Bisquick, cardamom, sugar, 3 tablespoons of the butter, and the milk, and stir into a soft dough. With floured hands pat the dough to a ½-inch thickness on a floured board and cut into 6 rounds using a 3-inch biscuit cutter or a large drinking glass. Place on an ungreased sheet pan and bake for 10 to 12 minutes, until puffed and golden brown. Let cool on a rack. This can be done up to a day ahead.

Drain the pears and reserve the liquid. Melt the remaining butter in a wok over medium heat, add the pears, and stir-fry until they are warmed through. Transfer to a bowl with a slotted spoon and stir in the vanilla. Raise the heat to high, pour the reserved pear liquid into the wok, and boil until it is reduced to a syrupy glaze and is lightly browned.

TO ASSEMBLE THE SHORTCAKES:

Split the biscuits in half, arrange the bottom halves on a platter, and top each one with a portion of pears and 1 tablespoon of the reduced syrup. Put the biscuit tops in place and pour another spoonful of syrup over the top. Add 1 tablespoon of sour cream and dust with powdered sugar if desired.

Ginger Lychee Sorbet

Fresh lychees are one of my favorite fruits, but they are available only for a few weeks in the summer. The rest of the year we must make do with the canned product. This sorbet is one of the only ways I know to give canned lychees the spark of fresh fruit. If you buy lychees in sweet syrup, you will need no additional sugar. Canned lychees are available in the Asian grocery section of many markets or in any Asian market.

Makes 1 pint or 4 servings

1 can (20 ounces) pitted lychees in heavy
    syrup
1 tablespoon pickled sushi ginger

Purée the lychees with their syrup and the ginger in a food processor or blender until smooth. Pour into a shallow pan and freeze until solid, about 4 hours or longer. Cut or break the frozen mixture into cubes and purée in a food processor until creamy. Store in the freezer in a tightly closed container for up to 1 week. If the mixture becomes solid, purée it again before serving.

Orange Blossom Green Tea Sorbet

The floral aura of this creamy exotic ice comes from green tea. Unlike pungent black tea, the leaves of green tea are not fermented, making them less bitter and astringent. In this recipe, green tea concentrate takes the place of brewed tea and sweetener. It is enriched with coconut milk, orange juice, and ginger for a frozen dessert that radiates the flavors of Southeast Asia.

Makes about 1½ pints or about 6 servings

1 bottle (16 ounces) Nestea Sweetened
    Ice Tea Concentrate, Green Tea and
    Honey Flavor
1 cup unsweetened coconut milk
¼ cup orange juice
½ teaspoon ground ginger
1 teaspoon dried orange peel, or 1 table-
    spoon finely grated fresh orange peel

Combine all the ingredients in a shallow pan and freeze until solid, about 4 hours or longer. Cut the frozen mixture into cubes and purée in a food processor until creamy. Store in a freezer in a tightly closed container for up to 1 week. If the mixture becomes solid, purée it again before serving.

Frozen Ricotta Mousse

This frozen confection is similar to home-made ice cream—minus the chores of cooking a custard, cooling, and churning. The ingredients are simply combined, frozen, and creamed in a food processor. The results are exceedingly creamy and surprisingly rich, delivering only a fraction of the fat found in many ice creams.

Makes about 1 quart or 8 servings

2 containers (15 ounces each) ricotta
*   cheese, whole-milk or part-skim*
½ cup honey
1 teaspoon vanilla extract

Combine the ricotta, honey, and vanilla, and pour into a shallow container. Freeze until solid, 4 hours or longer. Cut into cubes and purée in a food processor until creamy. Store in a tightly closed container in the freezer for up to 1 week. If the mixture becomes solid, purée it again before serving.

Apricot Sorbet

A can of fruit in heavy syrup is all you need to make the purest, most authentic fruit sorbet imaginable. Think about it: If you were going to prepare a pristine sorbet from scratch, you would start by picking the fruit at the peak of ripeness and then cook it in sugar until it almost melted. In the end you would have exactly what you get when you open a can of fruit in syrup. Just purée the contents of the can, flavor it as you wish, and freeze it into sorbet.

Makes about 1 quart or 8 servings

2 cans (15 ounces each) apricot halves in
*   syrup, heavy or light*
¼ teaspoon almond extract

Purée the apricots with their syrup and the almond extract in a food processor or blender until completely smooth. Pour into a shallow pan and freeze until solid, about 4 hours or longer. Cut into cubes and purée in a food processor until creamy. Store in a tightly closed container in the freezer for up to 1 week. If the mixture becomes solid, purée it again before serving.

Balsamic Fig Sorbet

This is without a doubt one of the best foods that will ever pass between your lips. The clove and cinnamon in the tea blend with the figs and the hint of balsamic vinegar into a creamy, spicy, fragrant frozen cloud. It is a gorgeous dessert, a refreshing snack, and an inspired palate cleanser.

Makes 1½ pints or 6 servings

3 cups water
1 cup sugar
3 spice tea bags, such as Celestial
   Seasonings Bengal Spice or Oregon
   Chai
6 Calimyrna or other pale-colored figs,
   stems removed, quartered
2 teaspoons balsamic vinegar

Combine the water and sugar in a saucepan and bring to a boil. Add the tea bags, take off the heat, and steep for 2 minutes. Remove the tea bags, add the figs, and set aside until the figs are soft, about 20 minutes. Add the vinegar and purée the mixture in a blender or food processor. Pour into a shallow pan and freeze until solid, 4 hours or longer. Cut into cubes and purée in a food processor until creamy. Store in a tightly closed container in the freezer for up to 1 week. If the mixture becomes solid, purée it again before serving.

White Wine Granita

Granita is shaved flavored ice, known as Italian ice in many parts of the United States. It is easy to prepare at home, but most people never do, which is a shame because the vast majority of commercially made ices are full of intense artificial flavors and dyes. This recipe for white wine granita combines light and natural flavors.

Makes 6 servings

1 bottle (750 ml.) white wine, any type
½ cup honey
Pinch of salt
¼ teaspoon raspberry vinegar

Whisk all the ingredients together until the honey and salt dissolve. Pour into a shallow pan and freeze until firm. Because of the alcohol in the wine, the mixture will never freeze into a solid. To serve, scrape the surface of the ice with a spoon and scoop the shavings into chilled wineglasses.

INGREDIENT SOURCES

All the ingredients for the recipes in *Almost from Scratch* are available in any well-stocked supermarket, but some stores, such as Trader Joe's, Wegman's, Central Market, and Whole Foods Markets, are geared toward highlighting new convenience cuisine ingredients. Not only do these stores stock these ingredients, but they continue to expand and improve their inventory. By the time this book makes it into print, there will be more ingredients delivering more flavor with less work than there were when I started writing, and I only hope that what you experience here will inspire you to give them a try.

If you can't find an ingredient in your supermarket, try a gourmet store or an ethnic market. You shouldn't have to go any further than that, but just in case, here are a few mail-order and Internet sources that might be of some help.

FOR CONDIMENTS:
Stonewall Kitchens, 800-207-5267, www.stonewallkitchen.com
Zingerman's, 888-636-8162, www.zingermans.com
Trader Joe's, www.traderjoes.com

FOR NATURAL, ORGANIC, AND HEALTH FOODS:
Whole Foods Market, www.wholefoodsmarket.com, to locate a
   store near you
Gaiam, 877-989-6321, www.gaiam.com

FOR HARD-TO-FIND GOURMET AND PROFESSIONAL INGREDIENTS:
Earthy Delights, 800-367-4709, www.earthy.com
Dean and DeLuca, 800-221-7714, www.deandeluca.com

FOR HARD-TO-FIND ETHNIC INGREDIENTS:
EthnicGrocer.Com, 866-438-4642, www.ethnicgrocer.com
Global Food Market, 818-879-0462 (fax),
    www.globalfoodmarket.com

FOR SEASONINGS:
Penzeys, 800-741-7787, www.penzeys.com
Vann's Spices at Earthy Delights, 800-367-4709, earthy.com

METRIC EQUIVALENCIES

LIQUID AND DRY MEASURE EQUIVALENCIES

Customary	Metric
¼ teaspoon	1.25 milliliters
½ teaspoon	2.5 milliliters
1 teaspoon	5 milliliters
1 tablespoon	15 milliliters
1 fluid ounce	30 milliliters
¼ cup	60 milliliters
⅓ cup	80 milliliters
½ cup	120 milliliters
1 cup	240 milliliters
1 pint (2 cups)	480 milliliters
1 quart (4 cups)	960 milliliters
	(.96 liter)
1 gallon (4 quarts)	3.84 liters
1 ounce (by weight)	28 grams
¼ pound (4 ounces)	114 grams
1 pound (16 ounces)	454 grams
2.2 pounds	1 kilogram
	(1000 grams)

OVEN TEMPERATURE EQUIVALENCIES

Description	°Fahrenheit	°Celsius
Cool	200	90
Very slow	250	120
Slow	300–325	150–160
Moderately slow	325–350	160–180
Moderate	350–375	180–190
Moderately hot	375–400	190–200
Hot	400–450	200–230
Very hot	450–500	230–260

INDEX